SENTINEL

MUGGED

Ann Coulter is the number one *New York Times* bestselling author of *Demonic: How the Liberal Is Endangering America*; *Guilty: Liberal Victims and Their Assault on America*; *If Democrats Had Any Brains, They'd Be Republicans*; *Godless: The Church of Liberalism*; *How to Talk to a Liberal (If You Must)*; *Treason: Liberal Treachery from the Cold War to the War on Terrorism*; *Slander: Liberal Lies About the American Right*; and *High Crimes and Misdemeanors: The Case Against Bill Clinton*.

She is the legal correspondent for *Human Events* and a syndicated columnist for Universal Press.

MUGGED

RACIAL DEMAGOGUERY FROM THE SEVENTIES TO OBAMA

ANN COULTER

SENTINEL

SENTINEL
Published by the Penguin Group
Penguin Group (USA) Inc., 375 Hudson Street,
New York, New York 10014, USA

USA | Canada | UK | Ireland | Australia | New Zealand | India | South Africa | China
Penguin Books Ltd, Registered Offices: 80 Strand, London WC2R 0RL, England
For more information about the Penguin Group visit penguin.com

First published in the United States of America by Sentinel, a member of Penguin Group (USA) Inc., 2012
This paperback edition with a new preface published 2013

Copyright © Ann Coulter, 2012, 2013
All rights reserved. No part of this product may be reproduced, scanned, or distributed in any printed or electronic form without permission. Please do not participate in or encourage piracy of copyrighted materials in violation of the author's rights. Purchase only authorized editions.

THE LIBRARY OF CONGRESS HAS CATALOGED THE HARDCOVER EDITION AS FOLLOWS:
Coulter, Ann H.
Mugged: racial demagoguery from the seventies to Obama / Ann Coulter.
p. cm.
Includes bibliographical references and index.
ISBN 978-1-59523-099-7 (hc.)
ISBN 978-1-59184-656-7 (pbk.)
1. Race—Political aspects—United States. 2. United States—Race relations—Political aspects. 3. United States—Politics and government—20th century. 4. United States—Politics and government—21st century.
I. Title.
El84.AlC658 2012
305.800973—dc23

Printed in the United States of America
1   3   5   7   9   10   8   6   4   2

Set in Minion
Designed by Sabrina Bowers

While the author has made every effort to provide accurate telephone numbers, Internet addresses, and other contact information at the time of publication, neither the publisher nor the author assumes any responsibility for errors or for changes that occur after publication. Further, the publisher does not have any control over and does not assume any responsibility for author or third-party Web sites or their content.

ALWAYS LEARNING   PEARSON

For the freest black man in America

CONTENTS

This book at least shut liberals up during the last months of the 2012 presidential campaign. The day before *Mugged* came out, MSNBC's Chris Matthews announced on his TV show that the word "apartment" was racist. (Mitt Romney had used it, you see.) But that was the last sighting of phony racism until shortly after the election, when my book tour was over and I went home.

Then suddenly—after not hearing a peep about racism for two solid months—Republican senators who opposed Susan Rice as President Obama's secretary of state were said to be opposing her solely because she is black.

Republicans made perfectly clear they objected to Rice because of her repeated claims on television that the Benghazi attack was provoked by some American's dumb movie trailer about Muhammad posted on YouTube, despite that being laughable. Also, just incidentally, the last two secretaries of state under a Republican president were Condoleezza Rice and Colin Powell.

No matter. Liberals were back in the game! Everything Republicans did was racist, and their losing the 2012 election proved it.

Some of our less-bright Republicans believed this, too, and rushed to embrace idiotic policies to prove they loved minorities. They would out-amnesty the Democrats! In polls, amnesty has never ranked particularly high among the concerns of Hispanics, but Republicans like Rand Paul and Marco Rubio were panicked by the reelection of an incumbent president. *Can we change our minds? Will you like us, too, Hispanics?*

Democrats are not big on amnesty in other contexts. They're still hoping to try George Bush for war crimes. But when it comes to immigration, a weird idea has taken hold that it's somehow unfair of America to skim the cream and try to get the best immigrants it can. Yes, it's unfair for that top model to date only rich, good-looking guys. She should be forced to date poor, short, fat losers. And maybe the Miami Heat should have to pick players by lottery. Why should blind midgets with no skill or native talent lose out to LeBron James?

It's one thing to apply quotas as a response to Democratic policies of Jim Crow, but to apply them to people who have never set foot in this country is utter madness. If they have grievances, they should go home and address the perpetrators. We owe them nothing.

As usual, when Democrats start getting huffy and self-righteous about "civil rights," their policy proposals not only have nothing to do with black people, they specifically harm black people. (*See* a woman's right to choose, gay marriage, the minimum wage.)

Amnesty for illegal aliens and guest worker schemes will dump millions of low-wage workers on the American workforce, hurting black workers most of all. I suspect we'd be hearing a lot less about "compassion" toward the rest of the world if illegal immigrants competed directly with urban elites, lawyers, politicians, and journalists.

Republicans have always stood with black Americans, and we should continue to do so when it comes to immigration. African Americans have roots in this country longer and deeper than most white Americans. We owe them something more than we do an illegal alien who has just run across our border.

The Republican Party was founded for the express purpose of ending slavery. (The Whigs were staunchly "pro-choice" on slavery.) After winning the Civil War and abolishing the barbarism of slavery, Republicans fought for the next hundred years against Democrats . . . who were busy founding the Ku Klux Klan, standing in the schoolhouse door, and concocting phony "literacy tests" for voting.

Recently, it's been a one-sided relationship between Republicans and black Americans, mostly on account of liberals' Alice-in-Wonderland version of history in which Republican and Democratic roles are simply reversed, making the Republicans the villains and the Democrats civil rights champions. Liberals lie a lot, but their lies about the history of civil rights has no equal. The truth is in this book.

Ann Coulter
April 2, 2013

CHAPTER 1

RACE WARS OF CONVENIENCE, NOT NECESSITY

The Democrats' slogan during the Bush years was: "Dissent is patriotic." Under Obama, it's: "Dissent is racist."

Liberals luxuriate in calling other people "racists" out of pure moral preening. They seem to imagine that in African American households throughout the land you'll find mantel portraits of Martin Luther King Jr., Robert Kennedy and Keith Olbermann. (More likely, those mantels would have portraits of Bernie Goetz.)

Beginning in the seventies, there was constant racial turmoil in this country, stirred up by the media, academia and Hollywood to promote their fantasy of America as "Mississippi Burning."

This was madness. There had been a real fight over civil rights for a century, especially in the previous two decades, but by the end of the sixties, it was over. Segregationist violence was gone, and all public places integrated. But in their minds, liberals lived in a heroic past, where they were the ones manning the barricades and marching against segregation. Liberals were hallucinating—about the present and the past.

Contrary to the myth Democrats told about themselves—that they were hairy-chested warriors for equal rights—the entire history of civil rights consists of Republicans battling Democrats to guarantee the constitutional rights of black people.

Not all Democrats were segregationists, but all segregationists were Democrats and there were enough of them to demand compliance from the rest of the party, just as today's Democrats submit to the demands of the proabortion feminists. The civil rights protests brought attention to injustice, and voters needed to know what was happening in the Democratic South. But the hoopla was unnecessary.

What really made the Democrats sit up and take notice was that blacks began voting, and would soon outnumber the Democrats' segregationist wing. That was accomplished by Thurgood Marshall winning cases in the Supreme Court, Republicans in Congress passing civil rights laws and Republicans in the White House enforcing both the court rulings and the laws—sometimes at the end of a gun.

Despite lingering hard feelings over the Civil War, Republican Dwight Eisenhower snatched large parts of the South from the Democrats in the 1952 presidential election.[1] Boosted by his war record in the patriotic, military-admiring South, this Republican candidate carried Tennessee, Virginia, Florida and Texas—and he nearly won Kentucky, North Carolina and West Virginia, losing Kentucky by a microscopic .07 percent. The Democrats' dream team that year was Adlai Stevenson—and Alabama segregationist John Sparkman.

(Eisenhower started a trend, but as far back as the 1920s Republicans were sporadically winning southern states. In 1920, Warren Harding won Tennessee and in 1928 Herbert Hoover won Virginia, North Carolina, Tennessee, Florida and Texas. Between Hoover and Eisenhower, Republicans didn't win a single presidential election, much less the South. The Hoover/Eisenhower southern states were the same states Nixon and Reagan would do best in—not the states Barry Goldwater carried in 1964. More on that to come.)

Eisenhower put a slew of blacks into prominent positions in his administration—unlike Barack Obama he chose competent ones—and quickly moved to desegregate the military, something President Harry Truman had announced, but failed to fully implement.[2]

It took a lifelong soldier who had smashed the Nazi war machine to compel total racial integration in the military. Eisenhower may have felt as his fellow Republican and soldier Senator Charles Potter did when he stood on crutches in the well of the Senate—he lost both legs in World War II—and denounced the Democrats for refusing to pass a civil rights bill. "I fought beside Negroes in the war," Potter said. "I saw them die for us. For the Senate of the United States to repay these valiant men . . . by a watered-down version of this legislation would make a mockery of the democratic concept we hold so dear."[3]

When Eisenhower ran for reelection in 1956, the Republican Party platform endorsed the recent Supreme Court ruling in *Brown v. Board of Education* desegregating public schools. The Democratic platform did not. Indeed, a number of Democratic governors proceeded to ignore the landmark decision. Ike responded by sending in the 101st Airborne to walk black children to school.

In his second term, Eisenhower pushed through two major civil rights laws and created the Civil Rights Commission—over the stubborn objections of Democrats. Senator Lyndon Johnson warned his fellow segregationist Democrats, "Be ready to take up the goddamned nigra bill again." Liberal hero, Senator Sam Ervin told his fellow segregationists, "I'm on your side, not theirs," adding ruefully, "we've got to give the goddamned niggers something."[4]

Vice President Richard Nixon pulled some procedural tricks as president of the Senate to get the 1957 bill passed, for which he was personally thanked by Dr. Martin Luther King Jr. But LBJ had stripped the first bill of enforcement provisions, so Eisenhower introduced another, stronger civil rights bill in 1960. All eighteen votes against both bills were by Democrats. Democratic opposition to civil rights was becoming what we call "a pattern."

Unfortunately for the cause of equality, Nixon lost the 1960 presidential election and there wasn't much enthusiasm for aggressively enforcing civil rights laws in either the Kennedy or Johnson administrations. That would have to wait for Nixon's return.

But with the electoral tide turning—thanks in large part to Eisenhower's civil rights laws and Thurgood Marshall's lawsuits—LBJ did a complete turnaround as president and suddenly decided to push through a dramatic civil rights bill. Black people were voting in large enough numbers that Democrats were either going to have to abandon the segregationists or never win another national election, so Johnson switched sides out of a sincere commitment to civil rights. (Northern blacks had begun moving to the Democratic Party with President Franklin Roosevelt's usual enticement of government largesse.)

Even with a Democratic president behind the Civil Rights Act of 1964, a far larger percentage of Republicans than Democrats voted for it. Eminent Democratic luminaries voted against it, including Senators Ernest Hollings, Richard Russell, Sam Ervin, Albert Gore Sr., J. William Fulbright (Bill Clinton's mentor) and of course, Robert Byrd. Overall, 82 percent of Senate Republicans supported the Civil Rights Act of 1964, compared to only 66 percent of Democrats. In the House, 80 percent of Republicans voted for it, while only 63 percent of Democrats did.

Crediting Democrats for finally coming on board with Republican civil rights policies by supporting the 1964 act would be nearly as absurd as giving the Democrats all the glory for Reagan's 1981 tax cuts—which passed with the support of 99 percent of Republicans but only 29 percent of Democrats.[5]

Nixon launched his national comeback with a 1966 column bashing Democrats as "the party of Maddox, Mahoney and Wallace" trying "to squeeze the last ounces of political juice out of the rotting fruit of racial injustice." One can see why Democrats would later be desperate to impeach him, especially Sam Ervin, a major segregationist who headed the Senate Watergate panel.

One of the main reasons Nixon chose a rookie like Spiro Agnew as his vice presidential nominee was Agnew's sterling civil rights record. Agnew had passed some of the first bans on racial discrimination in public housing in the nation—before the federal laws—and then beaten segregationist George Mahoney for governor of Maryland in 1966. That was the Mahoney in "Maddox, Mahoney and Wallace."

With the segregationist vote split between Democrat Hubert Humphrey and George Wallace in the 1968 presidential election,[6] Nixon won. In his inaugural address, he said, "No man can be fully free while his neighbor is not. To go forward at all is to go forward together. This means black and white together, as one nation, not two. The laws have caught up with our conscience. What remains is to give life to what is in the law: to ensure at last that as all are born equal in dignity before God, all are born equal in dignity before man."

President Nixon proceeded to desegregate the public schools with lightning speed. Just within Nixon's first two years, black students attending segregated schools in the South declined from nearly 70 percent to 18.4 percent.[7] There was more desegregation of American schools in Nixon's first term than in any historical period before or since.

During the campaign, Nixon had said, "people in the ghetto have to have more than an equal chance. They should be given a dividend." As president, he followed through by imposing formal racial quotas and timelines on the building trades. The construction industry got a lot of business from the federal government and yet had doggedly refused to hire blacks. They had been given long enough do so voluntarily. Nixon was fed up with the union's foot dragging and demanded results.

LBJ has been heaped with praise merely for having proposed an affirmative action plan for the building trades. But he backed down from pursuing the plan as soon as the first objection was raised. As with Truman's unenforced executive order desegregating the military, it took a Republican president to actually get it done.

The century-long struggle for civil rights was over. Attorney Thurgood Marshall had won his cases before the Supreme Court. President Eisenhower made clear he was willing to deploy the U.S. military to enforce those victories. President Nixon had desegregated the schools and building trades. Racist lunatic—and Democrat—Eugene "Bull" Connor was voted out of office by the good people of Birmingham, Alabama. The world had changed so much that even a majority of Democrats were at last supporting civil rights. After nearly a century of Republicans fighting for civil rights against Democratic segregationists, it was over.

That was the precise moment when liberals decided it was time to come out strongly against race discrimination.

For the next two decades liberals engaged in a ritualistic reenactment of the struggle for civil rights—long after it had any relevance to what was happening in the world. Their obsession with race was weirdly disconnected from actual causes and plausible remedies. They simply insisted on staging virtual Halloween dress-up parties, in which some people were designated "racists," others "victims of racist violence" and themselves, "saviors of black America."

The fact that New York City was the crucible of so much racial agitation in the seventies and eighties shows how phony it was. There was never any public segregation in New York. No one was moved to the back of the bus. There were no "whites only" water fountains. There were no segregated lunch counters. (Blacks could even get a sixteen-ounce soda in New York City back then!) But liberals love to drape themselves in decades-old glories they had nothing to do with.

Defending himself on *Hannity & Colmes* in 2004 after sneering about the competence of Condoleezza Rice, the first black female secretary of state in U.S. history, Democratic operative and fatuous blowhard Bob Beckel boasted: "I spent a lot of time out in the vineyards on the civil rights movement." Proving it, he said, "I've got scars on the back of my neck."[8]

Beckel was between twelve and fifteen years old during the big civil rights struggles—such as the 1961 Freedom Rides and the murders of three CORE workers by the Ku Klux Klan in 1964. He was still in high school when Martin Luther King was transitioning from civil rights to the "poor people's campaign" and white liberals were moving on to antiwar protests. Next, Beckel will be claiming to have been a member of 1927 Yankees.

Once-respected Mount Holyoke history professor Joseph Ellis also bragged about his work in the civil rights movement. He told one reporter that he had been followed and harassed by racist southern cops while on

the Freedom Trail in Mississippi. In June 2001, the *Boston Globe* looked
into the facts and discovered that this, along with many of Ellis's other fantasies, was a complete fabrication. He had never been a civil rights worker.[9]

For Carl Bernstein, the *Washington Post* reporter whose famous Watergate reportage with Bob Woodward became a book and movie, *All the
President's Men*, the moment of civil rights heroism came when he was on
a B'nai B'rith youth trip through the South and the train broke down in
Greensboro, North Carolina. Carl alleges that he led the other teenagers in
a sit-in at the train station cafeteria, refusing to leave the black restaurant
and nearly getting arrested. For this act of brave defiance, Bernstein claims
in his book, *Loyalties*, he was later reprimanded by B'nai B'rith leaders.

Reporter and author Adrian Havill searched for any evidence of the alleged sit-in for his book, *Deep Truth: The Lives of Bob Woodward and Carl
Bernstein*. He interviewed dozens of people who ought to have known
about it—other students on the trip, locals involved in trying to desegregate the station, B'nai B'rith leaders. Not one recalled such an incident. One
friend on the trip said, "It is apocryphal at best." No Greensboro newspapers mentioned it, and several Jewish leaders denied it ever happened.[10]

As long as they are in no real danger, liberals love to hallucinate racist
violence, with themselves playing the heroes defending poor blacks in
imaginary physical confrontations—or at least blistering editorials. Every
liberal over a certain age claims to have marched in Selma and accompanied the Freedom Riders.

A favorite liberal taunt is to accuse conservatives of clinging to an idealized past. *Poor, right-wing Americans vaguely sense the world is chang-
ing and now they're lashing out.* What about the idealized past liberals
cling to? They all act as if they were civil rights foot soldiers constantly
getting beat up by 500-pound southern sheriffs, while every twenty-year-
old Republican today is treated as if he is on Team Bull Connor. At best,
the struggle for civil rights was an intra–Democratic Party fight. More
accurately, it was Republicans and blacks fighting Democrat segregationists and enablers.

While liberals spent the decades after the civil rights era pretending
they were fighting 1962 battles—when most of them were five years old—
the rest of us had to live through race riots, denunciations of the police, extreme restrictions on speech, liberal racial pandering and a stream of racial
Armageddons.

For decades, one racist incident after another filled the news pages: a
racist police siege of Louis Farrakhan's mosque; trigger-happy cops shoot-

ing peaceful blacks, like Jose (Kiko) Garcia and Edmund Perry; Nazis on the Wappinger Falls police force; black children held down while having their faces forcibly painted white; the racist prosecution of Washington, DC mayor Marion Barry; police brutality against an innocent black motorist in Los Angeles; and on and on. Loads of these hate crimes turned out to be hoaxes, but they would be followed by retaliatory crimes against whites, which were not.

From race riots to race hoaxes to the automatic excuse machine for black criminals, the country had gone mad.

Contrary to what you might imagine, all this did little to improve the situation of blacks. In fact, it was exactly the opposite of what was needed.

After slavery, most of black America was starting at the bottom rung of social advancement. Not only that, but they had spent centuries in the backwoods culture of Southern hillbillies. Thomas Sowell points out that much of what is thought to be black culture is actually Southern "cracker" culture, imported, like Russell Brand, from the Northern provinces of the British Isles.[11]

In his book, *Black Rednecks and White Liberals*, Sowell traces behavioral patterns of various early Americans back to their original regions in the British Isles. Most colonialists in Massachusetts, for example, came from a small area in East Anglia. They were educated, religious and genteel.

White Southerners were another story. Much of the Southern population was made up of eighteenth-century immigrants from the "Celtic fringe"—Scotland, Ireland and Wales. As Sowell demonstrates with a mountain of hilarious examples, the unique cultural attributes of these British highlanders included wanton and brutal violence, hair-trigger tempers, an obsession with pride, shocking promiscuity, unalterable sloth, illiteracy and a total lack of respect for human life, including their own.

Today the only place we see this culture is on the TV show *Cops*—and in the black underclass.

The people of the Celtic fringe were practically a different species from those who settled New England. In the seventeenth century, rape was a capital offense in New England, while in some parts of the South it was treated as a misdemeanor on the order of petty theft.[12] Around the time of the Civil War, illiteracy was virtually nonexistent in New England, but more than 20 percent of Southern whites still couldn't read.[13] In military IQ tests administered during World War I, black recruits from northern states like Ohio, Illinois, New York and Pennsylvania scored higher than white southerners from Georgia, Arkansas, Kentucky and Mississippi.[14]

The very word "cracker" is thought by some scholars to refer to the prideful boasting of the transplanted British highlanders. Remnants of their fighting spirit has proved a boon to the U.S. military, but a few centuries ago, their skirmishing included fights that involved biting off noses, gouging out eyes, and ripping the ears off their opponents' heads. Far from objecting, local crowds would enthusiastically cheer the combatants on.[15] A millennium ago, even Roman armies couldn't subdue the barbarians of Scotland and instead built a gigantic wall, penning them in the north.

David Hackett Fischer gives an example of the "exceptionally violent" backcountry ways from 1787 newspaper accounts in his book, *Albion's Seed*: "robbers seized a man named Davis and tortured him at his own hearth with red-hot irons until he told them where his money was hidden. Then they burned his farm for their amusement and 'left the poor man tied to behold all in flames.'" The raiding parties "mutilated their victims for sport." These were families—and women were often the most violent.[16]

A British soldier, Major George Hanger, said of the backcountry Scots-Irish, "I have known one of these fellows [to] travel two hundred miles through the woods never keeping any road or path, guided by the sun by day, and the stars by night, to kill a particular person."[17]

It was these colorful folkways of the Celtic fringe that southern blacks were marinated in for centuries, but today are written about by twenty-first-century sociologists as a specifically "black culture."

These traits have nothing to do with Africa or the legacy of slavery. The quaint customs of southern rednecks came directly from their Scottish, Welsh and Irish ancestors and were passed on to southern blacks.

The East Coast–West Coast hip-hop rivalry, with its "diss tracks" and shootings and murders, are not a distant echo from the plains of Africa, but a modern version of the Hatfields and the McCoys, with much greater use of the F-word. For decades, raging right up to the twentieth century, these two Scottish families warred across the Kentucky and West Virginia border, leaving at least a dozen dead.

The Southern style of religious worship also lives on in black churches, as well as some white Protestant evangelical churches. It can be seen in the style, if not the substance, of Louis Farrakhan and the Reverend Jeremiah Wright. Citing Frederick Law Olmstead's direct observation of Southern religious services in the late nineteenth century, Sowell describes the technique thus: The preacher "nearly all the time cried aloud at the utmost stretch of his voice," "had the habit of frequently repeating a phrase," and exhibited "a dramatic talent that included leaning far over the desk, with his arms stretched forward, gesticulating violently, yelling at the highest key, and catching his breath with an effort."[18]

Voting Democrat is another bad habit blacks picked up from their neighbors. Southern blacks voted against their fellow Southerners only immediately after the Civil War and during the Democrats' Jim Crow period. But then things settled down and blacks began supporting the same southern Democratic demagogues as white southerners did. The smarmy disingenuousness of a Jimmy Carter, Bill Clinton, or John Edwards seems familiar and homey to southern whites and blacks alike.

It is a telling fact that although most blacks detested Ronald Reagan—a 90 percent black jury even found his attempted assassin, John Hinckley, not guilty[19]—a majority of black Alabamians came to support segregationist rabble-rouser Democrat George Wallace in his later years.

Wallace had stood in the schoolhouse door rather than allow the University of Alabama to be integrated; he appealed to white supremacists for political advantage; and he ran for president expressly as a segregationist. As late as 1970, Wallace had used a campaign flyer in his run for governor that proclaimed: "Wake Up, Alabama! Blacks vow to take over Alabama," accompanied by a picture of a blonde white girl on a park bench surrounded by seven leering black men.[20]

But just about a decade later, Wallace went to black voters and apologized, admitting he was a Christian sinner—and they forgave him. Wallace won 90 percent of the black vote in his last run for governor in 1982.[21]

Wallace spoke the language of the South; Reagan didn't.

Reagan was a straightforward Californian without an ounce of southern populism. He wasn't a demonstrative speaker, he didn't openly discuss his Christianity and there was nary an opportunity for audience participation during his speeches.

Even what is risibly called Ebonics—black dialect—can be traced back to the British highlanders, who used such words and phrases as "I be," "You be," "ax" (ask), "acrost" (across), "do" (door), "dat" (that). As Sowell says, "No such words came from Africa."

Luckily for southern rednecks, their wild and wooly ways weren't tolerated in the North. They were barely tolerated in the South, where these poor whites were used as a buffer against the Indians, but not much more could be done about them, inasmuch as the rednecks far outnumbered the gentry.

Long before there was discrimination against blacks, there was discrimination against white southerners. When large numbers of these country people moved north during World War II, they were aggressively excluded from neighborhoods, jobs and homes—not because of their skin color, but their accents.[22]

It was grossly unfair: Not all southerners were slothful, promiscuous drunks. But northerners couldn't be expected to examine each case individually to ascertain whether an applicant was Robert Penn Warren or Bull Connor, Flannery O'Connor or Casey Anthony. It was more efficient simply to discriminate against all southerners.

The identical thing happened with Irish immigrants in the nineteenth century. They brought many of the same primitive behaviors directly from the British Isles—but when their native folkways turned violent, they were met with Anglo-Saxon law and order.

The North's zero-tolerance policy for a backward culture forced the white trash out of both the Irish and southern rednecks, leaving just enough of them in their natural state to populate modern reality shows and the Kennedy family.

Unfortunately, such harsh but effective policies were briefly practiced and then guiltily abandoned when it came to southern blacks. In fact, New York City mayor John Lindsay expressly argued against bringing black people into the middle class through the immigrant model of assimilation in the Kerner Report, examining the reasons for the 1967 race riots.[23]

Although some blacks made it north in time to be acculturated to New England mores, just as the mass of black Americans were on the verge of shedding their adopted redneck culture in the sixties and seventies, the nation's elites decided to adopt a new set of rules.[24] A 1958 *Time* magazine article reported: "They are afraid to say so in public, but many of the North's big-city mayors groan in private that their biggest and most worrisome problem is the crime rate among Negroes."[25]

Instead of punishing violence, criminality, sexual promiscuity and other charming Celtic customs—as society had with white southerners— we would protect the exact same behavior among black southerners as priceless cultural artifacts of their African heritage. That's how we ended up with the intractable black underclass.

First, liberals set to work destroying the black family. The broken family isn't a black thing. As Sowell points out, there are numerous accounts of newly freed slaves who had been separated from their wives walking across entire states, looking for their families. Economic circumstances aside, the black family unit in the immediate postslavery era was a dream compared to what Democrats have done to it today. The same was true before slavery, with African wives clinging to their husbands as they were being taken into slavery by African raiders and having to be whipped until they would let go.[26]

Erol Ricketts, a demographer and sociologist with the Rockefeller Foundation, found that between 1890 and 1950, blacks had higher marriage rates than whites, according to the U.S. Census.[27] Until then, black women were more likely to get married than white women—and that was despite the high mortality rates among black men, which left fewer of them available for marriage and made more black women widows. In three of four decennial years between 1890 and 1920, black men outmarried white men, with a virtual tie in 1900 at about 54 percent.

Black Americans were moving forward on a well-trod path in this country when liberals decided it would be a great idea to start subsidizing illegitimacy.

Everyone knew—even FDR's secretary of labor, Frances Perkins, knew—that granting widows' benefits to unmarried women with illegitimate children would have disastrous consequences.[28] An early twentieth-century social welfare advocate, Homer Folks, warned back in 1914 that to grant pensions for "desertion or illegitimacy would, undoubtedly, have the effect of a premium upon these crimes against society."[29]

But under LBJ, that's exactly the system liberals implemented. The "suitable home" requirements for welfare—such as having a husband—were jettisoned as irrational and racist by liberal know-it-alls in the federal Bureau of Public Assistance.[30] By 1960, only 8 percent of welfare benefits intended for widows or wives with disabled husbands were being collected by such. More than 60 percent of Aid to Families with Dependent Children payments went to "absent father" homes. As a result, illegitimacy, particularly among blacks, went through the roof.

That was the very year the black marriage rate began its precipitous decline, gradually at first, with the marriage rate for black women falling below 70 percent for the first time only in 1970.[31] As late as that, a majority of black children were still living with both parents.[32] As Ricketts says, "The argument that current levels of female-headed families among blacks are due directly to the cultural legacy of slavery and that black family-formation patterns are fundamentally different from those of whites are not supported by the data."[33]

Rather, it resulted from the specific policy of paying women to have children out of wedlock—in Folks's words, putting a "premium upon these crimes against society."

By 2010, only 30.1 percent of blacks above the age of fifteen were married, compared to 52.7 percent of whites.[34] If blacks managed to get married again at their pre–Great Society rates, the entire black "culture of poverty" would be wiped out. Black people know this: The vital importance of the institution of marriage, felt by its absence, is reflected in the overwhelming, ferocious opposition to gay marriage in the black community.

Next, liberal judges and academics decided it was a bad idea to punish criminals. Instead, they suggested we try to *understand* the criminal, persuade him that the system is fair and give him 157 second chances.

This was not simply a failure to implement good policies. It was an aggressive plan to impose idiotic ideas dreamed up by self-righteous people who had worked it all out on paper. In a classic decision of the era, a New York judge refused to institutionalize Joyce Brown—*nom du insensé* Billie Boggs—a psychotic and schizophrenic woman living on the street, who was menacing passersby, defecating on herself, smoking crack, burning money and running into traffic.

Brown's family begged that she be put in an institution, but the American Civil Liberties Union disagreed. Norman Siegel, director of the New York Civil Liberties Union (NYCLU), said Brown was merely "eccentric and different" and had "no business being taken to Bellevue."[35] In an argument few could disagree with, her attorney, Robert Levy, said Brown was as sane as "a member of the board of the Civil Liberties Union."[36]

Judge Robert Lippman agreed with the ACLU. He explained that "the sight of her may improve us. By being an offense to the aesthetic senses, she may spur the community to action."[37]

Of course, the community had already been spurred to action, which was precisely why it was seeking to have her committed to a mental institution.

Ordinary people said: *You think not imprisoning criminals will lead to less crime? You say that by paying women to have children out of wedlock, we'll reduce the illegitimacy rate? Are you sure that a guaranteed income will encourage people to work harder?* They were ridiculed as unenlightened rubes.

Between 1960 and 1973, the number of FBI index crimes—which are serious offenses such as murder, rape, robbery, arson, assault, kidnapping and burglary—nearly tripled from 2,019,600 offenses a year to 5,891,924.[38]

Hundreds of thousands of Americans had to die, be raped or have their property destroyed or stolen because liberals had some neat new ideas about crime. As with all of the left's social experiments, it was the people at the bottom of society who bore the brunt of jaw-dropping crime rates.

It's striking that the race riots of the sixties were nearly nonexistent in the South, the locus of earlier Democratic segregationist and Klan violence. Rather, the hotbeds of violence were all the places where liberal ideas about crime and punishment prevailed—New York, Philadelphia, Rochester (NJ), Paterson and Newark, Detroit and Los Angeles.

All the while, the entire press corps dedicated itself to clamping down on anyone who looked askance at the dysfunctional black culture that liberals had done so much to cultivate. All Americans walked on eggshells for fear of being called a racist and having their reputations ruined. The elites' ceaseless defense of behavior that would never have been tolerated from a white person destroyed lives and got people killed—most of them black.

If liberal elites had spent years designing a plan to harm blacks, they couldn't have come up with a more ingenious one. Subsidize something, and you will get more of it. Tax it and you will get less of it. Both literally and figuratively, liberals taxed good behavior and subsidized bad behavior right about the time a lot of blacks needed to go through the same hard-knocks education that white southerners and Irish had.

Illegitimacy was directly subsidized through Aid to Families with Dependent Children (AFDC). The "tax" on crime was largely eliminated as liberal reformers shackled the police and rewarded criminals with reduced or nonexistent prison sentences. Honest discussion about the effects of these policies, such as exploding black crime rates, racial discrimination against white college applicants, and the black illegitimacy crisis was "taxed" by the penalty of being called a racist and possibly losing one's job.

Meanwhile, the black crime, dropout and illegitimacy rates continued their ever-upward spiral. Black college students were expected to major in "Being Black," instead of subjects that might get them jobs outside of a university or a government agency.

To hide their own role in the suppression of a black middle class, liberals promoted the myth that slavery alone had produced dystopian black lives. This is the quasi-theological underpinning of the modern welfare state. But the culprit wasn't slavery: It was the seventies. Anyone who looks closely at the footage of Martin Luther King's campaign will see impeccably attired audiences in sober business clothes. These were enormous middle-class gatherings, with married parents and intact families. That ethic, that population—black lawyers, doctors, shop owners—was destroyed by malignant reformers who then papered over their dirty work with the creation of a fraudulent black middle class engineered through affirmative action and government jobs.

Slavery—a policy defended to the death by Democrats—already meant that the great mass of black Americans were starting on the ground floor. But even that other Democratic innovation, the Jim Crow laws, couldn't stop blacks from progressing in the century following emancipation. It was modern Democratic policies guaranteeing that much of black America would fall back down.

From slavery to Jim Crow to "hope and change," liberals wrote the book on how to destroy a people. Democrats simply would not treat blacks as the equal of whites, deserving of rebuke for bad behavior just like a white person. Anyone opposed to mollycoddling blacks would be denounced as a racist.

It could be called "racism by mollycoddling," except that liberals don't actually want to hurt black people. They couldn't care less about black people. All they care about is their own glorious selves and how courageous, forward-thinking and fair-minded they are. At least the old Democratic racists were unabashed demagogues. Modern racists wrap themselves in unbounded self-righteousness.

This isn't a story about black people—it's a story about the left's agenda to patronize blacks and lie to everyone else. It wasn't black people's job to stop whites from acting like idiots. It took blubberbutts like Jim Dwyer, Anna Quindlen, Tom Wicker, Howell Raines and the *Los Angeles Times* to treat blacks as always right, never wrong, while self-righteously disparaging execrable, boring, rhythmless white people. Excluding their own hip selves, of course.

There was a whole industry of people that depended on the existence of racism, but Americans had not been delivering on being racists for years. By 1970, there were more child pornographers in the country than racists. So the media set about inventing them.

But no one could acknowledge that fact until the O. J. Simpson verdict.

Here we had a black celebrity, spectacularly guilty of murder but acquitted by a predominantly black jury. The verdict was wildly cheered by blacks across the nation. With those images, we were finally liberated from having to pretend America was run by the Klan. It was a watershed moment. It was the end of white guilt.

The media, politicians and academia had turned blacks into spoiled children who had never before heard the word *no*. After this one breathtaking miscarriage of justice, the American people said no and the White Guilt Bank was shut down overnight.

With that, America became a much healthier country. Blacks could never be brought into the culture while being so thoroughly infantilized by white liberals who oohed and aahed over every little thing they did.

The only people who had ever benefited from the left's lunacy on race were (1) professional blacks and (2) self-righteous white liberals, who congratulated themselves on their own ethnic sensitivity while moving heaven and earth to make sure their own kids didn't go to school with black kids.

In 1993, a few years before the Simpson verdict, *New York Times* columnist Brent Staples complained that "black prep school boys who study the classics and live within the law have found only marginal acceptance in American cultural reality." American culture, he said, preferred to celebrate the "angry black men."[39]

After the OJ trial, "angry black men" were a lot less attractive. Talented black people were in.

Blacks were the only people, as we discovered with the OJ verdict, who cheered criminals just because they were the same race. It's one thing to complain if an innocent member of your race is falsely accused. But when the guy turns out to be guilty, it's hard to imagine any other group instantly siding with the perp because of some shared characteristic. You didn't have white people rooting for Charles Manson, gays hoping Jeffrey Dahmer would be acquitted or Hispanics supporting Richard Ramirez, the Night Stalker. (Liberals rooted for Teddy Kennedy, but that's another book.)

After the OJ verdict, blacks' ferocious group identity began to weaken.

By 2007, an NPR/Pew poll showed that 53 percent of blacks said that those who couldn't get ahead were mostly responsible for their own condition, compared to 30 percent who said it was because of discrimination— a reversal of percentages from just a decade earlier.[40] (And if NPR came up with 53 percent, just imagine how much higher the actual figure must be!)

Even black people would admit, *Yeah it was a scam, but it was fun while it lasted.* You can push people too far and the OJ verdict pushed racial browbeating too far, just as raising taxes too high eventually leads people to stop paying them.

Much of the change came in subtle social signals. The daily hair-on-fire

racism stories, for example, virtually disappeared. No longer would pompous whites consider it a showstopper to announce at dinner parties that
America is still a racist country. Appeals to white self-condemnation no
longer worked. White people on TV stopped pretending that it was a hate
crime every time a black person got shot. Jesse Jackson was totally side-
lined. Even Al Sharpton's racial agitating no longer got front-page coverage. In fact, Sharpton's reputation dropped so precipitously that he was
forced to trade in his tracksuit for some dress clothes.

The OJ verdict lost everyone except the diehards in the media and the
universities—always the last to know. They'd still trot out their ground-
breaking America-is-a-racist-country insights now and then, but Americans weren't buying it.

Despite mounds of incriminating evidence, the jury acquitted O. J.
Simpson of a brutal double murder after only three hours of deliberation.
It came back to that implacable fact.

Completely inadvertently, that verdict ended up being one of the best
things that had ever happened to black America. Only with the waning influence of race hustlers and their white liberal enablers did the world discover that there were loads of competent blacks out there! Where had they
been all this time?

Liberals muddled through the next twelve years, disconsolate because
their claims of racism were falling flat. *Can't you let us have any of our cher-
ished illusions? Can't you let us keep being self-professed saviors to the
blacks?* For liberals, the OJ verdict was like telling them there was no Santa
Claus.

Enter half-white, half-Kenyan Barack Obama. He was a dream come
true for liberal elites: They could indulge in self-righteousness on race *and*
get a hardcore leftie into the White House at the same time! It was too great
a temptation to resist. So now we're back to liberals finding racists under
every bed again.

The "postracial" president has brought racial unrest back with a whoop.
Obama toys with it, but mostly he allows others to make despicable racial
smears on his behalf. As the *New York Times* described Obama's typical
campaign strategy back in 2008: "This has been [campaign manager
David] Axelrod's career, an eternal return to Chicago and to the politics of
race."

It's always the person with the least black heritage who is angriest at the
antiracism meetings. The ones who have never actually experienced anything resembling Jim Crow—in fact nothing but white suck-uppery—are

the most consumed with rage about things having nothing to do with their life experiences.

Responding to tapes of his insane racist preacher, Jeremiah Wright, Obama said that we need "to remind ourselves that so many of the disparities that exist in the African American community today can be directly traced to inequalities passed on from an earlier generation that suffered under the brutal legacy of slavery and Jim Crow."

Yes, let's bask in blacks' exquisite grievances against whites a little longer—just in case anyone missed *Roots, Do the Right Thing, Amistad, The Color Purple, Guess Who's Coming to Dinner?, Mississippi Burning, The Hurricane, Malcolm X, Monster's Ball, A Raisin in the Sun, To Kill a Mockingbird, Tuskegee Airmen, Ghosts of Mississippi, Ali, The Green Mile* and every ABC after-school special ever produced (except the ones about eating disorders) as well as your entire college education and the last fifty years of the *New York Times* and all other mainstream media outlets issuing hysterical updates on the unending civil rights struggle. In the last two decades, the *Times* has run more than 250 articles about the Selma march alone. Selma happened nearly half a century ago.

Our nation's routine condescension to black racists like Reverend Wright is insulting and creates utter disaster for blacks. Wright's rhetoric encourages easy moral excuses for murder, mayhem and a total disregard for the norms of civilized society. White criminals are at least treated with enough respect to be held morally responsible for their crimes. With black criminals, liberals believe it's always the lash of racism that made them do it, and racist cops, prosecutors, witnesses and jurors who convicted them.

We have recited the civic mantra for half a century: An institution that was wiped out 150 years ago is responsible for all bad behavior of blacks. This little mental exercise has led to a world in which blacks murder, assault, rape and sell drugs at rates that stagger the imagination, yet cannot understand why the avenues of prosperity remain closed to them.

Apparently endless jawboning about black grievances is not the soothing emolument liberals imagined it would be. Can't we return to the halcyon days between the OJ verdict and the Obama campaign, when whites weren't presumed to be harboring racist fantasies and blacks weren't presumed to be children?

No, we can't. Obama is up for reelection.

Obama has repeatedly returned to the well of racial divisiveness to serve his political ends. His 2008 presidential campaign managed to revive the white guilt that had long since dissipated, and then hinted that the one path to racial reconciliation was to make him president. Only then could we stop talking about race—a conversation he had initiated in the first place.

Alas, since he's been president, that's all we talk about.

The Obama presidency has been like the David Dinkins mayoralty all over again, with utter incompetence being papered over with appeals to white guilt.

At least Supreme Court justice Sandra Day O'Connor gave us a time limit on how much longer government discrimination against white people would be legal to make up for the historical injustices: twenty-five years.

With the Democrats it never ends.

It doesn't matter that the race-baiters were proved to be lying hucksters every five minutes throughout the seventies, eighties and nineties, up until the OJ verdict. Whenever the America-is-still-racist story fell apart, the media never told us the conclusions to the story, so they feel their false alarms shouldn't count.

The non-Fox media leapt on the Trayvon Martin shooting like Ted Kennedy on a case of scotch. Following procedure, as soon as their version of events began to collapse, liberals put the story in a lead casket and dropped it to the bottom of the ocean. The nation eagerly awaits their next example of America-is-a-racist-country, which will again turn out to be a hoax. But maybe there's still time to make up a good one before November 6.

Nothing can be left to cruel chance! Liberals are gearing up for the racial mau-mauing of a lifetime. To save Obama, liberals have gone right back to their old tricks. Let's review them.

CHAPTER 2

INNOCENT UNTIL PROVEN WHITE

From the end of the Civil War through the beginning of the twentieth century, law enforcement was nonexistent for black Americans in places controlled by Democrats. Because the Ku Klux Klan was an outgrowth of the Democratic Party—sometimes with overlapping memberships—government officials were often aligned with the terrorist thugs. The Klan was to the Democrats what the ACLU is today: Not every Democrat is an ACLUer, but every ACLUer is a Democrat. Same with the Klan.

When an African American marine, Robert F. Williams, returned to his hometown of Monroe, North Carolina, after serving in World War II, the Klan was riding high, utterly unmolested by the local police. Black doctors and lawyers were abandoning the NAACP in droves for fear of Klan reprisals.

Williams wasn't easily intimidated. So he revived the local chapter, instantly making himself a target of Klan violence. Once, a local Klansman nearly drove Williams off the road and over a seventy-five-foot cliff. The cars locked bumpers and the Klansman began whipping Williams's car back and forth across the highway, then tried to push the car into the intersection of a busy highway, which Williams avoided only by driving into a ditch. Williams banged on his horn to attract the attention of some nearby highway patrolmen. They just laughed and turned away.

When Williams reported the crime to a local policeman, the man refused to issue a warrant, saying he didn't see anything wrong with Williams's car. A crowd had gathered, so the officer told Williams they'd have to go back to the station to fill out a report. He explained that although Williams had the assailant's name, car type and license plate number, that still would not be enough for a warrant. He suggested Williams take it to the district attorney. The DA responded by calling the perpetrator and asking him if he did it. Williams's assailant denied it, and that ended the matter. (It sounded suspiciously like the way the media "investigates" Democrat scandals. *John Edwards denies he had an affair with Rielle Hunter and that's good enough for us!*)

As local law enforcement looked the other way—often having to break their necks to do so—it was open season on blacks in Monroe. The violent intimidation would have continued, too, except that Williams applied for and received a charter from the National Rifle Association—started by Union officers—and founded the Black Armed Guards.

The next time the Klan came to town, they planned to attack a black doctor. But on this occasion they were met by Williams's Armed Guards protecting the man's home. It only took one shootout for the local Democrats to finally ban the Klan from Monroe. As the saying goes, "It's not so much fun when the rabbit's got the gun." This miraculous policy change brought about by blacks willing to defend themselves is described in Williams's book, *Negroes With Guns*.[1]

(Noticeably, Justice Clarence Thomas, the only Supreme Court justice actually victimized by Jim Crow, has some rather lucid thoughts about the constitutional right to bear arms against racist mobs, as set forth in his concurrence in *McDonald v. City of Chicago*, upholding the Second Amendment against the states.)

Democrats eventually figured out that they were losing more votes than they were winning by supporting Jim Crow, so they dropped the segregationist wing of their party and started acting as if they had been battling segregationists all along, rather than harboring them, which was the truth. Liberals were mortified that Republicans, especially Eisenhower and Nixon, had led the fight to end segregation while—as Nixon said—Democrats were still squeezing "the last ounces of political juice out of the rotting fruit of racial injustice."

Driven by psychological deflection as well as their usual demagogic tendencies, Democrats turned around and started accusing everyone but themselves of racism, especially Republicans.

In the sixties, Democrats were slapping Orval Faubus on the back and courting George Wallace supporters. But once the danger was over, liberals decided to play-act being civil-rights champions.

Republicans had finally gotten all Democrats to start treating blacks as equal before the law and the next thing you knew, Democrats were treating blacks as *above* the law. Liberals have never been able to get the hang of a color-blind justice system. They went right back to their old tricks, looking for new victims and new villains. This time, black criminals were the victims and white cops were the villains—villains in the mold of Bull Connor. Who was a Democrat. The Democratic Party has always favored racial discrimination; it just switched which race should be discriminated against.

The new racial agitators came out full force in New York City, as well as in other big cities with virtually no history of race discrimination—but with lots of liberal journalists.

Suddenly, instead of worrying about black children in white schools, Democrats were terrified of the Klan taking over the New York City police force! They claimed the hotbeds of racism had migrated from the South to places like Queens, New York. In fact, all that had happened was that the Democrats' scapegoats had changed: Instead of poor southern blacks, the new patsies were working-class whites, often Irish, Italian and Polish—usually cops. This wasn't Mississippi in the 1960s, so liberals weren't putting themselves in any actual danger. But they got to pretend that they were very brave.

You can never rest with liberals. As soon as it seems as if some horror from the past has been excised, you look away for five minutes and the next thing you know, you're back on the five-yard line.

For many years, it was impossible to have a rational discussion about certain issues, especially race. It was all part of the cultural revolution emanating from the universities and the media, the distinguishing feature of which was that you had to say goodbye to everything you ever knew. There was sex, drugs and the pill—but also severe restrictions on what you were allowed to notice. Common sense was outlawed. If you objected to going to a certain part of town, for example, you'd be told it was just because you were afraid of blacks. *You wouldn't mind being raped and cut up by a white guy!* No, really, I would.

As certain subjects and words became taboo, we got the first glimmerings of political correctness, leading to people praising "the men *and women* of the Green Bay Packers." That's the whole point of taboos. People don't need edicts telling them not to stick pencils in their eyes. But to force society to abandon common sense required constant monitoring. Violators were severely punished.

To the satisfaction of *New York Times* editors, who managed to avoid all day-to-day contact with any black people, everyone walked on eggshells, afraid of making a career-ending slip of the tongue.

In 1988, Jimmy Snyder, known as "Jimmy the Greek," a football personality, was instantly fired from CBS News for attributing blacks' athletic prowess to breeding by slave owners: "During the slave period, the slave owner would breed his big black with his big woman so that he could have a big black kid—that's where it all started."[2] For devotees of Darwin's theory of evolution, Snyder's theory shouldn't have been controversial, much less offensive. But he had mentioned slavery, so he was a racist.

The one taboo so powerful that even an elderly sports commentator couldn't have missed it was that no one was allowed to notice the increasing criminality among blacks.

The black crime rate was skyrocketing—thanks, Great Society programs!—but the cases that routinely drew huge national attention, requiring months of soul-searching and exegeses about a larger societal problem, were the occasional white-on-black crimes.

Any violence committed by a white person against a black person was the occasion for marches, rallies, and conclusion jumping. Inasmuch as a white person physically attacking a black person was remarkably rare, the majority of these cases involved police officers. Every black person who was shot by the police, or who died in police custody, throughout the 1970s and 1980s, became a beloved member of our community, killed by racism. Most people will generally take the word of a cop over that of a criminal, but most people are not reporters for the *New York Times*.

It's time for a little retrospective on the lynch mobs of yesteryear, not only because they deserve it, but because the racial-grievance machinery has been warmed up again to defend the angel Obama. Let's review what life in America was like before the OJ verdict set us free.

ELEANOR BUMPURS—1984

In 1984, sixty-six-year-old Eleanor Bumpurs, a mentally disturbed black woman, stopped paying the rent on her $98.65 a month apartment in public housing. She claimed she was not paying the rent because various appliances in her apartment were broken. But when the government sent a maintenance man over, she refused to open the door and threatened to throw boiling lye in his face (and not because he was an overpaid public-sector worker with an outrageous pension).

Eventually, the maintenance man was admitted. He found everything in working order, except the buckets of feces Bumpurs kept in her bathtub.

As for that, she explained, "Reagan and his people had done it,"[3] qualifying her for a job with the *New York Times*.

A city psychiatrist was called in. He diagnosed Bumpurs as psychotic, emotionally disturbed and possibly dangerous."[4] The city's housing authority tried contacting Bumpurs's children, but receiving no reply, asked the police to take Bumpurs to a mental institution. She refused to unlock the door for the police and threatened them with boiling lye, too.

After cutting through the locks and opening the door, the six-man police emergency squad, armed with plastic shields and a Y-shaped restraining bar, found all three hundred pounds of Eleanor Bumpurs glowering at them, completely naked and brandishing a ten-inch carving knife. During the ensuing negotiations, Bumpurs knocked the restraining bar out of one officer's hands, causing him to fall, and lunged at another cop with her knife. Officer Stephen Sullivan fired two rounds from a shotgun at Bumpurs, killing her.

And it was all because she was black! The officers were white and Bumpurs was black, so a hue and cry went up about the cops' racist attack on a helpless black grandmother. Whenever police officers encounter three-hundred-pound naked white women trying to carve them up with ten-inch carving knives, they sit and have tea.

A Bronx jury indicted the officer who shot Bumpurs for second-degree manslaughter, a judge dismissed the indictment, and then an appellate court reinstated it. But because of the rallies and protests demanding "justice" for Bumpurs, no judge would take the case. (Cops always requested bench trials in brutality cases so that their fate would not rest in the hands of jurors, who could be influenced by political agitation.)

In the end, the case was assigned to a judge who was about to retire and would not be facing reelection.[5] Pre-OJ, everything was an ordeal if a black person was involved.

Spectators mobbed the courthouse, staging demonstrations inside and outside. They unfurled banners and shouted "Liar!," "Cover-up!," "Convict Stephen Sullivan!," "Stephen Sullivan murderer!" and "Sullivan guilty!" This required frequent recesses.[6] Days before the judge ruled, a bomb ripped through police union headquarters, blowing through a wall and destroying two sinks. A phone call later claimed the bomb had been sent to protest "racist murder and killer cops" in the Bumpurs case.

Sullivan was acquitted. Hundreds of police officers requested transfer out of the emergency squad.

MICHAEL STEWART—SEPTEMBER 15, 1983

It was also deemed a clear-cut case of racism in September 1983, when police arrested Michael Stewart, "artist." Transit police had caught Stewart on his way home from a New York City dance club at three a.m., scrawling graffiti on a subway station wall. On the basis of that fact, the media henceforth referred to Stewart as an "artist."

Stewart ran from the cops and fought violently when they caught him. He was charged with criminal mischief, resisting arrest and possession of marijuana.

Although some witnesses claimed they had seen the police beating Stewart at the subway station,[7] he apparently recovered. In the van to the precinct, Stewart arched over the back of his seat and began kicking the driver and officer in the front passenger seat. Upon their arrival at precinct headquarters, Stewart again tried to run. He was so combative that nearly a dozen officers were involved at some point in trying to subdue Stewart.

One officer who came out of the station, a sergeant who had been on the force for eighteen years, called Stewart a "violent psycho."[8] He said Stewart was bucking, kicking and screaming at the top of his lungs. Even when he was on the ground with his hands cuffed, Stewart kept trying to grab the officers' legs. Several cops were required to bind Stewart's ankles with gauze to get him to stop kicking. All this took place in front of the Union Square Precinct, which is surrounded by apartment buildings, restaurants and crowds of late-night revelers.

On the basis of Stewart's behavior, police believed he was emotionally disturbed and decided to take him to Bellevue for psychiatric evaluation. By the time they arrived, Stewart had stopped breathing and had to be revived. He fell into a coma, contracted pneumonia and, thirteen days later, he died.

Hospital tests determined that Stewart's blood alcohol level was .22, twice the legal limit, which according to the medical examiner was the equivalent of a dozen beers or eight whiskeys.[9] Or, in the words of a *New York Times* editorial about the "young artist and model," his "blood alcohol level was elevated."[10]

The officers were white and Stewart was black. So, naturally, *Times* editors asked themselves: What else could explain his death but that the NYPD was jam-packed with Klan members?

The *Times* ran more than a hundred stories on the case, described by black activists "as the latest example of 'racially motivated police violence,'" invariably referring to Stewart as an "artist."[11]

This was in the mid-eighties, when any accusation of racism created mass hysteria—and the *Times* was accusing everyone involved of racism. As a result, there were two grand-jury investigations, three criminal indictments, dismissal of the indictments, six more indictments, a jury trial and a federal investigation by a U.S. attorney. The first indictment had to be dismissed when it was revealed that a black grand juror had conducted his own investigation, including collecting press stories about the case, and presented his conclusions to the other jurors.[12]

Allegations of misconduct filled the newspapers—against the officers, the prosecutors and the medical examiner. And, as always seemed to happen in cases of alleged police racism, the family demanded a special prosecutor to investigate, because, you see, the regular criminal justice system could not be trusted.

There were multiple investigations that went on for years and years—by the police, the U.S. attorney's office, the Metropolitan Transportation Authority, the state's Board of Professional Medical Conduct, and Board of Regents.[13] And of course, the officers were criminally prosecuted. But no one was ever found guilty of any misconduct in the Stewart case. Except, arguably, Michael Stewart, whose vandalizing of the subway meant the taxpayers had to fund all these pointless investigations, not to mention the subway cleaning. Sorry, New York, no ice skating rink for you because Michael Stewart had to scrawl graffiti on a subway wall.

The autopsy in the case became a political football with the city's medical examiner, Dr. Elliot M. Gross, continuously altering his report as the screams of racism got louder.

His first report, after a six-hour examination in full view of two doctors hired by the Stewart family—who would later sue the city for $40 million in the case—concluded that the suspect had died of cardiac arrest, unrelated to his injuries.

This elicited the usual reaction, with Stewart's family accusing Dr. Gross of "some sort of collusion" with the transit police and calling his report a lie and cover-up.

So Dr. Gross revised his findings to say a spinal cord injury caused Stewart's death—a finding that was contradicted by a mayoral commission investigating Dr. Gross for misconduct, which concluded that the spinal cord injury had not caused Stewart's death.[14]

A second medical examiner performed a follow-up examination and confirmed Dr. Gross's original conclusion—that Stewart had died of cardiac arrest. Although the family accused the police of strangling Stewart, the reviewing doctor expressly found that the "tissues of the neck fail to disclose any evidence of trauma such as might be produced by strangulation."

Still later, Dr. Gross *again* revised his findings to say Stewart's injuries could have come from a beating.

Perhaps being accused of racism led Dr. Gross to produce more accurate reports. But the threat of being labeled a racist, becoming a social pariah, detested by all of humankind, has also been known to cause people to bend the truth.[15]

In order to prosecute the officers for manslaughter, the district attorney's office had to concoct a new theory of legal liability, allowing cops to be guilty of manslaughter simply for failing to protect suspects in their custody from harm.

In the middle of the investigation, the *Times* had weighed in with an editorial saying the city owed the public "rigorous prosecution of the Stewart case."[16] The police were never considered part of this "public" that was owed.

In what other criminal cases does the *Times* call for "rigorous prosecution"? It didn't call for "rigorous prosecution" in the case of the Central Park jogger brutalized and left for dead by a group of teenaged thugs. The *Times* didn't call for the "rigorous prosecution" of Jerry Sandusky. It certainly didn't call for the "rigorous prosecution" of Mike Nifong, the crazed prosecutor in the Duke lacrosse case, who tried to put innocent men in prison. Rigorous prosecution was only important when the police were on trial for allegedly beating a black criminal resisting arrest.

After a five-month trial—with lots of protests and audience participation—the jury acquitted all six officers. In a somber editorial on the verdict, the *Times* assumed that *some* officers had beaten Stewart, but the jurors couldn't decide which ones. Thus, the *Times* ruefully remarked that witnesses had testified that "they saw police officers beat and kick Mr. Stewart, but they were unable to identify specific officers."[17]

Except that wasn't why the jury acquitted the officers. As two jurors patiently explained to *Times* editors a few weeks later, they didn't believe any officers beat Stewart. Testimony from witnesses claiming to have seen Stewart being beaten, they said, was "inconsistent," "uncertain" and "vague."[18]

Suspiciously missing from the extensive media coverage of the Stewart case were the usual homey details about the victim—his family's recollections of him, his passions, how he loved school and had a "ready smile"—the "ready smile" detail was always when you knew the *Times* was writing about a dangerous sociopath.

Stewart's entire life was a blank slate, with the media identifying him exclusively as an "artist" and "model," and the police calling him a "violent psycho." However, one detail accidentally slipped out after the trial, when the *Times* mentioned that the jurors had heard "a reference to an outstanding warrant for Mr. Stewart's arrest."[19]

Liberals didn't know who Michael Stewart was and they didn't care—until his death allowed them to engage in their usual breast-beating about racism. Stewart is now memorialized in a Lou Reed song and a Keith Haring painting: a victim of police racism. Haring's painting is titled, "Michael Stewart—USA for Africa." For all we know, Stewart had never heard of Africa.

LARRY DAVIS—1987

A few years later, a black criminal, Larry Davis, killed four drug dealers in the South Bronx and one in Manhattan to steal their drugs. When the police came to arrest him, he shot six of them. For firing at uniformed police officers, the *Times* cheerfully reported, Davis became a folk hero in large parts of the black community. Davis eluded the police for seventeen days, and when he was finally led away, residents of the Bronx housing project where he was caught leaned out their windows, chanting "Lar-ry! Lar-ry!"[20]

Davis's lawyer, William Kunstler, argued that his client had shot uniformed policemen in self-defense and a mostly black jury in the Bronx agreed. This serial murderer/attempted cop killer was acquitted of all charges.

The *Times* had not called for "rigorous prosecution" of Larry Davis, nor was it unhappy with the verdict. Its editorial on his acquittal compared Davis's shooting six policemen to Bernie Goetz's self-defense shooting of four muggers a few years earlier.

In an editorial, the *Times* cautioned readers against "dismiss[ing]" the verdict, explaining:

"The jury, predominantly black, was influenced by the police department's recent history of overreaction and misconduct"—and then cited Michael Stewart and Eleanor Bumpurs.[21]

Although it was the *Times*'s own demagogic reporting that had helped turn those incidents into apparent acts of racism, the *Times* blamed blacks' negative perception of the police entirely on the police. Americans would have seen the OJ verdict coming if the *Times*'s readership hadn't been limited all those years to heads-up-their-butts, Upper West Side liberals.

LEMRICK NELSON—1992

After the officers in the Michael Stewart case were acquitted, an inconsolable *New York Times* published a somber editorial titled, "How to Remember Michael Stewart."[22] It began by saying that "a New York jury has refused to hold any police officers responsible for the death of Michael Stewart." Refused? Why not "has found police officers not responsible for the death of Michael Stewart"?

By contrast, several years later, when a predominantly black jury in Brooklyn acquitted Lemrick Nelson of murdering Yankel Rosenbaum—despite Nelson having the bloody knife on him, his being identified by a dying Rosenbaum as the perpetrator, and Nelson's confession to the police—the *Times* editorial the next day began: "A Brooklyn jury's acquittal leaves unresolved who killed Yankel Rosenbaum."[23]

That case began on August 19, 1992, when a car in a Hasidic rabbi's motorcade hit and killed a nine-year-old black child, Gavin Cato. This instantly incited three nights of black riots, pungent with anti-Semitism. Shortly after the accident, a mob of black teenagers surrounded Rosenbaum, shouting "Kill the Jew!" and stabbed Rosenbaum four times. Hours later, Rosenbaum died.

Cops chased Lemrick Nelson from the scene, caught him nearby and found a bloody knife on him. His jeans were bloodstained. Before the ambulance took Rosenbaum away, he identified Nelson as the man who had knifed him in front of cops, ambulance drivers and civilians. Rosenbaum then asked Nelson, "Why did you do this to me?"[24] Back at the police station, Nelson confessed.[25]

Stunningly, Nelson was acquitted of all charges by a majority black Brooklyn jury—or, as the *New York Times* described it, a "jury of seven women and five men."[26] Despite the overwhelming evidence against Nelson, the jurors indignantly insisted they based their verdict on "the law and evidence," as juror Mercidida Hernandez said. Juror Norma Hall said she didn't believe the police, and the jury foreman, John St. Hill, said there were "a lot of inconsistencies in the facts." After the verdict, the jurors went to a dinner with Nelson. Several of the jurors hugged him.[27]

In his federal civil rights trial more than ten years later, Nelson admitted he had stabbed Rosenbaum.[28]

Eight of the nine policemen who testified against Nelson were white, so the New York media blamed the police for the "black community" hating them, suggesting that the *Times* realized the importance of the jury's racial composition, despite burying that information.

The *New York Times* huffily editorialized about the verdict: "Has the Police Department lost all credibility with many of the neighborhoods it serves?" Instructing New Yorkers "to heed a jury's sobering message," the *Times* said the verdict sent a grave message to the police union to stop complaining about Mayor Dinkins's "supposedly oversympathetic responses when neighborhoods charge police misconduct." To "help us heal," the *Times* called for an independent board to review police misconduct.[29]

Showing the fierce independence that is the New York media, *Newsday* (New York) also blamed the police: "The verdict should give new urgency to the task of recruiting a police force that reflects the diversity of this city," it called on the police to "prove to skeptical communities that most cops deserve to be believed."[30]

(Sadly, the *New York Daily News* from that time is not on Nexis.)

Outside the courthouse, blacks cheered the result.[31] For many years in New York, every day was the OJ verdict.

KIKO GARCIA—1992

About the time police were being blamed for the acquittal of Lemrick Nelson, a far more serious charge of racism would be made—one that would leave a New York City policeman accused of murder. (Guess who's side Dinkins took?) Little remembered today, the facts are astonishing.

On July 3, 1992, undercover officer Michael O'Keefe and his partners spotted a man with a gun in a high drug-trafficking neighborhood in

Washington Heights. O'Keefe went to apprehend the man, Jose "Kiko" Garcia, while his partners circled around the block to cut off Garcia if he fled.

As soon as O'Keefe told Garcia he was a police officer, Garcia attacked him, launching the two into a four-minute, life-or-death struggle. As O'Keefe struggled to get Garcia's gun, the fight moved into an apartment foyer. The terrified officer screamed into his radio for backup, but his partners were giving chase to yet another Washington Heights man with a gun who had just run right in front of their car. Back in the apartment foyer, Garcia broke away and pointed his gun at O'Keefe. O'Keefe shot first, hitting Garcia in the stomach and then, as he spun, shot again, hitting Garcia in the side of his back. O'Keefe grabbed Garcia's loaded gun, and cuffed him.

Garcia, an illegal immigrant, convicted crack dealer, parole violator and cocaine addict was pronounced dead at the hospital. He became an instant martyr to the race agitators and one less vote for the Democrats.

The hardworking immigrant was first honored with three days of violent rioting in his Washington Heights neighborhood, estimated to contain one hundred thousand illegal immigrants. The riots left one person dead, 90 injured, 53 policemen hospitalized, 121 vehicles torched, 11 police cars damaged, and dozens of businesses burned or looted.[32] Even a police helicopter was struck by gunfire. An industrious Haitian couple stood and watched their livery cab blown up with a Molotov cocktail and burned to rubble. "This car is what we use to pay the rent, feed the kid and take care of our family overseas," the woman told the *Times*.[33]

Next, Garcia was honored with preposterous lies told by those in "the neighborhood," recycled in the press and given credibility by Mayor Dinkins.

About an hour after the shooting, neighbors Juana Rodriguez Madera and her sister Anna Rodriguez told detectives that they had seen nothing and heard only a baby crying and a "couple" of shots. But in no time they were blanketing the airwaves with vivid, minute-by-minute eyewitness accounts of the confrontation, in which they claimed—in various versions—that an unarmed Garcia had pleaded for his life as Officer O'Keefe beat and kicked him, then shot him in the back multiple times while he was face-down on the lobby floor.

About six months before this incident, the police had executed a raid on Madera's apartment in the building where the struggle took place and found cocaine, marijuana, drug paraphernalia, a loaded .38 caliber handgun and forty-two rounds of ammunition. (But, thankfully, no soda, salt, or saturated fats.) The police also found a videotape of Madera's nephew tossing small drug packets in the air, saying, "It's legal here; it's liberated," with Garcia visible in the background as the nephew's lookout.

Garcia's earlier drug conviction and his involvement with Madera in the drug trade was known to Mayor Dinkins before he paid a highly publicized visit to Garcia's family. The mayor offered the crack dealer's family his condolences, promising a full investigation and also announcing that the city would pay for Garcia's funeral expenses in the Dominican Republic. He invited the family to Gracie Mansion the next day.

Dinkins didn't so much as call Officer O'Keefe, the policeman who came within seconds of losing his life after being attacked by an illegal alien crack dealer, while he was trying to keep a black neighborhood safe.[34]

Manhattan District Attorney Robert Morganthau convened a grand jury to investigate Officer O'Keefe for murder—*murder*—in the shooting of Garcia, a clean-living hardworking man with a ready smile.

From the beginning, O'Keefe told one consistent story about what had happened.[35] By contrast, the drug-den sisters had a whole bunch of different stories. All the physical and forensic evidence supported O'Keefe's version—and often directly contradicted the sisters' testimony. This was according to the city's forensic experts, the Federal Bureau of Investigation—as well as a pathologist and criminologist hired by the Garcia family, who stood to make a lot of money if O'Keefe were found to have acted improperly.

Not a single bullet mark, for example, was found in the floor, despite the sisters' claim that Garcia had been lying on the ground unconscious while O'Keefe repeatedly shot him in the back. However, a bullet mark was found in a lobby pillar right where it would have passed through Garcia's stomach if he had been standing where O'Keefe said he was.

The bullet wounds on Garcia's body were consistent with his being shot once in the stomach, spinning from the impact, and then being shot in the side of his back—just as O'Keefe had said. The bullet wounds were inconsistent with the sisters' claim that Garcia was flat on his stomach, unconscious, as O'Keefe shot him three times in the back.

Apart from the handcuff marks, medical experts found only two bruises on Garcia's body—on his nose and head, exactly where O'Keefe said he had hit Garcia in the struggle. The absence of any other bruising strongly contradicted the sisters' claim that O'Keefe savagely beat Garcia all over his body, including his knees, shoulders and hands.

The bullets recovered from the foyer, a ballistics report on O'Keefe's gun, and Garcia's wounds all showed that only two shots were fired—as O'Keefe said. Not three—as the sisters testified.

As for why Garcia might have reacted violently to a policeman, the pathologists concluded that Kiko was a chronic cocaine user and that there was cocaine in his system at the time of death. The fact that he was an illegal immigrant, a convicted felon and a parole violator might also have influenced his decision to try to kill the cop.

But reporters were earnestly broadcasting every outlandish claim to come out of "the neighborhood"—a neighborhood that held the record for the most murders of any police precinct in New York.[36] CBS News called Garcia "a Dominican immigrant." (How about, "Heinrich Himmler, a Munich native"?) As the camera panned over his sorry living quarters, reporter Giselle Fernandez posed a question from his aunt: Does "this look like the lavish style of a drug dealer, as police allege?"[37]

Viewers might have been able to better answer that question if CBS had also mentioned that Garcia was a prodigious cocaine user, a convicted drug dealer and had appeared as a lookout on a home video seized during a drug bust months earlier.

A New York Times article cited "[p]eople on the street" contending that "the officer pushed Mr. Garcia into the building and then shot him." One man, Genefonsio Yiquiya, described a whole posse of police beating Garcia: "Undercover police hit him on the knee. After they break his legs, they pulled him in and shot him three times." He claimed he "heard Mr. Garcia screaming, 'Mama, Mama, they are killing me,' in Spanish." The Times also quoted, without correction, the Garcia family lawyer's claim that "this kid never was arrested; he wasn't a drug dealer."[38]

Soon the Times was referring to the illegal alien/coke addict/convicted drug dealer as "Mr. Garcia, a twenty-three-year-old father of two." ("Himmler, a forty-five-year-old father of two . . .") Mixed in were slanderous allegations from "the neighborhood" about O'Keefe being part of a criminal gang of cops, who stole money and cocaine from drug dealers.[39] Liberals have unadorned affection for any Third World dictatorship, but our police arrest a black man and it's always a fascist police state—in a negative way.

The Times was a model of journalistic skepticism compared to New York Newsday, which ran a banner headline on its cover: "Cop Shooting Victim: He Was Shot in the Back." Another Newsday article said it was "not clear what happened" because, although the police claimed Garcia was a convicted crack dealer, on the other hand, "the community"—i.e., drug dealers—said he was "a clean-living immigrant."[40] Who could possibly sort out these conflicting perspectives?

Newsday's Jim Dwyer dedicated an entire column to repeating the allegations of drug-den proprietress Madera. Describing Madera as a "mother of four," Dwyer said she "runs a small cafeteria in the kitchen of Apartment 110 at 505 W. 162nd St." The "cafeteria" noted by Dwyer was in the same apartment where she also stored drugs and guns, based on the recent police raid.

Dwyer also unskeptically reported that Madera saw O'Keefe beating Garcia from the second-floor landing, adding—as if the gritty street reporter had performed an inspection of the building himself—that the "lobby is visible from there only by kneeling."[41] In fact, it was not visible by kneeling, or even by lying prone—as was later established by city investigators as well as the Garcia family lawyer. Dwyer was so breathtakingly easy to fool, in no time he was hired by the *New York Times*, where he now holds the Anna Quindlen chair in Extreme Gullibility of Belief In Anything.

The drug-den sisters who claimed they had witnessed O'Keefe beating and shooting Garcia from a stairwell landing must have realized the grand jurors would be brighter than Jim Dwyer, so they explained they could see what was happening because they were lying down with their heads on the floor. All forensic experts concluded that, even lying down, it was impossible to see the lobby from the second-floor landing. The Garcia family's criminologist even used a laser beam to try to confirm the sisters' claim, but found that, at most, they could have only seen someone's feet. (Or maybe they saw the whole thing by "kneeling," as Jim Dwyer reported for *Newsday*.)

Also inconsistent with the sisters' description of a trigger-happy cop pitilessly torturing Garcia were tapes of Officer O'Keefe's high-pitched shrieks of "Ten-thirteen!" into his police radio, meaning "Officer in need of assistance": "Ten-thirteen! Ten-thirteen! 163 Street and St. Nick, send help! Ten-thirteen, 163 Street and St. Nick, send help!"[42] His partners barely recognized O'Keefe's voice, saying it sounded like a woman screaming.[43]

In the end, the grand jury concluded that O'Keefe was telling the truth and had acted in self-defense, and that the sisters were telling big stinking lies. (The rest of "the neighborhood" disappeared when it came time to make their statements under oath and not just to naïve reporters.)

After noting that the officer's account was corroborated by the autopsy, the toxicology tests and physical evidence at the scene, DA Morgenthau summarized the grand jury's conclusions as to the credibility of O'Keefe's accusers:

> Those accounts are unsubstantiated. The critical two witnesses have given different versions of events at different times. Their description of how they happened to see the shooting does not fit logically with the physical features of the lobby where it occurred. They deny matters which are provably true. And the version of events which they offered to investigators is not only not corroborated by the physical evidence in the case; it is actually contradicted by that evidence.[44]

The drug-den sisters had provably lied under oath to a grand jury—admittedly, not about something as important as whether they had used the N-word in the prior ten years—but in accusing a New York City cop of cold-blooded murder. As a result of their lies, the city was forced to waste two months of the grand jurors' time, as well as that of ten investigators and six prosecutors, who interviewed hundreds of people and presented more than a hundred exhibits to the grand jury.[45] If the sisters' claims had not been proved false by mountains of physical evidence, their lies could have sent a policeman to prison for life for the crime of risking his life to get a drug dealer out of a black neighborhood.

But—as with so many other lies about racism—no charges would be brought against the perjurious women. To the contrary, it was Garcia's family that was looking for a lawsuit. They responded to the grand jury's painstaking investigation by demanding a federal civil rights investigation of the police department[46] and a state investigation into the grand jury.[47] In Washington Heights, protestors dissatisfied with the grand jury's conclusion marched in protest, requiring yet another infusion of police into the neighborhood to prevent more riots.

The endless stream of false civil-rights claims on behalf of cop killers and drug dealers debased the cause of real civil rights and caused the immiseration of many people—always with dollops of abuse for anyone who dissented from conventional wisdom. When all the people the media had ridiculed turned out to be right, liberal zealots were still praised for their admirable goals. Why should it matter if they thought they were doing the right thing at the time? Hitler thought he was doing the right thing at the time. But on the left, you can never fail your way out of public life.

CHAPTER 3

GUILTY UNTIL PROVEN BLACK

In the world before OJ, racial intimidation ruled the day—except against liberals, who were immunized from charges of racism even if they had been Klansmen. Reporters became junior G-men ferreting out racist thoughts, knowing full well that the mere accusation of racism could destroy careers and reputations.

The racism hunters ruined lives, but they never paid a price. To the contrary, they got their butts kissed, collected awards, appeared on the David Susskind show and were the subject of "profiles in courage" testimonials. Any white person could get a standing ovation for accusing other white people of being racist. *Let's be honest, we live in a racist society.*

Why is that courageous? Normally, being honest consists of admitting something about yourself, not slinging slurs at others.

Defending the race-baiting courtroom techniques of famed black attorney Alton H. Maddox Jr., for example, Legal Services NYC attorney James I. Meyerson told the *Washington Post* that Maddox was "making all of us confront the barriers of our own racism."[1] "Our" racism means "yours"—not his. Liberal honesty consists of saying: *I didn't do it! They did!*

While white people lived under a presumption of guilt, black crimes were excused, lied about or unreported. White people have done their part by telling everyone not to be prejudiced against black teenagers. The next step is for black teenagers to stop committing so many crimes. That's the problem, but for decades it was hidden under a tsunami of excuses for black criminals and alerts about pervasive white racism every time any white harmed a black person.

EDMUND PERRY—1985

In the summer of 1985, Edmund Perry, a black teenager from Harlem, had just graduated from Exeter and was headed to Stanford on a full scholarship when he mugged a guy who turned out to be an undercover cop, and ended up dead.

Officer Lee Van Houten was patroling the St. Luke's Hospital parking lot dressed as a medical intern. Perry and his brother, Jonah, grabbed him from behind, threw him to the ground and started pummeling and kicking him. Van Houten screamed that he was a cop, but they kept pounding on him and shouting, "Give it up!" On the verge of unconsciousness, Van Houten pulled his ankle gun and fired at his attackers, hitting Perry who died a few hours later.

And then we were off to the races.

The *New York Post*: "COP KILLS HARLEM HONOR STUDENT"

The *New York Times*: "HONOR STUDENT, 17, IS KILLED BY POLICEMAN ON WEST SIDE."

The *Los Angeles Times*: "SAYS VICTIM ATTACKED HIM, MOTHER CHARGES RACISM; OFFICER KILLS TOP STUDENT, SETS OFF FUROR."

How about, "Hero Cop Attacked by Privileged Teen"?

Unfortunately for the twenty-four-year-old Van Houten, he was white, so the press had all the information it needed. Until that night, Van Houten had an unblemished record during his two years on the force and had never fired his gun in the line of duty. But instead of waiting for the facts, the media rushed out with a story about a trigger-happy racist cop. Van Houten's claim of self-defense was surrounded with quotes from others expressing skepticism.

When they're maligning Joe McCarthy, liberals are happy to remind us that an accusation is not proof of guilt. But all that innocent-until-proved-guilty claptrap flies out the window in the case of a politically incorrect crime. This is the racism exception to journalistic skepticism. For certain charges—racism, police brutality, rape—the media have decided to suspend all doubt about the accuser. The allegation alone is proof of guilt. If the accused says he's innocent, liberals stare in wonderment: *What kind of monster defends himself from a charge of racism?* You just had to hope no one accused you.

From the moment Edmund Perry was shot, the media noisily jumped on the bandwagon of a phony police brutality charge. When it turned out to be false, the *New York Times* silently looked at its shoes. It was the kind of story the elites wanted to be true, so it should be true. *We had such high hopes for that one. Damn!*

Typical was an article in the *Village Voice* on the Perry shooting that explained: "[L]ike so many other victims in this city," Perry was "just too black for his own good."[2] The *Voice*'s Nelson George went on to report fanciful accounts of the shooting from unnamed witnesses, as well as his own unfounded speculation. He hypothesized that Van Houten had been mugged by three other men; that he had not been knocked to the ground by muggers because, George claimed, the autopsy indicated Perry was shot from a distance and from a standing position; and that the officer was not on duty but "moonlighting" as a security guard.

None of this would be backed up by witnesses who testified to the grand jury and at trial. To the contrary, a number of witnesses, including black witnesses, supported Van Houten's account. If a conservative journalist retailed this many false facts about, say, Obama's birth certificate, he'd never get another serious job.

Most amusingly, George reported that Perry's friends and family had seen Officer Van Houten leave the hospital at one a.m. the night of the shooting, surrounded by "eight plainclothes and uniformed police" and . . . *he had no visible signs of injury!*[3] Of course, the only member of Perry's entourage who would have had the first idea what Van Houten looked like was his brother, Jonah, who participated in the mugging. But he said he wasn't there, so he couldn't very well claim to recognize the officer.

In any event, Van Houten was not walking out of St. Luke's surrounded by other officers at one a.m. because he was kept overnight for treatment to "cuts and bruises to his face, arms and back and injury to his neck," according to the *New York Times* and every other news outlet other than the *Voice*.[4]

Evidently, Perry's friends and family saw a different white guy leaving the hospital at one a.m with no visible scratches. (Just as when, in 2012, MSNBC triumphantly presented grainy videos of Trayvon Martin's shooter, George Zimmerman, in the police station hours after the shooting to proclaim him scratch-free—until more contemporaneous photos were produced showing bleeding welts on the back of his head.)

George characterized the police's position thus: "[W]hen Edmund saw a chance to mug a white person he took it. Really, what other motivation would a young nigger need?"[5] There was no evidence that Van Houten or anyone else had used the N-word. Only the liberal used it.

Perry's mother blamed her son's death on white resentment toward successful blacks: "White people hated to see his success. That's the only way I can figure it. They wanted to wipe him out."[6] It's not unusual for a mother to refuse to believe her son committed a crime. What's unusual is for the media to encourage such unfounded beliefs.

News accounts stressed not only that Perry was a graduate of Exeter on his way to Stanford, but that he was unarmed. In all white-on-black shootings, the media expect the white person to have RoboCop-like superpowers to detect weapons or the lack thereof, as well as the attacker's resumé.

A few weeks after the shooting, the *New York Times* editorialized about Perry, "a prized symbol of hope." In a telling bit of obtuseness, the *Times* said that "all New Yorkers have extraordinary reasons to wish for the innocence of the young man who was killed." I doubt very much that the cop being accused of murder hoped for that.

The *Times* criticized the police for saying they had numerous witnesses backing up the officer's story, but giving no details (after two whole weeks). Following *Times* guidelines, the paper blamed everyone but the black assailant: "Was deadly force necessary?" ... "Why didn't Officer Van Houten's backup team, following in a station wagon, intervene to prevent the beating and killing?" . . . "Why would [Edmund Perry] put his promising future at risk for a street crime?"[7]

One might also have asked: "Why would an undercover cop shoot a black kid for no reason?" But that did not pique the *Times*'s curiosity.

Then, twenty-three witnesses corroborated the officer's account in testimony to the grand jury. Some said that they heard Edmund planning the mugging with his brother Jonah, who was a sophomore at Cornell University. According to the district attorney, a "significant number" of witnesses said they saw the mugging. Other witnesses told the grand jury they heard Jonah saying his brother got shot when they were mugging a "D.T." or "detective."[8] God help Officer Van Houten if he had been mugged someplace other than a hospital parking lot with plenty of witnesses.

After considering the evidence, the grand jury cleared Van Houten of all wrongdoing and indicted Jonah for the mugging.

Needless to say, there would be no apology from the media for filling the air with accusations against a policeman. When the story first broke, everyone knew exactly where to place the blame. There was no tender search into a police officer's troubles, no praise for his educational achievements, no vaporous sorrow about the strain of his job, no "puzzle" to be solved. The cop was a racist. . . . The end.

But when it turned out Van Houten was telling the truth and that Edmund Perry had in fact mugged him, delicate reporting was called for. The truth about Perry was revealed amid great sorrow. It was no one's fault, but a problem of "confusion, frustration and pain" and "two worlds" colliding.[9]

Bard College produced a play about the incident, *Purgatory*, about "a lonely black teen-ager who tries to live in two worlds, one black and one white." One student explained, "I wanted to open people's eyes to the fact that racism is still very much alive, although it's not as visible."[10]

Again: PERRY MUGGED A COP.

For some journalists it was easier to deal with their grief by pretending they missed the news about all the witnesses supporting the cop's account. Even after the indictments, for example, Dorothy J. Gaiter of the *Miami Herald* wrote about Edmund Perry in an article titled, "To Be Black and Male Is Dangerous in U.S."[11] Based on not having been there, seen anything, or been on the grand jury, but rather on having met Edmund once, she announced: "I can't say whether he would do something that stupid."

So even if he mugged a cop, it wasn't wrong or bad, it was "stupid."

Having just allowed that she "couldn't say," Gaiter decided she could say, after all, and proceeded to ask: "How do you teach a boy to be a man in a society where others may view him as a threat just because he is black?" Numerous witnesses corroborated Van Houten's account that Perry had jumped him from behind, punched him in the face and demanded his money. Isn't it possible that Van Houten saw Perry as a threat for reasons other than "just because he is black"?

Reaching for the same "just because he was black" thesis as Nelson George in the *Village Voice*, Gaiter asked whether the policeman would have "shot to kill if Perry had looked like your typical prep-school student—that is, white?" Yes, Van Houten probably wouldn't have minded being kicked and stomped by a white man.

Racial filters paralyze logical thinking.

Numerous stories cited the fact that people "who knew the brothers well agree that it is unthinkable they were involved in a street mugging, as the police contend."[12] Do friends and family ever think their loved ones could have committed a crime? These consanguinity defenses were a staple of police brutality stories in the eighties. The beliefs and feelings of the officer's friends and family, however, were not deemed newsworthy. How could you trust the relative of a racist?

(One of the classics of the genre was a *Newsweek* article claiming "others" disputed Bernie Goetz's allegation that the four men he shot were mugging him. On close examination, the "others" turned out to be two of the muggers[13], who, by the way, later admitted to both the media and police that they were, in fact, mugging him.[14])

Somewhat amazingly, friends of the Perry family were not unanimous in their publicly stated refusal to believe the mugging story. Among the twenty-three prosecution witnesses, two were neighborhood acquaintances of the Perrys. One testified that Jonah told him on the night of the incident that his brother was shot when they were mugging someone. The other said Jonah told her that night that he tried to beat up a guy who turned out to be a cop.[15]

These intrepid souls told the truth, knowing they'd have to go back to the neighborhood.

Jonah did not take the stand in his defense and presented no witnesses to support his version of events. Rather, defense lawyer-cum-racial agitator Alton Maddox—soon to be concocting the Tawana Brawley hoax—accused the police of conducting a "frame-up" and claimed Van Houten was drunk on the night of the shooting. He presented no evidence for these charges.

Maddox attacked the family friend who testified that Jonah told her they had mugged a detective, accusing her of being a prostitute. He ridiculed the other Perry neighbor for his lack of education and having had troubles with the law. (And if there's one thing Alton Maddox cannot abide, it's a lawbreaker!) Throughout Maddox's summation, there were choruses of "Amen" from the gallery.[16]

In a courthouse jammed with Perry supporters, the jury acquitted Jonah of the mugging, leading to cheers from the courtroom.[17]

Still, the truth had come out and, whether or not Jonah was there (as the evidence indicated), there could be no question that Officer Van Houten had been mugged and had fired in self-defense. Instead of rounds of mea culpas from the media, the matter was quickly forgotten.

But not by the *Village Voice*'s Nelson George, who unabashedly included his essay on the Edmund Perry frame-up in a 1993 collection of his columns. The evidence had evidently not changed his opinion that something "stinks" in the NYPD.[18]

Why didn't we ever get any stories on the courageous neighborhood witnesses who testified against Jonah? Aren't they the heroes? They went against "the community" to tell the truth. *Yeah, I heard him say he mugged a cop.* Why aren't there any movies about such real bravery?

Instead, there was a movie about the mugger: *Murder Without Motive: The Edmund Perry Story*. Without motive? The motive was: *The cop was being mugged!* The IMDB movie summary states: "Edmund Perry appears to have things all going his way when he graduates from Phillips Exeter Academy with a scholarship to Stanford U. *when an unfortunate meeting with a police officer ends his life.*" (Emphasis added.)

Instead of turning every story about a black person shot or killed by a white person into an occasion to announce that "the simple fact is, America is a racist society," liberals might, just once, have asked the question: *Why do you suppose there would be a generalized fear of young black males? What might that be based on?*

Throw us a bone. Perhaps it's because a disproportionate number of criminals are young black males.[19]

What stinks in the Edmund Perry case is that the culture encouraged an entire ethnic group to develop a deeply adversarial relationship with mainstream society. Hollywood and the universities celebrated gansters and criminals. Black kids got beaten up for doing well at school. And when a Stanford-bound black teenager mugged an undercover cop, the *New York Times* trotted out the police brutality theory, later downgraded to "a tragedy."

MARLA HANSON—1986

Journalists needn't have worried about manufacturing a Hollywood-ready story. Hollywood was willing to alter the facts of actual cases all on its own in order to create a politically correct narrative.

In June 1986, model Marla Hanson's face was slashed by two black men. An Irish cop investigating the case determined that her assailants had been hired by Hanson's slimy landlord, upset that she had spurned his sexual advances. A white woman—a "white Hispanic" in the Trayvon Martin-era lingo—prosecuted the case, and a racial demagogue, Alton Maddox, represented the black defendants. At trial, Maddox attacked the victim with baseless accusations about her sex life and accused her of being prejudiced against blacks.

Maddox said, for example, that Hanson "saw two men coming toward her and feared she was going to be assaulted . . . sexually assaulted." He said Hanson had "racial hang-ups . . . Just the simple sight of two black men . . .

and she went absolutely nuts."[20] He said she invented the story to frame the black defendants.

Leaving aside the question of why the victim of a vicious crime would be more interested in falsely accusing two random black guys than in punishing the men who slashed her face so badly she needed a hundred fifty stitches and was left scarred for life, Maddox had not a shred of evidence for any of these claims. If Hanson had feared that the two black men approaching her were going to assault her, surely that is mitigated by the fact that they were.

Flash to the 1991 made-for-TV docudrama about the Marla Hanson case. In the movie, Hanson's champion was a black cop. The case was prosecuted by a black female. The defense attorney putting the victim's sex life and racial attitudes on trial was a white guy. It was like a Soviet documentary.

If Hollywood is cleaning up reality to send the right message, why not have eighty-five of one hundred U.S. senators be black? Or why not my fantasy: nine black Supreme Court justices, like Clarence Thomas, and I mean all nine *exactly* like Clarence Thomas.

MARION BARRY—WASHINGTON, DC, 1989

Another victim of white racism was Marion Barry, mayor of the nation's capital.

Despite Barry's being captured on videotape smoking crack cocaine and perjuring himself, the majority-black jury simply would not convict him—except on the single count his attorney had admitted to in open court: misdemeanor drug possession.

The DC police had happened upon the mayor's cocaine habit completely by accident. Two undercover officers were at the Washington, DC Ramada Inn, investigating suspected drug dealer Charles Lewis, when they happened to run into the mayor's security detail outside Lewis's room. After confirming that the mayor was inside, they promptly aborted the operation and turned it over to the FBI. Traces of cocaine were found in Lewis's hotel room—a room he had paid for with a city government credit card.[21]

During Barry's trial, Lewis testified in detail about his use of drugs with the mayor. A female witness told the jury that she had smoked crack with Barry in his hotel room in the Virgin Islands—and that he had then raped her. Two other women said they also smoked crack with Barry in the Virgin Islands and that he tried to have sex with them.[22]

But the key witness was the mayor's former mistress, Hazel Diane "Rasheeda" Moore, forever memorialized in Barry's immortal line, "The b—ch set me up." Moore had cooperated with the FBI, leading to the sting that produced videotapes of Barry smoking crack with her in a hotel room. She testified that she had smoked crack with the mayor at least a hundred times, sometimes two or three times a day during their three-year relationship.[23] For being his mistress, she said Barry gave her a lucrative city contract and then threatened to revoke it if she did not comply when he stood naked before her, demanding oral sex. [24]

The jury saw videotapes of the mayor smoking crack with Moore, along with Barry's videotaped testimony to the grand jury in which he denied ever having smoked crack or even knowing Rasheeda Moore.

Here was the mayor of the nation's capitol, which had a majority black population that was being decimated by the crack epidemic, caught on videotape smoking crack cocaine. But Barry checkmated the prosecution by entering the courtroom with a black power salute, wearing African kente cloth.[25]

Every day, when Barry emerged from the courthouse, a cheering throng of blacks began singing "We Shall Overcome."[26] Some threatened riots if Barry were found guilty.[27] Everywhere he went, there were standing ovations and cries of "Run, Barry, Run!"[28] George Stallings Jr., minister of a black separatist church Barry attended, affirmed that Barry was "more popular now than ever before."[29]

During his trial, Barry was the headline speaker at rallies for Nelson Mandela and Louis Farrakhan, presenting himself as a victim of white oppression in the mold of Mandela: "Let the people speak about what is happening in Washington, DC—not just here, but for the other black elected officials all over the land who have misfortunately [sic] been harassed and arraigned by U.S. prosecutors."[30] Jesse Jackson said the FBI sting of Barry reminded him of Soviet justice.[31]

The jury deadlocked on all courts, save the misdemeanor charge, despite the government's "overwhelming" case—as put by the presiding judge, U.S. District Court judge Thomas Penfield Jackson. Jackson said he had "never seen a stronger government case" but that some jurors simply "would not convict under any circumstances."

According to the *Washington Post*'s reporting on the case, Judge Jackson was right. There was a block of five black jurors who held out for acquittal on all but the misdemeanor count. Meanwhile, four young educated black women were adamantly in favor of conviction, believing the case against Barry was overwhelming on at least ten of the counts.[32]

But nothing would satisfy Barry's supporters on the jury. They denied that the bag of crack the FBI seized from Barry was crack, saying it looked more like sugar or baking soda. (The fact that the bag contained crack cocaine was contested by no one at trial.) They refused to convict on one of the possession counts because it referred to Barry smoking crack "on or about" January 1 to January 18—meaning the precise day was irrelevant—because they believed, irrelevantly, that Barry had actually smoked crack a few days earlier. They claimed the FBI "planted" evidence on Barry because he was black.

One of the pro-acquittal jurors, Valerie Jackson-Warren, was a DC Department of Corrections secretary. She explained her weighing of the evidence to the *Post*: "I believe [the government was] out to get Marion Barry. I believe that with all my heart." [33]

When other jurors were making arguments based on the evidence, one of Barry's supporters snapped at her, "I'm sick of you bourgeois blacks." Another told two black jurors who favored a guilty verdict that they should read a book about the oppression of blacks by whites.

After being sentenced to six months in prison, Barry went on the *Phil Donahue Show* and was greeted with "wild cheering" from the audience at the University of the District of Columbia. He complained about receiving any prison time at all, rather than community service.[34] Benjamin Hooks, executive director of the once-respected NAACP, embarrassed himself by appearing on the show with Barry to denounce the "vicious" prosecution of Barry and calling it part of the "incessant harassment of black elected officials."[35] He, too, said the "fair thing" would have been to sentence Barry to community service.[36]

By defending black elected officials like Barry, race hustlers left the impression that all black leaders were inevitably corrupt, incompetent or criminal. Why else would it be "racist" to punish a crack-smoking mayor?

EDWARD SUMMERS—JANUARY 1994

In January 1994, Edward Summers needed a new car. So he went to a shopping mall in Nanuet, New York, and waited in the parking lot until he saw Michael Falcone and Scott Nappi getting into Falcone's Jeep. He forced them at gunpoint to drive to a remote location three miles away, assuring them he wasn't going to hurt them. Summers then had the boys lie face down on the grass, straddled them, and shot each one in the head at point-blank range. Nappi flinched just as the gun went off, so the bullet lodged in his cheek, saving his life and making him a living witness to the entire crime.

Soon after Nappi had struggled to a phone and reported the fatal carjacking, the police spotted Summers driving Falcone's Jeep. He proceeded to lead the cops on a car chase reaching speeds of 130 miles per hour, crashed the Jeep, and leaped from the car to flee on foot. After being captured, Summers gave a detailed, forty-nine-page written confession. Nappi identified Summers as Falcone's killer.

The media refused to believe it. Summers was a college student from a middle-class black family, with married parents. Why would he steal a Jeep and commit murder? They had learned nothing and forgotten nothing.

Lynn Sherr's report on the crime for ABC News was titled: "Who Is Ed Summers?—Carjack Killer or Framed Innocent?" "Framed"? This was a case with a living witness and a written confession.

But Sherr reminded viewers that Summers was "an unlikely suspect, a loving son, a college student with a promising future," before asking: "What's the real story? Is an innocent man in jail?" Her report featured Summers's friends swearing he couldn't have done it, with Sherr adding: "Ed was a junior at South Carolina State University with good grades in pre-med. His friends say he loved his schoolwork and wanted to save lives, not destroy them."[37]

In a lengthy brief for the defense, *New York Magazine*'s Barbara Campbell went further, presenting Summers's crackpot alibi as completely believable. Despite having confessed, Summers later changed his story, claiming he had been forced into the Jeep by a terrifying neighborhood drug dealer named "Dino" who committed the carjacking, murder and attempted murder all on his own, then made Summers drive the Jeep back to New York.

The cops never found any evidence of a drug dealer named Dino. Nappi said that only one man had carjacked and shot them and that that man was Summers.

But Campbell found the "Dino" story highly compelling. She dismissed the overwhelming evidence against Summers with the overriding point: "The only question—the question Summers's astonished friends, teachers and the press raised over and over again—was . . . *why*?"

To the prosecutor's simple answer, "He wanted a Jeep," Campbell answered: This was not "simple at all." What the prosecution had apparently failed to consider, you see, was that Summers *said he didn't do it!* Only Barbara Campbell, liberal goo-goo at *New York Magazine,* understood the importance of the suspect's denial. "Summers maintains," Campbell reported, "that despite his being caught in the Jeep, despite the 'confession' (he signed no such document), despite his being identified by a victim, he committed no crime."[38]

Does anyone write this kind of nonsense on behalf of white criminals?

At trial, Summers's lawyers even presented a barber named Deno as a defense witness. Deno had agreed to take the stand for Summers to help his lawyers make the rather stupid point that there was someone named something like "Dino" in the neighborhood, proving that the police had not looked hard enough for anyone by that name.

It wasn't exactly a Perry Mason moment. We may presume the prosecution was not claiming there was no one in the Bronx named Dino, including harmless barbers. Summers's alibi was that this particular Dino was a major drug dealer, well known in the neighborhood and striking fear into everyone he met—which is why Summers had to do whatever Dino asked. That was the alibi.

Then, in a shocking twist, Summers's lawyer suddenly accused the astonished Deno of being the real killer! This poor schlub had taken a day off from work to help Summers and his thanks was to be accused of murder by Summers's lawyer.

The jurors were not overwhelmed by the Dino alibi. It was "smoke and mirrors," as one put it.[39] Not only had Nappi identified Summers as the killer, but the stocky five-foot-seven Deno did not resemble the slender six-foot-four "Dino" that Summers had described.

MICHAEL LASANE—1996

Journalists would never learn. In 1996, a black seventeen-year-old high school sophomore from the projects, Michael LaSane, abducted a special-education teacher, Kathleen Weinstein, and killed her for her gold 1995 Toyota Camry. We know this because, while Weinstein was in the car with him, she secretly turned on her pocket tape recorder, capturing the last half hour of her life as she tried to talk the young man out of killing her, telling him about her husband and children and asking him questions about himself. He parked the car and smothered her to death.

The tape, with LaSane's voice and personal details about him, left investigators a gold mine of information.

Nonetheless, as soon as the cops arrested LaSane with Weinstein's car, the *New York Times* asked in a headline: "Abduction Suspect Wanted a Car, But Would He Kill for It?"[40] The article quoted friends of LaSane's saying they thought he had been set up. Many also said LaSane had talked about getting a car for his seventeenth birthday. He "even had a model picked out: a gold 1995 Toyota Camry." He had the model picked out! Well, that changes everything.

There are soulless, remorseless killers of all races, but only black killers will be defended relentlessly by imbecilic liberals at places like the *New York Times*. We don't get credulous defenses of Scott Peterson or read about "lingering doubts" in the case of Phil Spector.

ROBERT CHAMBERS—1986

No one puzzled over why "Preppie Killer" Robert Chambers would kill Jennifer Levin. Chambers was arrested in August 1986 for murdering Jennifer Levin in Central Park after a night of drinking at the Upper East Side's Dorrian's Red Hand. He claimed Levin was his girlfriend and that their consensual rough sex had gotten out of hand.

This time, there were no wide-eyed journalists to champion a dubious alibi. No one would wonder why he would put his future at risk or questioned whether he could do something so "stupid." No one asked: "How do you teach a boy to be a man in a society where others may view him as a threat just because he is Irish?"

Oh no. Real life had finally produced a suspect as close as liberals were going to get to *Law & Order*'s version of the typical New York murderer: white—and, by God, liberals were going to make him privileged.

Journalists had batches of ready-made, sense-of-entitlement articles sitting around, but never got to use them. *Oh, it's just a low-class, common thug. Damn!* Chambers was white, and that was close enough. The media finally had their man, even if they had to fiddle with the facts to make him their man.

Raised mostly in Queens by his striving but not wealthy parents, an Irish nurse and an often absent, heavy-drinking father, Chambers had attended various prep schools and one semester of college—but was thrown out of most of them, most recently, Boston University. So he moved back in with his mother.[41]

And yet Chambers was still incessantly described as "rich," "privileged," "entitled," and "preppie."[42] He wasn't rich, privileged or entitled, and was only "preppie" in the strictly technical sense. (Edmund Perry could more accurately have been described as "preppie," but that didn't fit the story line.)

So with Chambers, instead of searching inquiries from wistful reporters asking: "Why would he do it?" the media were more than happy to delve into the dark side of the accused—his burglaries, psychiatric care, troubles with the law, cocaine habit, rotten grades and disciplinary problems in school and chronic unemployment.

Here's another interesting thing: You didn't see mobs of white people clogging the courtroom to heckle the prosecution or holding "No Justice, No Peace!" rallies defending Chambers. White people said: Go ahead, lock him up.

HOWARD BEACH—DECEMBER 20, 1986

Everyone was required to pretend that the real crime wave sweeping the nation was the epidemic of whites assaulting black people. As rare and precious as sightings of the aurora borealis, each one of these events would be covered like the 9/11 attack.

The media loved white goons! Where had they gone since those Democrat strongholds in the 1950s and '60s? Whenever a white perpetrator came along, journalists would write about the crime from this angle and that, roll out references to Selma and Birmingham, and polish up their incomprehensible spiels on the "social and political context" of "the Reagan Administration's [lack of] concern for the aspirations of minorities"—as the *New York Times* put it in one editorial.[43] Every false, meaningless platitude liberals believed was concentrated in their white-on-black crime stories.

The vicious attack on a group of blacks by a white gang in Howard Beach, Queens, was, as Joe Sobran called it, "the literary event of the season." It required around-the-clock coverage from newspapers, TV networks, the international press and major magazines including *Time*, *Newsweek*, *Maclean's* and the *Economist*. Mayor Ed Koch called it a "racial lynching" and requested a federal investigation. Even the governor's office got involved.

The deadly encounter in December 1986 began when three black men, Cedric Sandiford, Timothy Grimes and Michael Griffith, walked in front of a car full of white teenagers in Howard Beach, and the two groups exchanged epithets. A short while later, the whites returned, liquored up, with reinforcements and a baseball bat, spoiling for a fight. Grimes ran off unharmed, Sandiford got beaten and Griffith tried to flee by climbing through a hole in a fence—and ran directly onto a busy six-lane highway, where he was hit by a car and killed.

That same night, the white gang, or a similar one, beat up an off-duty white fireman and a couple of Hispanics in two separate incidents in Howard Beach. But those were overkill. The whites' attack on the black victims had secured their place in history, landing them on the cover of every newspaper in the city.

The FBI opened an investigation on the mugging of black victims and fifty police officers were assigned to investigate it. But no one heard about the gang attacks on white and Hispanic victims that same night in the same town.[44]

Although most of those involved were teenagers, there were criminal records on both sides. The ringleader of the white hoods, a British immigrant named Jon Lester, seventeen, had been arrested a month earlier for illegal possession of a firearm and attempting to steal a car. The victimized Grimes would be arrested days after the confrontation for stabbing his girlfriend in the back because she woke him too early.[45]

This was a turf fight instigated by teenage toughs, driven by alcohol and testosterone—both known to cause violence—not race. Lester had a black girlfriend, who sang his praises, saying, "He treated me better than all my other boyfriends, even my black boyfriends." She said he took her to see the movie *The Color Purple* on their first date and reacted movingly.[46] As one Howard Beach local said, the white kids were "punks" who "don't like anyone."[47]

White people felt no compulsion to defend the delinquents just because they were white—although residents of Howard Beach were a little testy about their whole town being portrayed as a racist cauldron on the basis of the actions of a few individuals. Thousands of black protesters repeatedly marched through Howard Beach, condemning racism and comparing the town to South Africa. One resident complained, "We don't go to Harlem when a black man kills a white man. So we don't want them coming here when it happens the other way around."[48]

The assault in Howard Beach was the sort of crime that probably happened dozens of times every week in the United States. The only unusual aspect to this particular crime was that the perpetrators were white and the victims black. Although there are no precise numbers on territorial battles among teenagers in which one of them runs onto a highway, gets hit by a car and dies, that year, blacks committed 49.1 percent of all homicides in the country, despite being only 12 percent of the population. Only 2.6 percent of all homicides in 1986 were white-on-black killings. Black criminals killed nearly three times as many white people (949) as whites killed blacks (378) and killed sixteen times as many black people (6,235) as whites did.[49]

Mayor Koch called the Howard Beach attack "the most horrendous incident of violence in the nine years I have been mayor."[50]

Earlier that year, a twenty-year-old white design student, Dawn Livecchi, answered the doorbell at her Fort Greene townhouse and was shot dead by a black part-time security guard, Anthony Neal Jenkins, who had followed her home from the grocery store.[51] Also that year, Robert Chambers had raped and murdered Jennifer Levin. One Queens woman interviewed by the *Times* about Howard Beach incidentally mentioned that her husband had been beaten so badly by a group of blacks that he remained in a coma two years later—this as Koch was uttering the words that the Howard Beach attack was "the most horrendous incident of violence" he'd seen as mayor.[52] Even the Howard Beach crowd didn't beat anyone into a coma.

The full-dress news coverage for the Howard Beach episode wasn't to highlight a rare, once-a-year occurrence. It was portrayed not as a man-bites-dog story, but a dog-bites-man story in a universe with packs of roving, rabid dogs. According to press accounts, whites attacking blacks was an epidemic—a nationwide "cancer" in the words of Mayor Koch. Of course, if that were true, this case wouldn't have attracted so much attention.

Liberals had finally gotten the freakishly atypical crime they had been searching for. They desperately wanted just one example to illustrate the popular America-is-still-racist thesis that was so rarely evident in real life.

Thus, in the deathless prose of columnist Jimmy Breslin, "Howard Beach suddenly has become what Birmingham once meant."[53] (A few years later, the ethnically sensitive Breslin was suspended for trashing a young Korean American colleague in the newsroom as a "slant-eyed bitch" and a "yellow cur."[54])

The winner of the most pompous, treacly, self-serving—and yet at the same time, revealing—commentary was *Atlantic* magazine editor Jack Beatty. In an op-ed for the *New York Times*, Beatty blamed Howard Beach on the Republican Party: "From Richard M. Nixon's 'southern strategy' to Ronald Reagan's boilerplate about 'welfare queens,' the legatees of the party of Lincoln have wrung political profit from the white backlash. Howard Beach shows that the politics of prejudice may have some vile life left in it yet."[55]

The attorneys for the black victims were Alton Maddox and C. Vernon Mason. It will not surprise those familiar with their work that the entire case quickly became a circus. The victims, Grimes and Sandiford refused to testify. They wouldn't even show up at lineups to identify their presumed attackers.

The purported reason for this lack of cooperation was to protest the failure of the police to arrest Dominic Blum, the driver of the car that stuck Griffith. Maddox and company claimed Blum had conspired with the Howard Beach gang, somehow arranging to be driving along that stretch of highway at the precise moment Griffiths ran onto it.

Even if that were logistically possible, the police found no evidence that the twenty-four-year-old Blum knew any of the defendants. He was a court officer and policeman's son, who happened to be driving home with his girlfriend after they had seen a play at Brooklyn College that night. He didn't even know he had hit anyone until he returned to the scene of the accident an hour later, thinking he'd hit a deer. Because of Maddox and Mason's screwball accusation against him, Blum needed police protection and was forced to move out of his home.[56]

Without the victims' cooperation, the police were only able to criminally charge the three teenagers who admitted to participating in the attack and the judge was forced to reduce the charges from murder and assault to reckless endangerment.

This provided another opportunity for accusations of racism. There were marches and demonstrations to denounce the judge for reducing the charge. Throngs of blacks filled the courtroom shouting "Injustice! Injustice!" Maddox stood outside the courthouse and proclaimed: "There will never be a conviction of a white man who murdered a black man in New York City."[57] He accused the police and court officers of misconduct and demanded that a special prosecutor be appointed to investigate his allegations and also to try the case because, again, the entire New York justice system was apparently shot through with racists.

The city had put fifty cops on this case, while virtually ignoring the beatings of non-black victims in Howard Beach the same night. When the defendants were tried, the judge created a new rule just for them, limiting the number of blacks the defense could excuse from the jury—a restriction on peremptory challenges that had never before been applied to the defense.[58]

But the justice system was racist.

With Al Sharpton staging marches through Howard Beach and more riots threatened, Governor Mario Cuomo complied with Maddox's insane request and appointed Charles Hynes, special state prosecutor, on the case. The governor also directed Hynes to investigate Maddox and Mason's fantastical accusations of police and prosecutorial corruption.

Hynes approached the case like an indulgent parent making excuses for a spoiled child. "I came to believe," he said, "that if police had acted sooner in running down Blum's account of his evening, Maddox might well have allowed Sandiford to cooperate."[59] Yes, and maybe if they had given him a lollipop, he would have been happy, too. The police had established Blum's whereabouts that evening within days of the attack, thus fully disproving the preposterous idea that the driver of the car had conspired with the Howard Beach thugs.

In the end, the three defendants were convicted of manslaughter. State Supreme Court justice Thomas Demakos sentenced Lester to a staggering ten to thirty-one years, requiring his sentences to be served consecutively. He was deported to Britain as soon as he had served his time.[60] The other two defendants got six-to-eighteen and five-to-fifteen-year terms, also to be served consecutively. But the foulest punishment was forcing the defendants to listen to the judge's little homily on how "racism breeds hatred."[61]

As was customary, the Howard Beach incident was followed by a slew of retaliatory crimes by blacks against whites, none of which would receive 1 percent of the attention the original attack had generated. The day after the attack, a dozen blacks beat and robbed a white seventeen-year-old boy sitting at a Queens bus stop, shouting, "Howard Beach! Howard Beach!" "He's a white boy, and they killed a black boy at Howard Beach."[62] One of the suspects was picked up a few days later. He was so intimidated by the rising white supremacist influence in New York City that he had gone on TV to brag about mugging a white kid.[63]

A few days after that, John Santiago, a lightskinned Hispanic, was beaten and robbed by a dozen black men shouting "Howard Beach! Howard Beach!" The mugging was almost called off when Santiago spoke Spanish to them, with one saying, "Leave him alone, he's not white." But the crowd was more persuaded by another assailant who argued, "He looks white."[64]

The retaliatory crimes were not reported with the fanfare of the Howard Beach incident. And that's despite the black assailants' specific mention of "Howard Beach," offering journalists another opportunity to remind readers that: America is still racist. The press couldn't have been less interested.

In all, the police said that thirty bias crimes were reported in the three weeks following Howard Beach, compared to four during the same period a year earlier.[65] The absence of any news reports on most of these crimes meant either that they were black-on-white crimes—or they were hoaxes. If there had been one other genuine white-on-black attack, we would have heard about it.

Right after the Howard Beach assailants were convicted, a year later, a white cab driver was beaten and robbed by eight blacks in Harlem, who said it was for Howard Beach. Only one newspaper, the *Chicago Tribune*, mentioned the attack, according to Nexis archives.[66] A week after that, two black men dragged the white wife of a police officer into the back of a van in Bensonhurst, Brooklyn, pulled her pants down and robbed her saying, "This is for Howard Beach" and "This will happen to other white women." That attack merited short, unsigned items in only two newspapers, the *Miami Herald* and the newspaper in the town where the attack occurred: the *New York Times*.[67]

ANN VINER AND EVELYN WAGLER

A corollary to the hysterical overreporting of any white-on-black crime is that black-on-white hate crimes will be utterly unreported by the media, except in the town where it happened.

Hollywood made a movie about Howard Beach (and the brave prosecutor who brought racists to justice). A street in New York is named after Michael Grimes. The *New York Times* still celebrates anniversaries of the Howard Beach attack. Michael Stewart, artist, is memorialized in paintings and songs. The shooting of black immigrant Amadou Diallo by four New York City cops who thought he had a gun has been featured in songs by Bruce Springsteen, Lauryn Hill, Cyndi Lauper and about four dozen other musicians. It has been written about in more than a thousand *New York Times* articles.

But does anyone know about Ann Viner? A week before the Howard Beach attack there was another interracial attack in a white neighborhood only a little father away from the *New York Times*'s building than Howard Beach is. A sixty-three-year-old white woman, Ann Viner, was attacked at her home in New Canaan, Connecticut, savagely beaten, dragged to her swimming pool and drowned by two twenty-year-old black men. It was the first murder in the affluent town in seventeen years, since a disturbed man killed four of his family members in 1970. That seems like a newsworthy story. But if you remember the wall-to-wall coverage this case got in the mainstream press at the time, immediately stop taking Ambien and call your doctor right away.

The *Times* briefly mentioned the New Canaan murder in three short news items, totaling less than a thousand words. The longest article, five hundred words, was the initial report on the murder—when there was still hope that the killers were not black.[68] No other major newspapers or magazines mentioned Viner's murder.

Twenty years later, the home invasion murders of a mother and two daughters in Cheshire, Connecticut, another white-picket-fence town, received, appropriately, a lot of coverage, including more than fifty articles in the *Times*. The killers were white.[69]

Say, has anyone heard of Evelyn Wagler? At twenty-four, Wagler, who was white, had just moved from Chicago to Roxbury, a black part of Boston. At around 9 p.m. one evening, she was set upon by six black youths, forced to douse herself in gasoline, and set on fire. Only a few newspapers picked up the AP report on her tortuous death in 1973.[70]

CHANNON CHRISTIAN AND CHRISTOPHER NEWSOM

There were so few cases of white-on-black crimes that each one could be lovingly covered for months on end—while equally heinous, and far more numerous black-on-white crimes barely made the police blotter. This suggested the possibility that, at least by the 1970s, white racism against blacks wasn't the country's most pressing problem. But the media and their designated black spokesmen kept everyone so riled up about ghosts, no one seemed not to notice that blacks weren't advancing. (They were probably living in fear of the black criminals white liberals kept defending.)

About the same time that the *New York Times* was giving saturation coverage of a stripper's (false) claim that she had been raped by white Duke lacrosse players, there was a non-hoax rape case also involving white college students in North Carolina's neighboring state of Tennessee. Channon Christian, twenty-one, and her boyfriend Christopher Newsom, twenty-three, were carjacked by five blacks. Both were repeatedly raped, sodomized with objects and tortured—bleach was poured down Channon's throat and on her bleeding genital area to eliminate the evidence while she was still alive. Newsom was shot in the head and set on fire, while Christian was tortured for several more hours before being put in a plastic bag and left in a garbage bin where she suffocated to death.

Other than a TV listing mentioning the Investigation Discovery channel's program on the crime,[71] the following constituted the *Times*'s entire coverage of this gruesome interracial rape-torture-murder, which itself was from the Associated Press:

> A man convicted in the killing of a young college student and her boyfriend has been sentenced to death. The man, Lemaricus Davidson, showed no reaction as jurors announced the sentence. Mr. Davidson, 28, was found guilty of abducting Channon Christian, 21, and her boyfriend, Christopher Newsom, 23, in Knoxville during a 2007 carjacking by several armed men. Both victims were raped. Mr. Newsom was shot and Ms. Christian suffocated after she was choked and stuffed in a garbage bag and a trash can. Mr. Davidson's brother was also convicted in the attack in August and was sentenced to life in prison without parole. Two other defendants await trial.[72]

Since the OJ verdict, the non-Fox media still refuse to cover black-on-white hate crimes, but at least they no longer ferociously defend the killers. The Tennessee murderers are not being defensively profiled by ABC's Lynn Sherr or *New York* magazine's Barbara Campbell. There are no *New York Times* editorials weeping over the guilty verdicts or *Village Voice* articles claiming the defendants were "just too black for [their] own good."[73]

If "hate crimes" were honestly prosecuted, we'd have another crime category where minorities lap the field. But the profusion of black-on-white hate crimes doesn't fit the "racist America" thesis the media have been trying to sell us, so these spectacular crimes don't make national news.

The people who report the news simply would not show a black person in an unfavorable light. When wild claims of racism were proved false, they'd just drop the matter, leaving wrecked lives in their wake, and tell themselves, "Our cause was good." With no disincentive to manufacture even the most preposterous claims of racism—and plenty to be gained by crying "racism"—the charlatans ran riot.

How on earth was defending criminals helping the black community? And why were only black people expected to instantly defend any member of their group?

One big change since the OJ verdict is that people will now openly talk about the obvious guilt of black criminals who are obviously guilty. No longer is that a social faux pas. There is also a lot less newsprint dedicated to exploring the difficult lives black criminals have had.

Apart from everything else, criminals are also incredibly lazy, rarely venturing beyond their neighborhoods to rape, kill and plunder. Why should we care about the criminals' tough luck when they're busy destroying the lives of other black people who have also been dealt a bad hand? But the victims of black criminals weren't the ones writing editorials on how to "heal" after this or that black criminal was shot by the police. White liberals were.

CHAPTER 4

HEY, WHATEVER HAPPENED
TO THAT STORY . . .

Whenever a much-celebrated claim of racism turned out to be a hoax—which was almost always—you'd just stop hearing about it. There would never be a clippable story admitting that the media's harrumphing had been in error: *Attention readers! That story we've been howling about for several months turned out to be a complete fraud.*

The hoax aspect was never what was heavily reported. Part one would be widely broadcast—the lie part. But only obscure right-wingers ever bothered with the follow-up when it turned out to be false. Liberals forgave the act of falsely reporting a crime on the grounds that that even though there wasn't a wolf, it raised our consciousness of wolves. Ordinary people just wanted to know: But was it true?

A little time would pass and then we'd get an all-new "Got racism?" media campaign. No matter how many times "hate crime" stories were disproved, reporters never tired of credulously reporting every allegation of racism to come down the pike. The media were incapable of remembering to get *all* the facts before launching moral crusades.

A normal person would hear some of the more outlandish allegations and think, "I can't believe it!"—not meaning, "Wow! What a blockbuster story!" but rather, "I would like to hear the facts because I literally don't believe it."

As soon as the truth emerged on each racial incident and the America-is-still-racist thesis collapsed, the story would just quietly disappear from the news pages, like Kennedy's trouble at the Chappaquiddick bridge. As a result, the official record shows some hate crimes and some unverified hate crimes with no clear resolution one way or another. As long as the fraudulent "hate crimes" didn't get counted as strike-outs, liberals always looked like Ted Williams. Since they didn't keep an accurate batting average, I'll do it for them.

WHITE GANGS AT COLUMBIA UNIVERSITY—1987

In March 1987, eight months before Tawana Brawley became a house-hold name, black students at Columbia University made the rather incred-ible charge that mobs of white students were beating up black students on campus. About a dozen blacks claimed to have seen or been victims of these racist attacks.

In the 1980s, American colleges were sturdy sentinels against the mer-est hint of a racist thought. There were seminars on racism, posters against racism, bake sales against racism, racism "awareness" days, articles de-nouncing racism, consciousness-raising sessions about racism. More re-sources were devoted to studying racism than studying history, chemistry or math. It would be hard to find a single person on an American college campus, at least post-1980, who would have one good thing to say about racism.

Moreover, the alleged perpetrators of these racist beatings at Columbia weren't teenaged toughs with criminal records in a working-class neigh-borhood: They were college students at an Ivy League school.

But blacks claimed that whites were so terrorizing them that they were afraid to walk alone on campus. According to their spokeswoman, Bar-nard student Cheryl Derricotte, it was "open season on black people."[1]

The usual nonsense ensued. There were sit-ins, administration building take-overs, and noisy rallies outside the fraternity house said to harbor the white racist thugs. Fifty people were arrested as a result of the anti-racism protests. Most of them were white.[2] Twenty-three Columbia students staged a sit-in at 1 Police Plaza in lower Manhattan to demand the arrest of the white students they claimed were beating up blacks on campus.[3]

Black students formed a group to protect themselves from the maraud-ing white mobs and—in what was always a good sign—hired C. Vernon Mason as their lawyer. "The message has gotten out," Mason said, "that black students are not safe on the Columbia campus and someone is going to have to answer for this."[4]

Newsweek quoted Frank L. Matthews, publisher of *Black Issues in Higher Education*, saying that he blamed the surge of college racism on white students' "reading the messages" from the Reagan administration.[5] Of course, another theory is that it was black students "reading the mes-sages" from a media that gave full-court press to even simulated racist in-cidents and refused to hold black people accountable for false reports.

If you are not a journalist, it will come as no surprise that, after painstaking investigations by both the police and the very politically correct university, the whole thing turned out to be a hoax. According to dozens of eyewitnesses, it was black students who had started a fight with white students late one night after a dance, and then made up the cock-and-bull story about roving white gangs targeting blacks.

None of the newspapers and magazines that had reported the original story about white racists stampeding through an Ivy League campus ever got around to mentioning that it was a lie—not the *New York Times*, the *Chicago Tribune*, *Newsweek* or *Time* magazine. Careful readers had to wait for this admission in the *Christian Science Monitor* about a year later:

> [T]he the university report on the incident, which relied on the signed statements of 22 eyewitnesses . . . differed substantially from the account given by the blacks and used by the news media in reporting the story. [I]n the Columbia account, the actual brawl was provoked by a group of five to seven blacks outside the hangout. [T]heir story of 'a white lynch mob' has since been discredited.[6]

No charges were brought by the university or the police against the students for filing a false police complaint.

The national news coverage of a story about Ivy Leaguers as latter-day Bull Connors triggered dozens more of these incidents at campuses around the country. These were all hoaxes, too. But no matter how absurd the idea of marauding white students attacking blacks on college campuses, the false charges kept coming and liberals kept believing them.

SABRINA COLLINS, EMORY UNIVERSITY

A few years later, in 1990, Sabrina Collins, a black premed student at Emory College, claimed to have been the victim of a campaign of racial harassment—"die, [N-word], die" had been painted on her floor, bleach poured on her clothes and typed death threats slipped under her door. Even her stuffed animals had been mutilated. As a result of these incidents, Collins fell mute and had to be hospitalized.

Hundreds of students held a rally to protest racism as a result of what had happened to Collins. One student, Leonard Scriven, denounced what he called the "pervasive system of racism" at Emory.[7] At a meeting of students and faculty about the incident, a newly formed black student group, Students Against Racial Inequality, submitted a list of demands, including more black students and faculty members, two new centers for the study of African American culture . . . and the firing of the director of public safety, Edward A. Medlin.

The public safety office had already responded to Collins's allegations by equipping her dorm room with additional locks, a portable motion detector and an alarm system. Safety officers patrolled her hallway as well as the area outside her dormitory building. The office of public safety had called in local, state and federal investigators. But the students against racial inequality wanted this poor guy's head.

After a thorough inquiry, the Georgia Bureau of Investigation concluded that Collins had perpetrated the racist acts on herself. Her fingerprints were the only ones on the letters and were arranged on the page in a pattern indicating that she had put the letter in a typewriter; the letters had been composed on a typewriter in the library she frequented; and, finally, the letters also spelled "you're" as "your"—as was Sabrina's habit.[8] The incidents had begun just as Collins was being investigated for an honor code violation for cheating in a chemistry class.[9]

No charges were pressed against Collins. The story vanished. Let's just hope the head of public safety was allowed to keep his job.

GILBERT MOORE JR., WILLIAMS COLLEGE—1993

Fake racist incidents on college campuses became as common as Madonna's music. Against a background of daily lectures against racism, some racist letter or graffiti would materialize, there would be a generalized gnashing of teeth about the pervasiveness of racism and then the perpetrator would always turn out to be a black student.

At Williams College in 1993, hideous racist messages were found on the door of the Black Student Union. An uproar ensued. Two days later, Dean Joan Edwards announced to general relief that the culprit had admitted responsibility and was being punished—but neglected to mention that the student was black until two weeks later, as the rumor mill went wild.

Junior Gilbert Moore Jr. said he had put up the racist notes as a response to actual racism at Williams—of which there was no evidence or he wouldn't have needed to fake it—and to encourage more dialogue about racism, because twenty-four hours a day, seven days a week was not enough. The college rose to the challenge—by suspending him for one semester. Enraged that a black student would be held responsible for anything he did, some black students denounced the harsh penalty, threatening to leave Williams. Moore concluded: "The system . . . has failed me."[10]

ALICIA HARDIN, TRINITY INTERNATIONAL UNIVERSITY—2005

Federal investigators must have been getting bored with the hoax hate crimes on college campuses they kept being asked to investigate. After OJ, even the media's hysteria was muted. Nonetheless, when three students at Trinity International University, a small Christian college near Chicago, received threatening racist letters in 2005, scores of newspapers across the country ran with the news.

A *New York Times* article on the alleged hate crime was bristling with references to the Christian nature of the school: "Christian College Secludes Students after Hate Letters . . . a small Evangelical Christian college . . . a conservative Bible-based school . . . more than 20 students held hands in a circle to pray . . . Affiliated with the Evangelical Free Church of America, the university mission statement says that its education is based on 'the authority of God's inerrant word, Holy Scripture,' and that it seeks an international identity with 'people drawn from every tribe and tongue.'"[11]

As is required by law, Jesse Jackson met with the victims of the letters, reporting that they "feel like a target is on their back because they are black." Charlie Dates, a black student getting his masters in divinity, did not sound especially worried. He told the *Times*, "Crazy people do crazy things. It's nothing to be terrified over."

There was big coverage for the initial allegation. You would not read in the *New York Times*, however, that the perpetrator turned out to be a black student, Alicia Hardin. She had staged the racist incident because she wanted to switch schools. But as soon as she confessed, the *Times* lost interest in the story.

So did most of the newspapers from around the country that had given banner coverage to the original story. Only a handful bothered informing their readers about the investigation's results. When the hoax part of the story was reported at all, it usually showed up in demure, hundred-word items buried deep inside the newspaper.[12]

Instead of bemoaning the runaway popularity of Fox News, the liberal media might consider cutting into Fox's popularity by not aggressively hiding the news.

None of the racist incidents sweeping college campuses ever turned out to be true. They were either the normal bumps and jostles that come with being a human being—or, more often, they were complete frauds perpetrated by wannabe victims.

TAWANA BRAWLEY—1987

After inspiring a rash of hoax hate crimes on college campuses, attorney C. Vernon Mason slipped away from Columbia and popped up in Wappingers Falls, New York, promoting a whopper of a racist hate crime.

One night in November, 1987, fifteen-year-old Tawana Brawley was found curled up in a ball inside a plastic bag, apparently unconscious. (Medical examiners later determined she was faking the unconscious part.) (As well as everything else.) She had feces and racist graffiti on her body. When she was finally able to communicate, she claimed that she had been raped and beaten over several days by three white men, including policemen, who then dumped her in the bag where she was found. Through her advisors, she later added three other white men to the list of her alleged rapists, identifying one by name: local prosecutor Steven Pagones.

The cavalry was called out in response to this shocking hate crime—the Dutchess County Sheriff's Department, the FBI, local and state police. Governor Mario Cuomo assigned Attorney General Robert Abrams to investigate the case.

But Brawley's advisors quickly turned the investigation into a clown parade, steadfastly refusing to cooperate and hurling wild invective at anyone trying to find the truth. Among many bon mots from Brawley's advisors, attorney Alton Maddox accused Abrams of masturbating to photos of Brawley. He suggested that Governor Cuomo was a Klansman, saying, "Mario Cuomo, the sheets have to come off!"[13]

Al Sharpton called Abrams "Hitler," Cuomo a racist, and demanded that Cuomo appoint Maddox special prosecutor on the case.[14] (Maddox later had his license suspended indefinitely for his conduct in the Brawley case.)

Eight months later, after a ridiculously time-consuming and costly investigation, the purported attack was exposed as a complete fraud.[15] It turned out that Brawley set the whole thing up to avoid explaining to her volatile stepfather why she hadn't come home for four nights straight. Brawley's boyfriend later told *Newsday* that she admitted to him she had cooked up the scheme with her mother.[16]

Among the suspicious facts noted in the grand jury's 170-page report were these:

- Brawley was well nourished, had clean breath, no bruises or injuries to her body and was not suffering from exposure, despite the temperature having dropped to freezing several times in the previous four days when she said she was being gang-raped in the woods.

- Witnesses saw her getting into the plastic bag by herself, and then hopping around in it before curling up into a ball on the ground.

- Hospital technicians who examined Brawley soon after she was discovered concluded that she was faking unconsciousness.

- The hospital rape tests were negative and no semen was found anyplace on her body.

- She had no recent bruises or other marks on her body consistent with a rape.

- During the period of the claimed attack, Brawley was seen in the apartment building nearby. Her clothes were in a washing machine in one of those apartments, as well as all the ingredients for her condition.

No charges were brought against the girl whose lies cost New York taxpayers $643,801[17]—about a million bucks in today's dollars. Couldn't we at least deduct the cost of investigating hoax bias crimes from the welfare budget?

Even her Amos and Andy advisors got off scot-free—at least until the OJ verdict.

Amazingly, the Tawana Brawley lunacy didn't put a dent in the endless accusations of racism. Over and over again in the eighties and nineties, patently false claims had to be aggressively investigated to prove no one was soft on racism.

The living embodiment of the rule that there would never be any consequences for black charlatans is Al Sharpton.

In addition to libeling innocent men in the Tawana Brawley hoax and whipping up mobs in Brooklyn's Crown Heights where a rabbinical student was stabbed to death, Sharpton famously incited an anti-Semitic pogrom against a Jewish-owned clothing store in Harlem, saying, "We will not stand by and allow them to move this brother so that some white interloper can expand his business." A deranged black man who was listening to Sharpton later decided to storm the store and start shooting, wounding several employees and setting a fire that killed seven people.

Surely, after all this, Sharpton became a pariah—oh wait! No, that's not what happened. Far from being exiled, he became famous, ran for president and Al Gore kissed his ring, *after* these events. Instead of becoming kryptonite, Sharpton became rich, famous, and a Democratic power broker.

Try to imagine Jerry Falwell or Pat Robertson getting away with any of that. Or this: In the 1980s, Sharpton was captured on an FBI videotape, biting an unlit cigar and wearing a leather cowboy hat, discussing purchasing a cocaine shipment from an agent posing as a drug dealer.

AL SHARPTON, NATIONAL ACTION NETWORK: So what kind of time limit are we dealing with, with this?

FBI AGENT: The coke?

SHARPTON: Yeah.

FBI AGENT: Could be—about the same time I have four million coming to us.

SHARPTON: End of April.

FBI AGENT: End of April, six weeks from now. Is that a good time, you think?

SHARPTON: Probably.

FBI AGENT: Now I can get pure coke, or, you know, 99 percent, for about 35,000 a kilo. But I gotta get, you know, more than one.

SHARPTON: Right.

FBI AGENT: You know, if we're going to do this thing . . .

SHARPTON: Now you're talking about some real . . . [18]

This tape was made in 1983, but the public didn't see it until 2002, nineteen years later. After the tape played on HBO's *Real Sports with Bryant Gumbel* in 2002, Sharpton threatened to sue, claiming that there was a second tape that exonerated him, but the second tape never materialized. Instead, government sources said they hadn't prosecuted Sharpton but instead used the tape to turn him into an FBI informant.[19] On *Meet the Press,* Sharpton denied committing a crime—he said he was just going along with the putative drug deal for fear of violence. He said he had given information to the FBI, and that the FBI had "spent money" on investigations, but denied being "a paid informant of law enforcement."[20] If the tape had been shown at the time, perhaps the nation could have been spared the Tawana Brawley hoax. That came in 1988, five years after Sharpton was discussing cocaine shipments with an undercover agent.

LAURIE HECHT—1988

There were even Munchausen syndrome bias crimes, with white women claiming to be victims of racism for having spoken up on behalf of blacks. Months after Brawley was discovered in the plastic bag, Laurie Hecht, a white legal secretary in Yonkers, claimed that her speech at a city council meeting in favor of low-income housing being built in white neighborhoods (far, far away from Park Avenue) produced a rash of death threats.

Hecht instantly received twenty-four-hour FBI protection and a police escort wherever she went. The College of New Rochelle awarded her an honorary Doctor of Humane Letters as the "lone voice of reason" promoting civil discourse. Touro College Jacob D. Fuchsberg Law Center offered her a scholarship.

The *New York Times* published touching articles about her grit and spirit, how she helped her neighbors and had lots of plants. She lightheartedly told the *Times* reporter, "I didn't get any death threats since Friday."[21]

Some might have noticed how she kept obsessively calling newspapers to tell them about her travails.

And then it turned out she was just a neurotic white woman desperate for attention. The FBI captured her on videotape scrawling racist graffiti in her own building moments before she reported the crime to the police. Telephone security equipment showed no calls to her apartment at the times she claimed she was receiving death threats.[22]

Still, no one in the media ever said, *Maybe we should reevaluate our policy of always believing any charge of racism by anyone at any time.* Even the sensational Tawana Brawley hoax came and went without hindering the racial-hysteria industry. On the ones they lost—which was all of them—it was considered bad taste for the falsely accused to high-five. Everyone just agreed to never talk about those examples again.

HOAXES—WHITE TODAY, 1992

Shock seized New York City in January 1992, when it was alleged that a black brother and sister, aged fourteen and twelve, walking to school in the Bronx early one morning, were attacked by white teenagers on a busy intersection. Calling themselves the Albanian Bad Boys, the teenaged assailants were said to have smeared the black children's faces with white shoe polish, saying, "You'll turn white today" and stealing $3 from them. The alleged assault was thwarted when the driver of a gypsy cab stopped to help.

After that, both the cab driver and the gang members seemed to disappear into thin air.

The racist paint attack was front-page news across the city and quickly became a national story. Having solved New York City's crime and budget problems, Mayor Dinkins immediately called the mother and offered the children counseling. He spent the entire next day meeting with government officials, religious leaders, politicians and the police in response to the incident, vowing that he would "leave no stone unturned" in bringing the perpetrators of this "dastardly deed" to justice.[23] He ordered the police and the Commission on Human Rights to investigate so that "those who committed this outrageous attack are brought to the justice they deserve."[24]

Everyone from the Bronx borough president to the police to the human rights commissioner and religious leaders denounced the bias crime and called on witnesses to step forward. The police canvassed the neighborhood and began hauling in suspects the very next day. A twenty-thousand-dollar reward was offered for any information about the attack and a direct appeal was made to the cab driver to come forward. A hotline was set up for anonymous tips.

The following week, a twelve-year-old Hispanic boy, Bryan Figueroa, claimed that the exact same thing happened to him! He said he was attacked at a school bus stop during morning rush hour. When the police showed up to interview him, he asked if he would get to meet the mayor, too.[25]

Dinkins called the purported second attack "shameful and heinous."[26]

A month later, despite blanket news coverage and a police dragnet, the police didn't have a single witness or suspect. They quietly admitted they believed both attacks were hoaxes. The *New York Times* broke the news gently, deep within the newspaper—Section B; page 3; column 5: "Police Puzzled by Lack of Leads in Bias Attacks on Black Youths." The police were "considering a variety of theories" the paper reported, but the only "theory" mentioned was that "the children may have fabricated their descriptions of the incident."[27]

It seemed that the mother of the first two children had been desperately trying to get them transferred to a different school—a request that had been denied but was immediately granted after the paint incident. Even before reporting it to the police, she had told school officials about the assault in order to again ask for a transfer. School officials were quick to assure the *Times* that the transfer request "had no bearing on the veracity of the reported attack." [28]

But, according to the *New York Post*'s Peter Moses, others at the school said they didn't believe it occurred because the boy had a history of blaming his problems on racism whenever he got in trouble.[29]

Asked about the possibility that the sensational crime had been a hoax, Mayor Dinkins said he wouldn't comment until the police "say that it didn't happen."[30]

Which would happen never. Instead, close observers of the case had to wait another three months for a small announcement on page 42 of the *Times* admitting that the police still had no leads, despite—at that point— hundreds of interviews.[31]

The only definitive proof that the paint attacks were hoaxes was that the police, the mayor and the *New York Times* suddenly dropped the subject, never mentioning the white-paint attacks again. Needless to say, there would be no investigation into whether the alleged victims had wasted police resources by falsely reporting a crime.

The shoe-polish hate crime had made the front page of the *New York Times* and the cover of *New York Newsday* in massive in-depth interviews with the "victims." The *Times*'s story, titled "Victim of Bias Attack, 14, Wrestles with His Anger," was 1,228 words long.[32] *Newsday*'s account, written by the most easily fooled journalist in America, Jim Dwyer, clocked in at 1,016 words and was titled "Race Victim's Mom: I Wanted a Better Life for My Kids."[33] The racist attack was talked about in France, Toronto, Seattle, Chicago, on the *MacNeil Lehrer NewsHour*, in endless stories on National Public Radio and still today, in Anna Quindlen's living room.

News coverage for the paint attacks turning out to be hoaxes was very, very, very, very, very, very, very much more subdued. The *New York Times* ran two obscure items on the police findings and *Newsday* inconspicuously revealed the hoax theory in a short item about various New York politicians deriding the idea that the attacks had been faked.

A year after the *New York Times* had quietly stopped mentioning the white-paint hate crime in the Bronx, the pea-brained Anna Quindlen included her *Times* column denouncing the attack in her book, *Thinking Out Loud*. She was either unaware that the attack had turned out to be a hoax or lacked the decency to cut it. Explaining that opposition to affirmative action is what led to the paint attack on black children (which, again, never happened), Quindlen preached:

> [Y]ou have to remember that kids learn their lessons from adults. That's what the mother of two black children who were sprayed with white paint in the Bronx said last week about the assailants, teenagers who called her son and daughter "nigger" and vowed they would turn them white. "Can you imagine what they are learning at home?" she asked.

On and on she went, blubbering about blacks who are "taught at age twelve and fourteen through the utter humiliation of having their faces cleaned with paint thinner that there are those who think that even becoming white from a bottle is better than not being white at all."[34] This would be like writing a book on the treachery of the Jews with the Dreyfus affair as your case in chief.

The *New York Post* had reported that the police and teachers from the children's school believed it was a hoax by February 1992. Even Quindlen's own paper hinted that the attack was a hoax in its still-no-leads article in May.

And yet Quindlen also included her anguished ruminations about a hoax hate crime in the paperback edition of her book, released in March 1994. *I'm not going to rewrite that column. That was my favorite column of the whole year!*

Liberals were so desperate for proof of white racism, they would believe anything.

CLINTON'S NONEXISTENT CHURCH BURNINGS AND SPECIAL FORCES RACISTS—1996

One of the more prominent hoax hate crimes was invented by Bill Clinton when he was president. In a 1996 radio address, Clinton said, "I have vivid and painful memories of black churches being burned in my own state when I was a child." No one else in Arkansas remembered a single church burning in Arkansas, ever. Definitely not when Clinton was a child.

The *Arkansas Democrat-Gazette* (Little Rock) checked with the state historian, current and past presidents of the Arkansas NAACP, the former president of the Regular Arkansas Baptist Convention, the chairman of the Arkansas Black History Advisory Committee—and all confirmed that there had been no church burnings in Clinton's own state.[35]

There was no apology from the White House, much less from Clinton himself, for this despicable slander on the state of Arkansas. The *New York Times*, the *Los Angeles Times* and the *Washington Post* didn't mention Clinton's tall tale—though all newspapers ran stories on the fraudulent claim that there had been an upsurge in arson at black churches.

In fact, the burnings of churches, black and white, had been declining in recent years. The hysteria about a new epidemic of black church burnings was completely counterfactual nonsense being put out by a liberal group in order to accuse right-wing rhetoric of inciting neo-Klanners.[36] Again, the lie part got a lot of coverage; the facts exposing the claim as a lie did not.

Then, during his 1996 reelection campaign, Clinton repeatedly trotted out a hoax hate crime against blacks allegedly committed by white Special Forces members.

At the 1996 Democratic National Convention, he said:

> We still have too many Americans who give in to their fears of those who are different from them. Not so long ago, swastikas were painted on the doors of some African American members of our Special Forces at Fort Bragg. Folks, for those of you who don't know

what they do, the Special Forces are just what the name says; they are special forces. If I walk off this stage tonight and call them on the telephone and tell them to go halfway around the world and risk their lives for you and be there by tomorrow at noon, they will do it. They do not deserve to have swastikas on their doors.[37]

He told the same yarn at a White House meeting with the Boys and Girls Nation,[38] in a speech to northern California Democrats,[39] in remarks at a magnet school in Arkansas,[40] and while chatting up a cocktail waitress in Des Moines.

As was already well known, the prime suspect was the black "victim" himself. This had been widely reported in the press. The soldier, not a member of Special Forces, by the way, was later discharged.[41]

Clinton thus became the first president in history to knowingly make a false statement while giving the keynote address at a major party convention. He did so to accuse the military of racism. *Just to cite one example of racism in America, here's a fraudulent one.*

If I were claiming America has a long way to come on race relations, I think I'd showcase the hate crimes that weren't complete fabrications. Someone should tell liberals that their argument about continuing racial problems would be more effective if they cited true cases of racism.

RACISM AS TRUMP CARD: JESSE JACKSON, MADONNA CONSTANTINE AND HENRY LOUIS GATES

The fact that an astonishingly high percentage of the hyped bias crimes kept turning out to be fakes—even with every journalist hunting for a real one in order to win a Pulitzer Prize—suggested that there wasn't a lot of racism still needing to be stamped out in America. But the media wouldn't rest.

Hoax charges of racism aren't rare because they are the trump card. These get-out-of-jail-free cards are too great a temptation to resist, especially in moments of crisis.

When the *National Enquirer* broke the story of Jesse Jackson's mistress and love child, he said that there must be "some motive" in revealing a "two-year-old story" and noted that the week Martin Luther King won the Nobel Peace Prize, he had been threatened with the exposure of his sexual liaisons.[42] (It was a "two-year-old story" only in the sense that his love child was nearly two years old—but this was the first the public had heard about it.)

On CNN's *Crossfire*, Al Sharpton said that "the timing of this, whether it was deliberate or not, to me is very, very suspect."[43] Of course, if it was not "deliberate," then there was nothing suspicious. *Whether intentional or not, it's still first-degree murder!*

On Fox News's *Hannity & Colmes*, civil rights lawyer Keith Watters was more explicit, blaming the scandal on "a lot of racists are attacking him, are using this to bring him down, because they don't like what he believes . . ." [44]

Not all black commentators jumped on the racism bandwagon. *Chicago Sun-Times* columnist Mary A. Mitchell expressed disappointment that some people were "more concerned about who leaked the story than they are that another respected leader and minister has set a poor example." Mitchell also said that, for years, reporters had ignored rumors about Jackson's private life—even when he ran for president—for fear of being called "racist."[45]

In 2007, Madonna Constantine, a black professor at Teachers College, Columbia University, claimed to be a victim of racism when she came under investigation for plagiarism. The racism charge was given added punch when, not long into the investigation, she claimed to have found a noose hanging on her office door!

A huge hoo-hah ensued, with student protests against racism until . . . the grand jury began looking at Constantine herself as the perpetrator of the hate crime. The noose investigation quietly disappeared, apparently unsolved, but the university fired Constantine for plagiarism the following year. [46] The only thing that saved this poor woman from being a complete buffoon was that Al Sharpton wasn't defending her.

Even respected Harvard professor Henry Louis Gates went to racial victimization in a moment of stress. Gates had just gotten off a fifteen-hour flight from China, he was tired and cranky and didn't have his house keys. After he and his driver had broken in, the police showed up, demanding to see Gates's ID as he stood in his own house. Gates blew up and accused them of racism.

It takes remarkable character not to do that. With clueless liberals salivating for instances of racism, blacks must think: *Really? I can do that? Oh look! A fish just jumped into my boat and bit my hook!*

Liberals send out engraved invitations to black people, begging them to claim racism, and then turn around and stalwartly refuse to believe that a false accusation of racism has ever been made. They'll still wheel out the fakes from time to time, confident that most people have forgotten the details.

In a society that has virtually no moral standards anymore, claims of racism are about the only thing that still get the moral-indignation juices flowing. But if a charge of racism is going to mean anything, the incessant false charges have got to stop. They help no one but serial fantasists. Hoax racism charges have wasted enormous amounts of police, prosecutorial and university resources, torn up communities and generated racial animosity where none had previously existed.

RETALIATORY RACE CRIMES THAT AREN'T HOAXES

It's not just that liberal media elites were making jackasses of themselves and wasting the police's time. Their constant burnishing of the facts in order to create the impression that America is a nation exploding in racism kept getting people killed.

In 1989, a group of black teenagers in Wisconsin reacted to the movie *Mississippi Burning* by attacking a white person. After ginning themselves up over the movie, one of the black kids said to the others, "Do you all feel hyped up enough to move on some white people?" They did, randomly choosing a fourteen-year-old white boy to beat to a pulp, leaving him in a coma with permanent brain damage.

The non-American director of *Mississippi Burning* justified his "fictionalizing" in the movie by saying he wanted people to react "viscerally, emotionally."[47] It worked. Now a young boy is brain damaged for the sin of being white.

The only reason we even know about that incident is that the defendants were charged with a hate crime and their case appealed to the Supreme Court on the First Amendment grounds. The first mention of this abhorrent—and genuine—hate crime in the Nexis archive is in a *Washington Post* article about the Supreme Court appeal.[48]

The New York media's hysteria over the "white today" shoe polish attacks was not dropped soon enough to stop a series of black-on-white backlash crimes—crimes committed in response to the fake bias incidents. And the retaliatory crimes weren't hoaxes.

Two black men in Brooklyn punched a white vagrant so hard he lost his teeth, telling him, "How about we paint you white, whitey?" (demonstrating their abject failure to grasp the point of the made-up hate crime). In the Bronx, a group of blacks beat and robbed white and Hispanic students, announcing they were looking for whites to assault. On a subway in Manhattan, three black men hit a white male passenger, telling him, "This is for what happened in the Bronx."[49]

About a week after the alleged paint attack, a fifteen-year-old white girl in Brooklyn was snatched from a bus stop at around 6:45 a.m. by two black men, thrown into their stolen Toyota Camry, raped, sodomized and robbed in what some believed was a retaliatory bias crime. Her attackers told her they raped her because she was "white and perfect."[50] The girl was treated for rape at a hospital and, by the end of the week, the police had found the stolen car she was raped in, partially charred from an attempt to burn it.[51] Mayor Dinkins offered a $10,000 reward for information about the attack—half the reward for the white-paint assault.

A few days later, a black man claimed he was beaten by a group of whites, who told him, "You aren't going to rape any more white women." Mayor Dinkins rushed to lambaste the attack, calling it an "absolutely appalling act of bias violence."[52] In short order, the man admitted he had made the whole thing up—as well as two earlier bias crimes he had reported.[53] So here we had a fake racist crime by whites inspiring a real crime by blacks, which led to another hoax hate crime by a black person.

There were nearly three times as many articles on the mythical white-paint attack as there were on the actual rape and sodomy of the fifteen-year-old girl for being "white." Nexis registers fourteen stories mentioning the rape, such as this one from the *New York Times*: "Police Find Bias Crimes Are Often Wrapped in Ambiguity."[54] Meanwhile, there were thirty-six major, lengthy in-depth features on the paint attack that never happened.

It took the rape of a girl for being "white and perfect" for reporters to realize that some interracial crimes were not bias crimes at all. Sometimes a crime was just a crime—for example, all black-on-white crimes. Newly aware that interracial crimes could happen for nonracial reasons, journalists couldn't stop making that point in the case of the fifteen-year-old white girl raped by two black men.

The man on the street quoted by New York *Newsday* said: "I don't think it was a bias crime . . . It just happened. . . . I think if it had been a black girl over there, they probably would have done the same thing."[55] Eerily, the man on the street always seems to say exactly what reporters are thinking!

A *Newsday* columnist weighed in, saying: "The rape of the fifteen-year-old was terrible. The fact that young girls are raped in this city every day doesn't make it any less terrible. But magnifying it into an act of racial retribution widens the gulf between blacks and whites."[56] Not as much as interracial rape widens the gulf, I'd guess.

So journalists were aware that reports of bias crimes could incite racial tension—at least when they were reporting crimes committed by blacks against whites. Why hadn't they noticed that with the white paint attack or Howard Beach? Why not, when they reflexively believed any hate crime alleged by a black person?

As soon as the next white cop shot a black criminal, the media would be right back to widening the gulf between blacks and whites.

On December 30, 1992, a group of eight blacks, two of them women, abducted a white girl, twenty-five-year-old Melissa McLauchlin, gang-raped, bound and tortured her before shooting her six times and throwing her body to the side of the road. This odious crime was committed in retaliation for "400 years of oppression."[57] These weren't common criminals grasping at straws; they were inspired by the idea that whites systematically oppress blacks. The ringleader, Joseph Gardner, was a naval petty officer whose mother worked in a sheriff's office. He had told the others that his New Year's resolution was to kill a white woman.[58]

In 1993, Colin Ferguson, a Jamaican immigrant, shot white passengers on the Long Island Rail Road, killing six, in retaliation for racism, as he explained in a note in his pocket titled, "Reasons for This." He said he had targeted Nassau County because it was predominantly white and had spared New York City because of its black mayor, David Dinkins. His lawyers, William M. Kunstler and Ronald Kuby, argued that Ferguson was not guilty by reason of "black rage" insanity.[59]

The stories the media pounded into us were the ones that comported with their fantasy of a world riven by white racism against blacks. Reporting that a hate crime was a hoax was not a high priority for them. The media would spend months hawking some three-alarm racism story, and then when it turned out to be a fraud, they'd whisper the ending and tiptoe out of the room, as if they were reading a bedtime story to a child.

The problem with liberals' constantly imputing racist hatred to white people was that it kept creating real racist hatred in black people—ending with real dead white people.

CHAPTER 5

THAT OLD BLACK MAGIC

The Reverend Jeremiah Wright wasn't the first nutty black clergyman admired by Democrats. If it seems surprising that Democrats would indulge Wright's deranged rants, consider how shocking it is that they don't even mind standard Christianity when practiced by black people.

Liberals' general view of Christians is that they are simpleminded nazis. In the 1980s, the *New York Times* famously quoted Professor Samuel S. Hill of the University of Florida for the proposition that evangelical Christians were "more easily led" than other voters.[1] Legions of liberals took him at his word and were led to disdain Christians.

In a feel-good piece on "Christian fascists" in the May 2005 *Harper's*, Chris Hedges reminisced about his Harvard Divinity School professor Dr. James Luther Adams, who had predicted in the 1980s that fascism would not come to America with swastikas but "carrying crosses and chanting the Pledge of Allegiance"—which, outside of Harvard, would make it hard to pick the fascists out of a crowd. *Fire at will, men, these people love Jesus AND America!*

In particular, Adams warned "to watch closely the Christian right's persecution of homosexuals and lesbians." This reminded him of, yes, Hitler.[2] Adams acolyte Chris Hedges took notice and realized: evangelical Christians were planning a holocaust against gays!

The evangelical ministers' position on homosexuality is what led Hedges to conclude they were fascists. Opinions can differ on homosexuality—unless you happen to be a clergyman with the Christian, Jewish or Muslim faith, because all three major world religions take a dim view of sodomy. Next, liberals will be attacking Christian ministers who criticize sin.

But while imagining that white evangelical Christians were on the verge of engineering a second Holocaust, liberals find *black* evangelical

Christians adorable—cuter than a bug's ear! Even when blacks oppose gay marriage, they get a pass.

Obama's presidential run brought out record numbers of African American voters in 2008. Unluckily for liberals, 2008 was also the year California had a proposition on the ballot that would ban gay marriage. Without the immense black turnout, California's Proposition 8 might have failed—it definitely would not have passed so decisively. Whites and Asians were split on the initiative, with bare majorities opposing it, 51 percent to 49 percent. Hispanics supported the ban, 53 percent to 47 percent. But black voters overwhelmingly voted for Prop 8 by a whopping 70 percent.

Liberals responded to the undeniable fact that blacks killed gay marriage by . . . attacking Mormons. After the vote, thousands of protesters gathered outside Mormon churches in Los Angeles, New York City and Chicago to slam opponents of gay marriage as haters and "morons." There were threats to challenge the Mormon Church's tax-exempt status.

Hollywood liberals and other predominantly gay groups made a sneering video accusing religious voters of stupidity for not knowing that the Bible condemned "shrimp cocktails" as much as sodomy—the two most popular items on the menu at any Hollywood party! Evidently, the New Testament hasn't made it to California yet. Liberals were so upset about the gay marriage vote, they were on the verge of claiming Proposition 8 was born in Kenya.

But even in the middle of this epic hissy fit over Prop 8, liberals managed to contextualize the black vote. The fact that seven out of ten blacks voted to ban gay marriage was merely "disappointing" and "painfully ironic."[3] No one challenged the black churches' tax-exempt status.

Dan Savage, the Maxine Waters of the gays, illustrated the double standard. To the Mormons, he said, "f—k you, Brigham Young." To the blacks, he rambled on incomprehensibly:

> The relative handful of racist white gays and lesbians—and they're out there, and I think they're scum—are not a bigger problem for African Americans, gay and straight, than the huge numbers of homophobic African Americans are for gay Americans, whatever their color. (Read that carefully: I did not say that black homophobia is a bigger problem than white racism; I said that the huge numbers of African-American homophobes are a bigger problem for gays and lesbians—including gays and lesbians of color—

than the comparatively small number of racist gays and lesbians. Which does not excuse racism among gays and lesbians, of course.)

Harvey Fierstein stopped reading at that point. Just reading that passage made me feel dizzier than a passed-over drag queen during last call at a rage in West Hollywood. Terrified of insulting black people—even black people against gay marriage—Savage took refuge in complete opacity.

In a 1994 college speech, Reverend Al Sharpton referred to "them Greek homos." At first he claimed that "homo" was "not a homophobic term," but then simply denied having said it, despite the existence of a videotape.[4] Nutty black clergymen got a pass on condemning sodomy and everything else.

As president, Bill Clinton had played both the gays and the blacks on gay marriage. First, he denounced Republicans for the Defense of Marriage Act, or DOMA. His press spokesman, Michael McCurry, called it "gay-baiting pure and simple."[5] Next, Clinton signed DOMA into law and bragged about signing it in campaign commercials on black radio stations during his 1996 reelection campaign.

If liberals were willing to forgive blacks for being Christians, they were thrilled with black religions that didn't take the God part all that seriously, but were actively hostile to America. While hysterical about white Baptists, liberals are complacent about psychotic cults involving persons of color. The Democrats have repeatedly endorsed black racist sects on the fringes of society. (Which is how we got the Reverend Al Sharpton.) Maybe if liberals had spent a little less time combing through Pat Robertson's sermons for secret Nazi references, and instead had taken a peek at certain demagogic black religious leaders, several employees of a Harlem clothing store, two policemen, a congressman and nine hundred people, about six-hundred of them black, would still be alive today. But their position was: *Forget Jim Jones, let's get back to what Jerry Falwell said about our beloved Teletubbies!*

Time and again, the Democrats' defense of some black pseudoreligious group would result in a violent explosion. Then, the entire incident would either be forgotten or reclassified under "Falwell" so that no one would notice the perpetual chaos being foisted on the country by mad black leaders who were sanctioned by the liberal establishment.

THE MOSQUE AND CHARLIE RANGEL

In 1972, members of the Nation of Islam mosque led by Louis Farrakhan ambushed four New York policemen, badly wounding three officers and murdering one.

The police had received an anonymous—and it later turned out, bogus—phone call, reporting an officer in distress on the second floor of West 116th Street. Unbeknownst to the responding officers, this happened to be Farrakhan's mosque. The first four cops on the scene either didn't realize (or didn't care) that the front doors of the mosque were uncharacteristically thrown open and the usual phalanx of armed "Fruit of Islam" Muslim guards were absent. The officers ran into the building and up the stairs in search of the injured policeman.

Once all four were in the stairwell, the doors behind them were slammed shut and bolted. At that moment, more than a dozen black Muslims, shouting "Allahu Akbar!" charged down the stairs. The Muslims kicked and dragged their trapped quarry to the bottom of the stairs and then out into the vestibule where they beat, kicked and stomped the policemen to a gruesome pulp. With all four officers on the ground and the vestibule awash in blood, the Muslims managed to wrench service revolvers from two of the battered officers. One of them shot Officer Phil Cardillo in the chest at point-blank range.

As all this was happening, the police dispatcher received a call cancelling the original 10-13 ("assist police officer") call and the policemen swarming toward the building turned back. But Officer Rudy Andre had already arrived and saw his comrade Vito Navarra lying outside the mosque, barely conscious. Andre assumed he was the "officer in distress" who had prompted the original call. Then Andre looked through the windows of the mosque's doors and saw the three other officers still being stomped by Farrakhan's Muslims. They were only yards away from him, but Andre couldn't get to them because the mosque's front doors were now bolted shut. After putting in an urgent call for backup, Andre shot through the door's window to unlock the door and disperse the mob.

By now, the ambushed cops were so drenched in blood that Andre didn't even realize Cardillo had been shot. The assailants all ran to the basement, with Andre in hot pursuit. There was only one way out, so the perpetrators were as trapped in the basement as the officers had been in the stairwell minutes earlier.

As police cars and ambulances arrived at the building, a crowd also gathered to jeer at the police and throw rocks and burning garbage at them. The crowd cheered when the cops were carried from the mosque on stretchers.

Amazingly, Cardillo was still clinging to life when he got to the hospital. Five days later, he would be dead.

Another beaten cop, Victor Padilla, was convulsing so badly when he arrived at the emergency room that doctors and nurses had to hold him down. Blood poured from the socket where his left eye had been gouged out.

Navarra, the officer Andre had found lying in the street, was bruised, bleeding and missing teeth. But, unlike the others, he did not require emergency admittance to the triage unit. So he left the hospital and went back to the mosque to identify the assailants, who were being questioned in the basement where Andre had cornered them.

When Navarra walked in, bloody and tattered, several Muslims retreated to the back of the room. The guilty knew they were moments away from being positively identified. In addition to Chief of Detectives Albert Seedman, who was conducting the interviews, Farrakhan was present. As soon as he saw the pummeled cop, Farrakhan tried to get rid of him, imperiously announcing that he would not be able to guarantee Navarra's safety "in this house of worship."

Seedman shut Farrakhan down, saying, "Everyone in this basement, including you, is a suspect in the shooting and beating of New York cops. No one other than me will be making any decisions in regards to this case."

But just as suddenly, Democratic congressman Charles Rangel materialized and informed Seedman that the police were to leave immediately. Deputy Police Commissioner Benjamin Ward—the first black man to hold that position—was in command, and he had just struck a deal with Rangel and Farrakhan: The cops would vacate the premises immediately, and in return Rangel and Farrakhan promised they would deliver the suspects to the police.

The police are still waiting.

Seedman refused to believe this was happening. But after a few phone calls, he got the order to vacate the premises directly from Commissioner Ward. He called Chief of Police Michael Codd to supersede the order, but the request was refused. Seedman called again and was told Codd had gone to lunch. With no other options, Seedman ordered the police to leave.

One black cop in the basement refused the order, saying, "There's an attempted murderer down here, and he's coming out attached to my cuffs."

But as Rangel had smirkingly indicated to Seedman, the order had been approved by Ward's boss, Police Commissioner Patrick Murphy. The cops were forced to clear out, walking past Muslims in the vestibule who were busily scrubbing the crime scene of evidence.

With Rangel operating as the mosque's bouncer, Navarra was prevented from identifying the assailants, and an airtight case vanished into thin air.

Soon the crowd on the street had grown to more than a thousand strong. Burning garbage, bricks and bottles filled the air. A female journalist was knocked to the ground, stomped, sprayed with lighter fluid and set on fire. Reporters were beaten and their equipment smashed. Stores were looted and destroyed. A stalled bus full of terrified passengers was bombarded with rocks and bottles, as hoodlums smashed its windows and tried to stuff burning newspapers inside.

One of the officers at the mosque, Randy Jurgensen, author of the book about the mosque incident, *Circle of Six*, describes what happened as he exited the building:

> We dropped our heads like fullbacks, squared our shoulders and surged forward. . . . They started to punch, kick and claw at us. I felt a horrific sting below my shoulder. Someone had bitten a chunk of skin out of my back. . . .
>
> We made it to [the police car], slamming the doors and locking them. The keys weren't in the car. BOOM! The windshield exploded, covering us in a million fine pieces of glass. If that wasn't enough, burning rags soaked in gasoline were tossed in. . . .

Commissioner Ward responded to the melee by ordering all white cops to leave the scene. He was later made police commissioner by Mayor Ed Koch.

Farrakhan and Rangel's promise turned out not to be one you could take to the bank. Despite assurances that they would personally escort everyone in the basement to the 24th Precinct, that never happened. A cop killer had been left in that basement on orders from Mayor John Lindsay's politically correct City Hall.

In response to a murderous ambush of his police, Lindsay apologized to Farrakhan for the officers' "invasion" of his mosque. The NYPD brass dirtied up the four cops by falsely portraying their entry into the mosque as unlawful and even implying that Cardillo had been killed by "friendly fire."

Neither Lindsay nor Murphy attended Cardillo's funeral, which was believed to be the first time a New York City mayor had not attended the funeral of a policemen killed in the line of duty.[6] Instead, Lindsay went skiing in Utah. Murphy took a "business trip" to London with his wife.

Murphy did have time, however, to meet with Farrakhan at police headquarters in order to apologize for the police's mistake in entering the mosque. Murphy would later describe Farrakhan as a man of "clear conviction, speaking in tones of deep resonance, whose larger style was not entirely confrontational."[7] Of course, he hadn't responded to the 911 call.

An open-and-shut investigation into a savage, premeditated cop killing had been shut down by a Democratic congressman.[8] If you've ever wondered how thorough a news blackout can be, and to what extent a politician can skate away from controversy, Rangel's knee-deep involvement in the Harlem mosque incident is a perfect example.

The *New York Times* sprang to action decades later by relentlessly flogging Representative Rangel on its front page. Not for covering up the murder of a policeman but for cheating on his taxes. Tax collection is a serious matter! But don't expect the *Times* to go after Rangel for protecting a cop killer.

The *Times*'s 2011 obituary for Patrick Murphy, the police chief who had conspired with Rangel and Farrakhan to cover up the coldblooded murder of a police officer, hailed Murphy as "a nationally recognized police figure with a track record that extended to Washington and Detroit." (If you were a police chief, would you put those two cities on your resumé?) The *Times* described Murphy as the man who "steer[ed] [the New York Police Department] through one of its rockiest periods as he instituted reforms to root out corruption in the ranks."

The entire mosque incident was brushed off in a single slippery sentence: "The next year, another officer, Phillip Cardillo, was fatally shot inside a Harlem mosque." Actually, he was murdered in cold blood and his assassin was protected by Patrick Murphy.

The *Times* was still dissembling about the mosque ambush in a May 12, 2012 article about a proposal to name a Harlem street after Phil Cardillo. The article described the 1972 ambush thus: The 911 call "turned out to be spurious, and a melee ensued," adding that mosque leaders "believed they were being invaded by a hostile police force." No. They set a trap for the purpose of killing cops. Everyone knew it—the police, the mayor and, certainly, the "mosque leaders." (In the *Times*'s defense, it may not have known.)

The ranks of ordinary cops included plenty of black officers. These were the ones on the street making arrests, at the mosque, visiting colleagues in the hospital afterward, and the ones who would be enraged for the rest of their lives at their betrayal by the mayor and top officials of the NYPD. But black cops were no more respected by liberals than white cops were. Only murderous, cop-killing, brick-throwing, garbage burning, taunting, spitting black miscreants at the Harlem mosque counted as "black" for purposes of the police brass and the politically correct media.

Phil Cardillo's murderer was eventually brought to justice, mostly through the indefatigable work of detective Randy Jurgensen. Meanwhile, the top echelons of the NYPD did everything in their power to block the capture and conviction of the murderer. Any investigation might raise questions about their own despicable conduct.

Blocked from using police surveillance equipment, Cardillo's partner privately said: "[They've] got a million motherf—king dollars' worth of equipment to collar dope heads, but for a dead cop, we can't get a camera and a roll of film. I wanna vomit . . . This job and those c—ksuckers downtown are a f—king joke. A dead cop, Randy, a dead cop. My partner."

Do not imagine that New York City was saved by anything other than Rudy Giuliani.

While Police Chief Murphy and his coterie were throwing every manner of roadblock in Jurgensen's way as he searched for Cardillo's murderer, a black Muslim from Farrakhan's mosque, Foster 2X Thomas was the hero of the case. Three years after the mosque attack, Thomas was arrested for using a stolen credit card. The polite young man immediately owned up to his crime and answered directly when asked about the ambush. As Foster explained in repeated interviews, he spoke the truth "because Minister Farrakhan always reminds the Muslims that we must tell the truth."[9]

Thomas had been working in the mosque bakery during the ambush and only emerged when he heard a commotion in the vestibule. Rushing in to defend his Muslim brothers, he was present when one of them shot the cop. He said it was Lewis 17X Dupree.

When Thomas testified against Dupree at trial, he was subjected to taunting from a hundred angry black Muslims glaring at him from the gallery. But, again, he matter-of-factly explained that he spoke the truth because Minister Farrakhan said Muslims must always be honest.

Unfortunately, the trial resulted in OJ-style justice with the truth coming out but with the jury hung, 10–2, for conviction. A black female juror refused to convict Dupree, and a white female juror refused to disagree with her. The second trial, with a less impressive presentation, ended in an acquittal. (Lewis 17X Dupree later ended up in prison on a federal felony conviction in North Carolina.)

For telling the truth, Thomas had to be shuttled about in seedy motel safe houses for three years until the trial and then placed directly into the federal witness protection program after the second trial.

But liberals don't celebrate men like Foster 2X Thomas. If only he had killed a cop or faked a hate crime, he would have been celebrated in movies, Hollywood petitions, Anna Quindlen columns and *New York Times* editorials. That was the chaotic, upside down world that liberals foisted on the nation in the 1970s right up to the OJ trial.

JIM JONES'S PEOPLES TEMPLE

Another shining example of the Democrats' promotion of a fringe black "religion" was their close association with Jim Jones's Peoples Temple. Though recent television biographies on Jones portray him as a religious leader in the mold of Jerry Falwell or Pat Robertson, Jones was the original left-wing community organizer, beloved by Democratic politicians throughout the land.

Jones's Temple was a black cult, even though Jones, like so many other jackass liberals who wreck black people's lives, was white. But more than 80 percent of Jones's followers were black,[10] and according to the most intensive study of Jonestown ever conducted—by the Department of Religious Studies at San Diego State University—the Peoples Temple was a "primarily black community in racial terms" and in "cultural identity."[11]

That, in addition to the fact that Jones bashed America, meant that no matter how obviously unhinged he was, Democrats fawned over him. Just as they would later be required to pay homage to Jesse Jackson and Al Sharpton, in the seventies Democrats had to kiss the ring of Jim Jones, atheist, communist and fake Cherokee. (What is it with liberals always claiming to be Cherokee?)

During Jimmy Carter's 1976 presidential campaign, Rosalynn Carter visited Jones's Peoples Temple of "apostolic socialism" and appeared on a stage with him, an act second in embarrassment only to the time she appeared on stage with her husband. Carter's vice presidential candidate,

Walter Mondale, wrote a letter to Jones, saying: "Knowing of your congregation's deep involvement in the major social and constitutional issues of our country is a great inspiration to me."[12]

Based in San Francisco, Jones was embraced by all of California's liberal elite, including then (and current) governor Jerry Brown, former governor Edmund Brown Jr., Democratic congressmen Phillip and John Burton, then assemblyman Willie Brown and San Francisco mayor George Moscone—who gave Jones a position on the city's housing authority.[13]

Jones modeled himself on a black preacher, Father Divine, giving sermons that were described as "fiery" and "charismatic." As one member put it, "He preached and he read good. And he shout. I used to like to see him shout."[14] An article in the *San Francisco Chronicle* described Jones as a "Southern-style gospel preacher" who "tossed Marxist phraseology into sermons."[15]

Like Farrakhan's mosque, Jones's temple was protected by locked doors and armed bodyguards. He was a bisexual who had sexual liaisons with many of his followers as well as those far outside his church: In December 1973, he was arrested in a Hollywood theater for attempting to molest an undercover policeman in a theater.[16]

Even before the mass suicide in Guyana, it was obvious that Jones was as mad as a March hare. His newspaper, *Peoples Forum*, was like a mini-*Nation* magazine, praising socialism, Black Panthers, Angela Davis and Huey Newton, and predicting a "Nazi" takeover of America. He warned his followers that fascists were planning concentration camps for black people, to do to them exactly what Germany did to the Jews.[17] Jones had relocated his so-called church to California from Indiana in the 1960s because he anticipated a thermonuclear war in 1967 and believed only Brazil and California would be safe.

He demanded that members remit jewelry, furs and homes to the temple as well as at least 25 to 40 percent of their money—another clue that he was a Democrat.[18] Many followers were forced to sign "confessions" to horrible crimes they had never committed.

During the "healing" sessions, Jones's wife, Marceline, would go into a bathroom with a cancer patient and emerge with old chicken gizzards in a jar, proclaiming—to cheers from the congregation—that the cancer had "passed." (This is covered in a lesser-known provision of Obamacare, by the way.) During "catharsis" sessions, members were disciplined with belts, paddles, fists, urine and vomit. Jones trained them out of their "hypocrisy" by having the entire congregation shout "shit!" over and over again.[19]

A year before the final bloodbath, Marceline Jones told the *New York Times* that Jones's hero was Mao Tse-tung and that his goal had always been social change through Marxism. She said he only "used religion to try to get some people out of the opiate of religion."[20]

The *Times* reported that Jones "was openly contemptuous of religion among his associates"[21] and, according to his wife, had once slammed a Bible on the table and said, "I've got to destroy this paper idol!"[22] One Jonestown survivor admitted that "even though it called itself a church, that was to legitimize it, to validate it, there was never actual Bible study."[23]

(And yet, Christopher Hitchens included Jim Jones's Marxist cult in a list of monstrosities caused by religion in his book, *God Is Not Great: How Religion Poisons Everything.* God can't get a break.)

For most of its existence, Jones's commune was left alone by the press. But on August 1, 1977, *New West* magazine ran a major exposé on Jones, based on interviews with more than a dozen former members willing to speak on the record. In response to credible allegations of child abuse, assault and fraud, San Francisco's liberal political establishment rallied around Jones.

The Democratic mayor and district attorney—whom Jones had helped elect—refused to investigate (a practice now known as "pulling an Eric Holder") with both Moscone and District Attorney Joseph Freitas Jr. summarily announcing that no laws had been broken.[24]

Willie Brown responded to the accusations by showing up at a rally at Jones's Temple, saying the attacks on the commune were "a measure of its effectiveness."[25] *Would it kill you to become a follower of Reverend Jones?*

Sadly, none of these elected Democrats accompanied the Peoples Temple to Guyana.

Would the political and media establishments have looked away if the Peoples Temple had not been left-wing and majority black? With few exceptions, it wasn't until after the mass suicide in Guyana that the major press took any notice of Jones at all. Why hadn't anyone in the media—apart from *New West* magazine—bothered exposing this lunatic before he led more than nine hundred people to suicide?

Not long after the *New West* investigative report appeared, Jones resigned from his position with the housing authority and fled with his followers to Guyana, a country he admired for its Marxist government. His entry was greased with letters of recommendation from Rosalynn Carter, Vice President Walter Mondale, and Carter cabinet member Joseph Califano,[26] among other eminent Democrats. His plan was to create "an experiment in socialism."[27] Terrific move. Those always go so well.

In Guyana, Jones began meeting with KGB agents at the Soviet embassy, hoping to move the commune to Russia. In anticipation of the move, Jones instituted mandatory Russian-language classes at Jonestown, refusing to let people eat—even the elderly—unless they spoke in Russian.[28] In Guyana, he also began the suicide drills, which he called "White Nights."[29]

After the cult's departure to Guyana, ex-members and relatives of members began kicking up a fuss, warning in interviews, newspaper articles, and letters to President Carter and the State Department that Jones was insane and was planning a mass suicide. Carter's State Department investigated and concluded that it had no basis for action.[30]

In November 1978 a Bay Area congressman, Leo Ryan, went on a fact-finding mission to Guyana. As he and his entourage were about to board their plane for home, Jones's followers sprayed them with machine-gun fire, killing Ryan and NBC correspondent Dan Harris. In all, five people were killed and ten wounded.

Back at the socialist paradise, Jones ordered his followers to commit "revolutionary suicide" to protest "the conditions of an inhumane world." Several cult members asked what happened to the plane to Russia. Jones told them Russia wasn't going to happen and tried to get on with the mass suicide. But they kept pestering him about Russia, until Jones assured them that "I'm right now making a call to Russia." But minutes later, he began exhorting them to take the grape drink and die "quickly, quickly, quickly, quickly, quickly. . . . Good knowing you!"

As hundreds died in front of him, Jones never mentioned God, but rather harangued his followers to stop their hysterics because "this is not the way for people who are Socialists or Communists to die. . . . I call on you to stop this now if you have any respect at all. Are we black, proud, and Socialist, or what are we?"[31]

More than nine hundred men, women and children died, most of them black. The majority died by drinking cyanide-laced Flavor Aid grape drink, an act memorialized in popular culture as "drinking the Kool-Aid." Cyanide poison causes death after several painful minutes of writhing, screaming and foaming at the mouth.[32] Some were apparently murdered with injections of the poison. Jones died of a gunshot wound to the head.

His wife, Marceline, left a will bequeathing all her money to the Communist Party of the Soviet Union, specifically directing that her daughter, Suzanne Jones Cartmell, was to receive nothing. Three members who escaped the mass suicide said that during the massacre, Jones's mistress, Maria Katsaris, gave them a heavy box, instructing them to take it to the

Soviet embassy. The box, which never made it to the embassy, had half a million dollars in it.

Jones's only religion was communism and a strange multicultural bisexualism—in other words, he was a mainstream Democrat. Even Jones's lawyers were part of the fabric of liberal America. One was attorney Charles Garry, white lawyer to the Black Panthers, who had defended Bobby Seale in the Chicago Seven trial. Garry pleaded the Fifth Amendment when called before the House Committee on Un-American Activities. Just one year before the Guyana massacre, Garry returned from a visit to Jonestown, proclaiming to the U.S. press, "I have been to paradise!"[33] Garry was visiting Jonestown again when Representative Ryan's party was shot. He bravely ran into the woods to escape.[34]

Jones's other lawyer was left-wing conspiracy theorist Mark Lane. Apart from his antiwar organizing with Vietnam Veterans Against the War— where it was proposed that the group assassinate conservative members of Congress[35]—and participation with the "Winter Soldier Investigation" (an event in which fraudulent non-soldiers "testified" to atrocities committed by American troops) Lane spent most of his life trying to prove a right-wing conspiracy was responsible for JFK's assassination. Sadly for him, the lone assassin was a fellow communist, Lee Harvey Oswald.

To hide the blinding fact that Jones was part of the mainstream Democratic elite in America, liberals instantly went to work reinventing him as a born-again preacher selling that old-time religion. *Time* magazine's article on Jones in the wake of the massacres began: "The sad story of a boy and his Bible."[36]

More recently, MSNBC's Rachel Maddow called Jones "a minister from a small town in Indiana"—which is on the order of calling Charles Manson a petty thief from Cincinnati. They both hit it big in spaced-out, left-wing, New Age California.

Tellingly, Maddow introduced the story on Jonestown by saying, "Now, for a story that is off our normally trod track of politics."[37] If Jerry Falwell, with as close an association with the Republican Party as Jones had to the Democratic Party, had led the students at Liberty University to assassinate a congressman and commit mass suicide, wouldn't that be a story about politics?

Within two years, the mainstream media in the United States, with very rare and brief exceptions, dropped the words "socialist," "communist," "Marxist," "Russia" and "Soviet Union" from all mentions of Jonestown. There would be no reminders of the Democrats' close connection to Jones. It was like the spontaneous disappearance of John Edwards from the news in 2008.

Most deceitfully, the chattering class began importing religious phrases into their descriptions of the atheistic, Marxist San Francisco community organizer. Thus, NBC repeatedly referred to Jones's "flock" and his "church," while saying his followers took the poison "as if lining up for communion."[38] How about, "as if standing in a Soviet bread line"?

There was certainly no reference to the racial composition of Jonestown or Jones's imitation of a black preacher and his constant references to himself as black.

The Democrats had mainstreamed insanity. Jones had all the earmarks of a demagogue—the meaningless slogans, the Castro-style stem-winders, and the hatred of the Bible and Christianity. He was a drug addict who enjoyed polymorphous sex and berated his critics as "haters." As is common in California, he staunchly supported communal living, no private property, the Soviet Union, and finally, death.

It is an arresting fact that more Republicans—to wit, Barry Goldwater and John McCain—have denounced Falwell and Robertson, than Democrats have ever denounced Jones. Then again, Falwell had criticized Teletubbies. All Jones did was murder nine hundred people.

"JOHN AFRICA" AND MOVE

Another black cult, MOVE (meaning unknown, other than, "Honey, I think it's time we move to the suburbs"), based in Philadelphia, billed itself as antiestablishment and rejected bathing, hygiene, medicine and electricity in order to return to the simplicity of life in Africa. Led by Vincent Leaphart, who called himself John Africa, MOVE's followers were required to adopt the surname "Africa," much as black Muslims' names must include "X," Communists call one another "comrade," and French revolutionaries called themselves "citizen." Totalitarians are obsessed with stamping out human individuality. Thus, MOVE's minister of information was named "Gerald Ford Africa."

There was constant friction with the group's neighbors on account of the hundreds of rats kept by MOVE; their "recycling" methods, which involved throwing trash and excrement onto the front yard; their armed assaults on neighbors; and nightly bullhorn broadcasts of their anarchist ideology. (MOVE's building was also consistently voted "worst place to trick or treat" by neighborhood children.)

In 1978, what began as a health inspection of MOVE's house led to a shootout that left one policeman dead. Nine members of the organization were convicted of his murder, but John Africa was acquitted.[39] One of the nine, defendant Delbert Orr Africa, accused the court of being "racially prejudiced [. . .] and society is genocidally bent toward destroying us." He also asked a police cameraman on the witness stand whether he was as "racially prejudiced as Mayor Frank Rizzo."[40] Naturally, liberal heartthrob Mumia Abu-Jamal was associated with this band of left-wing nuts, even demanding that he be allowed to represent John Africa in court despite his lack of a license to practice law.

A few years later, MOVE was creating the same problems with rats, garbage, terroristic threats and explosives at a different house in another part of town. After evacuating the neighbors, the police staged a predawn raid on the row house and began a deafening shootout with the cult members that lasted nearly two hours. The MOVE activists shot at the police with automatic weapons from a rooftop bunker fitted with peepholes and gun slots. Next, the fire department bombarded the house with water cannons for five hours. Still, the residents refused to leave.

Finally, in what turned out to be a miscalculation, at around 5:30 p.m., a police helicopter dropped explosive material on top of the house in an attempt to destroy the rooftop bunker. Instead, the explosive set off a conflagration that burned down the entire neighborhood, as well as killing eleven MOVE members inside the house.[41] MOVE, it turned out, had been storing drums of gasoline on the roof.

This was a major law enforcement screwup, so two grand juries were convened to consider criminal charges against the mayor and police. After a three-year investigation, no criminality was found.

Cries of racism were only slightly tempered by the fact that it was MOVE's black neighbors who had demanded action in the first place and also that the rooftop bomb had been approved by Philadelphia's first black mayor, W. Wilson Goode.

But that didn't slow down Al Sharpton and attorney Alton Maddox. Fresh from their Tawana Brawley triumph, the two called for Mayor Goode's arrest. Standing with John Africa's sisters, Sharpton denounced "the same grand jury system that has plagued us in New York and rendered a very racist and Nazi-like verdict in the Tawana Brawley case has even more so returned a ruthless verdict" in the MOVE case.[42]

How did MOVE's friends and family become martyrs? MOVE's neighbors had a right to be ticked off. Their houses were burned down, too, and they weren't the ones who had filled their homes with rats, garbage and explosives and then fired machine guns at the police. They were the true victims of both MOVE and a law enforcement screwup.

When did it become required for black leaders to automatically defend black criminals, while ignoring peaceable black people?

David Koresh's Branch Davidian compound was not bothering the neighbors when the ATF staged a military assault on his house. The only emergency the ATF was responding to was the threat of having its funding cut. As enraged as a lot of people were about the pointless, grandstanding government raid in Waco, Texas that left more than two hundred Americans dead, white people felt no obligation to sing Koresh's praises or carry on his message.

By contrast, John Africa has become a heroic figure in some quarters. In the mixed-up world where all that matters is race, in 2000, MOVE member Ramona Africa appeared on stage at the Harvard symposium "Race, Police and the Community" along with Abner Louima, an actual victim of police brutality in New York City.[43] Louima, a Haitian immigrant, had been arrested in a fracas at a nightclub, and then was viciously sodomized with a broomstick by a white police officer, Justin Volpe. who thought he had been sucker-punched by Louima. The attack was monstrous, but not racist: Volpe's most vociferous defender was his black girlfriend.

But what does a law enforcement mistake during a five-hour siege of a criminal nuthouse have to do with a psychotic policeman committing an assault on an innocent black man?

Celebrity cop killer Mumia Abu-Jamal still concludes his speeches and radio broadcasts with: "On the move. Long live John Africa. From death row, this is Mumia Abu-Jamal." An article in the *Village Voice* includes MOVE in a list of black victims of racism, such as Emmett Till.[44] Earth First! hailed MOVE as a civic-minded group that "fed poor children natural food and helped to uplift the community."[45]

MOVE was responsible for the deaths of more African Americans in the last four decades than the Klan. It's gotten quite a bit less bad press.

JEREMIAH WRIGHT

For a long time after these experiments with radical black cults, all was quiet on the western front. Dead and maimed cops in a Harlem mosque, nearly a thousand dead bodies in Guyana, a burned down neighborhood, eleven dead MOVE members and a murdered cop in Philadelphia—it was almost as if liberals *could* learn after being repeatedly hit in the head with a hammer.

And then the Obama era ushered in the Reverend Jeremiah Wright.

If a white pastor had said what Obama's preacher had said—not about black people, but literally, the exact same words—people might have noticed that he's crazier than the love child of David Duke and Ward Churchill (America-hating fake Indian). Both Churchill and the Reverend Wright, incidentally, referred to the attacks of 9/11 as the chickens coming "home to roost."

Imagine a white pastor calling Condoleezza Rice, "Condoskeeza Rice."

Imagine a white pastor saying, "Racism is the American way. Racism is how this country was founded . . . We believe in white supremacy and black inferiority. And believe it more than we believe in God."

Imagine a white pastor saying: "No, no, no, God *damn* America, that's in the Bible for killing innocent people! God *damn* America for treating our citizens as less than human! God *damn* America for as long as she acts like she is God and she is supreme!"

These taped comments of Wright's were defended in many media outlets as mere snippets, "culled" as Andrew Sullivan said, by dat ol' debbil, Sean Hannity, to the disadvantage of poor Senator Obama.[46] Ah, yes, the time-honored "taken out of context" ploy. But in fact, the outrageous quotes had been selected by Wright's own congregants for prominent display in videotapes sold by his church for promotional purposes. Apparently, those who knew Wright best—his own congregants—didn't feel these were careless pop-offs, but stand-alone gems that should be displayed to the public.

Two months before Wright was launched into the public consciousness, he was Obama's close confidant, friend, mentor, the man who married him and his wife, baptized his children and gave him the title of his best-selling book, *The Audacity of Hope*. But the moment America got a gander at this loon, he became just some "crazy uncle" Obama barely knew.

Nonetheless, Obama tried to justify Wright's deranged rants by explaining that "legalized discrimination" is the "reality in which Reverend Wright and other African Americans of his generation grew up."

That may accurately describe the libretto of *Porgy and Bess*, but it had no connection to reality. By Wright's own account, he was twelve years old and attending an integrated school in Philadelphia when *Brown v. Board of Education* was announced. When he was six years old, Jackie Robinson was admitted to major league baseball and Nat King Cole was the second most popular American in the country, after Bing Crosby. Wright's childhood was more like *The Jeffersons* than *The Confessions Of Nat Turner*.

Apart from the fact that Reverend Wright's world wasn't segregated, what about Wright's anti-Semitism? The anti-Semitic tone of his sermons was almost as clear as his rage against the United States. He called Israel a "dirty word" and a "racist country." He blamed Israel for 9/11, denounced Zionism and called for divestment from Israel. In addition to videos of Wright's sermons, Obama's church also offered for sale sermons by Nation of Islam leader Louis Farrakhan, whom Wright joined on a visit to Libya's Muammar al-Qadaffi in 1984. The church awarded Farrakhan the Dr. Jeremiah A. Wright Jr. Trumpeter Award in 2007, saying Farrakhan "truly epitomized greatness."

Why did crazy "uncle" Wright dislike Jews? But, again, who knows in what context this remark was made? Maybe they were trying to say that Farrakhan *isn't* great. Who knows? We weren't there. It's just a snippet.

In Obama's "conversation" on race (after his minister's tapes were publicized), he suggested that white Americans rise above anger with the likes of Reverend Wright—as if he represented all of black America—because his tantrums required "understanding." The media heralded Obama's speech as "eloquent," a "profile in courage," "rising above traditional divides,"[47] "honor[ing] the human dimension of his relationship with his politically threatening 'old uncle,' as he calls [Wright],"[48] and evidencing a "frankness about race," that "traced the roots of black church preaching deep into 'the bitterness and bias' of the black experience."[49] (And that's just from the *New York Times*.)

But Obama's oh-so-civil prescription—deeply admired in liberal quarters—bears, unfortunately, a strong resemblance to the patience that most adults reflexively extend to children. The problem is that black Americans, including Wright, are not our children, but our fellow citizens.

CHAPTER 6

PEOPLE IN DOORMAN BUILDINGS SHOULDN'T THROW STONES

It wasn't ordinary black people throwing rocks at the police and dropping cinderblocks on people's heads. Those were common criminals.

It wasn't ordinary blacks searching the world over for a single white person who would use the N-word—those were self-aggrandizing journalists.

It wasn't ordinary black people defending violent black cults and black cop killers, such as Mumia Abu-Jamal, John Africa's MOVE, Jim Jones's Peoples Temple, and the Black Panthers—that was the Democratic establishment.

It wasn't ordinary black people begging Jesse Jackson to be their leader. He was the black leader for white people. As black writer John McWhorter put it, Jackson's "self-aggrandizing machinations have left behind not a single successful project that would improve black lives beyond the boardrooms of his friends."[1]

It wasn't ordinary black people depicting every suspect ever shot by the cops as a victim of racism, every riot as the police's fault, every hoax hate crime as absolutely true, Al Sharpton as a respected spokesman for the black community, all cops as redneck racists. That was Jim Dwyer, the *New York Times*, Anna Quindlen, Hollywood scriptwriters, and John Lindsay.

Not only journalists, but the legal community did its part wreaking havoc in the black community. Starting in the sixties, ordinary people, black and white, watched in stupefaction as liberal social reformers came in and jettisoned thousands of years of human knowledge to rewrite criminal laws and government welfare policies. Liberals living in monochromatically white suburbs or doorman buildings in the cities said, *Let's try these new ideas that sound really cool, like school busing and deemphasizing prison!*

As Thomas Sowell describes the changes in his book, *The Vision of the Anointed*: The old view was to put criminals in prison. The new view, held by, for example, Lyndon Johnson's attorney general Ramsey Clark, Supreme Court justice William Brennan, and DC circuit judge David Bazelon, was to avoid sending criminals to prison and instead spend all our resources focusing on the "root causes" of crime. In the august words of Judge Bazelon, "poverty is the root cause of crime."[2]

The basic idea that liberal judges and politicians began to push on the country in the 1960s was that society should be nice to criminals so they would repay us with law-abiding behavior. As Attorney General Clark said: "The theory of rehabilitation is based on the belief that healthy, rational people will not injure others, that they will understand that the individual and his society are best served by conduct that does not inflict injury."[3] Of course, if that were true, they wouldn't have committed crimes in the first place.

Despite being completely insane, the reformers won out. Their policies were put into place and the stage was set to test two fundamentally opposed views of public policy and human nature. As Sowell writes:

All that was needed was empirical evidence.

THE RESULTS: Crime rates skyrocketed. Murder rates suddenly shot up until the murder rate in 1974 was more than twice as high as in 1961. Between 1960 and 1976, a citizen's chances of becoming a victim of a major violent crime tripled.[4]

Based on their having no understanding of human nature, the smart set turned American cities into petri dishes for crime and degenerate behavior without punishment. Thousands of Americans died, were raped and disfigured in criminal acts entirely made possible by the Warren court, the ACLU, liberal professors and activists, whose single-minded policy objective was to return criminals to the street.

In response to liberals demanding that we stop sending criminals to prison, normal people asked, "*Why would that work?*" But they were dismissed as unenlightened. Liberals had built a perfect system that had to be inflexibly imposed on the country. They got angry and sarcastic when anyone pointed out it wasn't going to work.

Sowell describes a former New York City police commissioner objecting to lenient Supreme Court rulings on criminal law at a 1965 judicial conference. He was "immediately met with ridicule by a law professor who asked, 'I wonder what rights we'd have left if we always yielded to the police hysteria.'"[5]

One of the first places to try out these advanced ideas in criminology was New York City, in the person of liberal celebrity, Mayor John Lindsay. Lindsay was the Obama of his day. For simply announcing his 1965 mayoral candidacy, Lindsay made the cover of *Look*, *Newsweek* and *Life* magazines. A *New York Times* editorial on his candidacy titled "A Man Who Can Be Mayor" hailed Lindsay's "good judgment," calling him "youthful, intelligent, energetic, liberal," "diligent," "courageous" and "conscientious."[6] When his victory was announced on election night, the *Times's* deputy managing editor Abe Rosenthal and metropolitan desk editor Arthur Gelb embraced, cheering "We've won!" [7]

While it's difficult to capture the totality of the destruction wrought by Lindsay's administration, his *New York Times* obituary is a start: a doubling of the welfare rolls; constant strikes by transit workers, teachers and sanitation workers; skyrocketing crime rates; a tripling of the city's debt; epic racial conflicts; demoralized police; and nonstop race riots.[8] The *Times* might have added: "He screwed up by taking our advice."

In a crowded field, Lindsay's greatest damage to the city was shackling the police in order to reduce civilian complaints. Meanwhile, citizens being mugged hit record levels. Between 1962 and 1967, robberies quintupled. Although it may have seemed as if the crime rate couldn't climb much higher, robberies doubled again from 1967 to 1972.[9] The left's official position was that crime was inevitable as long as there were inequities and if you really wanted to do something about crime, you'd support the Humphrey-Hawkins Full Employment Act.

After a while, the police learned to coexist with the new regime, soon discovering that not doing their jobs had its plus side. Life was better, they had fewer headaches and their work was a lot easier. Crime went through the roof, but guess what? There were no civilian complaints! Instead of *great year—we solved 129 crimes!* it became *great year—we had only 12 complaints!* The murder rate was higher than Mexico City's, but the police were heroes because no criminals were complaining about them.

There aren't a lot of ways the government can make things better, but the sixties and seventies proved that there are a lot of ways government can make things worse. It took decades to roll back the horrors imposed on the country by activist judges, beginning in the sixties. The battle was hindered by Johnson- and Carter-appointed judges honeycombing the judiciary for many decades to come. Some of these lunatics still walk among us today.

Meanwhile, the empirical evidence kept pouring in.

A 1982 Rand study of prison inmates in Michigan, Texas and California, found that each one committed a mean of between 187 and 287 non-drug crimes per year while out on the street.[10] A decade later, the Bureau of Alcohol, Tobacco and Firearms found that criminals with at least three convictions for a violent felony committed about 160 crimes per year.[11] By keeping career criminals in prison, the 1992 ATF study concluded, society would save $323,000 per year in actual monetary costs, not including physical and psychological damage to the victims of crime.

In 1994, the *Los Angeles Times* conservatively calculated the cost to taxpayers of a single quick gang shoot-out in which no one died, but a twelve-year-old girl was struck and paralyzed. Among the excluded costs were: Legal aid attorneys (the defendants hired private attorneys), jurors' time away from work, missed work by the injured girl's family, and the paralyzed girl's limited employment prospects. The shooting, in broad daylight in front of many witnesses, didn't require a lot of investigative time or court costs. One shooter pleaded guilty to a lesser offense, saving the costs of a trial, and the other was convicted after a quick five-day trial.

Still, the bare minimum costs came to well over $1 million—$1.7 million in 2010 dollars.[12]

Putting criminals in prison to prevent more crimes like that is a fantastic bargain for society. But for decades, America suffered under the delusional fantasies of liberal judges, mayors and attorneys general committed to the idea that punishing criminals was outmoded.

In 1970, not a single prison was under a court order. By 1990, more than five hundred municipalities had their prison systems being run by judges.[13] As a result, by 1993, the average time served for violent felonies, including murder and rape, was three and a half years.[14]

In 1994, Princeton professor John Dilulio looked at the consequences of a prison cap put on the Philadelphia prison population by a Carter-appointed judge, Norma Shapiro. In a single eighteen-month period, 9,732 prisoners released pursuant to Judge Shapiro's order were re-arrested for committing new crimes, including 79 murders, 90 rapes, 701 burglaries, 959 robberies, 1,113 assaults, 2,215 drug offenses and 2,748 thefts.[15]

It goes without saying that most of the victims were not well-heeled residents of Philadelphia's Main Line. In the country at large, blacks were becoming the victims of crime more than ever before. In 1992, black youths were nine times more likely to be murdered than white youths. Liberals lied, black kids died.

Despite pious assurances that locking up criminals wouldn't work, the prison-building boom that started to come online in the 1990s—as well as the gradual replacement of Democrat-appointed judges with Reagan and Bush judges—had an amazing effect on suppressing crime. Maybe by liberals' definition it didn't "work" because putting criminals in prison didn't help them become valued members of society. But it did keep them from killing people.

Much like doctors bleeding their patients, today we look back and say: "There was a time when people believed *that*?" These were judges, university professors and politicians imposing theories they had dreamed up at some all-night bull session at Harvard, ignoring policemen screaming at them, "*It doesn't seem like a good idea here on the ground!*"

Tut, tut, you must be one of those unsophisticated rubes worried about property values.

Even liberal historian Sean Wilentz has since said that liberal Democrats' reaction to criticism of their policies was "always to blame the people who were resisting for being narrow-minded or racist, not up to their own enlightened idea of the way Americans ought to be. There was a contempt, there was an elitism."[16]

Whenever we pause to think about great Americans, we should also pause to remember there were rotten Americans, too, such as John Lindsay, Justice William Brennan, Ramsey Clark, Norma Shapiro and countless other liberal activists, who, in life, never stopped getting their butts kissed. In death, they deserve to have their graves desecrated.

With a few shining exceptions (Jesse and Al), blacks have long been among the leading proponents of a strong police presence in their neighborhoods. No less an authority than Martin Luther King complained of the absence of police in poor black neighborhoods, saying crime was "the nightmare of the slum family" that had turned the ghettos into criminal "sanctuaries."[17]

In 1964, a Harlem riot raged for two days in response to a white police officer's shooting of fifteen-year-old James Powell. And yet, a *New York Times* poll in the wake of the riot showed Harlem residents ranked crime as a more important issue than police brutality.[18]

Two years later, in 1966, the NAACP's Roy Wilkins took a confidential survey of Harlem residents' opinions about police brutality. Fifty-seven percent said there was "none at all" or they were "not sure"; 31 percent said there was "a little" police brutality and only 12 percent said there was "a lot."[19] In 1968, the Harlem branch of the NAACP was calling for mandatory five-year sentences against muggers, ten-year sentences for drug pushers and thirty-year sentences for murderers.

But no one cared what blacks wanted. Liberal zealots were on the march. There were dissenting voices to the left's celebration of black criminals, but they were dismissed. When blacks rioted in Baltimore following Martin Luther King's assassination, Maryland governor Spiro Agnew invited more than a hundred black leaders to a meeting and gave an eloquent speech about rising black militancy. If more political leaders had had Agnew's moral authority as a civil rights champion to give a speech like this, the country, especially blacks, could have advanced in that moment by leaps and bounds.

Agnew began by noting that everyone in the room was a leader and contrasted them with "the ready-mix, instantaneous," "circuit-riding, Hanoi-visiting" "caterwauling, riot-inciting, burn-America-down"[20] type of leaders. Those, he noted, had not been invited to the meeting.

Then he said:

> It is deplorable and a sign of sickness in our society that the lunatic fringes of the black and white communities speak with wide publicity while we, the moderates, remain continuously mute. I cannot believe that the only alternative to white racism is black racism. Somewhere the objectives of the civil rights movement have been obscured in a surge of emotional oversimplification. . . . And I say that the road we have trodden is built with the sweat of the Roy Wilkinses and the Whitney Youngs—with the spiritual leadership of Dr. Martin Luther King—and not with violence.
>
> Tell me one constructive achievement that has flowed from the madness of the twin priests of violence, Stokely Carmichael and Rap Brown. They do not build—they demolish. They are agents of destruction and they will surely destroy us if we do not repudiate them and their philosophies—along with the white racists such as Joseph Carroll and Connie Lynch—the American Nazi Party, the John Birchers, and their fellow travelers.

He reminded them that white people of Maryland had "clearly repudiated racism in the 1966 election" (when he had defeated Democratic segregationist George Mahoney) and said that "the overwhelming majority of

Maryland's Negro citizens—responsible, hardworking, decent people" were "horrified" by the recent events and would be "unjustly victimized by a hardening of attitudes in the responsible, decent white community." Agnew called on the black leaders "as Americans, to speak out against the violence and hatred of Stokely Carmichael and Rap Brown. Otherwise, he said prophetically, "the heaviest losers will be the Negro citizens of America."[21]

Unfortunately, most white politicians reacted like Leonard Bernstein greeting the Black Panthers. They cooed over the violence and arson of black criminals, even justified it as an understandable reaction. What about the majority of blacks who weren't rioting? Did they feel Martin Luther King's assassination less poignantly?

As long as they had a free hall pass, black leaders tended to respond by condoning the violence, too. In response to the destructive Baltimore riots, Homer Favor of the Urban Studies Institute at Morgan State University said: "I feel unclean that I didn't burn down a building."[22] And that's how we ended up with many happy decades of peace and prosperity in bustling black neighborhoods from Baltimore to Newark, Detroit and Oakland.

Agnew was passé; radical white lawyers like William Kunstler and Clark Kissinger got the fawning press notices. For Kissinger, black criminals were just foot soldiers in his larger war against America, which he described as an "oppressive system of capitalism that exploits people all over the world, that destroys our planet, that oppresses minority people, that sends people to the death chambers in droves." (This was later turned into a sermon by Reverend Jeremiah Wright.)

Contrast that with the words of the great African American mathematician and writer Kelly Miller, born in 1863, who astutely observed that the "capitalist has but one dominating motive, the production and sale of goods. The race or color of the producer counts but little." The capitalist, he continued, "gives to every man the unhindered right to work according to his ability and skill. In this proposition the capitalist and the Negro are as one."[23]

Naturally, Kissinger was a big defender of cop killer Mumia Abu-Jamal, promoting the "call to justice" initiative which proposed a nationwide "Mumia Awareness Week." He was joined in this effort by Robert Meeropol, another prototypical black man, who is the son of executed Soviet spies Ethel and Julius Rosenberg.[24] Illustrating the importance of Mumia to the black community, he was defended by a star-studded list of other white liberals—Norman Mailer, Michael Moore, Noam Chomsky, Ben Cohen, Jonathan Kozol, Paul Newman, Susan Sarandon, Oliver Stone, Dean Ornish, Kerry Kennedy, Mike Farrell, William Styron, Alec Baldwin, David Byrne, Nadine Strossen, Trudie Styler, Joanne Woodward and Peter Yarrow.

Charles Garry, the lawyer for the Black Panters and Jim Jones's Peoples Temple, was another great example of a white liberal playing with black lives to advance his own self-image as a rebel without regard to the consequences for blacks. His help with the settlement in Guyana ended in a disaster for black people that was just a little more direct than liberals' standard methods.

Liberals put on shows trying to out bad-ass one another, but twenty years after the Harlem NAACP had been trying to tell us that blacks cared more about crime than understanding the criminal, things had only gotten worse. And black New Yorkers still cared more about crime than understanding the criminal.

After several decades of the media's nonstop drumbeat about racism everywhere in America (except in the nation's newsrooms), in December 1984, Bernhard (Bernie) Goetz shot four black men who were trying to mug him on the subway. Terror surged throughout Manhattan's smart set, but everyone else gave a celebratory whoop.

The youths, Darrell Cabey, nineteen, Troy Canty, nineteen, James Ramseur, eighteen, and Barry Allen, nineteen, told the police they were merely panhandling and had simply *asked* Goetz for five dollars. "We wasn't planning on robbing him," Allen said. "We had no intention of robbing him . . . He had no reason to be scared."[25] Members of the press, who had apparently hermetically sealed themselves off from any contact with New York City's streets and subways that decade, believed them.

Then, about a year later, one of the victims admitted to Jimmy Breslin, one of the columnists who had fallen for it, that, in fact, they "were goin' to rob him. They thought he looked like easy bait."[26]

Journalists might have surmised that had they not been brain-dead liberals. Together, Goetz's victims already had nineteen arrests and two convictions among them. Canty and Ramseur had served time in Rikers Island jail. Canty had been arrested four times since he was sixteen for criminal possession of stolen property, petty larceny, possession of burglar tools and criminal mischief. Cabey had been arrested for holding up three men with a shotgun, taking their money and jewelry and was charged with robbery, use of a firearm and possession of stolen property.

Allen had been arrested for attempted assault and a couple of larcenies for stealing money from video machines. He was on probation. Less than a year after the Goetz encounter, Allen was arrested for mugging an acquaintance in the elevator of their own apartment building.[27]

Ramseur had been arrested four times for petty larceny, criminal trespass, fare-beating, smoking marijuana in the subway and possession of marijuana. Five months after encountering Goetz, Ramseur viciously beat, raped, sodomized and robbed a young pregnant woman on the roof of his public-housing complex. He was in prison, serving a twenty-five-year sentence for this by the time of Goetz's trial.[28]

They had been carrying screwdrivers the night they mugged Goetz because, as they admitted, they were on their way to steal money from machines at a video arcade.

Within sixteen months of the subway shooting, the only Goetz victim who was not in prison or under court supervision for committing other crimes, was the one paralyzed by the shooting, Darrell Cabey. The earlier armed robbery charges against Cabey were dismissed as a result of his condition.[29]

As with the Trayvon Martin case in the era of Obama, the New York press relentlessly showed pictures of the subway "youths" as little kids. A message was being sent. We don't see Hitler's baby pictures. We don't see the Duke lacrosse players' baby pictures. When publishing these first-communion photos of politically correct victims/criminals, the media should be required to run disclaimers: *"Full disclosure: These kids were actually nineteen years old at the time of the shooting"* or *"Photo of spokesperson model, not Goetz's actual victim."*

Polls taken in the month immediately following the shooting showed that half of all New Yorkers enthusiastically supported what Goetz had done—and black people supported him every bit as much as whites did.

In a January 1985 *Daily News* (New York) poll of New York City residents, 52 percent of blacks approved of Goetz's shooting the muggers, compared to 49 percent of all New Yorkers.[30] A Gallup poll the same month showed that 52 percent of whites approved of the shooting compared to 49 percent of blacks.[31]

Georgetown professor Daniel Robinson raised doubts about the poll results, saying that if Goetz "had simply scared the devil out of the four, I think most people would be just as happy."[32] Unfortunately, there were no poll questions on whether Goetz should have "scared the devil" out of the muggers.

Talk radio shows were overwhelmed with callers praising Goetz. When the police set up a hotline for tips about the incident, it was bombarded with callers expressing their support for the shooter and offering to pay his defense costs.[33]

The Guardian Angels, a voluntary patrol made up predominantly of black and Hispanic youths, supported Goetz a hundred percent and began collecting money at the subway for his defense. Roy Innis's Congress of Racial Equality supported Goetz, saying, "We applaud this kind of public spirit against crime."[34]

Commenting on the enthusiastic response to Goetz's self-defense, eminent political science professor Walter F. Berns said: "I am encouraged by what I see as a greater disposition to regard punishment of criminals as not only necessary but moral as well. There is a move by highly respected criminologists to, in effect, rehabilitate the idea of punishment. In a sense, the intellectuals are coming around to where the public has been all the time."[35]

The experiment with "root causes" was over. The world only needed Rudy Giuliani to come in and make it official. (The government official who decided there would be no federal civil rights prosecution of Goetz? U.S. Attorney Rudolph W. Giuliani.)

But the media kept trying to refocus the public's attention on Goetz's possible racism. Days after the shooting, a *New York Times* article on the incident warned: "Just beneath the surface of last week's debate was the question of whether the shooting may have been racially motivated. The four teenagers were black, the gunman was white."[36]

Newsweek sneered that the "reality" of the shooting "was never very heroic" and called Goetz "a distressingly ordinary man."[37]

Washington Post columnist Richard Cohen blamed Goetz for getting mugged, demanding to know why he didn't sit on the other side of the car from the trouble-making black youths. He hypothesized that Goetz "went looking for young blacks." Fear of crime, Cohen noted, "is a code for fear of young blacks."[38] Meanwhile one of the shooting victims himself said, "I heard he had been robbed by some black guys before, so in a way I can understand why he might have been afraid."[39] The mugger grasped crime statistics better than Cohen did.

After a few months of the media haranguing the public to view the shooting as a racial incident and Goetz as a racist nut, ABC bragged that its poll showed support for Goetz had dropped 12 percent among blacks. *Congratulations, media!*

White liberals kept trying to turn the Goetz shooting into a racial incident, but a lot of black people apparently didn't get that memo.

In Claremont Village, the South Bronx project where the four teenagers lived, there was no love lost for the victims. A *Washington Post* reporter interviewed people in Darryl Cabey's building as the paralyzed boy remained in a coma and found surprising unanimity. Eighteen-year-old Yvette Green said "If I'd had a gun, I would have shot him." Darryl Singleton, twenty-four years old, called Cabey, "a sweet person," but said, "if I had a gun, I would have shot the guy."[40]

One woman told the *New York Times*, "Maybe he shouldn't have shot them, but I can't feel bad if four kids up to no good got hurt."[41] A black man wrote to Cabey's mother: "[Y]ou get no sympathy from us peace-loving, law-abiding blacks. We will even contribute to support the guy who taught you a lesson, every way we can . . . P.S. I hope your wheelchair has a flat tire."[42]

One of the trial witnesses called by Goetz's attorney was Andrea Reid, a young black woman, who had been in Goetz's subway car with her husband and child during the shooting. As she assessed the situation, those "punks were bothering the white man," adding "those punks got what they deserved."[43] (She testified reluctantly, explaining that she had met the mother and brother of one of the muggers at a party.[44])

Noticeably, defense lawyer Barry Slotnick did not try to keep blacks off the jury, nor did he need to. Three blacks and one Hispanic on the jury voted to acquit Goetz of all thirteen charges except for the minor charge of carrying an illegal firearm. Juror Robert Leach, a black bus driver from Harlem, was one of Goetz's most vehement defenders, even persuading his fellow jurors not to convict Goetz for unlawful possession of the guns he had given to his neighbor, Myra Friedman. Leach said he didn't believe Friedman's testimony.[45]

But when the verdict was announced—attempted murder: not guilty, assault: not guilty, and reckless endangerment: not guilty—the usual racial agitators had their usual response.

Al Sharpton slammed the verdict, saying the jurors had "legalized the rampant opinion that if you see young blacks look menacing, then it's okay to shoot them—and don't worry about prosecution." [46]

Don't worry about prosecution? Au contraire! The district attorney had empaneled two grand juries just to get an indictment against Goetz on anything other than the illegal firearm possession charge, delaying the trial until April 1987, more than three years after the shooting.

New York Governor Mario Cuomo remonstrated that "some people" would read the verdict as a "license now to carry a weapon and to shoot everyone who looks mean to you."[47] And, naturally, the *New York Times* ran an article titled, "Blacks See Goetz Verdict as Blow to Race Relations."[48] This included NAACP director Benjamin L. Hooks Jr., ("inexcusable," "a terrible and grave miscarriage of justice") and Representative Major Owens, Democrat of Brooklyn ("The hysteria in the white community will be, 'Yeah, we were right, let's go get 'em.'")[49]

The *Times* had not requested comment from defense witness Andrea Reid, juror Robert Leach, CORE president Roy Innis, any of the Guardian Angels or the muggers' South Bronx neighbors.

For decades, liberal elites rewarded the worst possible black behavior while ignoring amazing courage in the black community. Only a white liberal could think Al Sharpton has been a blessing to black people. As, again, McWhorter says: "Sharpton would be hard-pressed to point to one positive development in black New York, much less black America, that he could take credit for."[50]

This is not to say all problems of black people are caused by white people. But it has been white liberals in positions of power—in the media, academia, Hollywood and the judicial system—who thought it was fun (and quite hip!) to elevate all the worst elements of the black community as heroes and martyrs.

The beginning of Clarence Thomas's dissent in *Grutter v. Bollinger*, about the University of Michigan's affirmative action program, should be tattooed on every liberal's buttocks. Thomas wrote:

> Frederick Douglass, speaking to a group of abolitionists almost 140 years ago, delivered a message lost on today's majority:
>
> "[I]n regard to the colored people, there is always more that is benevolent, I perceive, than just, manifested towards us. What I ask for the negro is not benevolence, not pity, not sympathy, but simply justice. The American people have always been anxious to know what they shall do with us. . . . I have had but one answer from the beginning. Do nothing with us! Your doing with us has already played the mischief with us. Do nothing with us! . . . And if the negro cannot stand on his own legs, let him fall also. All I ask is, give him a chance to stand on his own legs! Let him alone! . . . [Y]our interference is doing him positive injury."[51]

Fittingly, *New York Times* columnist Bill Keller attacked Thomas for his dissent in this case, characterizing it as "the angry exclamation of a black man who feels personally patronized and demeaned" and calling Thomas an affirmative-action appointment.[52] Liberals demand gratitude for their condescension.

CHAPTER 7

LIBERAL-BLACK RELATIONS

Their Landlord and *Their Friend*

It was the misfortune of black Americans that they were just on the verge of passing through the immigrant experience when these damaging ideas about welfare and crime took hold. It could have happened to the Italians, Germans, Jews or Irish, but luckily for them, there were no liberals around to "help" when they arrived.

Until liberals started driving the bus, black Americans were doing better in individual pursuits than immigrants.[1] For about a century after the Civil War, black Americans had good reason to have a chip on their shoulder, but, somewhat amazingly, most did not—until liberals put it there.

Notice the absence of sullen resentment in massively accomplished black Americans in the first generation or two out of slavery—Kelly Miller, James Weldon Johnson, Paul Laurence Dunbar, W.E.B. DuBois, Booker T. Washington, Archibald Henry Grimké, George Washington Carver, Jack Johnson, Huddie William Ledbetter (Lead Belly), Louis Armstrong, Thurgood Marshall, Joe Louis, Jackie Robinson (whose middle name, Roosevelt, was in honor of the Republican president by that name[2]) and many others. And, unlike the immigrants, they had very good reasons to be aggrieved.

Liberal icon Franklin D. Roosevelt put a Ku Klux Klanner on the Supreme Court and refused to desegregate the military, but he was more than happy to put blacks on "Irish Welfare"—government jobs. With the proliferation of government work and welfare under the New Deal, black progress was instantly frozen, ineluctably tied to the growth of government. That is why, in the thirties, for the first time in seventy years, the black vote migrated from the Republican Party to the Democrats. That was, of course, limited to northern blacks: Democrats in the South still weren't letting blacks vote.

The black writer and anthropologist Zora Neale Hurston observed the change and commented: "Throughout the New Deal era the relief program was the biggest weapon ever placed in the hands of those who sought power and votes. . . . Dependent upon the Government for their daily bread, men gradually relaxed their watchfulness and submitted to the will of the 'Little White Father,' more or less. Once they had weakened that far, it was easy to go on and on voting for more relief, and leaving Government affairs in the hands of a few."[3]

Liberals took blacks as their pets and then tried to kill them by patronizing them to death.

In the rainbow of diversity that is the left in this country, a remarkably large number of these white friend-of-the-blacks came from as far west as Riverside Drive, south to Columbus Circle, all the way east to Central Park—and as far north as Morningside Heights. Their basic assumption was that anyone outside of Manhattan—especially white people in Queens—sympathized with the Ku Klux Klan.

Michael Moore managed to be both self-flattering and groveling in his book, *Stupid White Men*. Nothing gives liberals a better sense of their own courage like attacking the only group it's okay to malign and winning standing ovations from cretins.

Liberals have got to get some new material. They've been working that bit about sneering at nonexistent racists forever. *Goddamn it, this may cost me my career but I'm going to speak up for racial equality and let the chips fall where they may!*

It's apparently hard for some people to grasp that it's not brave to tell an audience what it already believes.

Start with the title of Moore's book. Really. White men have contributed nothing? Since you brought it up—no one wrote a book called *Smart White Men*—shall we compare SAT scores, cultural contributions and inventions of white men compared to others? It's one thing to say pink is white, or beige is white. But to say black is white is to have no compunction about sounding like a complete idiot in public.

Reminiscent of a modern-day Jimmy the Greek, Moore urges whites to marry blacks and procreate so we can breed the whiteness out of the country.[4] Hacks think statements like that make black people like them, when it's just creepy and weird. Only a very, very few blacks get to be Al Sharpton. The rest of them have to live in the same world we all do.

Liberals pioneered the method of calling anyone who disagrees with them on politics a racist, based on standards that they themselves could never withstand. It's a favorite hobby of MSNBC hosts to count the number of black faces at a Tea Party rally or the Republican National Convention. James Meredith, the first black person to attend the University of Mississippi in the face of violent attacks, worked for Jesse Helms. How many blacks work for Michael Moore?

How about Chris Matthews? He is an aggressive bean counter when it comes to the number of blacks at Tea Parties—as if the Tea Partiers can control who shows up at their rallies.

Blacks as a group are overwhelmingly one-party voters. Jews have more Republicans. As a result, any group that espouses Republican principles obviously isn't going to have a lot of black people—although probably more than the schools Chris Matthews's children attended.

While living cheek-by-jowl with the nation's capital, which happens to be a majority black city, Matthews's kids managed to go to schools that are probably about 3 percent black. When Matthews had an opportunity to associate with blacks by sending his children to public schools, he chose not to. His obsession with race is all about self-congratulation. As Ralph Waldo Emerson said: "The louder he talked of his honor, the faster we counted our spoons."

The Tea Parties weren't as white as Chris Matthews's office. They weren't as white as Matthews's neighborhood or television audience. (It's doubtful that even Eugene Robinson watches *Hardball*.)

This is *New-York-Times*-Charlie-Rose-PBS thinking. We're not racist, they are. This pompous self-perception allows liberals to be offensively, self-righteously preening in the positions they take, such as demanding school busing for other people but sending their own kids to private schools.

If we attended a party at the Matthews home in Chevy Chase, Maryland, how many blacks would we see? Could we at least wave to the black neighbors? The *New York Times* write-up of his son's wedding[5] included a panoramic shot of the church, showing nearly a hundred guests. Not one of them is black. You may check for yourself here: http://www.nytimes.com/2010/04/04/fashion/weddings/04vows.html?pagewanted=all.

A Republican saddled with the facts of Matthews's life would be convicted of racism in five minutes.

No one is required to be a friend to someone else because it's good for society, and people should be able to hire anyone they please. But you better have your own house in order if you're going to run around accusing everyone else of racism based on a dearth of black associates.

Like Matthews, *New York Times* columnist Tom Wicker made a career of proclaiming that America was a deeply racist country. But he sent his own kids to lily-white private schools and then retired to the whitest state in the nation, Vermont. Wicker being so right-thinking and the scourge of racists, people were curious about why he didn't send his kids to New York public schools. Did he just screw up? Asked about the hypocrisy of sending his own children to sanitized private schools, Wicker said, "It gives me a lot of intellectual discomfort, but I am not going to disadvantage my children to win more support for my views."[6]

It's not a question of winning support for his views, it's whether he really held those views to begin with. The surest proof of racism is not what people say, but what they do. The only thing in his whole life Wicker could have done that wasn't just running his mouth was to send his kids to public schools, and he didn't do it. On what basis did Wicker have a right to self-congratulation on his racial attitudes? Because he worked especially hard to make sure other people's kids had to go to crime-ridden schools?

It's often said that those who are unduly bothered by gays are latent homosexuals. Isn't it possible that people obsessed with racism are themselves racist?

Treating blacks like special-needs children, liberals bury them in ludicrously gushy praise. In a field where the competition is brisk, MSNBC's Rachel Maddow stands out. When not spinning conspiracy theories, Maddow can usually be found patronizing her very, very special black guest, Melissa Harris-Lacewell with fulsome, flowery praise.

Harris-Lacewell (who became Melissa Harris-Perry toward the end of 2010) is professor of being a black woman, which is one of the most demanding, hardest-to-qualify-for positions at any university (you have to be a black woman). She is never treated like some regular nerd guest. Maddow is compelled to tell her she's "amazing," "wicked smart" and "one of the smartest people I've ever talked to about anything, anytime, anywhere." (Then again, the smartest person at MSNBC is the guy who replaces the toner, so that last one might not be false praise.)

Here are a few examples:

■ 1/19/09: Joining us now is a woman who couldn't sound stupid if she practiced it for a week, Melissa Harris-Lacewell, associate professor of politics and African American studies at Princeton University.

■ 7/29/09: Melissa Harris-Lacewell, associate professor of politics and African American studies at Princeton University, I think that's a tremendous insight. That sort of insight is the whole reason that I sought you out in the first place and had you back on the show so many times. It's really invaluable. Thanks, Melissa.

■ 10/8/09: Melissa Harris-Lacewell, associate professor of politics and African American studies at Princeton University. You're wicked smart. Thanks for joining us, Melissa. It's great to see you.

■ 1/8/10: Melissa Harris-Lacewell, associate professor of politics and African American studies at Princeton University, the perfect person to talk to about this. I knew you'd have the academic rigor of the pretesting down. Thank you very much, Melissa. It's great to see you.

■ 2/22/10: Melissa Harris-Lacewell, Princeton professor, MSNBC contributor of which we are very proud, the *Nation* columnist, thanks for coming on the show, Melissa. I appreciate it.

■ 4/7/10: Melissa Harris-Lacewell, Princeton professor, MSNBC contributor, and one of the smartest people I've every talked to about anything, anytime, anywhere.

■ 8/3/10: Every Tuesday, you've been doing this to me, Melissa, every Tuesday my whole adult life. Melissa Harris-Lacewell, the *Nation* columnist, MSNBC contributor, Princeton professor—always a very, very welcome guest here. It's great to see you.

■ 8/5/10: Melissa Harris-Lacewell, Princeton professor, columnist for the *Nation*, MSNBC contributor and somebody who is very, very smart, who I always enjoy talking to. Thanks, Melissa.

■ 9/16/10: Princeton University professor and MSNBC contributor, Melissa Harris-Lacewell, who didn't write what she just said right there. She just said it because she can do that. You're amazing. Melissa, thank you.

■ 10/19/10: Melissa Harris-Perry, Princeton professor and MSNBC contributor and person from whom I most regularly learn the most by talking to on TV—Melissa, thank you so much for your insight. I really appreciate it.

Those are not the words of someone who is comfortable around black people.

For comparison, here's Maddow describing a white male guest: "Chris Hayes, Washington editor of the *Nation*, it's always good to see you."

But at least MSNBC hosts never confuse Chris Hayes with any other white guests. On October 21, 2009, MSNBC's Contessa Brewer introduced Jesse Jackson as "Al Sharpton." (At least it wasn't *Reggie* Jackson.) Then, on November 8, 2010, *Hardball* host Chris Matthews called Representative Elijah Cummings "Congressman [James] Clyburn." If that had happened at Fox News, the power would have been cut.

Managing not to confuse Harris-Lacewell with any other black people, Matthews once introduced her by saying he was really going to listen to her because "I do find it interesting. No, I mean it. I mean it. I mean it, Melissa. I want to listen because I do find a lot to be learning here."[7]

If ever there was a metaphor for charges of racism being a scam pushed by white liberals for their own advantage, it was pasty white fruitcake Keith Olbermann inventing a bogus claim of racism in an attempt to eliminate his main rival.

Agriculture state school graduate Olbermann (major: Communications) spent weeks of his MSNBC show demanding that Fox News fire Bill O'Reilly for criticizing a radio-show caller who said she knew someone who told her that Michelle Obama hated America. O'Reilly said he'd need more than that, adding that he had sympathy for public figures such as the Clintons and Obamas, adding:

> And I don't want to go on a lynching party against Michelle Obama unless there's evidence, hard facts that say this is how the woman really feels. If that's how she really feels, that America is a bad country or a flawed nation, whatever, then that's legit. We'll track it down.

No black person noticed anything untoward in O'Reilly's comments, but luckily they had Keith Olbermann to speak on their behalf, based on his having zero experience with black people. Olbermann heard the word "lynch" and immediately thought of the Klan. *Keith, you're all that stands between democracy and fascism. Take the rest of the week off.*

It was absurd to take any offense at all, but Olbermann twisted a figure of speech into an actual threat and claimed that the phrase, "I don't want to go on a lynching party against Michelle Obama unless there's evidence, hard facts" was a threat to lynch Michelle Obama—provided O'Reilly could get the goods on her. Olbermann had heroically converted O'Reilly's telling a caller she was nuts into, "I'm waiting to lead a lynch party, but I need the evidence—HURRY UP!"

Not everyone who wasn't popular in high school has to spend the rest of his life seeking revenge, but Olbermann refused to accept that. With feigned incredulity, night after night, he would update his viewers: *You won't believe it, but miraculously O'Reilly still has a job.*

I have an explanation, Keith: You are a gigantic fruit.

In a strange coincidence, Bill O'Reilly happened to be Olbermann's time-slot competitor at 8 p.m. and O'Reilly was walloping him in the ratings.

Night 1, Keith Trying to Get His Main Competitor Taken Off Air:

". . . the obscenity, the moral obscenity involved in a national discussion of whether to launch a lynching party against the black woman married to the black man running for president."

" . . . [A] fair observer concludes this man is not color blind, he is not reckless with language, he has that insidious kind of low grade prejudice that we see in ordinary American society still, low grade prejudice against black people."

And then, the main point:

"I mean, do people have to then start—never mind talking to him—but talk to people who are keeping him on the air? Call Westwood One, the radio proprietors of his show, or his boss at Fox News, Roger Ailes or the advertisers and say get rid of the guy, suspend him, whatever . . ."

Night 2, Keith Trying to Get His Main Competitor Taken Off Air:

"Our runner-up, racist Bill O'Reilly: His remark on a radio show was simple and straightforward and honorable. 'I don't want to go on a lynching party against Michelle Obama unless there's evidence.' He has neither been fired nor suspended."

Night 3, Keith Trying to Get His Main Competitor Taken Off Air:

On this occasion, Olbermann brought in a very special guest, carried on a litter and fanned with giant palm fronds by dwarves in loincloths: the

Reverend Jesse Jackson. Keith acted as if he had landed the Jackie Kennedy interview three days after JFK's assassination, but Jackson just seemed puzzled by Olbermann's histrionics.

Quickly getting straight to the heart of the matter—firing O'Reilly—Olbermann hinted that a boycott might be just the thing, asking Jackson: "What do you think is appropriate? I mean, is this a dismissal-level event? Is it suspension; is it a sponsor boycott, or what it is right now, which is nothing? . . . Has Fox responded sufficiently, in your mind?"

And would it be appropriate to award me fifteen share points in the ratings to punish O'Reilly?

Even Jackson was perplexed by this relentless pursuit of O'Reilly, saying at one point: "I guess it's not for me to say it, but it is a burden upon the FCC."

Melodramatically, Olbermann closed with, "The Reverend Jesse Jackson, joining us from Atlanta. I'm sorry it was under these circumstances, but it's always a pleasure to speak with you, sir."

Months later, he was still harping about O'Reilly's plot to lynch Michelle Obama—provided he could get the goods on her. Alas, O'Reilly was not fired, but Olbermann was.

Liberals were always self-aggrandizing blubberbutts patronizing blacks. After the OJ verdict, the rest of the country just stopped being interested.

CHAPTER 8

RODNEY KING—THE MOST DESTRUCTIVE EDIT IN HISTORY

The apotheosis of liberal race-mongering and excuse-making was the Rodney King televised tape and consequent Los Angeles riots.

There will always be barbarians ready to strike at civilization. What the media did with the Rodney King tape was the equivalent of bearbaiting the outlaws. Much like the NBC producers editing the 911 call in the Trayvon Martin case to falsely portray the shooter as a racist, people at Los Angeles's KTLA television network edited the Rodney King tape to make it look like a senseless act of police brutality against an innocent black man. In fact, what the public saw was the officers' final efforts to subdue a deranged suspect after all other methods had proved futile.

News producers at KTLA deliberately cut the first thirteen seconds of the videotape, revealing only the last sixty-eight seconds of an eighty-one-second tape. Even the full tape obviously wouldn't have captured the police officers' entire ordeal with King, but it would at least have given some context—such as showing King's last lunge at one of the police officers.

KTLA won a Peabody Award for its presentation of the tape.[1] I hope it was worth nearly burning Los Angeles to the ground. The people at that TV station who made the decision to edit the tape are responsible for fifty-four dead human beings, thousands of injuries and a billion dollars in property damage.

King was a violent ex-con on parole, though by all accounts he was perfectly charming as long as he hadn't been drinking. But he had been drinking a lot the night of March 2, 1991, when he decided to go for a drive with two friends. Even five hours after his arrest, his blood alcohol level was twice the legal limit.[2]

Melanie and Tim Singer, a husband and wife team on the California Highway Patrol, spotted King's Hyundai flying down the 210 freeway, and tried to pull him over. For nearly seven miles, King led the Singers on a high-speed chase at speeds clocked at up to 115 miles per hour and 85 miles per hour in residential neighborhoods.³ King later explained that he had tried to outrun the cops because "I was scared of going back to prison and I just kind of thought the problem would just go away."⁴

The chase ended when King shot through a red light, nearly causing an accident, and came to a stop. In addition to the Singers, the first officers at the scene were Sergeant Stacey Koon, Laurence Powell, Theodore Briseno, Timothy Wind and a rookie cop, Rolando Solano. Everyone's adrenaline was pumping, a condition reflected in the policemen's motto: "You run, you get beat."

Tim Singer approached the car and ordered the three occupants to exit the vehicle and lie on the ground. King's black passengers did so. They went home without a scratch that night.

While Tim Singer frisked the passengers, Melanie Singer approached the car and told King to get out. Reluctantly, King did so, but instead of lying on the ground, as instructed, he proceeded to dance and babble to himself, wave to the police helicopter hovering overhead and then began to meander about, crouching, kneeling, getting on all fours at one point, laughing and smiling.

Seeing King reach behind him, and thinking he might have a gun, Melanie Singer drew hers and told King to keep his hands away from his backside. In response, King grabbed his posterior and wiggled it at her. He also made a clicking noise, a prison gesture of disrespect.⁵

So the officers knew King had been in prison and, given his behavior, they were beginning to suspect he was high on angel dust (PCP). As one of King's passengers later told the jury, "he was acting strange."

As Singer approached King with her gun drawn, the senior officer, Sgt. Koon, ordered her to back away. He didn't want to risk a fatal encounter.⁶

Following proper procedure, Koon began with verbal commands for King to lie down, but the suspect ignored him, continuing his peculiar behavior, laughing and talking to himself. Next, Koon ordered the four officers to swarm King, two taking his arms and two taking his legs, in order to handcuff him. But King tossed all four officers off his back like rag dolls. Later that night, Powell told a fellow officer—by now, there were a few dozen on the scene—"I was scared. The guy threw me off his back. I thought I was going to have to shoot him." ⁷

At that point, the officers were convinced King was on angel dust, a specific fear for cops because "dusted" perps seemed to have superhuman strength and to be impervious to pain. King's two passengers, Bryant Allen and Freddie Helms, later testified that they thought King was on angel dust that night, too. [8]

Koon shot King with a Taser dart, which got a howl out of King, but not much else. He shot a second dart, and this one seemed to work at first—but not for long.

The video being shot by a random citizen, George Holliday, from a nearby apartment balcony, began here.

Instead of being subdued by the second Taser dart, King leaped up and lurched toward Officer Powell, drawing his first smack with a metal baton.

But the public never saw that.

Unable to subdue King with four men and two darts from a Taser gun, the police were running out of options. LAPD policy prohibited officers from using the choke hold on suspects and discouraged them from struggling with "dusters." So that left the batons.

Following a by-the-book procedure for subduing aggressive suspects without killing them, the three more senior officers began hitting King with their metal batons, under the supervision of Sgt. Koon. If King moved, they whacked him. It was only this part of the confrontation that KTLA allowed viewers to see, repeated on an endless loop on TV.

In all, the officers hit King more than fifty times with metal batons. Finally, they double-handcuffed him, the procedure for suspects on PCP, and put him in an ambulance to the hospital. King and the officers were all alive. When Koon first heard that the arrest had been captured on videotape, he said: "This is great! They got it on tape! Now we'll have a live, in-the-field film to show police recruits. It can be a real-life example of how to use escalating force properly." [9]

At the officers' trial, expert defense witness Sergeant Charles Duke analyzed the baton strikes blow by blow, saying each one was appropriate. But you would have had to sit through actual legal evidence presented in a real courtroom to know that. The jury did, and acquitted the officers.

Nearly everyone who saw the full tape agreed that the thirteen seconds helpfully edited out by KTLA dramatically changed their impression of the incident. That may not seem like much, but, in 2012, fewer seconds were cut by NBC from the 911 call in the Trayvon Martin case—and yet that tiny edit completely altered the meaning of the call. Seeing the six foot four, two-hundred-forty-pound Rodney King rising like a phoenix and charging at Officer Powell would have done a lot to explain the officers' fear of him.

On ABC's *Nightline*, the forewoman of the state court jury, Dorothy

Bailey, told Ted Koppel that when she first saw the King video on television, "I was revulsed. . . . I thought they were hitting that poor man too
hard and too long." But during the trial she said she discovered that "there
was a great deal more to this case than the small bit of video that had been
shown on television."[10]

Roger Parloff, a liberal lawyer and legal reporter who sat through most
of the first trial, wrote an article in the *American Lawyer* concluding that
the jury's verdict was correct. Even though he had actually seen the trial,
Parloff said, he was afraid to tell the truth: "I can't remember a time when
I have ever felt so hesitant to say what I believe." Here was a member of the
media worried about the media. "After all," he said, "imagine if the media
were to summarize [my] article the way it summarized the trial."[11]

Lou Cannon, who covered the trial for the *Washington Post* and later
wrote a book about it, said the full recording was "vital" to understanding
why the first jury acquitted the officers. He said he had "assumed that the
videotape of the King beating would assure conviction," but not after seeing the full tape.[12] After watching a two-hour summary of the trial on videotape, the renowned economist Walter Williams, who is black, denounced
"the news media's dereliction and deception" in its presentation of that
tape.[13]

But the public didn't see the full tape. Everyone with a TV saw only the
KTLA-edited version that ran continuously for the next year on all the net-
works—"like wallpaper," in the words of CNN executive vice president Ed
Turner.[14]

Even the jurors on the second, federal civil rights trial were leaning toward acquittal when their deliberations began—and that was after the explosive riots sparked by the first jury's acquittal of the officers. That was
after the mayor of Los Angeles had declared the officers guilty of a crime,
saying of the first verdict, "The jury told the world that what we all saw
with our own eyes was not a crime." That was after even the president of
the United States had proclaimed the officers guilty.

A few days into the Los Angeles riots, President George Bush addressed
the nation from the Oval Office and said: "It was hard to understand how
the verdict could possibly square with the video. Those civil rights leaders
with whom I met were stunned. And so was I and so was Barbara and so
were my kids." Then he announced that he would be pursuing a federal
prosecution of the acquitted policemen.[15]

The federal jury knew its job was to convict the officers, whatever the
evidence—and it did. A measure of the second jury's trepidation is re-

vealed by the fact that the forewoman of the first jury—the mean, racist jury that acquitted the officers—appeared on *Nightline* with her full name. The foreman on the second jury would only go by "Bob" on the very same show.

Neither jury thought race was a factor. The police department investigation concluded that adrenaline and fear, not racism, fueled the confrontation. Even Rodney King didn't think his race was a factor in the beatdown (at least until the second trial, when he suddenly recalled hearing the officers call him the N-word). To summarize, both juries, the police and Rodney King said it wasn't racism.

The media's conclusion? Racism.

The riots that erupted hours after the officers' acquittals were entirely the fault of KTLA. That station was looking for more of an Emmett Till–type story, so it deliberately fed the public misinformation. KTLA knew exactly what it was doing. Yes, the rioters were more responsible, but to paraphrase Jesus, ye have criminals with you always. If KTLA had simply run the full eighty-one-second tape, the public would have been prepared for the possibility of acquittal. Everyone would have said, "Well, he *was* lunging at the cop, I wonder what else he did. . . ."

Not only did the media show only part of the videotape, ad nauseum, but they did everything in their power to turn up the dial on ghetto rage. King was instantly dubbed a "black motorist"—as if he had been out for a Sunday drive after lunch with the parson in the tin lizzy, wearing a jaunty cap and goggles, as opposed to a drunk, violent ex-con leading police on a dangerous high-speed chase.

Foreshadowing the OJ trial, the media considered it highly probative that earlier in the night, Officer Powell had referred in a private communication to a domestic violence call as something "out of *Gorillas in the Mist*." But forepersons on both juries said that race did not figure into their deliberations at all. In fact, "Bob" reported that it was the younger jurors, rather than the two black jurors, who seemed to see things from King's point of view.[16]

It was not as widely reported—meaning it was reported in a single newspaper—that Officer Koon had once given mouth-to-mouth resuscitation to a black transvestite prostitute with sores on his mouth after the man collapsed in a police station lockup. When the prostitute died, the medical examiner confirmed that he had had AIDS. Koon explained to one stunned officer that he did it because the transvestite prostitute "was created in the image and likeness of God, and if he could keep him alive, he was going to do that." [17]

Ted Koppel asked the forewoman of the first jury if the ensuing riots had given her "any second thoughts at all about what you had done?"[18] The jurors? They did their job, and properly according to everyone familiar with the evidence.

How about KTLA? That TV station was rewarded by the industry for deceptively editing a video in order to create the false impression of racist cops savagely wailing on a random "black motorist." Anyone with a passing familiarity with the facts of the case—say, someone working at a television news bureau—had to know an acquittal was highly likely on the basis of the actual facts of the case. Just for fun, KTLA's producers and news directors piled up kindling, firewood and lighter fluid and waited to see what happened.

THE LA RIOTS

The LA riots were a calculated explosion—and a guaranteed media ratings booster!

In a poll, 87 percent of black respondents said they did not approve of the riots. 37 percent thought the riots were totally unjustified, period, while 50 percent disapproved of the riots but understood why the rioters responded to the acquittals the way they did. Only 9 percent thought the riots were justified.[19] (Among white liberals, 99 percent agreed with the statement, "the riots were great TV.")

A *Los Angeles Times* poll asked what would prevent a future riot. The runaway favorite, among several options, was "more moral leadership," garnering 50 percent support from both blacks and whites, as well as from about a third of Latinos.[20]

We would not be getting that moral leadership from Congresswoman Maxine Waters. She responded to the officers' acquittal in the King case by taking to the streets, chanting "No justice, No Peace!"[21]

U.S. News & World Report said the five days of mind-bogglingly destructive riots were "bred out of decades of racism and police brutality and nourished by the enraging conditions of ghetto life: unemployment, poverty, family breakdown, gangs, drugs, welfare and Reagan-era cutbacks in aid." [22]

KTLA shouldn't have taunted the wolfpack, but that doesn't mean we want to understand the wolves' feelings.

In the most infamous incident from the riots, a white truck driver, Reginald Denny, drove his eighteen-wheeler into the middle of the mayhem, unaware of what was going on because he was listening to country music on the radio. At the corner of Florence and Normandie, rioters smashed his passenger window with a rock, dragged Denny from the car and began beating him to a pulp.

As Henry Keith Watson stood on Denny's neck, other black thugs repeatedly kicked and stomped him, smashed his head with a claw hammer, and threw a five-pound oxygenator—stolen from another bloodied white truck driver—at his head. In a final gruesome act, Damian "Football" Williams picked up a slab of concrete and heaved it directly on Denny's head, knocking him unconscious for five minutes and fracturing his skull in ninety-one places. Williams then did a victory dance around Denny's body, pointed at Denny and flashed gang signs to the hovering news chopper that was filming the entire attack.

Other black rioters took photos of Denny's brutalized body, spat on him and stole his wallet. One black man stopped on his motorcycle and fired a shotgun at the gas tank on Denny's truck, mercifully missing.

Bobby Green, a black truck driver who lived in the neighborhood—one of the more affluent and stable in South Central LA—saw the beating of Denny on TV and rushed out to the street to rescue him. With the help of three other blacks running interference in their cars, Green drove Denny's truck, with Denny in it, to a hospital. They got there just in the nick of time. Denny went into seizure as soon as they arrived.

The riots did finally produce a hate crime involving paint, but, unlike the hoax attack in the Bronx earlier that year, this one actually happened. It was captured on videotape. After savagely beating and kicking Fidel Lopez until he was unconscious, rioter Damian Williams painted the unconscious man's face black, then pulled down Lopez's pants and painted his penis and testicles black, as another attacker joyfully announced on his videotape of the attack, "He's black now! He's black now!"

Lopez would have been one of the dead, but an ex-con, ex-pimp black minister, Bennie Newton, threw himself over Lopez's body and told the crowd, "Kill him and you have to kill me, too."[23] Where's the Hollywood movie about Bennie Newton?

Representative Waters did not champion the heroic blacks like Green or Newton, who risked their necks to save the lives of brutalized victims. She championed Damian Williams and the other violent animals who did the brutalizing. Williams's mother told the *Los Angeles Times* that no sooner had

Williams been arrested than Waters "just showed up at the door" and said "'I'm Maxine Waters'" and offered help to Williams and the other young men in the neighborhood, saying, "her doors were open."[24]

Waters insisted on calling the bloody, pointless riots a "rebellion," as if a larger cause were at stake, something other than thievery, murder and mayhem. As she explained: "If you call it a riot, it sounds like it was just a bunch of crazy people who went out and did bad things for no reason. I maintain it was somewhat understandable, if not acceptable. So I call it a rebellion." Yes, their *cause juste* was that they wanted new TVs and free liquor.

The people who bore the brunt of this "rebellion" were the Korean Americans who moved into South Central to do business, primarily running small markets after the big grocery chains pulled out, an act that had been a mystery . . . until the LA riots.

In one of the accounts of the riots, Sergeant Lisa Phillips said she and her partner were trying to rescue a Korean girl who was stuck in her car, being besieged by hundreds of rioters:

> We ran up to her car. My partner, Dan Nee, grabbed her—she was bloody, strapped in with her seatbelt. We thought she was already dead.
>
> We were running back to the car when my partner gets hit with a rock and goes down into the street. The woman goes flying out of his arms, and the crowd laughed. That is one thing I will never forget. The crowd spontaneously burst into laughter.[25]

That's what Maxine said was "understandable, if not acceptable." Calling their celebrated anger "righteous" and a "reaction to a lot of injustice," Waters said: "There were mothers who took this as an opportunity to take some milk, to take some bread, to take some shoes. They are not crooks." [26]

U.S. taxpayers already supply the unlucky and the lazy with food stamps, free school breakfast and lunch programs, the Special Supplemental Nutrition Program for Women, Infants, and Children (WIC), free and subsidized housing for the poor, free medical care for the poor, direct cash payments to the poor—all at a cost of hundreds of billions of dollars each year. Half a dozen federal agencies administer a score of programs to ensure that the poor in America are housed, fed, clothed and cared for. The only thing missing is a government worker to lift the spoon to the poor person's lips. The disadvantaged are fed so well, the leading health problem among them is obesity. But when a black mob erupts in a murderous rage, looting liquor stores and killing white and Korean victims, a U.S. congresswoman tells us it's because they needed milk and bread.[27]

As was getting to be a habit, the media blamed the cops for the behavior of blacks. *U.S. News & World Report* said, "the prolonged, televised absence of police at the riot's epicenter virtually invited thousands of would-be looters to believe they could steal and rampage with impunity."[28] Virtually invited! They pulverized Asians, Hispanics and whites and did a billion dollars worth of property damage. The rioters even attacked a carload of nuns. What else could the little darlings be expected to do? It was the cops' fault for not stopping them.

The elites treated blacks like children—unusually violent children— who could not be held accountable, even when they were captured on news cameras beating random passersby nearly to death.

■ ■ ■

Fifty-four people were killed in the riots. Thousands more were injured— and consider that Reginald Denny counts as injured, not killed.

Every single member of the crack KTLA news team that deliberately fed the public the misinformation that led to this carnage ought to spend the rest of his life looking over his shoulder, worried about a relative of Reginald Denny or a financially ruined Korean sneaking up on him.

But far from hiding, the people responsible for the misleading tape brag about their Peabody Award.[29] At least we have their names.

KTLA's Ryan Cowan was the first to see the tape.

Reporter Stan Chambers took the tape to the police for comment and was the on-air reporter who presented the deceptive tape to unsuspecting viewers. Before the tape aired, Lieutenant Fred Nixon of the LAPD's Press Information Office made the obvious point to Chambers that "As you and I both know, it's impossible to look at a videotape and tell precisely what the justification was."[30] And he was talking about the full eighty-one-second tape.

There was some hint of the justification in the first thirteen seconds with King lunging at Officer Powell. So KTLA cut that part out. I could win all arguments, too, if I could alter the evidence. Chambers boasts on the KTLA Web site that the tape "spurred a national debate on race relations and excessive use of force by police."

Newscaster Ron Olsen also touts his Peabody Award for the edited tape that incited the LA riots.

News director Warren Cereghino was the man responsible for putting the edited tape on the air and then giving it to other networks, according to author Lou Cannon.[31]

KTLA's executive producer Gerald Ruben responded to criticism of the network for distributing such an inflammatory tape by saying, "If we hadn't aired it, someone else would have." That's the perennial justification of the criminal: *If I hadn't raped her, somebody else would have.*

Years later, KTLA arranged for lingerie models to traipse through the set during the weather forecast to spice up the news. At least no one got killed with that ratings ploy.[32]

After the riots, Accuracy in Media chairman Reed Irvine complained to ABC News about its use of the edited King tape. Vice president Stephen Weiswasser responded in a letter, saying: "It is our view that the part of the tape not regularly shown does not shed light on the jury's action, one way or the other." [33]

As the kids say: Duh. Of course the altered video didn't "shed light on the jury's action"—the jury saw the full tape and did what any jury would do. The edited tape does, however, shed light on the *riots*, which was the point.

In the end, the elite's more exciting version of the news became reality: The police officers who beat Rodney King were prosecuted a second time and two of the four convicted by jurors who were well aware not only of the deadly riots but of the calumnies directed at the first trial's jurors.

Four months after the cops were duly convicted, the trial of Damian Williams and his cohorts began. Representative Waters sprang into action by demanding that the charges be dismissed. "The whole community," she said, "is going to organize to ask the district attorney and the judge to dismiss the charges against Williams."[34] In her statesmanlike way, Waters suggested that the trial of Denny's attackers was an opportunity to take "revenge" for the acquittals in the Rodney King case.[35]

John Mack, president of the Los Angeles Urban League, said he didn't want Williams's trial "to send out a message to all of the African American residents, and especially young African American men, that we're going to throw the book at these three guys and the same thing is going to happen to you if you get out of line."[36]

I'm sorry, but isn't that *precisely* the message we want to send?

Reginald Denny's assailants were acquitted of all felony charges—save Damian Williams, who was convicted on one count of mayhem. Williams and Watson were found guilty of only misdemeanor assault. The jury hung on all other charges.

In response, not one white person looted, despite being "virtually invited" to by the absence of police on Rodeo Drive. In that case, we were required to accept the jury's verdict and not expect a reaction, much less a second, federal civil rights trial, despite the blindingly obvious fact that the defendants attacked Denny because he was white. The jurors had spoken, the case was over, the criminal justice system had run its course—let's all accept that justice has been served and move on.

Upon his release from prison, Williams received a job from Waters.[37] This lunatic was allowed to roam free, causing havoc wherever she went because, as Shelby Steele said, "the larger society feels it doesn't have the moral authority to call her on it."[38] For years, it was required that, whenever race was mentioned, all thinking be shut down.

■ ■ ■

So much evil has been done by liberals in the name of race relations.

- KTLA created a situation where if there were an acquittal of the Rodney King officers—highly likely given the facts—the city would burn.

- The black stripper, Crystal Mangum, falsely accused Duke lacrosse players of gang-raping her, but was never prosecuted for her lies. Within the next few years, she was charged with child abuse, arson and attempted murder—and convicted of child abuse. (As we go to press she is on trial for murdering her boyfriend.)

- Two years after Lemrick Nelson was acquitted for the murder of Yankel Rosenbaum—and the *New York Times* concluded that the verdict "leaves unresolved who killed Yankel Rosenbaum"[39]—he pleaded guilty to slashing a fellow student with a razor blade.

- Within less than a year of being shot by Bernie Goetz, two of the "youths," mere panhandlers according to much of the press, had committed violent crimes—Barry Allen had mugged an acquaintance and James Ramseur had raped and sodomized a pregnant woman.

- Half a dozen white people were beaten, robbed or sexually assaulted in response to hysterical media coverage of a hoax paint attack in the Bronx and a gang attack in Howard Beach.

Rewriting the facts to prove racial discrimination in lending, in 1992, the Federal Reserve Bank of Boston produced a famous study allegedly proving that blacks were discriminated against in mortgage lending. The study was a sham. It was riddled with preposterous errors, suggesting, for example, that some loans required the banks to pay interest to borrowers. Once the errors were removed, no evidence of discrimination remained.

But the study fit the America-is-still-racist myth, so the Federal Reserve charged ahead and imposed suicidal mortgage lending policies on banks. Among other things, the new guidelines directed that banks stop requiring borrowers to have a credit history and mandated that banks accept welfare payments and unemployment benefits as down payments.[40]

It would be like ordering professional baseball teams to ignore how a player hits, runs and catches, but to accept broken bones as a qualification.

The bad loans, destined to default, were spread throughout the economy in the form of mortgage-backed securities—bundling the good loans with the crap loans. When the loans collapsed, so did the economy. Our financial system had to be blown up so that millionaires at the Boston Fed and Federal Reserve could feel good about themselves for rooting out nonexistent racial discrimination.

How many lives have been ruined to fulfill liberals' fantasy that America is still a racist country?

And now the media are impatient for another Rodney King explosion to help Obama's reelection campaign. Then, if he is not reelected, the media will have primed the public to believe that only racism can explain it. *Isn't ObamaCare wildly popular with the public? College graduates love living at home with their parents! The economy is great!* They plot their reporting of the news to make people believe Obama can't lose—except for racism.

CHAPTER 9

TRIAL OF THE CENTURY
Mark Fuhrman's Felony Conviction

In 1995, Americans discovered it was considered a graver offense to use "the N-word" than to cut a woman's head off. (Unless you happened to be a black rap artist or comedian, in which case the nonstop use of that epithet would get you an Emmy, Grammy, Oscar or NAACP Image Award.)

Only one felony conviction came out of the O. J. Simpson trial for a double murder so brutal that one victim's neck was severed to her spinal cord: the perjury conviction of Los Angeles detective Mark Fuhrman, for lying about having used the N-word nine and a half years earlier. Meanwhile, despite mounds of incriminating evidence, the jury acquitted OJ of murdering Nicole Simpson and Ron Goldman after only three hours of deliberation.

The end of paralyzing groupthink on race began with the verdict in the O. J. Simpson trial. Unknown to the elites, the world changed at 10:07 a.m. on October 3, 1995, when an estimated 150 million people[1] turned on their TVs to watch the verdict. As blacks across the country erupted in cheers at the acquittal, it was the end of white guilt in America.

Thanks to the miracle of television, nearly everyone in the country had seen the same evidence the jury saw, unfiltered by the KTLA newsroom or hapless reporters like Jim Dwyer of the *New York Times*. Ninety-five million Americans had watched the slow-speed car chase that ended with OJ's arrest.[2] For the next year, a small cable channel, Court TV, was getting ratings as if it were running the Super Bowl every night.

People saw the Congressional Black Caucus give Johnnie Cochran a standing ovation three days before his closing argument.[3] They saw the juror who was a former Black Panther give OJ the "black power" salute after the verdict was read. And they saw blacks across the country cheering the outcome—most shockingly at the esteemed, historically black Howard University School of Law. The sight of black law students whooping and

applauding OJ's acquittal had the same emotional impact as watching Pal-
estinians celebrate the 9/11 attack.

In black neighborhoods throughout the country, car horns honked in
victory when Simpson was acquitted.[4] At a McDonald's in Clayton, Missouri, the all-black staff burst out in cheers and high-fives, while the mostly
white customers watched in disbelief.[5] At one high school in St. Louis
(being filmed for TV) black students cheered for five solid minutes.

At another high school, twenty black students beat, kicked and stomped
a younger white student while shouting "Black power!"[6] Outside the Los
Angeles Criminal Courts building, a Hispanic man was assaulted by an
angry crowd of blacks merely for saying he thought OJ was guilty.[7] In Colorado, a black man beat up his white girlfriend because she disagreed with
him about the verdict. He told her Nicole Simpson deserved it and maybe
she did, too.[8]

White people took it all in and said: That's it. This has drained the last
reserves from the Guilt Account. Henceforth, mau-mauing appeals to
white self-condemnation were futile. Accusing someone of racism suddenly stopped working, as if there were a glitch in the subway system and
MetroCards didn't open the turnstile anymore.

Okay, you got us back. I hope OJ was worth it.

The corpus delicti at the trial was Mark Fuhrman's use of the N-word in
the previous ten years. The main witness, which in a technical sense was
about two murders, was screenwriter Laura Hart McKinney, who said
Fuhrman had used the word in her presence nearly a decade earlier.

Whether Mark Fuhrman had used the N-word became an issue because, despite its monumental irrelevance to Simpson's guilt or innocence,
defense attorney F. Lee Bailey had been allowed to ask Fuhrman if he had
"addressed any black person as a nigger or spoken about black people as
niggers in the past ten years." Bailey's query commingled two very different questions: 1) whether Fuhrman had called an actual person the N-
word (no); or 2) whether he had ever *used* the N-word (yes).

A normal person would hear that question and assume it meant: "Have
you personally referred to blacks with the N-word?" and not "Has the word
passed your lips, perhaps because you were repeating a Chris Rock joke,
singing along with a Tupac song or reading Joseph Conrad's *Nigger of the
'Narcissus'*?"

The media was thrilled by this development. It was just a few years since
Rodney King and the Los Angeles riots and there were a lot of reporters sitting around, bored, waiting for another America-is-racist story. These

overblown racism incidents, with their flood-the-zone coverage, were as good for ratings as dead-pretty-white-girl stories are today.

There were some dubious claims about Fuhrman using the N-word. Kathleen Bell said she heard Fuhrman use the N-word in a marine recruiting station, whereupon she fled the room, crying. Three other marines who were present remembered no such thing. Also casting doubt on Bell's story was the fact that, soon after Fuhrman drove her to tears, she tried to set him up on a date with a friend of hers. [9]

So McKinney was the star witness for the most important charge in the trial of the century. She had taped Fuhrman years earlier when he used the N-word while proposing dialogue for her screenplay. Fuhrman was trying to impress the screenwriter with his gritty street language. Apparently, it worked. The two had had a sexual relationship.

Fuhrman was inventing dialogue, not, he said, using "my own words, my own experiences, or my own sentiments."[10] As he put it, he "had to exaggerate things to make the screenplay dramatic and commercially appealing." Hollywood producers, he surmised, were not going to want a "nice warm and fuzzy movie about good cops." So in his make-believe dialogues, Fuhrman played a racist cop who used the N-word a lot.

McKinney admitted on the stand that Fuhrman had never used the N-word, except when they were working on the screenplay. No one testified that Fuhrman had referred to any actual black person with the N-word. Rather, he had used the N-word the exact same way Bailey had: by putting it in someone else's mouth; in his case, an imaginary cop (to be played by Gene Hackman).

Fuhrman was right about what Hollywood wanted. Quentin Tarantino was showered with awards for his movie *Pulp Fiction*, in which the N-word is used approximately one billion times, including an Oscar for best original screenplay awarded in March 1995, the very month Fuhrman took the stand.

The date was important in another way. It was March 1995 when Fuhrman testified that he had not used the N-word "in the past ten years" and McKinney's tapes were from 1985. This was a case of perjury by calendar: If the trial had taken place just a few months later, there would be no possible claim of perjury, even under the racism-hunters' Fuhrman-specific definition of the crime.

As the nation would hear over and over again in defense of President Bill Clinton's actual perjury a few years later—generally from the same people demanding a life sentence for Fuhrman—a lie under oath must be "material" to the outcome of a case in order to constitute perjury. To take one completely random example, questions about a president's sexual relationship with a White House intern are material to a sexual harassment claim against him by another subordinate—as was specifically ruled by a federal court. A cop in the OJ case who lied under oath about what his wife made him for dinner the night before would be strange, but not perjurious.

It's quite a stretch to argue that Fuhrman's "lie" about using the N-word was material to whether OJ killed Nicole Simpson and Ron Goldman. The defense's theory was that if Fuhrman had used the N-word in the previous decade, he might have planted evidence against OJ. But this requires one to assume, first, that use of the N-word in any context proves racism, making F. Lee Bailey, George Carlin, Ice Cube and Quentin Tarantino racists; and, second, that it was possible for Fuhrman to plant the evidence against OJ.

Philosophers may debate whether any use of the N-word proves racism, but it was established to everyone's satisfaction that Fuhrman couldn't have planted the glove—to Judge Lance Ito, California attorney general Dan Lungren and even Simpson defense lawyer Alan Dershowitz. A half dozen other detectives were swarming all over Nicole's condo before Fuhrman even arrived. They saw only one glove at the scene of the crime. Another half dozen were with him at OJ's estate when Fuhrman saw the matching glove in the yard and pointed it out to them. And there were the bushels of other evidence, such as bloody footprints leading away from the murder scene, consistent with the rare and expensive, size-twelve Bruno Magli shoes, which OJ had been photographed wearing, despite his denying he owned the "ugly-ass" shoes.

But the country was crazy. About the same time as the OJ trial, a black man sued a computer encyclopedia company for emotional distress because when he was looking up the Niger River, he mistyped and got the encyclopedia's entry on the N-word. [11]

In court, OJ's defense lawyer, Johnnie Cochran, summarized the N-word accusations by calling Fuhrman "this perjurer, this racist, this genocidal racist." He told the mostly black jury that Fuhrman wanted to "take all black people out and burn them, or bomb them. That's genocidal racism."

Spurning subtlety, Cochran said Fuhrman was similar to "another man not too long ago in the world, who had those same views, who wanted to burn people, who had racist views and ultimately had power over people in his country. . . . This man, this scourge became one of the worst people in the world, Adolf Hitler, because people didn't care, didn't try to stop him." Only the jury could stop this incipient Adolf Hitler! Fred Goldman, Ron's father, may have been the only person who took exception to Cochran's comparing a Los Angeles detective to Adolf Hitler.[12]

It was the same argument Jim Jones had made: White America wants to do to black people what Hitler did to the Jews. It must be a mesmerizing accusation: With that claim, Jones got nine hundred people to commit suicide and Cochran got twelve people to acquit a murderer.

No one in the media considered it ironic that in a trial of a black man for the slaying of two white people, the only person called a "genocidal racist" was a cop who had used an ugly word in a nine-year-old screenplay. Cochran said Fuhrman was "America's worst nightmare." Evidently, having a large black man sneak up to your house late at night and cut your throat to the spinal cord is just an unpleasant dream. Maybe we should check with Nicole and Ron on their worst nightmare . . . oh no, we can't.

The defense team had hired OJ's accomplice, Robert Kardashian, as a lawyer solely to prevent him from being asked about the bulging Louis Vuitton garment bag he was seen carrying away from OJ's residence the day after the murder, leading to speculation that the bag contained bloody clothes and the murder weapon. This constituted the second worst thing he ever did after spawning the Kardashian sisters.

These were the people who wanted the book thrown at Fuhrman for allegedly perjuring himself about using the N-word.

When it was over and Simpson was set free, the media was ravenous for payback—not against the man who had carved up two human beings and walked away, but against the person accused of using the N-word.

Fuhrman apologized to the nation, to the Goldmans, to the Browns and to the prosecutors. He apologized on *Oprah*, on Diane Sawyer's *Dateline NBC*, on ABC and on the *Geraldo Rivera Show*. Say, how many years has it been since Al Sharpton hasn't apologized for foisting the Tawana Brawley hoax on the nation and accusing an innocent man of rape?

Fuhrman was subsequently investigated by the FBI, the Los Angeles County Public Defender's Office, the California Attorney General and the Los Angeles Police Department for any infraction in his twenty years on the force.[13] Who could survive such a career autopsy? Yet the investigations turned up nothing against Fuhrman—nothing except rave reviews, including from his minority partners, colleagues and friends.

Months after the verdict the *New York Times* reported that one former Fuhrman partner, a black man named Carlton Brown, praised Fuhrman as "a consummate detective." He scoffed at the McKinney tapes, saying he himself might have invented stories of beating up white people if he had been talking to a screenwriter. Another partner, Roberto Alaniz, a Hispanic officer, said Fuhrman "exemplified exactly what a police officer should be." [14]

One of Fuhrman's best friends in the department was a black female assistant district attorney, Danette Meyers. She called Fuhrman "one of the best detectives in the city." Meyers said that if a suspect was hungry, Fuhrman would sometimes take him to lunch. She said Fuhrman invited her home to dinner with his wife and children. Once, after she received a death threat, he offered to be her personal bodyguard on his own time.

None of Fuhrman's black and Hispanic colleagues, the *Times* reported, ever heard him make a racist remark. Fuhrman was part of an early-morning department basketball league composed of mostly black officers, one of whom remarked: "If you really hate African Americans, why would you get up at 5:40 to play basketball with me?"

The investigation into Fuhrman's life and work performed by the Los Angeles public defender's office—which, as the *Times* noted, was likely to be "aggressive"—found "virtually no complaints against him." In all major cases Fuhrman worked from 1988 to 1995, there was not a single accusation of racial misconduct, nor of planting evidence. Indeed, the public defender's office found "some compliments paid to Fuhrman by arrestees," including minorities.[15]

The Los Angeles Police Department's investigation turned up about a half dozen complaints that had been lodged against Fuhrman between 1984 and 1990. Almost all were ruled groundless, though he did receive disciplinary actions twice, once for grabbing a pedestrian's wrists and once for leaving a note with an "improper remark" on a car windshield.

About a year after OJ had gotten off scot-free for two brutal murders, California's Republican attorney general, Dan Lungren, hauled Fuhrman back from his new home in Idaho to charge him with perjury for denying that he had used the N-word in the prior ten years, when in fact he had not used it for only the previous nine and a half years.

Although Fuhrman would likely have won in court, he decided to forego a criminal trial—against the vehement advice of his lawyer—and accepted a plea of no contest to a felony charge of perjury. He was sentenced to three years parole and ordered to pay a $200 fine. Unlike OJ, Fuhrman was now a convicted felon, unable to vote or own a gun.

Editorial boards across the nation erupted in rage, demanding that Lungren justify himself—not to explain why he had brought charges at all, but rather why Fuhrman was given such a light sentence.[16] As OJ hit the golf course the mob demanded jail time for the man who used the N-word.

The full demagnetizing of the race card would take time, because our stupidest fellow citizens write the news. As the country stared in disbelief, the elites acted as if nothing had changed. Their America-is-still-racist stories were always a scam and Simpson's acquittal didn't change that. The multitude is foolish, Edmund Burke said, but "the species is wise, and when time is given to it, as a species, it always acts right."

Eventually, even liberals would catch on to the fact that Americans were done with treating blacks like children. But not yet.

So for a few more years, the race narcissists continued to issue the same hoary platitudes, after normal people had moved on.

Daryl Gates, former chief of the Los Angeles Police Department, reacted to the verdict by saying: "I take the responsibility for Mark Fuhrman. The miserable, no-good son of a bitch."[17]

The *Sun-Sentinel* (Fort Lauderdale, Florida) called the Fuhrman sentence a "powderdpuff sentence" for a crime that "should have brought a term near the maximum."[18] The *San Francisco Chronicle* said the Fuhrman plea was further evidence of the Republican attorney general's "selectivity [in] his tough-on-crime views." The *Seattle Post-Intelligencer* said the plea agreement constituted a "blow to a judicial system."[19] The *Florida Times-Union* (Jacksonville) called the punishment "not nearly as severe" as a wrist slap.[20] The *Buffalo News* (New York) said: "He deserved at least some of that jail time."[21] The *Herald-Sun* (Durham, North Carolina) said Fuhrman "should have gone to prison."[22] The *South Bend Tribune* (Indiana) belittled the sentence and Fuhrman, saying he not only lacked "credibility, but he also lacked character."

The prize for Most Outraged naturally went to the newspaper in one of the whitest towns in America (0.3 percent black): the *Lewiston Morning Tribune* (Idaho), which called Fuhrman's deal "another injustice from O.J. Simpson's murder trial" and his alleged perjury "one of the most infamous crimes of the decade," adding, "he has more in common with O.J. than anyone thought."[23]

Pulitzer Prize-winning columnist—and yet still a Man of the People—William Raspberry dedicated an entire column to quoting a cab driver on how outrageous the Fuhrman sentence was: "'And the punishment! . . . It's nothing. Probation and a small fine. . . . Perjury is serious stuff, and they treated it like he accidentally misspoke himself or something. What they did is no punishment at all.'" [24] Pulitzer Prize-winning columnist Carl Rowan said the plea deal had dropped "another barrel of racial poison into the bloodstream of American life," and this "teensy rebuke of Fuhrman" would "heighten general distrust of and disrespect for the criminal justice system."[25]

Apparently, it's not enough that every black person with a column wins a Pulitzer Prize except the two who actually deserve it—Thomas Sowell and Walter Williams—Mark Fuhrman should have gone to prison for using the N-word so black people would trust the system.

Vice President Hubert Humphrey once said, clear as a bell, that the two most horrible words are "nigger" and "honky." (The second two worst were "Lyndon" and "Johnson"). Very soon after that, it got to the point that one couldn't even say the N-word in order to call it a terrible word. This is how America would make up for slavery!

Most blacks must have been bemused at all this nonsense over a word. How does hearing the N-word measure up to being punched in the face? How about compared to being almost decapitated? The principal way blacks suffer at the hands of white people in America are affronts to their dignity. The principal way whites suffer at the hands of black people are stabbings, shootings and rapes. Even as words go, Fuhrman's case demonstrates that the worst thing you can be called isn't the N-word. It's "racist."

Americans could not face up to the fact that a mostly black—and all-Democratic—jury would not, under any circumstances, convict a black celebrity like OJ for a double murder. The evidence against OJ might have been discovered by Jesus Christ and the jury would have voted "not guilty." OJ could have taken the stand and admitted it, and the jury would have voted "not guilty."

The country got a preview into the thought process of the jurors when Jeanette Harris was dismissed as a juror in early April 1995 and proceeded to give a round of interviews. Glowing with admiration for OJ, Harris said: "Whether he did it or not, he presents this picture of a person handling a great deal." She was concerned that OJ hadn't "been allowed to grieve," but was unimpressed by the tearful testimony of Nicole Brown's sister Denise, who she believed was "acting."

Even if OJ did beat Nicole, Harris said, "that doesn't make him guilty of murder." Whereas whether Fuhrman had ever used the N-word was highly probative on the question of whether he planted evidence.

Harris also said that "from day one, I didn't see it being a fair trial." According to the *Washington Post*, Harris was "considered one of the jury's most sober and attentive members."

Most memorably, Harris described the evidence presented by the prosecution as "a whole lot of nothing."[26] At this point in the trial, the evidence included drops of blood leading away from the two victims to Simpson's Ford Bronco, to his driveway, to his front door, into his foyer and then to his bathroom; and a bloody left-hand glove found on the grounds of OJ's estate the night of the murders that matched a right-hand glove found at the murder scene.

And consider that this was even before evidence had been adduced on the key question of whether Mark Fuhrman had ever used the N-word, throwing the glove evidence into turmoil.

Overall, Harris seemed less concerned with OJ's guilt than with the racism of some of her fellow jurors and court personnel. She alleged that the deputies had given white jurors more time at the Ross and Target department stores and that a white woman on the jury had kicked her without then saying "excuse me."[27] As she told Larry King, "growing up in Los Angeles, you're faced with racism every day."

Normally, something that happens every day stops being noticeable, like crickets in the country or traffic noises in the city. But with Harris, constancy seemed to have sharpened her racism sensor, perhaps with a little nudge from a media consumed with talking about racist America every single day.

After the trial, two black female jurors quoted in the *Los Angeles Times* said they knew OJ didn't do it and the evidence didn't convince them otherwise. One explained: "In plain English, the glove didn't fit." The other juror said she thought the glove was planted, but she too acknowledged that she believed OJ was innocent before the trial began.[28]

Manifestly, none of the evidence was of the slightest interest to the jurors. But no one dared blame the mostly minority jurors for the "not guilty" verdict. (For my younger readers, blaming black people for anything they did used to be illegal in the United States.)

Inasmuch as the media couldn't blame the jurors, the prosecutors (one was black) or defense lawyer Johnnie Cochran (also black), there was only one acceptable target for the media's wrath: Mark Fuhrman. He used the N-word in 1985. Ergo, the jury had no choice but to acquit OJ.

As Geraldo Rivera said of Fuhrman: "History will always say that he is, by far, the single most responsible person for O. J. Simpson walking free."[29] I would vote for the jurors being a smidgen more responsible, but, then, I don't get a kick out of patronizing black people.

Ron Goldman's sister, Kim, called Fuhrman a "despicable human being," asking: "What if he told the truth? How would that have affected the case? What if he just came clean and it all came right out in the open? How would it have affected the case? And I will never know that."[30]

I know the answer to that, Kim! *It would have made absolutely no difference.*

The media were as unanimous as the OJ jury: It was Fuhrman's fault. The *San Francisco Chronicle* said Fuhrman's "perjured testimony"—about using the N-word—"helped undercut the prosecution's case."[31] Yes, in addition to the fact that jurors thought a trail of blood from the crime scene to OJ's house and a bloody glove in OJ's yard matching the one at the crime scene was, and I quote, "a whole lot of nothing."

Calling Fuhrman "a major factor in Simpson's acquittal," The *Sun-Sentinel* said the "trial might have had a completely different verdict" if Fuhrman hadn't lied about using the N-word.[32]

The *Post-Intelligencer* said "documented racism" was "a key element in Simpson's acquittal by a jury, nine of whose members were African Americans."[33] (And that white juror kicking Jeanette Harris didn't help things either!)

On and on it went. Some newspapers went so far as to endorse the jury's verdict. The *South Bend Tribune* (Indiana) said the jurors were correct to ignore questions of OJ's "guilt or innocence" given that Fuhrman was "a racist and a liar."[34] Durham, North Carolina's *Herald-Sun*—which a decade later would be championing the false rape claims against Duke lacrosse players by a stripper who is now on trial for murder—said Fuhrman was "so overtly prejudiced against blacks that, yes, it's reasonable to agree . . . that Furhman was part of a police conspiracy to frame OJ for the killings of Nicole Brown Simpson and Ronald Goldman."[35]

Oh, come on.

Would these holier-than-thou journalists have reacted the same way if a Jewish jury refused to convict Bernie Madoff because one of the Securities and Exchange investigators had used the H-word word (Hymie)? If anything, an all-Jewish jury might have given him the death penalty. Would they have cheered a jury for letting off Leona Helmsley if an officer with the Internal Revenue Service had used the C-word?

Of course not. But it was the official position of the elites that blacks could not be treated like the rest of us adults. *Well, of course he threw a tantrum! You forgot to give him a cookie.*

Even the change in trial venue was premised on the idea that blacks cannot be treated like our fellow citizens. Not enough black people lived near Brentwood, so the OJ trial had to be moved to downtown Los Angeles. If a white person is arrested for committing a murder in Washington, DC, no court would order him tried in some whiter neighborhood, such as western Virginia.

The chattering class may have reprised its role as Chief Patronizers of Black America, but the rest of the country had changed. Thus, while the unanimous legal opinion given in the media was that Furhman's perjury would cost the Goldman family a win in civil court,[36] that jury ordered OJ to pay the Goldman and Brown families $33 million in damages.

Simpson took the stand in the civil case and, as respected legal reporter Stuart Taylor wrote, there was "ample evidence that Simpson lied rampantly and shamelessly under oath in his civil trial and deposition."

Guess who wasn't prosecuted for perjury? Suddenly perjury wasn't such a terrible crime, after all.

The police officers in the Rodney King case were tried twice. Mark Fuhrman was prosecuted for perjury over whether he had used a word ten years (or only nine and a half years) earlier. But OJ wasn't tried for perjury for denying, as Taylor notes, "that he ever hit or slapped his former wife, or that he ever received his girlfriend Paula Barbieri's message breaking up with him the day of the murders, or that he ever owned 'ugly ass' Bruno Magli shoes of the type that left bloody footprints at the murder scene."[37]

Still, no matter how much politicians, prosecutors and the media tried to convince Americans that Fuhrman was a greater criminal than OJ, the insanity on race was over. No one was buying it anymore.

The media couldn't even convince themselves—at least when they were making business decisions in corporate suites and not chitchatting on TV. A few months after the verdict, OJ marketed a video of himself arguing that he was innocent, for $29.95 each. TV stations refused to run commercials advertising the video.[38] The star of the trial of the century sold fewer than 40,000 copies. Around the same time, a Weather Channel video about storms sold 100,000 copies.[39]

OJ's acquittal and Fuhrman's conviction was the last gasp of the white racial guilt that had gripped the nation for so long. The blinders were off and, no matter how much pompous liberals tried, blacks would no longer be treated as subhuman beings.

CHAPTER 10

POST-OJ VERDICT: PARADISE

Right up until the OJ verdict, the race hustlers were riding high, to no one's benefit. It's hard to believe now, but when Jesse Jackson ran for president in 1984, he came in third in a field of seven candidates in the Democratic primaries. Jackson received more than 3 million votes, about 20 percent of all votes cast, winning primaries in South Carolina and Louisiana outright—and almost beating the eventual nominee, Walter Mondale, in Virginia. This made Jesse Jackson a major figure in the Democratic Party, ensuring him a speaking spot at the Convention and the right to make demands and impose rules changes.

In the 1988 presidential campaign, Jackson did even better, coming in second in a field of six Democrats, winning nine states, and walloping third-place Al Gore by more than a two to one margin. Jackson ended up with nearly 30 percent of all primary votes cast, not far behind nominee Michael Dukakis's 43 percent. (In Jackson's defense, he'd make a better president.) That same year, David Dinkins became both the first black mayor of New York and—judging by the results—the last black mayor of New York.

But after the OJ verdict, the reign of the race hustlers was completely over. Not surprisingly, Democrats were the last to know. Even journalists knew before the Democrats did. (Except at CNN.)

During the 2000 presidential race, all the Democratic candidates flew to New York to kiss Al Sharpton's ring. Bill Bradley was the first and most ardent of Sharpton's suitors, attending a public meeting with Sharpton and his National Action Network in New York and absurdly leading the audience in a chant of "No Justice, No Peace!"[1] Al Gore met with Sharpton on the sly, at first denying that he had done so, but eventually admitting to having bumped into Sharpton at his daughter Karenna's Upper East Side apartment.[2] Bradley was slaughtered in the primaries, winning only 2.7 million votes, or 19 percent of the votes cast. Jesse Jackson had done better than that.

By the time Al Sharpton ran for president in the 2004 election, well after OJ, he didn't win a single state in the Democratic primaries. He had only "single-digit showings in contests from coast to coast," as the *New York Times* put it. Sharpton couldn't even get a majority of black votes in his home state of New York. Twenty years earlier, Jesse Jackson had won 85 percent of the black vote in New York and 25 percent of the vote overall.[3]

The only fun Sharpton has anymore is tormenting Howard Dean.

In 2004, presidential candidate Vermont governor Howard Dean, never having met a black person, cowered before Sharpton during a Democratic presidential debate when Sharpton demanded to know if Dean had a "black or brown" person on his cabinet. Dean said he had "a senior member" of his staff who was black. Toying with a terrified Dean like a cat with a mouse, Sharpton summarily dismissed the staff member as irrelevant.

Throughout the rest of the debate, Dean burbled and apologized to Sharpton for not having enough brothers on his staff. At some point, Dean announced that he had more endorsements from the Congressional Black Caucus and the Congressional Hispanic Caucus than any other candidate on the stage. Trying again, he said, "I will take a back seat to no one in my commitment to civil rights in the United States of America." Still later in the debate, Dean apologized to John Edwards for saying he wanted to be "the candidate for guys with Confederate flags" in their pickup trucks.[4]

Days after the debate, Dean announced that he had requested a black roommate at Yale and even produced the roommate to attest to his racial broadmindedness.[5] As soon as the other black candidate, Carol Moseley Braun, dropped out of the race, Dean hired her for his campaign.

It apparently never occurred to Dean to mention that blacks account for 0.5 percent of Vermont's population, making it extremely difficult for any Vermont governor to put blacks in his cabinet. Nor did it occur to him that he was talking to Al Sharpton. Dean's epitaph should read: "Al Sharpton's Last Lickspittle."

Except for the occasional Vermont governor, no longer do we have to endure pompous whites treating blacks like children: "Do you like your ice cream? Is that good?" Now everyone laughs at Jackson and Sharpton, and other black people will laugh with you. These days, people roll their eyes when Janeane Garofalo says criticism of half-black Obama is "racism, straight-up." With the OJ verdict, blacks had finally triumphed over liberals' condescension.

In 1984, CBS's Dan Rather gushed that Jesse Jackson's address to the Democratic National Convention was "one for the history books"—and that was before Jackson gave his speech. Similarly, on ABC, David Brinkley said, "We are seeing something truly historic" while waiting for Jackson to take the stage. NBC's Tom Brokaw called Jackson's execrable speech "splendid and memorable." The Democratic governor of Florida, Bob Graham, said of the speech: "America is never going to be the same after tonight."[6]

Flash-forward through the eighties, through the OJ verdict, to Jackson's speech at the 2000 Democratic National Convention. We find NBC's Tom Brokaw sharing a laugh with author Bill Bennett about Jackson's usual rhymes.

> BENNETT: I thought some of the phrases were resonant, not quite as resonant as they've been in the past. They should rhyme. I'm waiting for a rhyme from the Reverend Jackson.
>
> BROKAW: You want to go from the outhouse to the courthouse . . .
>
> BENNETT: Yeah, exactly.
>
> BROKAW: . . . to the state house to the White House.
>
> BENNETT: To the White House, exactly.[7]

Even Steve Pagones, the falsely accused prosecutor in the Tawana Brawley case, finally got paid after the OJ verdict. In the middle of that hootenanny, Sharpton had said "If we're lying, sue us. Sue us right now."[8] Steve Pagones, named by these charlatans as one of Brawley's rapists, did just that, in October 1988, just weeks after the grand jury reported its findings. About a year and a half later, he won his defamation suit against Brawley, which was meaningless because she had no assets. But then nothing happened with his lawsuit against Sharpton, Maddox and Mason for years. And years.

No one had an appetite for stirring up the racial hatred crew, so one judge after another recused himself from the case, depriving Pagones of his day in court for nearly a decade.

Everyone just moved on, and to hell with Pagones. Sharpton ran for mayor of New York. He marched in Howard Beach and Crown Heights, protested outside Freddy's in Harlem, defended MOVE in Philadelphia. After a Central Park jogger was viciously beaten by a mob of black teenagers, he showed up at the trial, claiming he was there to "observe how differently a white victim was treated and how the accused in this case have been mishandled [sic] a lot differently from the people she [Brawley] accused."[9]

Pagones's life was ruined, a sacrifice to the race hustlers. White America's eternal hope was: *Maybe this will finally satiate them . . . As long as it's not me being accused of racism, please God, don't let it be me.* But the racial hatred machine could never be satisfied. Every sacrificial lamb just made the hucksters hungry for more.

It took the race-based acquittal of a double murderer in the trial of the century for Pagones to finally get his day in court. Less than six months after the OJ verdict, an amazing thing occurred: A judge was at last assigned to Pagones's case.[10] Two years later—a full decade after the grand jury declared Brawley's accusations false—Pagones won his defamation suit and was awarded damages of $185,000 from Mr. Mason, $95,000 from Mr. Maddox, $65,000 from Mr. Sharpton and $187,000 from Ms. Brawley.

By January 2001, black leaders and businessmen had paid off Sharpton and Maddox's debt to Pagones. The disbarred Mason was having his wages garnished.[11]

Pagones would still be waiting for his day in court, if not for OJ. Ironically, one of the men paying Pagones on Sharpton's behalf was Johnnie Cochran.

There were other factors tamping down racial hysteria around the time of the OJ trial.

First, the generation that witnessed racial discrimination against blacks is getting old. Anyone who grew up watching *The Brady Bunch* entered a world in which blacks were only the beneficiaries of race discrimination—as Allan Bakke found out in 1974 when he was denied admission to the University of California medical school because he was white. That's the life experience of anyone who is under fifty years old. Accusations of racism have as much sting for such people as being accused of involvement in the Teapot Dome scandal.

Second, there was Rudy Giuliani's overturning thirty years of liberal crime policies in New York. Just six months before Nicole Simpson and Ron Goldman were murdered, in January 1994 Giuliani replaced the utterly incompetent David Dinkins as mayor of New York and, over the next few years, turned the "ungovernable city" into the safest big city in the country. A major part of Giuliani's success derived from his absolute refusal to be cowed by accusations of racism leveled at him by the likes of Al Sharpton, the *New York Times* and the Clinton Justice Department.

Former mayor Ed Koch had been called a bigot merely for supporting Giuliani. The head of a black police organization, Eric Adams, promised racial violence if Giuliani beat the city's first black mayor, saying blacks would arm themselves with bullets.[12]

A little more than a week after Giuliani's inauguration—and hours before the new police commissioner was sworn in—there was a melee in Harlem. A 911 call had come in claiming there was an armed robbery in progress on the third floor of a building at Fifth Avenue and 125th Street—which happened to be Louis Farrakhan's mosque, though the police didn't know it. It was an ambush, eerily similar to the one in 1972. Two police officers arrived at the nondescript building and ran to the location of the alleged holdup, completely unaware that the third floor was a mosque. They were met by Farrakhan's "Fruit of Islam" guards, roughed up and thrown down the stairs after having a gun and police radio stolen from them.

A standoff ensued with the police outside and the Fruit of Islam guards inside. To the alarm of liberals, the mayor was demanding arrests. "You have officers injured," Giuliani told his negotiating team over the phone. "You have stolen police property. Why aren't you going in?" [13] As the new police commissioner, William Bratton, said: "For twenty-five years, [African Americans] and other groups in the city had been treated gingerly by City Hall. Now Giuliani had come in and said, 'Everybody's going to be treated the same.'" [14]

Giuliani didn't get arrests that night, but the police were allowed to enter and search the mosque, retrieving the stolen gun and radio.

Afterward, racial healer Al Sharpton tried to butt into a meeting of mosque leaders with Bratton and Giuliani, but the mayor refused to meet with an "outside agitator" like Sharpton, and cancelled the meeting. Shock waves shot through all of Charlie Rose-New York. Sharpton was in such a tizzy, he vowed that Giuliani would be impeached by spring.[15]

But then guess what happened? Nothing. The mosque leaders came back the next day for the meeting without Sharpton. While Sharpton gassed on about Giuliani's "arrogance" in choosing whom to meet with, the mosque's leader, Don Muhammad, came out of the meeting saying,

"We do not wish to be viewed as persons disrespectful to the law."[16] Sharpton can get thirty losers to protest, but if you just ignore him, he'll eventually go home.

With all the usual proponents of racial reconciliation turning out to denounce Giuliani—Rangel, protector of cop killers; C. Vernon Mason, counsel to hate-crime hoaxer Tawana Brawley; the Reverend Wyatt T. Walker, who called Giuliani a "fascist"; and Sharpton—Giuliani made a big point of ignoring them and allying himself with respectable black leaders. He particularly incensed the race hustlers by attending the Martin Luther King Day dinner held by Roy Innis of the Congress of Racial Equality. It was the biggest event of its kind in the city, with more than fifteen hundred people attending, including Richard Pryor.[17] The self-appointed Spokesmen for All Black People didn't want fair dealing for black people, they wanted their butts kissed.

The *New York Times* issued a patronizing editorial after Giuliani cancelled the meeting with Sharpton, informing the mayor that "[g]overning is messy, unpredictable and raw, especially in this inherently fractious city." The *Times* patiently explained that "presiding over New York City demands flexibility, and above all a willingness to reach out to alienated communities." David Dinkins had lost an election and the *Times* acted like it was 9/11 and we all needed "healing." The paper actually called on Giuliani "to lead the healing process." [18]

Of course, a lot less "healing" would be necessary under Giuliani because the policies he implemented (over the hot indignation of liberals) cut the city's murder rate from about 2,000 a year to 714 the year Giuliani left office. By studiously ignoring the advice of the *Times*, Giuliani reduced the murder rate by 20 percent in just his first year in office—an accomplishment celebrated in the *Times* with an article titled: "New York City Crime Falls But Just Why Is a Mystery."[19]

This is how miraculous Giuliani's transformation of New York was: The *Times* endorsed his reelection and mocked his opponent Ruth Messinger for denying that he had improved the city's "quality of life," citing—as the first example—the dramatic reduction in crime. Messinger, the *Times* said, "was arguing against the voters' own sense of reality."[20]

(That's with the exception of voter Richard Goldstein of the *Village Voice*, who claimed on MSNBC'S *Hardball* that he felt "less safe" in Giuliani's New York City than he did twenty years earlier.[21] This was a position Goldstein developed after taking a vow to never leave his apartment, never read a newspaper, never watch TV and never allow visitors.)

By the end of Giuliani's two terms in office, the Reverend Calvin Butts, pastor of Harlem's Abyssinian Baptist Church, was describing Giuliani as King Josiah of the Bible, who "brought order, peace, the law back to the land." Without Giuliani, he said, "we would have been overrun." [22]

The third factor lessening the grip of the race hucksters in the 1990s was Bill O'Reilly's relentless pursuit of Jesse Jackson, which began a few years after the OJ verdict.

Starting in 1999 and continuing for years thereafter, O'Reilly bird-dogged Jackson on his nightly Fox News show, persistently inviting Jackson to come on the show and answer questions about his funding.

Until then, multinational corporations had quaked at phone calls from Jackson. But O'Reilly turned the tables, shining a floodlight on Jackson's operation. That's when the marks stopped paying up and then it was the minister's turn to sweat and curse. Until O'Reilly's brave campaign, anyone who asked about Jackson's finances would be told: *We don't keep those records. How'd you like to be called a racist on national TV?*

All it took was a single television host standing up to the class bully to prove that the racial scam artists were always paper tigers. O'Reilly's dogged reports on Jackson can fairly be credited with driving him from public life.

But if the world were still the kind of place where a cop who used the N-word was more despised than a double murderer, would anyone have risked being turned into the next Mark Fuhrman, despised from coast to coast? A few years after the OJ verdict, even Mark Furhman wasn't Mark Fuhrman, but rather a bestselling author and sought-after television guest.

It was a different world—the birds were singing, the sun was shining and lives were no longer being held hostage to frivolous charges of racism. In the eighties, any white person could get a standing ovation for droning on about racism. But after OJ, all the grandstanding nonsense—"That's right, I'm courageous enough to say white people are racist"—was over.

With the decline of the racial agitators, it turned out there were other black people in America besides Jackson and Sharpton. We got a brief glimpse of wildly talented blacks during the Clarence Thomas hearings back in 1991, when, one after another, they testified on Thomas's behalf. Then—poof!—they all disappeared again.

Perhaps it was the advent of the Internet and cable news, but, post-OJ, there seemed to be a renaissance of black people with opinions different from Jesse Jackson's—Deneen Borelli, Ron Christie, Ken Blackwell, Niger Innis, Star Parker, Jesse Lee Peterson, Angela McGlowan, Michael

Meyers, David Webb, Allen West—and those are just a few from Fox News. There was also Marc Lamont Hill, Juan Williams, Sherrod Small—there are so many that you don't even notice it anymore. Where had they been all that time? They were probably sitting at home, wondering why no one in the media ever asked them their opinion, instead going to Jesse Jackson for the "black perspective."

Blacks had won the final civil rights battle: The right to be treated like adults. Liberals would have to find new victims to patronize.

CHAPTER 11

LIBERALS ARE THE NEW BLACKS

As harmful as it was to blacks to have liberals take them on as their special projects, at least liberals got the beneficiary group right, even if their idea of "help" was idiotic. If any group deserves special treatment, it is the descendants of slavery and Jim Crow in this country. Civil rights aren't supposed to be bounties for every self-obsessed group with a grievance.

But these days, liberals use blacks as a cat's paw to promote the issues they really care about: national health care, blocking voter ID laws, abortion on demand, stripping the nation of religious imagery, amnesty for illegal aliens, gay marriage and girls in the military. These are not policies that help blacks, nor are they supported by most black people. But Democrats believe blacks should be like children: seen and not heard. Shut up and vote for us.

Democrats are always itching to expand the list of civil rights victims and thus enlarge their pool of debtors. Instead of basing favored treatment on a history of widespread injustice in America, liberals thought it should also be based on other forms of suffering, such as: being a housewife, having an abortion, having been born in Mexico, or being gay. If a single pelican had died as a result of the BP oil spill, pelicans would have replaced blacks as liberals' new victim group.

The trend of describing every left-wing cause as a "civil rights" issue began before the ink on the Civil Rights Act of 1964 was dry. These days, you could be forgiven for not realizing that civil rights ever had anything to do with black people. Indeed, according to the *New York Times*, in June 2012, "gay rights was the fastest-moving civil rights movement in our nation's history"![1]

Instead of discrimination based on skin color, judges began outlawing discrimination based on being a smelly homeless person menacing library patrons.[2] Instead of hoax racism charges, we started getting hoax rape charges. Instead of blacks being denied admission to public schools and universities, gays were "denied" the ability to marry one another.

It must make blacks feel great being compared to smelly homeless people, daft women and lesbians who want to marry one another. Princeton ethics professor Peter Singer compares black people to apes, citing the black liberation movement as a model for the liberation of apes. We must "extend to other species," he says, "the basic principle of equality that most of us recognize should be extended to all members of our own species."[3]

Modern "civil rights" lawsuits are almost never about black people—they're about women, Hispanics, gays, the foreign born, transgendered Eskimos in wheelchairs and so on. According to the Web site of the U.S. Equal Opportunity Employment Commission, for more than a decade, 65 percent of all civil rights claims had absolutely nothing to do with race discrimination.[4] Claims of sexual harassment alone doubled between 1989 and 1993. The vast majority of those, by the way—95 percent—involved no groping, touching or demands for sex, but rather were "hostile environment" claims.[5] Having to endure being called "honey" in the workplace is much like being lynched.

Civil rights now include the right not to have Bible verses printed on your paycheck, according to one Pennsylvania court,[6] or not to see construction signs that say "Men at Work," according to the Kentucky Commission on Civil Rights,[7] or the "civil right" not to inform your husband that you're aborting his child.[8]

Blacks are just props to dress up the left's pet causes.

In the 1998 Maryland gubernatorial race, Bob Shrum, consultant to the Democratic incumbent Parris Glendening, ran an ad against his Republican challenger Ellen Sauerbrey claiming she had voted against "the civil rights act." Featuring pictures of sad black people and ominous music, the ad concluded with: "The real Ellen Sauerbrey—a civil rights record to be ashamed of."

The only "civil rights" bill Sauerbrey had voted against had nothing to do with black people. It was a sexual harassment bill so nutty that the majority-Democrat Maryland legislature voted against it. A black legislator, Democrat Richard Dixon, complained that even calling it a civil rights bill was "a misnomer and misleading." He had voted against it, too. Kurt Schmoke, the black Democratic mayor of Baltimore, publicly denounced the Shrum ad, saying he refused to "participate in a campaign to try to persuade people that [Sauerbrey] is a racist." Only the *Washington Times* and *Hotline* reported the attacks on the Shrum ad by various Maryland black leaders. Released the last week before the election, the ad increased Glendening's black support in a tight race and he won the election.

Anyone who would make utterly baseless accusations of racism deserves to have his picture posted on Web sites, similar to sex offender Web sites. The public needs to be warned about such social predators, who instill racial hatreds to score political points. The rapid expansion of "civil rights" to encompass every left-wing cause—except real civil rights—proves that liberals never took the nation's debt to black Americans seriously in the first place.

The most outrageous policy proposals are invariably described as the promotion of "civil rights." As long as liberals label something a "right," they never have to explain why it's a good idea.

Thus, for example, the main argument for gay marriage is to baldly assert that it is a "civil right" and accuse opponents of opposing "civil rights." Some would say that if you want to overturn a six-thousand-year-old institution like marriage, the burden should be on you to tell us why. The obligation shouldn't be on defenders of marriage. But liberals sneak out of this obligation by chanting the mantra of "civil rights."

Why isn't a flat tax a "civil right"? Why not the right to smoke or to consume twenty-four-ounce sugary sodas? These days, calling something a "civil right" means nothing more than that liberals want it and they don't feel the need to explain.

When gay marriage was first thrust on the nation by the Massachusetts Supreme Court during the 2004 presidential primary campaign, Senator John Kerry said what was at stake was "somebody's right to live equally under the same laws as other people in the country."

But of course, gays do live equally under the same laws as other people. There are no special speed limit laws or trespassing laws or murder laws for gays. What gays can't do is get married to members of the same sex. Nor can heterosexuals, immigrants, whites, blacks, the rich, the poor or the homeless.

The Democrats' comparison of gay marriage to civil rights ultimately led to the ridiculous spectacle of Kerry basically accusing a black woman of being a bigot because she did not appreciate the comparison of gays to blacks under the equal protection clause. It had to happen.

At a "town hall" meeting in Mississippi during the campaign, a black woman in the audience asked Kerry to reject the comparison of gay marriage to civil rights. "I don't care what they say," she said, "there is no correlation between gay rights and civil rights in terms of what black Americans have gone through."[9]

In response, Kerry said it was important to recognize that "we have a Constitution which has an equal protection clause." (Because black people had probably forgotten that.)

The woman "was not satisfied" with Kerry's answer, in the delicate phrasing of the *New York Times*. She said: "My point is, homosexuality is an idea. You have never heard a doctor say, 'Mr. and Mrs. John Doe, you have a bouncing baby homosexual.' It's an idea."

Kerry again invoked the equal protection clause: "American citizens deserve the protection of the equal protection clause." The left's promiscuous expansion of civil rights had reached absurdity: John Kerry was lecturing a black woman in Mississippi about the meaning of the equal protection clause.

Liberals have spent decades acting as if they are the blacks' biggest best friends—by defending black criminals like Damian Williams—but as soon as they have to choose between feminists and blacks or gays and blacks, it's no contest. Feminists and gays win. Gays have more money and the ladies have more votes.

A few years ago, when the black actor Isaiah Washington got in a fight with a fellow cast member and called him a "faggot," even he suddenly became Bull Connor.

If you thought blacks were already being taken for granted by the left, wait until Democrats notice that Hispanics outnumber blacks.

The reason that is happening is that Senator Ted Kennedy needed his own civil rights bill, just like brothers John and Bobby. Teddy thought: *Let's treat people who live in other countries like they're blacks who suffered through slavery in this country!* His 1965 immigration bill ensured that the vast majority—85 percent—of new immigrants would come from the third world, while severely limiting immigration from the nationalities that had populated America before there was a welfare state.[10]

Blacks already paid a price when the new immigrants flooded into low-skilled jobs, driving down wages. The eminent Harvard economists George Borjas and Lawrence Katz calculated that immigrants arriving between 1980 and 2000 had the effect of lowering the wages of the average American worker by 3.3 percent—but lowered the wages of high school dropouts by 8 percent.[11] During the same time period, the drop-out rate for blacks was roughly twice that of whites.[12] Similarly, Vanderbilt law professor Carol Swain, author of *Debate Immigration*, says illegal immigration "hurts low-skilled, low-wage workers of all races, but blacks are harmed the most because they're disproportionately low-skilled."[13]

The problem with defining "civil rights" as anything that benefits the Democratic Party was expressed beautifully by "T. J. in California" during a CNN call-in segment on "civil rights" for illegal immigrants:

> I have a comment. My comment as an African American is, I am outraged that these people would think it's all right to hijack the civil rights movement. We were enslaved. We were brought here unwillingly. And when I see people saying it's the same thing as jumping the fence for a domestic upgrade, it's not fair. I think it's a horrible thing. I think that if you have a car, do whatever you have to do. And I don't care, by the way, if they're from Saturn. Whatever your cause is, it's not the same as being a slave. And I think they need to find their own song and find their own martyrs or whatever they want to call them. But comparing it to slavery and the African American experience is a slap in the face to every African American in the United States of America.[14]

CNN's illegal-immigration activist, Alisa Valdes-Rodriguez, was unimpressed and continued insisting that amnesty for illegal aliens was the same as the black struggle for civil rights. Illegals, she said, "have the same history that you do. . . . These two struggles are extremely related." True, illegal aliens had crossed the border illegally, she said, but: "Was it legal to bring slaves to the United States?" *QED. I rest my case, Your Honor.* (Actually, it was.)

But no aspiring victim group has commandeered the black experience like the feminists. I can't help but notice that women voters substantially outnumber blacks.

In 1970—a mere six years after the Civil Rights Act of 1964—New York State legalized abortion on the grounds that killing the unborn was just another "civil right." State senator Manfred Ohrenstein of Manhattan explained: "It was the end of the civil rights era, and we viewed this as a civil right."[15]

Two years after that, the Supreme Court found that abortion was a constitutional right—just like equal protection under the law, except not actually written in the Constitution. In the Court's haste to make abortion a basic right of every American, liberals didn't notice that there is no abortion clause.

The abortion ladies even used an anti-Ku Klux Klan law to try to shut down abortion clinic protests. The Ku Klux Klan Law of 1871 forbade con-

spiracies against a "class of persons." But abortion protesters weren't conspiring against a "class of persons." They were "conspiring" against abortion, just
as Planned Parenthood "conspires" for abortion. Mercifully, the majority
opinion by Justice Antonin Scalia noted that the law prohibited conspiracies
based on invidious discrimination against a race or class of people, and concluded that "Women seeking abortion is not a qualifying class."[16]

But the vote was 6–3, with dissenting justices John Paul Stevens, Sandra
Day O'Connor and Harry A. Blackmun finding abortionists and women
having abortions a "class of persons" analogous to black people being
lynched by Democrats in the South.

Feminists latched their cause to the suffering of blacks—and then completely forgot about the blacks. A majority of blacks oppose abortion, so
they probably wouldn't mind a judge who did so, too—especially if he also
happened to have prosecuted the Klan in Mississippi.

In 2001, President George W. Bush nominated district court judge
Charles Pickering to the Fifth Circuit Court of Appeals. As a Republican
prosecutor in Mississippi in the sixties, he had put his life, and the lives of
his wife and children at risk, by standing up to the Klan.

This wasn't a Hollywood movie; it was real life. Back then, the Klan
held Mississippians in terror, committing dozens of murders and at least
seventy-five church bombings. Pickering signed affidavits for the arrest of
Klan members and voluntarily testified against the Imperial Wizard of the
Ku Klux Klan being tried for the murder of NAACP leader Vernon Dahmer. The FBI was required to provide full-time protection for Pickering
and his family.

Not only that, but while phony liberals like Al Gore, Bill Clinton and
Tom Wicker sent their children to 99-percent-white private schools to
avoid the diversity of public schools, Pickering sent his kids to overwhelmingly black Mississippi public schools. He served on the boards of the Mississippi Baptist Convention and the William Winter Institute for Racial
Reconciliation at the University of Mississippi.

Not surprisingly, Pickering's nomination to the federal appellate court
was supported by past presidents of the Mississippi NAACP and Charles
Evers, brother of slain civil rights leader Medgar Evers.

But the feminists opposed Pickering because of his opposition to abortion. So Senate Democrats blocked the nomination of this civil rights hero
to a federal appeals court on the grounds that he was bad on "civil rights."
Senators Charles Schumer and Edward Kennedy demanded to see Pickering's unpublished opinions "involving civil rights, labor and reproductive

issues."[17] They didn't care about civil rights—it was the "reproductive issues" that got their dander up.

Doing the bidding of the abortion ladies, the Congressional Black Caucus and the national NAACP came out against Pickering, claiming his "record on civil rights is a grave concern."[18] Yes, his "record on civil rights" was also of concern to his family when they risked death so that he could prosecute the KKK.

Nearly exploding with rage, Charles Evers challenged these modern "civil rights" leaders on CBS's *60 Minutes*:

CHARLES EVERS: You know, maybe you don't know, you know that Charles Pickering is a man who helped us break the Ku Klux Klan. Did you know that?

CLARENCE MAGEE, NAACP: I heard that statement made.

CHARLES EVERS: I mean, I know that. Do you know that?

CLARENCE MAGEE: I don't know that.

CHARLES EVERS: I know that. Do you know about the young black man that was accused of robbing the young white woman. You know about that?

CLARENCE MAGEE: Nope.

CHARLES EVERS: So Charles Pickering took the case. Came to trial and won the case and the young man became free.

CLARENCE MAGEE: I don't know about that.

CHARLES EVERS: But did you also know that Charles Pickering is the man who helped integrate his churches. You know about that?

CLARENCE MAGEE: No.

CHARLES EVERS: Well, you don't know a thing about Charles Pickering.

Pickering's nomination was blocked by the same political party that had once harbored the Klan he had battled for so many years. The Democrats' refusal to confirm him marked the precise moment that "civil rights" ceased having anything to do with black people and became a front for abortion rights and other feminist enthusiasms.

In 2007, then-governor Eliot Spitzer spoke to a proabortion group in Manhattan, vowing to protect a woman's right to partial-birth abortion, grandly proclaiming: "New York State will continue to be a beacon of civil rights."[19] Puncturing a baby's skull and suctioning its brains out is another one of those fast-growing "civil rights movements."

The feminists' most risible misappropriation of the black experience was the 1994 Violence Against Women Act. To justify VAWA, women claimed to suffer in twentieth century America as much as blacks had during the Jim Crow era.

Feminists wanted their own civil rights law. So when they were riding high during the first two years of the Clinton presidency—with Hillary as copresident, Janet Reno as the first female attorney general and Al Gore as first lady, in addition to huge Democratic majorities in Congress—Democrats enacted VAWA.

The real civil rights laws were generally passed under Congress's authority to enforce the equal protection clause and to regulate interstate commerce. With Democratic elected officials in the South denying black Americans their basic constitutional rights, the federal government had to step in and provide a federal remedy for federal rights. Hotels and restaurants that refused to serve blacks made it difficult for blacks to travel across state lines, giving Congress authority to ban such practices under the interstate commerce clause.

Liberal women believed their situation in America, circa 1994, was comparable.

Democrats claimed Congress had authority to pass VAWA based on the exact same constitutional provisions underlying real civil rights laws. Led by Senator Joe Biden, congressional committees set to work collecting evidence for the proposition that state criminal justice systems were a living nightmare for women, so teeming with woman-hating Cro-Magnons that federal judges were required to ride into town and secure women's basic civil rights. In the alternative, they found that violence against women had a major impact on interstate commerce.

Operating on the theory that women were being treated just like blacks in 1961 Alabama, the Democrats claimed that there was a "pervasive bias in various state justice systems against victims of gender-motivated violence," including the perpetuation of "an array of erroneous stereotypes and assumptions." This apparently included the erroneous assumption that women want to have sex with their husbands: VAWA included a cause of action for marital rape.[20]

Congress also found that violent crimes based on gender deterred "potential victims from traveling interstate, from engaging in employment in interstate business, and from transacting with business, and in places involved in interstate commerce; . . . by diminishing national productivity, increasing medical and other costs, and decreasing the supply of and the demand for interstate products."[21]

Presumably crimes of violence generally would have an even larger effect on interstate commerce, but VAWA provided a tort remedy only for violent crimes "committed because of gender or on the basis of gender, and due, at least in part, to an animus based on the victim's gender." As explained by Pat Reuss of the National Organization for Women, VAWA was carefully limited because it would not cover "a rapist who rapes men, women, dogs, and simply is a horrible, vicious assaulter." Only rapes committed because of the victim's gender.[22]

Essentially, VAWA duplicated state criminal laws on rape and domestic violence, except instead of being crimes, rape and domestic violence became torts, to be litigated in civil court for monetary awards.

Fittingly, the first case brought under VAWA involved a white woman in the South falsely accusing two black men of rape. On September 21, 1994, Virginia Tech student Christy Brzonkala and a female friend were returning from a late night of drinking when they stopped by the dorm room of two black football players, Antonio Morrison and his roommate, James Crawford. After some sexually suggestive chitchat, Crawford and Brzonkala's friend left, and Brzonkala was alone in the room with Morrison. She and Morrison then proceeded to engage in . . . interstate commerce.

More than six months later, after overhearing Morrison boast in the college dining hall that he liked to get girls drunk and have sex with them, Brzonkala claimed both men had raped her. She did not go to the police, but to university officials. After two administrative hearings, the school cleared Crawford of any misconduct whatsoever—he wasn't there—and found Morrison guilty only of "using abusive language" toward Brzonkala. (After they had sex, he told her, "You'd better not have any f—ing diseases.")

Brzonkala still didn't pursue criminal charges against her alleged rapists. Instead, she sued Morrison, Crawford, Crawford's alibi witness and Virginia Tech under the newly enacted VAWA. As professor Jeremy Rabkin has said, VAWA enshrined into law "the feminist doctrine that every affront to women is tantamount to rape."[23]

There's a reason we have criminal rules of evidence and burdens of proof for serious accusations such as rape. But Brzonkala wanted to punish Morrison and Crawford by having them labeled rapists and making them pay her money without having to prove her charges beyond a reasonable doubt in a criminal court. This, VAWA allowed her to do.

After Brzonkala went public with her story about being raped by two Virginia Tech football players, the state attorney general ordered a criminal probe—something she had never requested. Following a two-month investigation, the state police's findings were presented to a grand jury—which, in Sol Wachtler's famous phrase, would indict a ham sandwich. The grand jury—which was all white, by the way—refused to indict the black football players.

But Brzonkala still had her civil suit against her alleged rapists and the university under VAWA. She demanded damages from Virginia Tech of $8.3 million—a number chosen because it was the exact amount the university had won in that year's Sugar Bowl. She also requested an injunction "directing Virginia Tech to provide at least five hours of mandatory sexual assault awareness education to student athletes . . . and to bring nationally recognized speakers on sexual harassment and sexual assault issues to its university forum at least twice a year."

The conservative public interest law firm Center for Individual Rights took Morrison and Crawford's case, arguing that Congress had no constitutional authority to pass a law creating a federal civil action for violence against women. The Supreme Court agreed and this feminist lunacy was ruled unconstitutional. Yale law professor Judith Resnik compared the Court's decision to those upholding slavery. [24]

The two most celebrated interracial rapes in the last quarter century illustrate the shift in civil rights from blacks to the ladies: the alleged gang rapes of Tawana Brawley and Crystal Mangum. In many ways, the cases were identical: there was mass hysteria, we had a nationwide consciousness-raising session on the scourge of white men raping black women—and then both accusers turned out to be lying.

There was one big difference in the alleged rapes: The Tawana Brawley incident was a race hoax; the rape claim against the Duke lacrosse players was a feminist hoax.

The transition from the oppression of blacks to the oppression of women was smoothly accomplished because feminists are concentrated in academia and media, which happen to be the most closed-minded, reason-free, quick-to-accuse, unfair, standardless environments in the universe. Sometime in the 1990s everything became rape—metaphorical rape, historical rape, institutional rape. We didn't hear a lot about actual rapes, however.

The left has got to understand that it is wrong to falsely accuse people of crimes. Calling someone a rapist is a very serious charge. It doesn't matter if it's drawing attention to an important issue. Making false rape claims ruins people's lives. But liberals have given women unlimited free shots to cry "rape!" with no penalty, ever, for false charges.

Once the feminists take over, not only do blacks get moved to the back of the bus, but facts and honest scholarship fly out the window. The uproar over white-on-black rape is an example of the feminists advancing under the flag of black people to promote their own agenda.

Contrary to feminist blather, white-on-black rape is an exceedingly rare crime. If there were a single unequivocal example of a white-on-black rape in modern times, a lesbian folk singer would have written a song about it and won an Oscar for the accompanying documentary.

For those hoping not to look foolish by jumping to conclusions the next time a black woman claims to have been gang-raped by white men, here are some recent Department of Justice statistics for white-on-black rape:

- 2008: White Offender/Black Victim—Rape/Sexual Assaults: 0.0

- 2007: White Offender/Black Victim—Rape/Sexual Assaults: 0.0

- 2006: White Offender/Black Victim—Rape/Sexual Assaults: 0.0

- 2005: White Offender/Black Victim—Rape/Sexual Assaults: 0.0

- 2004:White Offender/Black Victim—Rape/Sexual Assaults: 0.0

- 2003: White Offender/Black Victim—Rape/Sexual Assaults: 0.0

- 2002: White Offender/Black Victim—Rape/Sexual Assaults: [Sample based on 10 or fewer]

- 2001: White Offender/Black Victim—Rape/Sexual Assaults: [Sample based on 10 or fewer]

- 2000: White Offender/Black Victim—Rape/Sexual Assaults: [Sample based on 10 or fewer]

- 1999: White Offender/Black Victim—Rape/Sexual Assaults: 0.0

- 1998: White Offender/Black Victim—Rape/Sexual Assaults: [Sample based on 10 or fewer]

- 1997: White Offender/Black Victim—Rape/Sexual Assaults: 0.0[25]

During the same time period, blacks were raping whites at a clip of several thousand per year—and raping black women at a rate of many multiple thousand per year, according to Department of Justice victimization surveys. (Victimization surveys are obviously the most accurate measure of who is committing crimes because someone who has just been beaten or raped is not going to lie about the race of his assailant for the good of the race.)

When a black stripper, Crystal Mangum, accused members of the Duke University lacrosse team of gang-raping her, no one in the media paused to consider the likelihood of her having been the victim of a nonexistent crime. At no point did liberals say, "Wait a minute, maybe there wasn't a rape." As soon as the charge was made, they said, "Well, we know there was a rape. Now let's psychoanalyze the perpetrators and draw larger conclusions about it."

Mangum's alleged rape instantly inspired rafts of articles about "frat boys," "patriarchy" and "white male power." One white male sports columnist managed to use the phrase "frat boys" five times in a single column about "good old frat boys having a good old frat-boy time ... rich-boy, frat-boy arrogance and entitlement."[26]

Certain words always say more about the speaker than the person being described. People who call others "entitled," "privileged" or a "frat boy" or refer to someone's "daddy" are fantasists who enjoy imagining Thurston Howell chasing them with his polo mallet. Liberals treat WASPdom as an obscure and mysterious cult instead of the ethnic background of a majority of Americans at least into the 1990s. "Frat boys" haven't held any kind of power since at least the 1920s.

There isn't even a Protestant on the Supreme Court, much less an Eastern establishment, old money, Ivy League, social club Protestant. The only traditional WASPS in the presidency in the past century have been FDR and the two Bushes—the second raised in Texas. As Richard Brookhiser, author of *The Way of the WASP*, puts it, these days, the very phrase, "the Protestant establishment" sounds like a joke.[27]

Consequently, for Duke professors, Mangum's putative rape was like Christmas morning. Within a few weeks of Mangum leveling her charge, eighty-eight professors had rushed out with a full-page newspaper ad titled, "This Is What A Social Disaster Looks Like," that simply assumed the lacrosse players' guilt. It was too good a story to wait for the facts.

One hint of the turn civil rights had taken was given by the signatories to the advertisement. Obviously, the African American Studies Department was overrepresented, with 80 percent of the department signing, but they have to justify their existence somehow. Nipping at the heels of the African American Studies Department was the Program in Women's Studies, with 72 percent represented, followed by the Department of Cultural Anthropology, coming in at 60 percent.[28]

Among the more prominent professors signing the letter were:[29]

Anne Allison, white feminist nut. Her work includes the book *Nightwork: Sexuality, Pleasure, and Corporate Masculinity in a Tokyo Hostess Club* (1994). After the rape charge, she began teaching a new class titled, "Hook-up Culture at Duke" that would explore what "the lacrossse scandal tell[s] us about power, difference and raced, classed, gendered and sexed normativity in the U.S."[30]

William Chafe, white male. On the Duke faculty page, he describes his research as reflecting his "long-term interest in issues of race and gender equality." Perhaps barking up the wrong tree, he also enjoys women's soccer, flannel shirts, the LPGA, the Indigo Girls, and Jodie Foster movies.

Miriam Cooke, white feminist nut. Her specialty is providing a feminist interpretation of the Koran. (Her entire doctoral dissertation was a single sentence that read, *Women: shut up or be killed.*)

Kim Curtis, white feminist nut and political-science professor, promptly failed two of her students on the lacrosse team, for which the university ended up having to make a cash settlement with the players, in addition to giving them passing grades.

Cathy Davidson, white feminist nut. Her books include *The Book of Love: Writers and Their Love Letters, The Oxford Book of Women's Writing in the United States* and *The Oxford Companion to Women's Writing in the United States*. She's currently working on *The Oxford Companion to the Oxford Companion to the Oxford Book of Women's Writings on Women's Love Letters in the United States*, which she will require all her students to buy.

Ariel Dorfman, white male. His "most famous" play, according to Wikipedia, is *Death and the Maiden*, a light romantic comedy about a former torture victim meeting the man she believes tortured her.

Michael Hardt, white male, specializing in class oppression and imperialism, with a minor in advanced victimology. His book *Empire* has been called the new "Communist Manifesto,"[31] because the original wasn't communisty enough.

Alice Kaplan, white feminist nut. Her most recent work of scholarship is a book about the Paris years of Jackie O., Angela Davis and Susan Sontag.

Claudia Ann Koonz, white feminist nut. Her area of expertise is women during the Nazi era.

Pedro Lasch (born Gerry Rivers), white male. He describes himself as: "artist, researcher, educator, activist, cultural organizer."

Walter Mignolo, white male. His latest book is the captivating thriller, *The Darker Side of Western Modernity: Global Futures, Decolonial Options (Latin America Otherwise)*.

Diane Nelson, white feminist nut, Professor of Cultural Anthropology, Latin American and Caribbean Studies, and Women's Studies. She urges students to "actively make alternative histories." (Hey—let's start one now with a fake rape story!)

Kathy Rudy, white feminist nut in the Women's Studies Department. Her work includes "anti-speciesism" and an essay, in which she describes coming to Duke as an undergraduate and moving "quickly into the lesbian community because there was a growing sentiment in feminist discourse that lesbianism was the most legitimate way to act out our politics. . . . I managed to live most of my daily life avoiding men all together [sic], and spent most of my social time reading, dreaming, planning, talking, and writing about the beauty of a world run only by women, . . . free of [men's] patronizing dominance." Then one day she couldn't change a flat tire and reconsidered everything.

Pete Sigal, white male. He teaches "Sexual History Around the Globe."

Rebecca Stein, white feminist, whose Duke Web page states that her work on Israeli cultural politics has appeared in such journals as *Jour-*

nal of Palestine Studies, GLQ: A Journal of Gay and Lesbian Studies and
Interventions: International Journal of Postcolonial Studies.

One begins to understand why today's students don't enjoy reading.
Also why the Duke University Press is referred to as "the laughingstock of
the publishing world."[32]

As is evident, the rush to judgment in the Duke case was led by the
chroniclers of white-male patriarchy, anti-speciesism and the gender-
power-and-privilege crowd—not the descendants of slaves. The stripper
could have been white for all they cared. The race angle gave the story a little frisson, but the main point was that a member of the lower class had
been raped by white male oppressors—from *the lacrosse team*, no less.
Cathy Davidson, one of the signatories, later explained that the "social disaster" referred to in the ad included the fact that "women's salaries for
similar jobs are substantially less than men's."[33]

The black experience in America had been ripped off by feminists.

White female termigants Nancy Grace and her partner in righteous
anger, Wendy Murphy were the Alton Maddox and Al Sharpton of the
Duke lacrosse case. After it was established that none of the players' DNA
was found on the accuser, Nancy Grace had this exchange with a Duke student on her Headline News show:

STEPHEN MILLER, DUKE CONSERVATIVE UNION: Well, I think I
speak for many students when I say that we're very, very concerned that two innocent people may have possibly—

GRACE: Oh, good lord![34]

In April 2006, Wendy Murphy explained that the lacrosse players see
"women as objects, that they would degrade a woman, rape her, strangle
her, beat her senseless. Why wouldn't they, then, write an e-mail saying,
'And, oh, by the way, the next time I do this, I think I'll just cut right to the
chase and kill her outright.' I think it shows a state of mind of utter disrespect for that woman in particular, for women in general."

She said the players were "thinking, 'I was entitled to do this. I'm a
member of a wealthy white boy's school in a community that allows me to
do what I want when I want. They've gotten away with a lot for a very long
time. Why not go home and celebrate?' . . . The e-mail shows that these
guys were of the mind that whatever had happened to this woman was just

another day at the beach. They'll rape her, sodomize her and tomorrow they'll kill her."[35]

A month later, as the case continued to disintegrate, Murphy said, "I never, ever met a false rape claim, by the way. My own statistics speak to the truth."[36] She said: "Over 99 percent of cases indicted are in fact legitimate," adding, "the guys are guilty. I have scientific, statistical proof."[37]

Even feminists only claim that 2 percent of rape claims are false, which itself is an unsubstantiated factoid from Susan Brownmiller's 1975 book, *Against Our Will*.[38] Brownmiller's only "source" is a mimeograph of a speech by a state court judge, to the New York State Bar Association, in which he made a passing remark about a single New York precinct with an all-female rape squad. Nothing more is known about what the rape squad studied, how it analyzed the information or the precise results. No trace of it exists.

According to the FBI, a higher percentage of rape claims are false than any other criminal complaint, 8 percent compared to 2 percent for other crimes.[39] More detailed studies have found much higher rates of false rape charges. A study of all rape allegations in a Midwestern city over nine years found 41 percent were false[40] and a study of more than a thousand rape allegations on air force bases over the course of four years concluded that 46 percent were false. In 27 percent of the cases, the accuser recanted.[41]

Even after Jesse Jackson had thrown in the towel, Murphy was still convinced the stripper was telling the truth. Nine months into the investigation, prosecutor Mike Nifong amended his filing to say there was no rape, and he further admitted to the court that Mangum had the DNA of at least five other men in or on her—but none from any of the lacrosse players. Murphy responded by hypothesizing nonexistent evidence, saying Nifong might have photos from cooperating witnesses at the party. Yes, and he might also have photos of Big Foot and the Easter bunny dancing the Charleston at the Loch Ness monster's house. He might have had photos of Wendy Murphy assaulting the stripper.

Murphy said that dropping the rape charge from a rape prosecution was a brilliant strategic move, because by dumping the vaginal rape charge, "we're not going to hear about the sex she had with five or ten or fifteen other guys, and that's a good thing for the prosecution."[42]

Feminist blogger Amanda Marcotte (the potty-mouthed activist briefly hired by the John Edwards presidential campaign) was still going strong long after the rape had been exposed as a fraud. At the point when Nifong had been removed from the case and ethics charges brought against him by the state bar, she blogged:

I've been sort of casually listening to CNN blaring throughout
the waiting area and good fucking god is that channel pure evil.
For awhile, I had to listen to how the poor dear lacrosse players at
Duke are being persecuted just because they held someone down
and fucked her against her will—not rape, of course, because the
charges have been thrown out. Can't a few white boys sexually assault a black woman anymore without people getting all wound
up about it? So unfair.[43]

Demonstrating her deep sensitivity to racial issues, Marcotte's book,
*It's a Jungle Out There: The Feminist Survival Guide to Politically Inhospita-
ble Environments* had to be pulled and reissued because the illustrations
were so laughably racist. The book's drawings portrayed various scenes of
a buxom blonde battling African savages in loin cloths.[44]

Hysteria over the alleged rape by Duke lacrosse players was entirely a
feminist enterprise. That's modern civil rights.

It's not about Democratic governors blocking the schoolhouse door: It's
about giving women the right to make false charges of rape. It's about
"equal pay" for women with education degrees, compared to men with engineering degrees. It's about the Augusta National Golf Club not admitting women as members. And it's about bringing "nationally recognized
speakers on sexual harassment" to speak at universities at least twice a year
to supplement the speeches on sexual harassment already given every hour
of every day on college campuses.

And it's about abortion, gay marriage and amnesty for illegal aliens.

It's fantastic that the Democrats have finally come out in favor of civil
rights. It would have been a lot more help, though, if they had done so
when their own party was denying blacks the right to vote, to go to school,
to sit in nonsegregated diners and to use the same water fountains as
whites. But Democrats' commitment to civil rights has always been directly proportional to how much it helps them politically. These days,
blacks are nothing more than window dressing for the issues liberals really
care about.

And the left's most important political cause since sometime in 2007
has been Barack Obama. Even he doesn't take the legacy of slavery seriously. As the cover of *Newsweek* proclaimed, Obama is our "first gay president."

CHAPTER 12

CIVIL RIGHTS CHICKENHAWKS

A staple of Democratic campaigning is to accuse Republicans of being racists. Republican candidates can expect to have their entire life histories probed to find out if, as twelve-year-olds, they caddied at an all-white golf club or ever lived in a predominantly white neighborhood. When liberals can find no archaic restrictive covenant on some piece of property owned by the Republican, they invent stories about Republicans opposing civil rights, having a "despicable" history on race relations and pursuing an imaginary "southern strategy" to win racists over to their party.

Liberals' neurotic obsession with this apocryphal "southern strategy"—it's been cited hundreds of times in the *New York Times*—is supposed to explain why Democrats can't get nice churchgoing, patriotic southerners to vote for the party of antiwar protesters, abortion, the ACLU and gay marriage. They tell themselves they can't win the South because they won't stoop to pander to a bunch of racists—which should probably be their first clue why southerners don't like them.

The premise of liberals' southern strategy folklore is the sophisticated belief that anyone who votes Republican is a racist. They are counting on no one noticing, much less mentioning, the real history of racism in this country.

The single most important piece of evidence for the Republicans' alleged southern strategy is President Lyndon B. Johnson's statement, after signing the Civil Rights Act of 1964, that "we just delivered the South to the Republican Party for a long time to come." That self-serving quote is cited by liberals with more solemnity than Patrick Henry's "Give me liberty or give me death."

Johnson's statement is of questionable provenance. The sole source for the quote is LBJ assistant Bill Moyers, whose other work for the president included hunting for gays on Barry Goldwater's staff and monitoring the

FBI's bugs on Martin Luther King's hotel room, then distributing the sala-cious tapes to select members of the Johnson administration and the press.[1] If this were my case-in-chief for an important point, I'd want better sourcing than a sanctimonious liberal fraud.

An aquaintance of Johnson's who is *not* a partisan hack, dirty trickster and MLK-adultery publicist is Robert M. MacMillan, Air Force One stew-ard during the Johnson administration. MacMillan reports that when LBJ was flying on Air Force One with two governors once, he boasted that by pushing the 1964 civil rights bill, "I'll have them niggers voting Demo-cratic for two hundred years."[2]

Regardless of whether Johnson actually said the Democrats' passage of the Civil Rights Act of 1964 had delivered the south to Republicans, who cares?

That's not proof! Liberals always produce this quote as they're bran-dishing a signed confession to the murder of JonBenét Ramsey. *We have the smoking gun!* But LBJ's statement was the opposite of a confession; it was a self-glorifying tribute to his own high principles. (These were princi-ples of recent vintage: Johnson had ferociously opposed civil rights laws up until five minutes before he became president.)

Do you doubt that LBJ said it?

We'll assume he said it.

Do you have some other explanation?

Yes. He was bragging about his bravery while simultaneously smearing Republicans.

How about this: *When Bush attacked the Taliban, he said, "We just de-livered the Northeast to the Democrats for a long time to come."* Would that be accepted as proof of the liberal Northeast's tendency for treason?

But that's not the only problem with Johnson's self-serving quote. Both parts of his analysis are false. First, the Democrats didn't pass the Civil Rights Act of 1964. That bill, along with every civil rights bill for the pre-ceding century, was supported by substantially more Republicans than Democrats. What distinguished the 1964 act is that it was the first civil rights bill that Democrats finally supported in large numbers. Congratula-tions, Democrats!

Second, that's not what happened: The south kept voting for Democrats for decades after the 1964 act. The very year Johnson said it, even Goldwa-ter couldn't win the South. You don't get a better test case than that.

Goldwater was one of only six Republican senators to vote against the 1964 act, on libertarian grounds, and the other five did so only because they supported Goldwater's presidential nomination.[3] Although a much larger percentage of Republicans had supported the 1964 Civil Rights Act than Democrats—Republican leader Everett Dirksen publicly rebuked Goldwater for his vote[4]—Goldwater was the GOP's presidential candidate that year.

Goldwater went on to win five southern states in 1964—Alabama, Georgia, Louisiana, Mississippi and South Carolina. But he lost eight—North Carolina, Virginia, West Virginia, Kentucky, Tennessee, Arkansas, Texas and Florida. That's not a sweep anyplace except Chicago.

Democrats argue that it isn't the number of states Goldwater won, but which states he won. Goldwater's southern support came from the exact same states that Strom Thurmond captured when he ran for president as a segregationist "Dixiecrat" in 1948—Alabama, Louisiana, Mississippi, and South Carolina—with Goldwater adding only Georgia.

That would be a reasonable argument, but only if your entire historical knowledge begins and ends with 1964. Far from preparing the GOP for a southern takeover, Goldwater's 1964 campaign nearly destroyed the party and created no foundation at all—not even in the South. (That's what purist libertarianism gets you.)

The southern states Goldwater won were the very states that Nixon and Reagan would go on to lose, or almost lose, in their triumphant elections of 1968 and 1980. On the other hand, Democrats Jimmy Carter and Bill Clinton would do pretty well in the Goldwater states in their southern sweeps of 1976 and 1992.

Republicans did not flip the states Goldwater won. Those states went right back to voting for the Democrats for many decades to come. Republicans always did best in the southern states Goldwater lost, which happened to be the same ones Republicans had been winning with some regularity since 1928.

These are the facts:

In 1928, Republican Herbert Hoover won Virginia, Tennessee, Florida, Texas and North Carolina. (See Appendix A for electoral maps.)

In the thirties and forties, FDR and Truman dominated national elections throughout the country, so there is little to be learned about southern voting patterns from those dark days.

In 1952, Republican Eisenhower won Virginia, Tennessee, Florida and Texas, losing Kentucky by a razor-thin 0.07 percent margin.

In 1956, Ike again won Virginia, Tennessee and Florida and added Texas, Kentucky and Louisiana.

In 1960, Nixon won Virginia, Tennessee, Florida and Kentucky.

You will note that 1928, 1952, 1956 and 1960 are years before 1964.

In 1968, Nixon won thirty-two states overall, including six southern states—all the usual Republican favorites: Virginia, Tennessee, Florida, Kentucky, North Carolina and South Carolina. These were the exact same states Republican Hoover had won in 1928, plus South Carolina. Nixon lost Alabama, Georgia, Louisiana and Mississippi—four of the five states Goldwater had won.

Four years after Goldwater's run, the segregationist vote went right back to the Democrats. Democrat Hubert Humphrey picked up about half of George Wallace's supporters that year; Nixon got none of the segregationist vote, as the polls demonstrated.[5] Nixon's early poll numbers were the same as his vote, whereas Humphrey miraculously gained 12 percentage points on election day—just a little bit less than Wallace lost.

Then, in 1976, despite Nixon's malevolent plot to corral racist Democrats, Jimmy Carter swept the entire South. All eleven states of the Old Confederacy—except the great commonwealth of Virginia—flipped right back and voted Democratic. The electoral map of Jimmy Carter's victory in 1976 virtually splits the country down the middle, with Carter taking the entire South, a few solidly Democratic northeastern states and his vice president's home state of Minnesota and neighboring Wisconsin. On the entire continental United States, Carter did not win a single state west of Texas. Of 147 electoral votes in the South, Carter won 127 of them.

Was that because Carter was appealing to bigots? Or is it only appealing to bigots when Republicans win in the South?

In 1980, Reagan won a landslide forty-four states. Reagan crushed Carter in the southern states Republicans had been winning off and on since 1928—Virginia, Tennessee, Florida, Texas and Kentucky. (Republicans had won at least four of those states in five previous elections—three predating Goldwater's 1964 campaign—in 1928, 1956, 1960, 1968 and 1972.)

But despite it being a landslide election, Reagan still lost, or barely won, the Goldwater states, narrowly winning Alabama, Mississippi, and South Carolina[6] and losing Georgia outright. Reagan prevailed in only one Goldwater state by a significant margin: Louisiana. But so did Eisenhower in 1956. Even in an election in which the Democrats carried only six states in the entire country, one of those six was a Goldwater state.

Noticeably, Reagan won among young southern voters—and lost among their seniors, i.e., the ones who had voted in 1948 and 1964. The segregationists never abandoned Democrats. Eventually, they died or were outvoted by other, younger southerners.

Extensive college polling in 1980 put Reagan in third place in the northeast, well behind John Anderson and Jimmy Carter. But at southern colleges, Reagan massacred both Anderson and Carter. Thus, Reagan won 14 percent of the student vote at Yale but 71 percent at Louisiana Tech University.[7] Are we supposing the LTU students were Goldwater men at age three? Dixiecrats before birth? No matter how you run the numbers, neither Nixon nor Reagan ever captured the Goldwater voters. Republicans certainly weren't winning the Dixiecrat vote. Even in 1968, twenty years after Thurmond's 1948 campaign, Nixon carried only one of Thurmond's states, despite taking six southern states in all. After Thurmond's presidential run, the Dixiecrats went right back to voting for the Democrats for another half century.

Of course, Nixon and Reagan did sweep the entire South in their 1972 and 1984 reelections. Also the Midwest, the Colorado Mountains, the windswept prairies, the Pacific Northwest and the Hawaiian Islands. Nixon walloped his opponent, George McGovern, in every state of the union except Massachusetts. The same thing happened in 1984, when Reagan won forty-nine states, losing only his opponent Walter Mondale's home state of Minnesota—and Dutch nearly took that. A political party that attributes such landslide victories to a secret Republican plan to appeal to racists has gone stark raving mad.

Revealing what intellectuals really thought at the time, as late as 1972, liberal luminary Arthur Schlesinger Jr. openly acknowledged in the pages of the *New York Times* that the segregationists would be voting for McGovern—not Nixon—writing that "voters hesitate between McGovern and George Wallace." Note that he did not say voters hesitated between Nixon and Wallace.

So firmly were the segregationists in the Democratic fold, that Schlesinger went on to praise them for their integrity. The Wallace votes in the primaries, Schlesinger said, showed that voters cared deeply about—I quote—"integrity."[8] That's what liberals said before they decided to do a complete historical rewrite.

And of course, McGovern gave an obligatory tribute to the segregationist Wallace in his acceptance speech at the Democratic Convention that year.[9] This was in 1972, the exact midpoint between Goldwater and Reagan, when the imaginary "southern strategy" should have been complete, according to the fevered propaganda of the left.

It wasn't until 1988, a quarter century after Goldwater's run, that a Republican presidential candidate finally won all five of his southern states in anything other than forty-nine-state Republican landslides. Bush won only a forty-state landslide that year.

In addition to Goldwater's states, Bush also won California, Maine, Vermont, Illinois, Michigan, Iowa and Delaware. And yet no one talks about Republicans' secret strategy to appeal to Ben & Jerry's lesbians to explain their Vermont triumph in 1988.

Four years later the South would flip right back and vote for Clinton, who carried six southern states, including two Goldwater states.

Not only that, but from the moment of LBJ's woe-is-me prediction in 1964 that Democrats had lost the South forever, Democrats continued to win a plurality of votes in southern congressional elections every two years for the next thirty years, right up until 1994.[10] Republicans didn't win the Dixiecrat vote—the Dixiecrats died. If the Republicans were scheming to capture southern racists—of which there is no evidence—it didn't work.

In presidential elections for forty years, between 1948 and 1988, Republicans never won a majority of the Dixiecrat states, except in two forty-nine-state landslides. Whatever turned the South away from the Democrats—their enthusiasm for abortion, gays in the military, Christian-bashing, springing criminals, attacks on guns, dovish foreign policy, Save the Whales/Kill the Humans environmentalism—it wasn't race.

By contrast, Democrats kept winning the alleged "segregationist" states right up to the 1990s. In 1976, Carter won all the Goldwater states. Even as late as 1992, Clinton carried two of the southern states won by Goldwater: Georgia and Louisiana.

Were these southerners voting for Goldwater out of racism, but supporting Clinton for other, noble reasons? If anything, it was the opposite. Clinton's mentor was J. William Fulbright, a vehement foe of integration who had voted against the Civil Rights Act of 1964. At his gubernatorial inauguration, Clinton publicly embraced Orval Faubus, the man who stood in the schoolhouse door in Little Rock rather than comply with the Supreme Court's school desegregation ruling.[11] (That's when Republican Eisenhower sent in the 101st Airborne to enforce civil rights in Arkansas.)

Goldwater didn't vote against the 1964 act because he supported segregation—he had long since desegregated his family's department stores, as well as the Arizona National Guard. He was a founding member of the Arizona NAACP. Goldwater voted against the 1964 act because he was a libertarian opposed to the act's restrictions on private property, which he believed to be beyond Congress's powers under the commerce clause of the Constitution. Unlike the Democrats who voted against the act, Goldwater had supported every other civil rights bill until that one. Much of this was finally admitted by the *Washington Post*—in Goldwater's obituary.[12]

It's bad enough to cite some gaseous remark by a politician as if it proves something. But for liberals to keep citing Johnson's self-serving blather when the subsequent facts completely contradict it requires either raw mendacity or Chris Matthews–level stupidity.

Democrats have had a stronger hold on Massachusetts for the last half century than Republicans have had on the South. How do we know they're not using code words to appeal to Puritan witch-hunters?

It's amazing the lengths liberals have gone to in order to hide the truth.

In any discussion of who the segregationists were, liberals switch the word "Democrats" to "southerners."[13] But it wasn't southerners opposing civil rights; it was Democrats. The Civil Rights Act of 1957, for example, was supported by all forty-three Republicans in the Senate, but only twenty-nine Democrats. It was opposed by eighteen Democrats, including northerners such as Wayne Morse of Oregon, Warren Magnuson of Washington, James Murray of Montana, Mike Mansfield of Montana, and Joseph O'Mahoney of Wyoming.[14]

There were also plenty of southern integrationists: They were Republicans.

When a Republican in the South was as rare as one in Hollywood today, these brave conservatives battled Democrat segregationists. But their lonely fight has been meticulously excised from the historical record by the left.

In 1966, pro-integrationist Republican Winthrop Rockefeller became the first Republican governor of Arkansas since Reconstruction, replacing rabid segregationist Democrat (and Bill Clinton pal) Orval Faubus. Rockefeller pushed for integration of the schools and appointed the first African American to a cabinet level position. Rockefeller's win carried another Republican integrationist, Maurice Britt, into the lieutenant governor's office.

Also in 1966, Republican Howard Baker ran on an integrationist platform, taking his campaign "directly to blacks" to become the first Republican senator from Tennessee since Reconstruction.[15] Years later, Baker would serve as the Republican majority leader in the Senate and President Reagan's chief of staff.

Both Baker and Rockefeller won statewide southern elections as Re-

publicans championing civil rights two years after Goldwater won his supposedly game-changing victory in four Dixiecrat states by sneakily
appealing to racists.

Also in 1966, Republican and civil rights supporter Bo Calloway ran
against a virulent racist Democrat, Lester Maddox, for governor of Georgia. While Calloway was in Congress backing the Voting Rights Act of
1965,[16] Maddox was in Atlanta, chasing blacks from his segregated restaurant with a shotgun. Maddox eventually closed the restaurant rather than
serve black people.

In the governor's race, Maddox was endorsed by future president Jimmy
Carter. The vote was too close to call, so the Democratic state legislature
gave it to Maddox. Calloway appealed, but the Supreme Court upheld the
legislature's decision—with the vote of former KKK member Justice Hugo
Black—who was appointed by Democratic president Franklin Roosevelt.

Republican Charles Pickering of Mississippi spent the sixties literally
risking his life to prosecute the powerful Democratic Ku Klux Klan. From
its inception, the Klan was—as liberal historian Eric Foner writes—"a military force, serving the interests of the Democratic Party. . . ."[17]

Republican Spiro Agnew wasn't in the South, but—again—not all segregationists were southern: All segregationists were Democrats. In 1966,
Agnew ran against Democratic segregationist George Mahoney for the
Maryland governorship. Four years earlier, as Baltimore County Executive, Agnew had enacted some of the first laws in the nation that outlawed
race discrimination in public accommodations.[18] In a specific rebuke to
fair-housing laws, Mahoney's campaign slogan was "your home is your
castle—protect it." Running for governor, Agnew vowed to enact a state
fair-housing law and to repeal Maryland's antimiscegenation statute. He
developed a close working relationship with black leaders, meeting with
them frequently during the campaign and while in office.

Even back in the fifties, Republicans were battling Democratic segregationists in the South. Republican Horace E. Henderson took on the segregationist "Byrd machine" in Virginia by running for lieutenant governor
as a pro–civil rights Republican—and losing. He brought a lawsuit to challenge the legality of the Democrats' discriminatory poll tax, a position that
prevailed in the Supreme Court.

There are more proabortion Republicans today than there were Republican segregationists in the twentieth century. The segregationists were
Democrats, just as they are the proabortion party today.

When not calling Democrat segregationists "southerners," liberals call them "conservatives"—much like the media label the most extreme Soviet communists or Islamic jihadists "conservatives." Brave integrationist stances taken by southern Republicans, putting their lives in danger, are labeled "moderate" positions, even "liberal." Liberals lie about history by manipulating words.

Thus, a *Harvard Crimson* article on Agnew's strong integrationist views in the 1960s is titled: "Earlier Agnew Took Moderate Stances." A Web site on American presidents amazingly refers to Agnew's sterling civil rights record as "to the left of his Democratic challenger"—a segregationist.[19] Even David Hackett Fischer capitulates to the standard phraseology, writing: "Truman managed to be liberal on race and conservative on property. . . ."[20]

Liberals simply take everything that is good in history—which they generally fought against at the time—and retroactively label it "liberal." Everything bad—which they generally supported—is branded "conservative." Reagan wanted to smash communism, Carter warned Americans not to have "an inordinate fear of communism."[21] So in what Alice-in-Wonderland lingua franca are hardened communists "conservatives"? In another twenty years, history books will be describing Reagan's aggressive posture toward the Soviet Union as the "progressive" stance and calling Jimmy Carter's appeasement strategy the "conservative" position.

There is no sense in which race discrimination is "conservative." Liberals were for race discrimination in the fifties; liberals are for race discrimination today. (As long as their kids still get into a good college.) There was never a period of time when race discrimination was a Republican policy, except maybe briefly when Nixon imposed affirmative action on the building trades doing business with the government in the sixties, but they deserved it. (A policy for which LBJ is showered with praise for thinking about—but never actually implementing.)

When journalists and historians are forced to admit some Democrat was a segregationist—something that often slips their minds—the news is delivered amid a blizzard of excuses.

The appalling civil rights record of liberal hero and lifelong Democrat Sam Ervin is explained away on Wikipedia: "Defenders of Ervin argue that his opposition to most civil rights legislation was based on his commitment to the preservation of the Constitution in its pristine formulation that he repeatedly stated encapsulated civil, human and equal rights for all. There is little if any evidence that he engaged in the racial demagoguery of many of his Southern colleagues."

Ervin's precious commitment to the Constitution seemed to leave him when it came to big, government-spending programs. As for racial pandering, Robert Caro reports that Ervin said of the 1957 civil rights act: "We've got to give the goddamned niggers something" and "We're not gonna be able to get out of here until we've got *some* kind of nigger bill."[22] This quote will surely be excised from future editions of Caro's book.

The only reason anyone knows that recently departed Democratic Senator Robert Byrd was a member of the Klan is because conservatives kept screaming it from the rooftops in response to liberals' monumental lies about who the segregationists were. Byrd was no mere segregationist; he was an officer with a racist vigilante group.

Liberal journalist John Nichols wrote fondly of the former Klanner in the *Nation*: "I covered Byrd during much of that last quarter century and, like the vast majority of his fellow senators, developed an appreciation for the sincerity of the man's rejection of the past."[23]

The *Washington Post* lies outright, describing Senator William Fulbright (in their lingo) as "a progressive on racial issues." Fulbright was a full-bore segregationist. He voted *against* the 1957, 1960, 1964 and 1965 civil rights bills. He was a signatory to the Southern Manifesto.[24]

It helps that liberals refuse to learn any history and instead endlessly repeat popular liberal folktales.

In November 2008, Adam Nossiter wrote in the *New York Times* that Virginia and North Carolina "made history last week in breaking from their Confederate past and supporting Mr. Obama."[25]

To review some first-grade history, the Confederates were Democrats and the Union, led by Abraham Lincoln, was Republican. Thus, to be "breaking from their Confederate past," Virginia and North Carolina would have to vote for a Republican, not a Democrat. North Carolina and Virginia first broke "from their Confederate past" in 1928, when both states went for Herbert Hoover.

If Mr. Nossiter is rewriting history to switch sides in the Civil War, both Virginia and North Carolina have voted for Democrats for president more than a dozen times since the end of the war. Most recently, Virginia went for LBJ in 1964 and North Carolina voted for Carter in 1976.

If instead Nossiter is using "Confederate" to mean "segregationist" or "Barry Goldwater-supporting," neither Virginia nor North Carolina voted for either Thurmond or Goldwater.

If Mr. Nossiter is referring to the fact that two southern states had miraculously voted for a black to be president, it was the first time for the rest of the country, too.

Moreover, if he thinks it's amazing that two Southern states voted for *any* black person, then he must be unaware that the former Confederate states were the first to send blacks to Congress. This is missing from liberal history books because the dozens of black politicians elected to Congress after the Civil War were all Republicans. The first black governor in the country was P. B. S. Pinchback, acting governor of Louisiana in 1872. (The *Washington Post*'s Eugene Robinson claimed in 2008 that "in the nation's history we've had only two black governors—Douglas Wilder in Virginia and Deval Patrick in Massachusetts."[26] He forgot Pinchback, a Republican.)

The first black lieutenant governor in the nation was Oscar James Dunn, elected in Louisiana in 1868, who was, of course, a Republican. Two years later, black Republican Alonzo J. Ransier was elected lieutenant governor in South Carolina.

The nation's first black governor since Reconstruction was elected not merely in the South but in one of the two states Adam Nossiter specifically cited as "breaking from [its] Confederate roots" to vote for a black man. Virginia made Douglas Wilder the country's first *elected* black governor in 1989.

What on earth is Nossiter talking about? What could he possibly mean by saying Virginia and North Carolina "made history last week in breaking from their Confederate past and supporting Mr. Obama"? Liberals have submerged themselves so deeply in their self-flattering fantasies about racist Republicans and heroic Democrats that it's impossible to make any sense of what they say. They don't read history books. Liberals only read books about cats.

One thing that's clear is that Nossiter intended to praise Virginia and North Carolina for voting for Obama. He went on to explain that Obama's victory in those states could be attributed to "an influx of better educated and more prosperous voters in recent years." Liberals seem to imagine the entire South—the first region of the country to send lots of blacks to Congress—is an English-speaking Taliban in need of instruction by white liberals.

Most of the time, liberals are at least smart enough to steer clear of any details in order to avoid making inane statements, like Nossiter. Note the complete absence of facts in this outburst from Joe Klein: "Traditionally— at least since Nixon's 'southern strategy'—Republicans have been truly despicable on race, and there are more than a few stalwarts who continue to bloviate disingenuously in support of a 'colorblind' society, by which they mean a tacit relapse into segregation."[27]

I'm sorry—was Joe Klein some hitherto unacknowledged hero of the civil rights movement? Was he with King? Why does he get to play the Freedom Rider, while some thirty-year-old Republican is suddenly on Team Bull Connor? Contrary to Klein's suggestion, it seems highly unlikely that Republicans are trying to bring back segregation inasmuch as that was a Democratic policy, never supported by the Republican Party. Having endlessly perseverated these nonsense fairy tales to themselves and the public, liberals turn around and race-bait Republicans to advance Democratic policies having nothing to do with blacks.

In 2002, liberals were exultant when Senator Trent Lott toasted Senator Strom Thurmond at his 100th birthday party, saying: "I want to say this about my state: When Strom Thurmond ran for president, we voted for him. We're proud of it. And if the rest of the country had followed our lead, we wouldn't have had all these problems over all these years, either."

Liberals leaped on the meaningless praise at an old-timer's birthday party to remind everyone that Thurmond had run for president on a segregationist platform! This led to a new round of racism accusations against the Republican Party—which Thurmond joined sixteen years after his 1948 segregationist presidential run.

In 1948, Thurmond did not run as a "Dixiecan," he ran as a "Dixiecrat." As the name indicates, the Dixiecrats were an offshoot of the Democratic Party. When he lost, Thurmond went right back to being a Democrat.

Assuming—contrary to common sense—that Lott was intending to praise Thurmond for his segregationist stance two decades earlier, what we had here was: one former Democrat praising another former Democrat for what was once a Democrat policy. The Lott incident reminded us that Republicans have to be careful about letting Democrats into their party.

All segregationists were Democrats and—contrary to liberal fables— the vast majority of them remained Democrats for the rest of their lives. Many have famous names—commemorated in buildings and statues and tribute speeches by Bill Clinton. But one never hears about their segregationist pasts, or even Klan memberships. Among them are: Supreme Court justice Hugo Black; Governor George Wallace of Alabama; gubernatorial candidate George Mahoney of Maryland; Bull Connor, Commissioner of Public Safety for Birmingham, Alabama; Governor Orval Faubus of Arkansas; and Governor Lester Maddox of Georgia.

But for practical purposes, the most important segregationists were the ones in the U.S. Senate, where civil rights bills went to die. All the segregationists in the Senate were of course, Democrats. All but one remained Democrats for the rest of their lives—and not conservative Democrats. Support for segregation went hand in hand with liberal positions on other issues, too.

The myth of the southern strategy is that southern segregationists were conservatives just waiting for a wink from Nixon to switch parties and join the Reagan revolution. That could not be further from the truth. With the exception of Strom Thurmond—the only one who ever became a Republican—they were almost all liberals and remained liberals for the rest of their lives. Of the twelve southern segregationists in the Senate other than Thurmond, only two could conceivably be described as "conservative Democrats."

The twelve were:

- Senator Harry Byrd (staunch opponent of anti-communist Senator Joseph McCarthy);

- Senator Robert Byrd (proabortion, opponent of 1990 Gulf War and 2002 Iraq War, huge pork barrel spender, sending more than $1 billion to his home state during his tenure, supported the Equal Rights Amendment,[28] won a 100 percent rating from NARAL Pro-Choice America and a 71 percent grade from the American Civil Liberties Union in 2007);

- Senator Allen Ellender of Louisiana (McCarthy opponent, pacifist and opponent of the Vietnam War);

- Senator Sam Ervin of North Carolina (McCarthy opponent, anti-Vietnam War, major Nixon antagonist as head the Watergate Committee that led to the president's resignation);

- Senator Albert Gore Sr. of Tennessee (ferocious McCarthy opponent despite McCarthy's popularity in Tennessee,[29] anti-Vietnam War);

- Senator James Eastland of Mississippi (conservative Democrat, though he supported some of FDR's New Deal, but was a strong anti-communist);

- Senator J. William Fulbright of Arkansas (staunch McCarthy opponent,[30] anti-Vietnam War, big supporter of the United Nations and taxpayer-funded grants given in his name);

- Senator Walter F. George of Georgia (supported Social Security Act, Tennessee Valley Authority and many portions of the Great Society);

- Senator Ernest Hollings (initiated federal food stamp program, supported controls on oil, but later became a conservative Democrat, as evidenced by his support for Clarence Thomas's nomination to the Supreme Court);

- Senator Russell Long (Senate floor leader on LBJ's Great Society programs);

- Senator Richard Russell (strident McCarthy opponent, calling him a "huckster of hysteria,"[31] supported FDR's New Deal, defended Truman's firing of General Douglas MacArthur, mildly opposed to the Vietnam War);

- Senator John Stennis (won murder convictions against three blacks based solely on their confessions, which were extracted by vicious police floggings, leading to reversal by the Supreme Court; first senator to publicly attack Joe McCarthy on the Senate floor; and, in his later years, opposed Judge Robert Bork's nomination to the Supreme Court).

The only Democratic segregationist in the Senate to become a Republican—Strom Thurmond—did so eighteen years after he ran for president as a Dixiecrat. He was never a member of the terroristic Ku Klux Klan, as Hugo Black and Robert Byrd had been. You could make a lot of money betting people to name one segregationist U.S. senator other than Thurmond. Only the one who became a Republican is remembered for his dark days as a segregationist Democrat.

As for the remaining dozen segregationists, only two—Hollings and Eastland—were what you'd call conservative Democrats. The rest were dyed-in-the-wool liberals taking the left-wing positions on issues of the day. Segregationist beliefs went hand in hand with opposition to Senator Joe McCarthy,[32] opposition to the Vietnam War, support for New Deal and Great Society programs, support for the United Nations, opposition to Nixon and a 100 percent rating from NARAL. Being against civil rights is now and has always been the liberal position.

The media intentionally hide the civil rights records of lifelong, liberal Democrats to make it look as if it was the Republican Party that was the party of segregation and race discrimination, which it never was. If Senator Joe Lieberman ever becomes a Republican, someday liberals will rewrite history to accuse Republicans of being the party of partial-birth abortion. (Lieberman is a member of two of the world's smallest groups: Orthodox Jews for Partial-Birth Abortion and Democrats for a Strong National Defense.)

Delusionally carrying on about the Lott contretemps at Thurmond's birthday party, *Newsweek*'s Jon Meacham declared: "Trent Lott and the GOP grew up together in the South. They both have a painful secret."

First: The Republicans most definitely did not grow up in the South. They only began to win a plurality of House votes there in 1994—coincidentally, about twenty years after the Democratic Party went insane. Reagan barely won Mississippi in his landslide election of 1980 and Mississippi didn't elect a Republican governor until 1991.

Second, when Lott was growing up, he was a Democrat. He was a Democrat through college. He was a Democrat after college. Lott was a Democrat his entire life, until he ran for Congress in 1972—the year the entire country, except Massachusetts, went Republican. Indeed, until 1972, Lott had been the administrative assistant to a congressional Democrat. Then, the Democratic Party ran George McGovern for president as part of a strategy to turn the party into a group of far-left kooks from places like New York City, San Francisco, and Los Angeles. Lott became a Republican the same year that New York, California, Illinois and Minnesota became Republican, albeit more fleetingly.

Meacham also said Bush had distanced himself from Lott by "evoking Lincoln—the only port a Republican president has in this kind of storm."[33] Liberals seem to think Meacham is an intellectual, so he must be a monstrous liar because that is preposterous.

Here are a few other "ports" Republicans have "in this kind of storm":

Republicans passed the Thirteenth Amendment, ending slavery, with 80 percent of Democrats voting against it.

Republicans enacted the Fourteenth Amendment, granting freed slaves the rights of citizenship—unanimously supported by Republicans and unanimously opposed by Democrats.

Republicans passed the Fifteenth Amendment, giving freedmen the right to vote.

Republicans passed the Civil Rights Act of 1866, conferring U.S. citizenship on all African Americans and according them "full and equal benefit of all laws"—unanimously supported by Republicans, who had to override Democrat President Andrew Johnson's veto.

Republicans passed the Reconstruction Act of 1867.

Republicans sent federal troops to the Democratic South to enforce the constitutional rights of the newly freed slaves.

Republicans were the first targets of the Ku Klux Klan, during Reconstruction.

Republicans continued trying to pass federal civil rights laws for a century following the Civil War—most of which the Democrats blocked—including a bill banning racial discrimination in public accommodations in 1875; a bill guaranteeing blacks the right to vote in the South in 1890; anti-lynching bills in 1922, 1935 and 1938, and anti-poll tax bills in 1942, 1944 and 1946.

A Republican president, Theodore Roosevelt, invited Booker T. Washington to dine at the White House in 1901, making him the first black American to do so.[34]

Republican party platforms repeatedly called for equal rights, demanding in 1908, for example, equal justice for black Americans and condemning all devices that disfranchise blacks for their color alone, "as unfair, un-American and repugnant to the Supreme law of the land."

Republicans called for anti-lynching legislation in their presidential platforms throughout the 1920s, while the Democratic platforms did not.

Republicans demanded integration of the military in civil services in their party platform in 1940; again, the Democrats did not.[35]

Republicans endorsed *Brown v. Board of Education* in their 1956 presidential platform; the Democrats did not.

Republicans sent the 101st Airborne Division to Little Rock to enforce the Court's school desegregation ruling to stop the Democratic governor from blocking the schoolhouse door.

Republicans fully implemented the desegregation of the military, left unfinished by a Democratic president.

Republicans introduced and passed into law the Civil Rights Act of 1957 opposed and watered down by Democrats.[36]

Republicans reintroduced and passed another civil rights bill in 1960, maneuvering it past Democratic obstructionism, with all votes against the bill coming from Democrats.

Republicans created the Commission on Civil Rights.

Republicans voted in far greater numbers for the Civil Rights Act of 1964 than the Democrats, though this was the year Democrats finally stopped aggressively opposing civil rights bills.

Republicans effectively desegregated public schools throughout the nation in the first few years of the Nixon administration.

Republicans desegregated the building trades, introducing, for the first time, racial quotas and timetables for those doing business with the federal government.

Republicans appointed the first black secretary of state as well as the first black female secretary of state.

Republicans appointed one of two black justices ever to sit on the Supreme Court, over the hysterical objections of Democrats. . . .

Meanwhile, the Democrats passed the Violence Against Women Act and think they're civil rights champions.

Bill Clinton smeared the entire South in his comments on Lott's toast, saying: "I think what they are really upset about is that he made public their strategy," adding, "How do they think they got a majority in the South anyway?" Clinton won six southern states in 1992! How does he think he got that? His "role model"[37] was the segregationist Democrat J. William Fulbright, whom he worked for and called "my mentor." [38]

Fulbright voted against every important civil rights bill in the fifties and sixties. He signed the Southern Manifesto opposing desegregation in response to the Supreme Court's ruling in *Brown v. Board of Education.* (Ninety-seven of the ninety-nine signatories to that document were Democrats.) Just three years after Fulbright opposed the Civil Rights Acts of 1965, Clinton was working on his reelection campaign. As president, Clinton invited Fulbright to the White House for a special ceremony to give the old segregationist the Presidential Medal of Freedom. Another segregationist, Albert Gore Sr. was in attendance. In his tribute, Clinton praised Fulbright for being "among the first Americans to try to get us to think about the people in Russia as people."[39] The people in Russia! Alas, Fulbright was incapable of thinking about black Americans as people.

While exploding in a joyful frenzy about Lott—who was seven years old when Strom Thurmond ran for president as a Dixiecrat—the media were undisturbed by a former Ku Klux Klansman sitting in the U.S. Senate for more than half a century. He was a Democrat.

Democrat Bob Byrd had been a "kleagle" (recruiter) and "exalted cyclops" (head of the local chapter) of the Ku Klux Klan. But he got liberal insta-forgiveness. During his fifty-one years in the U.S. Senate, Democrats made Byrd secretary of the Senate Democratic Caucus (1967–1971), Senate majority whip (1971–1977), Senate majority leader (1977–1981 and 1987–1989) and Senate minority leader (1981–1987).

After World War II, which Byrd somehow managed to avoid despite being in his late twenties, he wrote to the Grand Wizard of the KKK saying the Klan was needed "now more than ever" and that he was "anxious to see its rebirth in West Virginia."

He wrote another letter to a racist senator proclaiming that he—war avoider Byrd—would never fight under the American flag "with a Negro by my side. Rather I should die a thousand times, and see Old Glory trampled in the dirt never to rise again, than to see this beloved land of ours become degraded by race mongrels, a throwback to the blackest specimen from the wilds."[40]

The uncomfortable fact of Byrd's official positions with the Klan was always gently brushed over, when not completely ignored. The April 2003 *Vanity Fair* magazine paid homage to Byrd in a "Profiles in Courage" tribute written by former Clinton spokesman Dee Dee Myers, who quickly disposed of his Klan days, saying: "despite briefly aligning himself with racists a half-century ago . . ." On his death in 2010, Bill Clinton complained that newspapers had even mentioned Byrd's "fleeting" membership with the Klan, which Clinton excused by saying, "He was trying to get elected."[41]

Less than two years after the hysteria over Lott's toast to Strom Thurmond, one of Lott's fiercest critics, Democratic senator Chris Dodd, made his own hail-fellow-well-met toast—to the former KKK kleagle Bob Byrd. On the occasion of Byrd's seventeen thousandth vote in the Senate, Dodd said Byrd "would have been a great senator at any moment. . . . He would have been in the leadership crafting this Constitution. He would have been right during the great conflict of Civil War in this nation."

During the Civil War?

The *Hartford Courant* defended Senator Dodd's offensive gasbaggery about Byrd being "right" during the Civil War, saying Dodd's civil rights record is "impeccable." He "erred," the *Courant* said. "He didn't commit a capital offense"[42]—unlike Trent Lott for his less egregious remark about a less egregious man.

At least Strom Thurmond did a complete about-face on his racial views when he became a Republican. Thurmond voted to make Martin Luther

King's birthday a national holiday and voted to confirm Clarence Thomas to the U.S. Supreme Court.

Meanwhile, Byrd is the only senator to have voted against both blacks ever nominated to the Supreme Court: Thurgood Marshall and Clarence Thomas. He also voted against the appointments of federal judge Janice Rogers Brown and Secretary of State Condoleezza Rice. Both are black women.

Apparently Nixon's "southern strategy" didn't work on Robert Byrd.

In addition to Senator Dodd's fulsome praise, Byrd has been extolled by Senator Teddy Kennedy as having "the kind of qualities that the Founding Fathers believed were so important for service to the nation."

Byrd's extraordinary transformation from Ku Klux Klan kleagle to liberal profile-in-courage winner was mostly accomplished by the simple expedient of his switching from opposing the rights of blacks to opposing the rights of unborn babies. In 2007, NARAL Pro-Choice America gave Byrd a grade of 100 for his stellar service in the war against unborn babies. At least he's consistent: Abortion is disproportionately performed on black babies.[43]

Liberals have always been very picky about whose racist pasts could be mentioned. The most beloved Democratic president in the liberal firmament is Franklin D. Roosevelt, and he nominated a former Klan member to the Supreme Court. But the left's secular religion holds that FDR was the greatest president who ever breathed, so that nasty business with the Klan was swept under the rug.

This is why liberals love the public schools: The populace has been so dumbed down that Democrats can spout any counterfactual nonsense and people will believe it. With their infernal repetition, liberals spread amazingly self-flattering myths and no one ever bothers to look up facts. The left's victory will be complete when all high school seniors believe the Confederates were Republicans, like Adam Nossiter of the *New York Times*.

CHAPTER 13

YOU RACIST!

Any fact that makes Americans less likely to vote for a Democrat is now called a racist smear.

The mythos of Republican dirty campaigning is entirely liberal projection. The real secret of modern political campaigns isn't Republicans' sneaky appeals to racial resentment, it's liberals' Miss Grundy lecturing about racism intended to rile up black voters and intimidate white suburbanites who are terrified of appearing racist.

Liberals love telling blacks they are woebegone wretches horribly oppressed by whites. They *love* that. But since even the Democrats aren't subjugating blacks anymore, no one is. So the Democrats make up stories of racist incidents committed by Republicans.

The caption accompanying a *Newsweek* story about racism is a good example of the miasma of lies, myths and irrelevant associations that sustain the Republicans-are-racist thesis:

"After Nixon's narrow loss to JFK, Goldwater stormed the GOP; by '68, Nixon was back with his 'Southern Strategy'—one that helped elect Lott to the House in 1972; . . . As the party became more apparently mainstream under Reagan and Bush, Lott rose through Congress, singing different songs to different audiences; PHOTO: Hardball: Bush at the controversial Bob Jones University in 2000; the McCain family, which was smeared in the GOP South Carolina primary that year; Lott at the Thurmond birthday party."[1]

Where to begin?

Goldwater did not "storm the GOP." He was nominated after a contentious convention fight and went on to lose in a historic landslide, as a blunt, purist, abortion-supporting libertarian only the Cato Institute could love. Republicans got nothing from his candidacy and wouldn't win the southern states he carried for another three decades, except in epic landslides.

Newsweek's other markers on the left's racist *via dolorosa* are some of the most popular ones. They get traded in and out as the truth emerges, and then people forget what the truth was, so liberals can trot the discredited ones out again.

In 2002, the *New York Times*'s Bob Herbert cited four other liberal chestnuts, which, he claimed, proved that the "Republican Party has become a haven for white racist attitudes and anti-black policies."[2]

Excluding random name calling ("southern strategy"! "Dixiecrats"!), Herbert's evidence against the Republicans was:

1. "the Willie Horton campaign ad"

2. "Bob Jones University"

3. "[In] Reagan's 1980 presidential run . . . his first major appearance in the general election campaign was in Philadelphia, Miss., which just happened to be the place where three civil rights workers—Andrew Goodman, Michael Schwerner and James Chaney—were murdered in 1964."

4. "During that appearance, Mr. Reagan told his audience, 'I believe in states' rights.'"

How many times do we have to disprove these tall tales? Let's go through them in chronological order.

PHILADELPHIA, MISSISSIPPI—1980

Reagan's Philadelphia speech is classic Democratic princess-and-the-pea campaigning.

Romney is speaking in Chicago—what can I be offended about?

I'm working on it—give me a minute.

Hurry! I'm going on TV in thirty minutes. Where's my indignation button?

I've got it! "How anyone can give a speech on the economy less than three weeks away from the fifty-seventh anniversary of Chicago native Emmett Till's death! In Chicago, no less!"

● ● ●

During Obama's 2008 campaign, doleful reminiscences of Reagan's kick-off speech in Philadelphia reached an all-time election year high. Former president Jimmy Carter nearly brought Keith Olbermann and Chris Matthews to tears, saying:

"When [Reagan] made his speech in Philadelphia, I wept, because he expressed the essence of racial discrimination clearly. . . . And since then, the Deep South has been dominated by the Republican Party, using the race issue as a subtle and sometimes overt mechanism to gain a majority. . . . And I remember when my opponent in 1980 opened his campaign, Ronald Reagan, it was in the little town in Mississippi where the three civil rights workers were buried in a dam."[3]

Also, in 2008, Irv Randolph wrote in the *Philadelphia Tribune* that Republicans "have a well documented history of injecting race in presidential campaigns" and then gave as his case-in-chief (besides the GOP's alluring "southern strategy"): "In the 1980 presidential campaign, Ronald Reagan called for states' rights in a speech in Philadelphia, Miss., where three civil rights workers had been murdered 16 years earlier."[4]

Roger Simon wrote in Politico.com of Republicans' history of exploiting racial fears: "Ronald Reagan began his presidential campaign in 1980 by giving a speech at a county fair in Philadelphia, Miss, where three civil rights workers—James Chaney, Michael Schwerner and Andrew Goodman—had been murdered in 1964."[5] (Wait until he finds out about Reagan introducing AIDS into the black community! Or was that Bush?)

On MSNBC's *The Ed Show* in 2010, Bob Shrum, author of the lying, racism-accusing ad in the Maryland gubernatorial campaign, said, "You know, Ed, [opposing Obama] is perfectly appropriate for a Republican party, a modern Republican party, that's driven out all the moderates and was born in the southern strategy. We all know what the southern strategy was about. Ronald Reagan opened his campaign for president in 1980 in Philadelphia, Mississippi, where those civil rights workers were killed."[6]

As is evident, Reagan's Philadelphia speech is a liberal folktale classic.

First, and least important, the speech wasn't Reagan's first major campaign speech. It was one of several summer events more than a month before the traditional Labor Day kickoff speech. That's why the *Washington Post* headlined a September 1, 1980, article, "Candidates' Labor Day Speeches Mark Start of Presidential Race," stating: "The official campaign for America's 48th presidential election begins today, with President Carter in his native South and Ronald Reagan wooing Democratic voters in the industrial East."[7]

Reagan's opening day campaign speeches were given in Liberty State Park, New Jersey, and Detroit, Michigan.

Second, Reagan's earlier, summertime, speech wasn't in Philadelphia, Mississippi, where the three CORE workers were killed. It was at the Neshoba County fairgrounds, seven miles away. There happens to be a major state fair there every year. Contrary to what you may have thought, the state fair has nothing to do with the three CORE workers being killed several miles away in 1964.

But if we're blaming politicians for hideous crimes that happened within several miles of the towns where they give speeches:

- Obama kicked off his 2008 presidential campaign in Springfield, Illinois, where, just a few years earlier, Mark Winger had beaten his wife to death with a hammer and murdered a van driver after framing him for the crime.

- Obama gave a major speech during the 2008 primaries to seventeen thousand people at the Reunion Arena in Dallas—the very town where John F. Kennedy was shot!

- Obama, the most pro-abortion president we've ever had, gave his 2008 convention speech in Denver, not far from where JonBenét Ramsey was murdered and a mass murder of schoolchildren in Columbine occurred.

If liberals truly believed there was something uniquely horrible about the Neshoba County Fairgrounds, why did Michael Dukakis give a campaign speech there during his 1988 presidential campaign?[8]

Third, now that liberals have told us the symbolic value of where the opening day speech is given, guess where Jimmy Carter gave his while Reagan was in Liberty Park and Detroit?

Carter actually did kick off his campaign in Tuscumbia, Alabama—home to the national headquarters of the Knights of the Ku Klux Klan.[9] Yes, that would be the same Jimmy Carter weeping over Reagan's "Philadelphia speech" on MSNBC in 2008. Carter kicked off his campaign in the town where the KKK was based. Then—not sixteen years earlier.

Reagan even made a crack about Carter's choice of opening day venues, telling a man wearing a Carter mask in Detroit that he was supposed to be in Alabama "in the city that gave birth to and is the parent body of the Ku Klux Klan."[10] The KKK responded by denouncing Reagan for using his jab at Carter to try and curry favor with black voters.[11]

The remaining exhibit of Reagan's racism for a speech (which was not his opening speech) at the Neshoba County Fair (which was not the site of the civil rights workers' murders) was that Reagan mentioned . . . "states' rights." Obama's official position on gun rights during the 2008 campaign was to say he supported states' rights, and his reelection suck-up to gays on gay marriage is to say it's a states' rights issue. I guess "states' rights" is no longer considered secret code for racism.

WILLIE HORTON—1988

The nadir of dirty campaigning is supposed to be the Willie Horton ad run by George H. W. Bush in 1988 against Governor Michael Dukakis of Massachusetts. Willie Horton appears in textbooks only as an example of how race is used in an ugly way in American politics.

Evidently, most people do not remember the ad because liberals invoke it as if we all agree that it was obviously racist, and Republicans' only response is to say, "Al Gore used Willie Horton first!"

The truth is: It was the greatest, fairest, most legitimate ad ever used in politics. Learn your history, Republicans.

The campaign ad described actual Dukakis policies that had effects on real people, clearly illustrating why Dukakis was the kind of left-wing loon who should never be let anywhere near the White House. It was so devastating that all liberals could do was to cry "racism."

As governor, Michael Dukakis signed a bill eliminating the death penalty. Then, the wacky Massachusetts Supreme Judicial Court—the same court that discovered a right to gay marriage in a document written in 1779 by John Adams, and that kept a manifestly innocent man, Gerald Amirault, in prison for eighteen years—ruled that prison furloughs had to be extended to first-degree murderers, who were never supposed to be released under any circumstances.

The whole idea of prison furloughs is to acclimate prisoners to life on the outside before their release back into the community. It's for check-kiters, drug dealers, extortionists and other convicts serving a term of years—not first-degree murderers like Horton, who were never going to be reintroduced into the community. First, liberals tell you life in prison without possibility of parole is just as good as capital punishment, then they start giving weekends off to lifers. Even the overwhelmingly Democratic

Massachusetts legislature realized the court's ruling was insane, and quickly passed a law prohibiting first-degree murderers from being furloughed.

With great fanfare and the enthusiastic support of the ACLU, Dukakis vetoed the bill. It was this precise veto, showily executed by Dukakis, that allowed a savage murderer, Willie Horton, to be released from prison.

The crime that had put Horton in prison was loathsome: He had robbed a gas station of about three hundred dollars and, after getting the money, stabbed the teenaged station attendant, Joseph Fournier, nineteen times then stuffed his body into a garbage can, where he was found by a friend. This was Horton's second stint in prison, having earlier served time in South Carolina for attempted murder.

But under a furlough policy that existed solely because of Michael Dukakis, Horton was released from prison.

While out of prison on his Dukakis-enabled furlough in 1987, Horton broke into a Maryland couple's home, beat the man, Cliff Barnes; bound, blindfolded and gagged him; stabbed him twenty-two times; and then spent the next several hours raping and slashing Barnes's fiancée, Angela Miller. Barnes listened to it all helplessly from the basement. Miller didn't know if Cliff was dead or alive. Early the next morning, as Horton was raping Miller again, Barnes managed to escape and call the police—twelve hours after he had first encountered Horton in his home. Realizing Barnes had escaped, Horton fled in the couple's Camaro and was captured after a shootout with the police.[12]

The Maryland judge who sentenced Horton—to two life terms—refused to return him to Massachusetts, saying he didn't want to take the chance that Horton would ever be released again. Which was too bad, because Horton had dinner plans with Dukakis during the following month's weekend furlough.

Everyone knew it was crazy to be springing first-degree murderers. Everyone except the Massachusetts Supreme Court, the ACLU . . . and the doctrinaire liberal nut the Democrats were running for president.

After their ordeal, Barnes and Miller flew to Boston to request a meeting with Dukakis. All they wanted was an apology and an explanation. But even after a convicted murderer had used his Dukakis-granted furlough to commit a barbarous crime, the governor refused to admit that furloughing remorseless murderers was a mistake. Dukakis hid from the couple and issued a statement reaffirming his strong support for furloughing first-degree murderers.

The Bush campaign thought voters should know about this. In one of the proudest moments in Republican election history, the campaign produced an ad describing the Dukakis furlough program—the perfect emblem of liberal idiocy on crime.

The furlough ad destroyed Dukakis. It exposed him as the kind of reflexive left-wing zealot who would do something stupid and get us all killed. Dukakis was one of the most ridiculous characters ever presented to the American people as a presidential candidate, and because of the Willie Horton ad, the voters knew it.

There was nothing the Democrats could do. As one Dukakis aide said to a reporter: "OK, you write our response to Willie Horton. You write the catchy phrase. You come up with the 30-second spot. You come up with the jingle. What are we supposed to say? That Horton wasn't let out of prison and that he didn't rape that woman? What the hell are we supposed to say?"[13]

First, Democrats tried lying. They falsely claimed prison furloughs were a Republican policy. It would be like saying prisons are a Republican policy. The issue wasn't furloughs—and it wasn't prisons—it was prison furloughs *for first-degree murderers*. No other state in the union had furloughs for prisoners sentenced to life without parole. That was Dukakis's innovation.

With no place to go, no stinging comebacks, no answers at all, liberals went to their old reliable charge: racism. For those of you who have ever been to our planet, it will not come as a surprise to learn that Horton was black.

But you wouldn't know that from the Bush ad, which went to heroic lengths to hide Horton's race. It certainly did not show a picture of Horton. Rather, in accordance with the stultifying politically correct codes of our day, the Bush campaign did everything possible to hide Horton's race, to the point of showing a "revolving prison door" with all-white criminals passing through it. It was like an Aaron Sorkin production.

Horton's photo did appear in a thirty-second commercial produced by a private group, but the scariest photo in that ad was the one of Dukakis. This ad was seen by about seven people: It ran only on cable and this was back in 1988, when public-access channels had larger audiences. The private group's commercial described Dukakis's furlough policy and Horton's crimes. Only a liberal would imagine that Angela Miller and Cliff Barnes wouldn't have minded being raped and tortured for twelve hours— if only Horton had been white!

And yet the Bush campaign commercial on Horton has gone down in liberal history as the most beastly, monstrous act of racist demagoguery in campaign history. As Peter Brimelow says: "A 'racist' is a conservative winning an argument with a liberal." A Louis Harris poll taken in October 1988 showed that Dukakis's furlough policy had influenced voters more than any other issue in the campaign.[14]

It was the greatest ad in political history, a one-sentence explanation of why people like Michael Dukakis should never be allowed to run any part of government. I'll stop writing about the Horton ad when liberals stop lying about it and conservatives stop apologizing for it.

BUSH'S RESTRICTIVE COVENANT—1988

There was more race mongering against Bush for the Willie Horton ad than any racism in either of the Horton commercials. Five days before the election, the *Washington Post* ran a breathless article about a "whites only" restrictive covenant on a parcel of land owned by Vice President Bush.

Restrictive covenants have been unenforceable in this country since 1948, when the Supreme Court held them unconstitutional in *Shelley v. Kraemer*. The language of such covenants still appears on deeds, principally because, as a legal matter, no one knows how to get them removed. But any restrictive covenant is a dead letter, utterly meaningless. It would be like trying to enforce a contract for murder.

And yet days before the election, a column in the *Post* said that Bush's deed "was not only dirty, it was illegal." Needless to say, Bush quickly denied even knowing about the null and void covenant and denounced such restrictions as "repugnant." But the crackerjack *Post* reporter droned on and on: "It is not 'irrelevant.' It is not legal. It is not smart. It is not cute."[15] If liberals spent less time looking for apocryphal constitutional provisions about abortion and ObamaCare, they might notice that there is an an actual Equal Protection Clause and accompanying case law.

BOB JONES—2000

The imbroglio over George W. Bush speaking at Bob Jones University was about that school's policy against interracial dating. That may have been silly. It may have been theologically incorrect. But it wasn't racist. Whites couldn't date people of other races every bit as much as blacks couldn't date people of other races.

In fact, the policy had nothing to do with blacks at all. The issue arose when an Asian family threatened to sue the school back in the 1950s when their son met and almost married a white girl at the school. So the school banned interracial dating.[16]

Nonetheless, the school's dating policy had been a liberal fixation for decades.[17] Missing in action when there was real racism to fight, Democrats kicked into high gear for fake racism. Merely for speaking to these peaceful Christians in 2000, Bush was ritualistically censured and made to apologize. Which he did. A few months later BJU dropped its nonracist, utterly irrelevant policy banning interracial dating.

Yet that's cited as proof of Republican "racism."

BATTLE FLAG—2000

Like clockwork, every election year the Confederate flag becomes a major campaign issue. This always thrills the Democrats because it finally gives them an issue to run on: their new-found support for the Union side in the Civil War. Which Democrats opposed during the actual war.

Democrats love talking about the Confederate flag because they relish nothing more than being morally indignant. They can't take the moral high ground on abortion, adultery, illegitimacy, the divorce rate, drugs, crime, a president molesting an intern and then lying to federal investigators—or anything else of any practical consequence. Democrats stake out a clear moral position only on the issue of slavery. Of course, when it mattered, they were on the wrong side of that, too.

Bush's big moment of racism was to say, during the 2000 Republican primaries, that the people of South Carolina could decide for themselves what to do about the battle flag. In 2008, when Howard Dean said he wanted to "be the candidate for guys with Confederate flags in their pickup trucks," no one had asked him—he just said it.

Bush hadn't said anything about the Confederate flag, but NBC's Brian Williams demanded that he take a position—coincidentally, just before the South Carolina primary.

WILLIAMS: Governor Bush, a few blocks from here, on top of the state capitol building, the Confederate flag flies with the state flag and the U.S. flag. [Crowd boos.] It is, as you can hear from the reaction of tonight's crowd of 3,000 people from South Carolina, a hot-button issue here. The question is: Does the flag offend you personally?

BUSH: The answer to your question is—and what you're trying to get me to do is to express the will of the people of South Carolina—

WILLIAMS: No, I'm asking you about your personal opinion—

BUSH: The people of South Carolina, Brian, I believe the people of South Carolina can figure out what to do with this flag issue. It's the people of South Carolina—

WILLIAMS: If I may—

BUSH: I don't believe it's the role of someone from outside South Carolina and someone running for president to come into this state and tell the people of South Carolina what to do with their business when it comes to the flag.

WILLIAMS: As an American citizen, do you have a visceral reaction to seeing the Confederate flag—

BUSH: As an American citizen, I trust the people of South Carolina to make the decision for South Carolina.[18]

In a breathtaking bit of legerdemain, John Edwards once said of the Confederate flag: "I had such a strong reaction to seeing it there, the first time."[19] Strong–good, or strong-bad? Journalists didn't ask. Oh, to run for president as a Democrat!

The Confederate flag is a totally synthetic issue that liberals use to slander southerners and insult blacks. Liberals take sadistic pleasure in telling blacks that everyone hates them—except themselves. Trust no one but a liberal, the truest, most loyal friend anyone has ever had.

The Confederate flag is a reflection of the South's warrior ethic that black Americans share more than white New Yorkers. Despite the media's obsessive claims that the Confederate flag is a symbol of racism, in 2001 about 30 percent of blacks in Mississippi voted to keep the 1894 state flag, which displays the Confederate flag in the upper left corner.

What is commonly known as the Confederate flag—by Vermonters, for example—is the Southern Cross, the battle flag Confederate troops carried into the field. It was not the official flag of the Confederacy and never flew over any Confederate buildings. It was the flag of the Confederate Army.

Confederate soldiers fought because they lived in the South—not because they held a brief for slavery. As the historian Shelby Foote described it: "You have to understand that the raggedy Confederate soldier who owned no slaves and probably couldn't even read the Constitution, let alone understand it, when he was captured by Union soldiers and asked, What are you fighting for? replied, I'm fighting because you're down here."[20]

At an abstract level, of course, the war was about slavery, but that's not why the soldiers fought. They didn't own slaves—their honor is really inviolate. And they were spectacular soldiers.

The Confederate battle flag is a symbol of military valor, not racism. Although the South was outnumbered by the North in men of military age 4.4 to 1, was outgunned in firearms production 32 to 1, and had only one-third the wealth of the North, "the south was superior to the north in the intensity of its warrior ethic," as David Hackett Fischer says in *Albion's Seed*. In 1852, there was one militia officer for every 216 men in Massachusetts; there was one officer for every sixteen men in North Carolina.[21]

The Confederate soldiers also fought for Robert E. Lee, who was as much a symbol of the South as the battle flag. Lee opposed slavery and had freed all his slaves. He fought on the Confederate side because Virginia was his home. His men, many of them hungry and barefoot, followed him because of his personal qualities of honor and because they lived in the South, too. When General George Pickett rallied his men before their history-making charge at Gettysburg, all he needed to say was: "Don't forget today that you are from old Virginia."

A small number of blacks served in the Confederate army, presumably for reasons other than their support of slavery. In February 2003, a Confederate funeral was held for Richard Quarls, a slave who had served in the Confederate States Army alongside his master's son and fought in several battles. Quarls's great-granddaughter said he was proud to be the only black person from Tarpon Springs to attend the 1916 National Convention of the United Confederate Veterans in Washington, DC, where he saw the president. He drew a Confederate soldier's pension, which his wife continued receiving until her death in 1951. When he was freed, after the war, Quarls changed his name to Christopher Columbus.

The 2003 memorial service was organized by the Sons of Confederate Veterans and the United Daughters of the Confederacy after Quarls's unmarked grave was discovered. Though Quarls had died in 1925, the service was packed, with about a hundred fifty people attending, including Quarls's descendants, community leaders, Civil War reenactors and Confederate daughters. Also attending was Quarls's great-great-great-grandson, Michael Brown, an enlisted man in the U.S. Air Force. They sang "Dixie." Quarls's great-granddaughter told the newspapers: "He was a proud man and would have been honored to see this."[22]

It is the proud military heritage of the South that the Confederate flag represents—a heritage that belongs to all southerners, black and white. The whole country's military history is shot through with southerners. Obviously boys from all over fought in this country's wars, and fought bravely, but it is simply a fact that southerners are overrepresented in this country's heroic annals.

Among the sons of the South are: Sergeant Alvin York, who received the Medal of Honor in WWI for leading seven men to capture a hundred twenty-eight Germans, including four officers (Tennessee); Audie Murphy, the most decorated soldier of WWII (Texas); General Lucius Clay, commander of the Berlin Airlift (Georgia); Admiral Chester W. Nimitz, Pacific commander in chief of the navy during World War II (Texas); General Douglas MacArthur, who commanded Allied forces in WWII in the Southwest Pacific (Arkansas); General William Westmoreland, commander of U.S. troops in Vietnam (South Carolina); Lieutenant General Lewis Burwell "Chesty" Puller, considered by many to be the greatest marine ever and the only one to be awarded the Navy Cross five times for heroism and gallantry in combat (Virginia); and Tommy Franks, who led the attack on the Taliban (Texas).

The large number of blacks in the military is a reflection of the disproportionate number of southerners in the military.

Freddie Stowers, the only African American to receive the Medal of Honor for his service in World War I, was from South Carolina. After his commanding officers had been killed, Stowers led his combat unit up a hill occupied by the Germans. Stowers and his men took out a German machine gun nest and were advancing toward a second German trench when Stowers was hit by machine gun fire. He kept going. Then he was hit a second time. As he lay dying, he ordered his men to continue. They did, and drove the Germans from the hill. Seventy-three years later, President George H. W. Bush awarded the medal posthumously to Stowers in a White House ceremony attended by Stowers's sisters.

Five black marines were posthumously awarded the Medal of Honor for their service in Vietnam for diving on exploding enemy grenades to protect their comrades. Three of the five were from the South.

The majority of military bases in the continental United States are named after Confederate officers—Fort Bragg, Fort Benning, Fort Hood, Fort Polk, Fort Rucker. Former senator and secretary of the navy James Webb describes southern soldiers in his military novels whispering "and for the South," under their breath when reciting their duty to their country. They go to war not for Old Glory, he writes, "but for this vestige of lost hope called the South." This is a shared cultural ethic among all southerners, not just the "Sons of the Confederacy."[23]

It is pride in the South's military history—encompassing both races— that the Confederate battle flag represents, a pride in values that exist independently of the institution of slavery. The American flag could just as well be said to symbolize slavery: Slavery was legal in the United States for far longer than the Confederate flag ever flew.

Northern liberals and race demagogues try to turn the Confederate flag into a badge of shame, in the process spitting on America's gallant warrior class. As with desegregation, Republicans could have used some of this Democratic dudgeon back when the war was being fought.

SOUTH CAROLINA—McCAIN—2000

The alleged smearing of "the McCain family" in South Carolina was a total hoax. According to the myth, before the 2000 South Carolina primary, the Bush campaign made phone calls to voters implying that McCain had an illegitimate black child. As Linda Wertheimer reported on National Public Radio: "Mysterious callers posing as pollsters asked voters how they felt about John McCain's black child."[24]

That never happened. After a massive investigation by the media into Bush's mudslinging against their then-heartthrob McCain, they turned up nothing. Bush even took the unusual step of ordering the release of all phone scripts being used in the robocalls. Still nothing. And that was with hundreds of thousands of these calls being made, thousands of which should have ended up on answering machines throughout the state.

The closest anyone came was one single email sent by a Bob Jones professor, Richard Hand, to a dozen of his friends, claiming McCain had fathered two children with his first wife before marrying her. Hand did not claim that the children were black. He had no connection to the Bush campaign. McCain had, in fact, adopted his first wife's children from a prior marriage, which Hand simply assumed were fathered by McCain. Hand discovered his error and apologized for his incorrect email before any votes were cast.[25]

It's always the same jumble of fact-free invective repeated to the point of delirium. Liberals say conservatives speak in code to communicate with bigots, but they're the ones with code words for their racist myths—southern strategy, McCain in South Carolina, Bob Jones, Trent Lott, dog whistles, Goldwater, Reagan's kickoff speech, Strom Thurmond's birthday party, the "other," white fear, white picket fences, and on and on. (Also, when liberals say they have gone "duck-hunting," that's code for "antiquing.")

CODE WORDS—LAW AND ORDER, WELFARE

Liberals claim Republicans speak in racist code words for the simple reason that Republicans aren't saying anything that's objectively racist. The idea of looking past people's words and actions to discover some secret motive comes straight from the communist playbook. *The kulaks are bad; the proletariat, good. But wait! Some proletariat don't listen to us—they're bad! They're "lumpen proletariat."* Facts aren't important, it's what is in your hearts. As determined by liberals.

On the *Charlie Rose Show* in 2007, *New York Times* columnist Paul Krugman claimed that "race is central to how the conservative movement got where it is in America today." He said Ronald Reagan's political career "was largely based on tacit race-baiting."[26] Even Charlie Rose took exception to such inanity, and suggested that anticommunism was somewhat more central to Reagan's worldview.

"Well, Okay. If you want," Krugman allowed. "There was some of that." But he barged on, saying Reagan "had passion on two things, communism and welfare cheats. And he didn't have to say what color the welfare cheats were. It just always got through."

That was remarkably stupid, even for Paul Krugman. For those of us who know something about Reagan, his big issues were anticommunism, tax cuts, abortion and small government. Even when he did talk about welfare, it was to criticize government bureaucrats who kept people dependent on government for their own interests.

Thus, for example, in Reagan's famed speech at the Neshoba County fair, he said he didn't believe people were on welfare "simply because they prefer to be there." Rather, he said, it was the welfare bureaucrats who kept them "so economically trapped that there's no way they can get away. And they're trapped because that bureaucracy needs them as a clientele to preserve the jobs of the bureaucrats themselves."[27]

To be fair to liberals, even Charlie Rose was perplexed by Krugman's claim, noting that distaste for welfare might have some rationale other than hatred of black people.

The other big "dog whistle" proving the Republicans' "southern strategy" is any mention of law and order. Why must Republicans prattle on so about crime? It's one thing to talk about crime a little bit. But if you start talking about it too much, you're a racist. (Which is hard to square with liberals' stalwart refusal to acknowledge an inordinately high crime rate among young black men.)

In *Newsweek*, Jon Meacham said that when Nixon "talked about 'law and order,' it was not hard to figure out what he meant." [28] I'm not certain, but I think he meant: law and order.

In the 1960s crime was exploding, the courts were issuing criminal-law decisions to warm an ACLUer's heart and the colleges were exploding with violent student protests. Only a race-obsessed neurotic could think the public's concern about crime was really about racism.

But the "concern-about-crime-is-racist" thesis kept popping up as a statement of raw, irrefutable fact. A few years later, Jonathan Alter wrote—also in *Newsweek*, in case its readers missed it the first twenty-seven times—"In 1968, Richard Nixon used code words like 'law and order' to exploit racial fears as part of his 'southern strategy.'"[29]

So welfare and crime it is! Those are the ground-zero code words, the dog whistles, the irrefutable proof of racism in Republican hearts. We're all agreed on that, yes?

Those also happen to be the two issues liberals tout as Clinton's major policy triumphs. At the end of the Clinton administration, an article in the *New York Times* gushed that he had "co-opted the Republicans' longstanding political advantage on issues from crime to the economy to welfare." It was one of his "striking strengths," the *Times* said.[30]

Why was it racist when Republicans talked about crime and welfare but brilliant policy making when a Democrat "co-opted" those issues?

Two years later the *Times* ran a column by Joe Klein also praising Clinton for being "candid about crime in the inner cities, about the disastrous consequences of out-of-wedlock births and the need for welfare reform."[31] But when a Republican is candid about crime or welfare, it's racist.

There was no new twist to Clinton's crime and welfare policies. As a "third-way," Democratic Leadership Council–admiring, triangulating Democrat, Clinton had merely claimed credit for Republican policies. When Democrats were losing politically on welfare and crime, they accused Republicans of racism. When Clinton capitulated to Republicans on those issues, he was hailed as a genius.

Clinton's sole contribution to the Republicans' welfare bill—besides claiming credit for it—was to sign it, kicking and screaming, and only at the point when it would have been too embarrassing for him not to, having specifically campaigned on reforming welfare.

As for law and order, Clinton's contribution was to harass and stymie the one man most responsible for declining crime rates: New York City mayor Rudy Giuliani. By virtually abolishing crime in one of the nation's largest cities, he brought down the national crime rate. And the entire time he was doing it, Giuliani was hounded by liberals for being . . . guess what? Yes, racist.

In Giuliani's first three years as mayor, the drop in crime in New York City alone was responsible for 35 percent of the reduction in crime nationally. As even the *New York Times* admitted in 1996, Giuliani "has already done as much to re-elect [Clinton] as any Democratic mayor" by lowering New York's crime rate "so dramatically that it has driven down those of the country."[32] Soon other cities were emulating New York's crime fighting practices, multiplying the effects of tough-on-crime policies that began in the mid-1990s under Giuliani.

And how did Clinton help this project? As Giuliani was implementing novel policing techniques that would change the nation, the Clinton administration denounced him as a racist. Democratic attacks on Giuliani's crime policies kicked into high gear in 1999, just as Hillary Clinton was preparing to run for the Senate from New York. In order to dirty up

Giuliani, her then-probable opponent, President Clinton unleashed the Justice Department, two U.S. attorneys and the U.S. Commission on Civil Rights on Giuliani's police.

The accidental shooting of a black man by four New York policemen in early 1999 gave the Clintons an opening. The cops had shot Haitian immigrant Amadou Diallo when he reached for his wallet and they thought he was reaching for a gun. One cop flinched, lost his balance and fell backwards, leading the others to believe he had been shot by Diallo, so they started firing. In response, the entire Democratic establishment wanted New York City put under federal monitors.

A footnote to the Diallo case that has been wiped from the record is that the cops had stopped Diallo because they were looking for a black man who had beaten and raped more than fifty black and Hispanic women in the previous six years, beginning in the Dinkins administration. Two months after the Diallo shooting, the cops caught the actual rapist, Isaac Jones, who looked strikingly similar to Diallo, lived a mile from where Diallo was shot and was heavily armed. The police found a cache of weapons in Jones's car, including a 9mm MAC 11, a .380 semiautomatic pistol and a .22 caliber rifle.

The *New York Times* published more than two hundred articles on the Diallo shooting between the time he was killed in February 1999 and when Jones was apprehended a few months later. In the coming months, there would be hundreds more articles on Diallo. That's almost as many as it published on Mitt Romney's dog. But the *Times* saw fit to mention Isaac Jones—a vicious rapist who had been terrorizing black and Hispanic women until Giuliani's police stopped him—in only one solitary article on page B-4.[33]

Immediately after the Diallo shooting, President Clinton used a presidential radio address to say that he was "deeply disturbed" by allegations of "continued racial profiling."[34] Racial profiling? Black women had identified a black man as their rapist. Hillary piped in with her deep concerns, too—even going so far as to accuse the four officers of "murder." All four were later acquitted by a jury that included four black women.

Two United States attorneys in New York opened investigations into police profiling and use of excessive force in New York City, as did state attorney general Eliot Spitzer.

It didn't go unnoticed that Hillary was gearing up for a presumed campaign against Giuliani as her husband, the president, was siccing federal investigators on the mayor. At a press conference, Attorney General Janet

Reno was asked how Hillary's anticipated run against Giuliani would af-
fect the investigation of the NYPD.[35] Giuliani's spokesman remarked, "We
just hope that all of the Clinton administration officials and Democratic
attorney general Spitzer don't bump into each other as they rush to conduct their investigations."[36]

If the president and his wife were really concerned with the use of ex-
cessive force by the police, they might have started a little closer to home.
There were four times as many fatal police shootings in Washington as in
New York that year—1.14 per one thousand cops to 0.28.[37] At the very
same time, Clinton was helping keep New York City safe by pardoning
Puerto Rican terrorists who had detonated more than a hundred bombs in
New York and Chicago and who vowed to continue their bombing cam-
paign if released.[38]

And that's how Clinton whipped the nation's crime problem.

It's racist for Republicans to actually do something about crime or welfare, but after it works, the Democrats will claim credit, despite having
fought Republicans every step of the way. It's the exact same thing Democrats did with civil rights: They battled Republicans for a hundred years,
and when civil rights were finally achieved, Democrats claimed all the
glory.

The Democrats' only consistent theme is accusing their opponents of
being racists.

JAMES BYRD

In the 2000 presidential race, the NAACP ran a notorious ad suggesting
that Bush didn't care about the dragging death of James Byrd, a black man,
in Texas. Showing a video of a pickup truck dragging a chain, Byrd's
daughter said, "So when Governor George W. Bush refused to sign hate
crimes legislation, it was like my father was killed all over again." Under
Bush, two perpetrators of this heinous crime were put to death and the
least culpable defendant got life in prison. Death! It was surely small con-
solation to them that they were not also adjudged guilty of "hate."

HILLARY LEAVING THE GOP

In 2008, CNN's Anderson Cooper reported that Hillary left the Republican Party after discovering the Republicans' dasdardly plan to win the South by appealing to racists.[39]

Hillary's dash from the racist Republican Party became a gem Cooper would repeatedly present to viewers. Again and again Cooper asserted that it was Nixon's racist southern strategy that sent erstwhile "Goldwater Girl" Hillary Clinton fleeing from the Republican Party. "In the summer of sixty-eight," Cooper said, "she snagged an internship with a House Republican conference under then minority leader Gerald Ford and attended the Republican National Convention in Miami, where the party adopted the infamous southern strategy, exploiting racial tensions to win white voters."[40] It was as if "Appeal to racists" were an actual plank in the GOP platform.

Cooper's interlocutor, Alan Schechter, who was billed as Hillary's thesis advisor, concurred, noting that "if the Republican Party hadn't moved to the right at that time" she might have remained a Republican. (We really dodged a bullet there!)

One expects Cooper to be an illiterate. But Schechter surely recalled that less than a year after Hillary allegedly fled the Republican Party because of its (nonexistent) racism, she was publicly humiliating the first black person elected to the U.S. Senate since Reconstruction. (The earlier ones were Hiram Revels and Blanche Bruce, both Republicans from Mississippi.)

Senator Edward Brooke of Massachusetts, also a Republican, was the Wellesley graduation speaker in 1969—the spring following Hillary's famed exit from the Republican Party. Unfortunately for Brooke, this was also the year Hillary became the first person to give a student address at commencement. She used this honor to attack Brooke's speech. "I find myself reacting," she said, "to some of the things that Senator Brooke said." She then lectured the honored guest, saying, "the problem for empathy with professed goals is that empathy doesn't do anything."

Brooke later remarked, charitably, that Hillary "came that day with an agenda, pure and simple." Hillary's father, watching her bizarre attack on the elected official, said he wanted to "lie on the ground and crawl away."[41] Four decades later, Barbara Walters claimed to have had an affair with

Brooke, marking the second time he was publicly humiliated by a liberal white woman.

Could we review the pure grain alcohol–level insanity of claiming that the "Goldwater Girl" was fine with a candidate who voted against the Civil Rights Act of 1964, but was driven screaming from the party by Nixon's calling for "law and order"? Do liberals even listen to themselves?

With the Vietnam War demonstrations, the peace-and-love generation spawning Charles Manson, Timothy Leary's acid experiments, and the Supreme Court's *Miranda* decision, there was considerably more going on in 1968 and 1972 than resentment of the civil rights movement. Everything wasn't always about the blacks. Except with Democrats. They were either denouncing blacks to get votes or they were denouncing Republicans for nonexistent racism to get votes.

Ironically, Democrats are going back to their demagogic segregationist roots by constantly stirring up racial hatreds to motivate a small slice of the population to vote for them.

Race obsessives in the South were Democrats then, and they're Democrats today. Genuine racists were a distinct minority, but they were a minority that voted on one issue. Opportunistic politicians played to their fears to win 100 percent of the vote of this minority group, giving them an automatic 10-point advantage in any election.

Which party does that sound like today?

Which party's presidential candidate lyingly told them that the U.S. Constitution once considered blacks three-fifths of a human being?

The three-fifths clause had nothing to do with the moral worth of black people or even their right to vote. Rather, it allowed southern states to count nonvoting black slaves and freedmen as part of the population in order to increase the size of their all-white, slavery-supporting congressional delegations. It was southern politicians who wanted blacks to count for more, not less, in order to have more seats in Congress.

The candidate of which party falsely suggested to blacks that as governor of Texas, George W. Bush had not sought the highest penalty for thugs who dragged a black man by a chain from the bumper of their pickup truck?

Two of the three perpetrators were sentenced to death; the third received life in prison.

Which party ran a presidential candidate who made the demonstrably false statement that in the 2000 election "more than one million African

Americans were disenfranchised in one of the most tainted elections in history."

After a six-month investigation into alleged voter disenfranchisement in Florida in the 2000 election, the U.S. Commission on Civil Rights did not find a single black person who had been improperly denied the right to vote. The one million figure is an estimate of the number of spoiled ballots, which averaged about 3 percent of all votes cast in Florida that year.

The answer is: Gore, Gore and Kerry—Democrats. This isn't normal political pandering, like kissing babies and promising to fight for labor unions or prolife causes. These are malicious lies told to black people to make them fear imaginary oppressors, so they will turn to the big, strong Democrats to protect them.

CHAPTER 14

DREAMS OF MY ASSASSINATION

There was a sudden upsurge of racism in America starting right around February 10, 2007, when Obama announced he was running for president. It got so bad that by the end of the year MSNBC was forced to dedicate nearly its entire prime-time news coverage to racism in America.

When Barack and Michelle Obama appeared on *60 Minutes* the day after Obama declared, CBS's Steve Kroft asked Michelle if she were "worried about some crazy person with a gun." I don't recall Laura Bush being asked if she feared for her husband's safety the day after he announced his candidacy. Or ever. But Michelle doubled down, saying, "I don't lose sleep over it, because the realities are that, you know, as a black man, Barack can get shot going to the gas station."[1]

As a black man? The only reason black men are more likely than others to be victims of homicide in America is because of other black men killing them. The danger doesn't come from *being* black, but from *being shot by* blacks. Except Obama didn't live in a public housing project. He lived in Chicago's Hyde Park, where he was no more likely to be shot "going to the gas station" than his white neighbor Bill Ayers.

Unless . . . unless Michelle was talking about the mythical white racists running wild in America, slaughtering black men, putting crack cocaine in their neighborhoods[2] and impotence-inducing drugs in fried chicken, Kool cigarettes and grape soda![3] (These are all actual myths that have been pushed in black neighborhoods, one by U.S. congresswoman Maxine Waters.)

The point was to constantly call America racist—so racist that even a pleasant black man like Barack Obama was at enormous risk in running for president. Then we'd all feel guilty about living in an awful country packed to the gills with racists and vote for Obama to teach America a lesson. Another incidental benefit of the racist assassins myth was that it required that Obama not be criticized—for fear of setting off the racist hit squads.

The media were happy to oblige the Obamas' fantasy of white racists terrorizing black Americans. Obama had the far-left politics of Paul Krugman without looking like Paul Krugman. This made him a precious jewel that had to be protected at all costs, much like a member of the Kennedy family.

Endless news stories told of the grave danger facing Obama because he was a black man running for president. No facts were ever cited. There were none. Instead reporters cited "fears." The fear was so all-consuming that for a while, there were more special reports on the danger of a white supremacist killing Obama than the danger of women dying from anorexia.

It was classic liberal magical thinking: They're afraid, so it must be a national problem. *I couldn't sleep last night, I was so worried about an assassination attempt on Obama! What does that say about this country?* It could either mean the country is racist, or—hear me out—it could mean liberals are neurotic nuts.

It wasn't clear where journalists were getting their information about white people mobilizing to assassinate a black candidate for president. The Secret Service is tight-lipped about security to avoid giving people ideas or revealing the agency's methods. In any event, neither the Secret Service nor any other government agency was ever cited as the basis for these frantic claims.

Rather, journalists quoted one another, invented facts, cited anonymous "reports" and their own fears as evidence that Obama was in a state of mortal danger.

News reports about the heightened danger toward Obama generally consisted of one liberal quoting another liberal about their shared delusions of a burgeoning white supremacist uprising.

Before Obama even said he was running, CNN issued a somber dispatch on the "personal safety factors" in Obama's deliberations, beginning with quotes from Jesse Jackson about his apprehensions when he ran for president ("I had the most sensitivity to the fact that we had to have security at home") and concluding with Obama's aides confirming that "of course, racism and security issues were among the factors Obama and his wife considered."[4]

An ABC News report on the danger to Obama largely consisted of black people denouncing supposed white racists:

> What do these bigots want?. . . . I mean, they don't want a black man to run this country. . . . [T]here are people in our country who are racists. I mean, for us to deny that or . . . when he was talking about becoming a candidate, people around in the coffee houses were saying, you know, he's gonna be an assassination target. I mean, that was the thing, because if he gets that close, then, I mean, that's America.

All we had were liberals' subjective fears, which turned out to have as much relationship to reality as liberal fears usually do.[5] Frank Rich wrote that "the biggest fear" about Barack Obama had been that "a crazy person might take a shot at him." The *New York Times*'s Bob Herbert raised the "widespread" belief that Obama "might be assassinated because of his race" and cited a poll showing "that 6 in 10 Americans said that they were worried that someone would try to harm Senator Obama if he became the Democratic nominee."[6]

In February 2008, Nobel Prize–winning novelist Doris Lessing was quoted far and wide for her prediction that Obama would be assassinated because he is black. She said it "would certainly not last long, a black man in the position of president. They would murder him."[7]

This mysterious "they" apparently failed to activate. Reagan took an assassin's bullet to the chest within two months of becoming president. Just a year after Ford assumed the presidency, two people pointed loaded guns at him and pulled the trigger. Lessing's prediction was just another hysterical liberal fantasy about racist America. We get lots of overwrought predictions about racist Americans, but we never, ever get the admission, *Okay, I overreacted.*

Newsweek reported: "As the wife of the first African American to stand a good chance of becoming president, Michelle Obama is understandably nervous about her husband's safety."[8]

The *New York Times* ran a front page article titled "In Memories of a Painful Past, Hushed Worry About Obama." It began, "There is a hushed worry on the minds of many supporters of Senator Barack Obama, echoing in conversations from state to state, rally to rally: Will he be safe?" The hard evidence just piled up from there: Two sisters "pray daily for his safety," a mother "feared that winning would put [Obama] in danger" and a woman "expressed worries that a message of hope and change, in addition to his race, made him more vulnerable to violence."[9]

Liberals can never understand that their demented reactions to things doesn't constitute proof.

In November 2008, the Associated Press proclaimed in a headline: "Obama has more threats than other presidents-elect." The article admitted that the "Secret Service would not comment or provide the number of cases they are investigating."[10] So what was their source? Mark Potok, a senior fellow at the Southern Poverty Law Center (SPLC) and source of all white-supremacist hysteria, said it was "not surprising that a black president would galvanize the white supremacist movement."

In other words, they had nothing. Less than nothing, actually. Although the AP claimed that "[c]hatter among white supremacists on the Internet has increased throughout the campaign and since Election Day," the AP reporter didn't actually check to see if that was true. In fact, there was no such uptick, according to Alexa, the Internet traffic tracker.[11] As long as liberals liked the point of a story, there would be no fact checking.

A month later, Rachel Weiner warned in the *Huffington Post*: "As America's first black president-elect, Obama is a walking provocation to racists everywhere." Secret Service agents, she said, were "suddenly the only thing standing between the free world and catastrophe." Her evidence was a man-on-the-street saying "some idiot out there's going to put a bullet in that silver-tongued devil and then there'll be a race war."[12]

Never has so much hysteria been experienced by so many, based on so little.

Much was made of Obama's getting Secret Service protection earlier than any other candidate in history. *New York Times* columnist Frank Rich wrote about the fear that Obama's "very presence unleashes the demons who have stalked America from Lincoln to King." He then stated ominously: "After consultation with Congress, Michael Chertoff, the homeland security secretary, gave Obama a Secret Service detail earlier than any presidential candidate in our history—in May 2007, some eight months before the first Democratic primaries."[13]

Similarly, columnist Leonard Pitts announced: "No other presidential candidate, no matter his or her polarizing positions, has felt it necessary to seek protection from the Secret Service. But last week we learned that Obama has sought and will receive that protection, the only candidate ever to do so this early in the process."[14]

ABC News reported that it had "learned that because of an undisclosed threat or threats, plural, the U.S. Secret Service is providing new protection for only one candidate, Senator Barack Obama." Senator Dick Durbin—who was among those requesting protection for Obama—told ABC that the extra security probably had to do with race.[15] If he was the one requesting it, didn't he know?

In the *New York Times* article on the "hushed" worry about Obama's safety, the paper also noted that "Mr. Obama has had Secret Service agents surrounding him since May 3, the earliest a candidate has ever been provided protection."[16]

Nine months after Obama's Secret Service protection had begun, ABC again reminded viewers: "Last May, Senator Barack Obama . . . was issued a full-time Secret Service detail, an unusual event so early in the election season, but one that reflected the potential threat against him."[17]

In January 2009, an article in *Slate* said, "Barack Obama received Secret Service protection earlier than any other candidate in history because of what is euphemistically referred to as 'the historic nature of the campaign' (i.e., the fact that he is a black guy)."[18]

None of this was true. The reason Obama's Secret Service protection started so early was not because he was black. It had nothing to do with the ghosts of Lincoln and King. It was because campaigns start earlier these days. Hillary Clinton already had Secret Service protection as the wife of an (impeached) ex-president. Obama declared he was running for president on February 10, 2007. Three months later, he got Secret Service protection.

Reagan announced he was running for president on November 13, 1979. You know when he got Secret Service protection? The very same day. And you want to know why? For the exact same reason Obama got it: He was a major party candidate and he asked for it.[19]

Drama queen, thy name is liberal.

In an interview with South Dakota's *Argus Leader* newspaper in May 2008, Hillary explained why she was not dropping out of the Democratic primaries, despite angry demands from MSNBC hosts that she do so. She said: "You know, my husband did not wrap up the nomination in 1992 until he won the California primary somewhere in the middle of June, right? We all remember Bobby Kennedy was assassinated in June in California."[20]

A normal person would read that and see that Hillary was pointing out that primaries had often continued well into June, citing her husband's case as well as a famous historic event that everyone would remember happened during June primaries.

Liberals would have been happier if a Republican had said it, but Hillary would do. It was just the provocation they had been waiting for, giving them an opening for another gusher about the dire threat facing a black man running for president in America. (One would think that Sirhan Sirhan, the Palestinian nationalist who shot RFK, would more likely be a campaign contributor to Obama than his assailant.)

There were hundreds of articles about Hillary's monstrous gaffe, although she had said the same thing a few months earlier to *Time* magazine without anyone raising an eyebrow. But this time, the Obama campaign struck, wailing about fears surrounding his historic candidacy. Within hours, *Newsday* cited an Obama staffer saying Hillary was "done" and reported that Obama's supporters interpreted the Clinton remark "as a suggestion the Illinois senator was a potential target."[21] Obama spokesman Bill Burton said Hillary's remark, was "unfortunate and has no place in this campaign."[22]

The *New York Times*'s Bob Herbert said the comment was "tasteless," "purely self-serving" and sent "a shiver of dread through millions."[23] Also in the *Times*, Roger Cohen called Hillary's innocuous reference to the date of Kennedy's assassination, "stomach-turning."[24] The *Washington Post*'s Eugene Robinson called her remark, "ungenuine, unprincipled and insane."[25]

Hillary was forced to apologize and, best of all, her remark led to a "special comment" from the gigantic fruit, suitable for framing.

KEITH OLBERMANN: She actually said those words.

Those words, Senator?

You actually invoked the nightmare of political assassination?

You actually invoked the specter of an inspirational leader, at the seeming moment of triumph for himself and a battered nation yearning to breathe free, silenced forever?

You actually used the word "assassination" in the middle of a campaign with a loud undertone of racial hatred—and gender hatred—and political hatred?

You actually used the word "assassination" in a time when there is a fear, unspoken but vivid and terrible, that our again-troubled land and fractured political landscape might target a black man running for president? Or a white man. Or a white woman!

You actually used those words, in this America, Senator, while running against an African-American man against whom the death threats started the moment he declared his campaign?

You actually used those words, in this America, Senator, while running to break your "greatest glass ceiling" and claiming there are people who would do anything to stop you?

You!

Senator—never mind the implications of using the word "assassination" in any connection to Senator Obama—

What about you?

You cannot say this!

There is no good time to recall the awful events of June 5th, 1968, in Los Angeles, of Senator Bobby Kennedy . . .

There is no good time to recall this. . . . And certainly to invoke it three days after the awful diagnosis, and heartbreaking prognosis, for Senator Ted Kennedy is just as insensitive, and just as heartless.[26]

With less melodrama, this was also the position of the same mainstream media that had been pushing the Obama assassination scenario from the moment he announced his candidacy.

And on it went, until finally, on December 3, 2009, the head of the Secret Service provided the one element that had been missing from all these maniacal reports: actual facts. At a Homeland Security hearing, Secret Service director Mark Sullivan was forced to cough up the truth while being browbeaten by Representative Eleanor Holmes Norton about the unique danger facing President Obama:

REP. ELEANOR HOLMES NORTON: Let me tell you what my concern is, Mr. Sullivan. It is well known, it has been in the press over and over again that this president has received far more death threats than any president in the history of the United States, an alarming number of death threats. I am not going to ask you for the details on that. But here we had the first state dinner, not of just any old president, but of the first African American president. Was there any attempt to increase security, given all you know, which is much more than we know, about threats to this president of the United States?

MR. SULLIVAN: Ma'am, no matter who the president is—

MS. NORTON: I am asking about this president, and my question is very specific. Given death threats to this president, was there any attempt to increase the security at this event? Yes or no?

MR. SULLIVAN: I cannot talk about that. Number one, I will address the threats. I have heard a number out there that the threat is up by 400 percent. I am not sure where that number—

MS. NORTON: Is it up at all? We are not asking for the—

MR. SULLIVAN: I think I can answer you, ma'am. It is not at 400 percent. I am not sure where that number came from, but I can—

MS. NORTON: Well, please don't—

CHAIRMAN THOMPSON: Just a minute. We can't hear the gentleman.

MS. NORTON: Please don't assign to me a number in my question. I just asked you if the threats were up. Are the threats up?

MR. SULLIVAN: They are not. The threats right now, the inappropriate interest that we are seeing, is the same level as it has been for the previous two presidents at this point—

MS. NORTON: This is very comforting news.[27]

The threats against Obama were not up. He was getting the same number of threats as presidents Clinton and Bush had.

It appeared that the principal source of false information about the rise of racist hate groups in response to Obama was Mark Potok of the SPLC.[28] Every few months, he would issue the same news bulletin about increased chatter from white hate groups regarding Obama, and the mainstream media would run all-new stories about racism on the rise against the first black president.

The media so dearly wanted to believe Potok's reports that they never bothered running a simple Internet search to see if they were true. It was like the explosion of heterosexual AIDS we kept hearing about in the 1980s. It was always right around the corner, but thirty years later, we're still waiting for that big heterosexual outbreak.

Steve Gilbert of the Sweetness & Light blog tracked the media's endless repetition of Potok's claims throughout Obama's candidacy and presidency, running their articles next to charts showing that hate group activity on the Web had grown not one iota. Thus, in June 2008, the *Washington Post* reported that Obama's clinching of the Democratic primaries had "sparked an increase in racist and white supremacist activity, mainly on the Internet," citing the SPLC.

While the *Post* went the extra mile to interview the racist leaders boasting about their rising popularity, the newspaper didn't trouble to check their actual Web site traffic. Sweetness & Light did, and it turned out that in addition to being racist nuts, white supremacists are liars.

There was no spike in traffic to their Web sites. In fact, Stormfront's traffic had been on the decline in the months before the *Post* was reporting a burst of activity. [29] As Gilbert said, "according to Google Trends online, interest from regular users in 'white supremacy' has remained about the same over the last year, [i]n contrast to our news media, whose references to 'white supremacy' have spiked twice."[30]

A few months later, in October 2008, *USA Today* claimed: "Supremacist groups are on the rise." It, too, cited the Southern Poverty Law Center.[31] Sweetness & Light again posted charts from Alexa showing absolutely no growth in hate group activity on the Web—at least for all those Web sites big enough to be ranked at all.

Then again, in January 2009, CNN reported that: "Hate crimes experts and law enforcement officials are closely watching white supremacists across the country as Barack Obama prepares next week to be sworn in as the first black president of the United States."[32] SPLC's Mark Potok was cited for the claim that "leaders of these groups are frustrated by Obama's win."

Although CNN acknowledged that there was "no known organized effort to express opposition to Obama's rise to the presidency," it said that the Ku Klux Klan had called for members to wear black armbands. As many as one household did so.

Unaware of the many Internet traffic tracking Web sites, CNN reported that it was "difficult to pinpoint how many people subscribe to white supremacist views, because the Internet allows people to follow the movement under the cloak of anonymity." Again, Sweetness & Light posted Alexa charts showing the white supremacist Web sites flatlining.

In June 2009, Potok was on MSNBC's *The Ed Show*, again warning about increasing white supremacist activity. "We've seen a lot of activity," he said, "really in the last just half year or so. I think the election of Obama has definitely spurred some people to become very angry. I think it's fairly clear, in fact, that this shooter at the Holocaust Museum was angered in large part because of Obama's election."[33]

The Holocaust Museum shooter was James von Brunn, who hated Bush, hated McCain and hated "neoconservatives." He was a 9/11 "truther" and detested Christianity as much as what he called "the Holocaust religion."[34] He is what is known in professional law enforcement circles as a "nut."

Most of the hate group Web sites repeatedly cited by Potok—and recycled in the mainstream media—didn't even have enough visitors to register on Web site trackers. The two that did—Stormfront and the Ku Klux Klan—remained steady or declined since Obama first announced his candidacy.

With so many reporters poring over the hate Web sites, it's amazing the media themselves hadn't created a spike in their readership.

When it comes to claims of racism, empirical evidence is irrelevant. It's not the number of racist Web sites that's important, but their mythopoetic resonance with the master political narrative of the day. If blacks murder more whites than whites murder blacks, it doesn't matter because that's not the story. As racism becomes less of a factor in American life than agoraphobia, the media work overtime to find illustrations—true or not—of their larger thesis.

Even after the head of the Secret Service had stated under oath in December 2009 that there had been no increase in threats against Obama compared to previous presidents, Potok was back on NPR, warning of the rise of white supremacist groups opposed to Obama. "It is worth remembering that while Obama was still a candidate," Potok said, "before he had even, you know, actually been elected, there were two different racist skinhead plots to assassinate him—one in Denver, one in Tennessee."[35]

The Denver "plot" consisted of three methheads with long criminal records driving around Glendale, Colorado, in a rented car, high as a kite, with guns, methamphetamine, wigs and bulletproof vests. They had no agreement, no plan, no schedule and no capacity to get past a 7-Eleven clerk, much less past security at the Democratic National Convention. But one of the delinquents told the arresting officer they planned to shoot Obama when he gave his acceptance speech at the Convention. As the Denver U.S. attorney described it to the *New York Times*, "It was one methhead talking to another about life."[36]

The "plot" in Tennessee involved two unemployed petty criminals who told police they planned to kill 102 black people, decapitating 14, and then assassinate Obama from a speeding car, while dressed in white tuxedos and top hats. The plot didn't get very far inasmuch as they were arrested after shooting out windows in a black church and putting racist graffiti on their car.[37]

I think we're all in favor of locking up deranged criminals (except liberals), but are we now counting the dream journals of druggies and deadbeats as "assassination attempts"?

In 2012, Potok was still at it. MSNBC's Web site on March 7, 2012, said: "The election of President Barack Obama in 2008 triggered an explosion in the number of militias and so-called patriot groups in the United States, the Southern Poverty Law Center reported in its annual tally of such anti-government organizations."[38]

In response, Sweetness & Light again posted the latest Alexa graph, which again showed zero increase, even a slight decrease, in racist Web site activity, as "previously noted."[39]

Liberals have got to calm down. All presidents are in danger and all decent people are horrified at the idea of any president being assassinated. Although liberals could be a little more horrified.

When Bush was president, there was both a book and movie fantasizing about his assassination. The book was reviewed in the *New York Times* and the *Washington Post*.[40] The *Post*'s Linton Weeks calmly stated: "It's a work of the imagination and no attempts on the president's life are actually made." Would that be enough if the fictional assassin's target had been Obama?

The 2006 mock documentary depicting President Bush's assassination won six awards, including the Prize of the International Critics at the Toronto Film Festival. How would that go over if it were about President Obama? Lots of awards?

In 2012—years after Bush had left the presidency and the world was safe under our hero Obama—the HBO show *Game of Thrones* contained scenes with Bush's decapitated head on a pike. The producers claimed it was just a cost-cutting measure because they happened to have Bush's head lying around.[41]

Throughout Bush's presidency, liberals were openly joking about assassinating him.

In 2006, Senator John Kerry responded to Bill Maher's comment that he could have "killed two birds with one stone," by saying, "Or, I could have gone to 1600 Pennsylvania and killed the real bird with one stone."[42]

At the International Women's Peace Conference in Dallas, Texas, on July 11, 2007, Nobel Peace Prize laureate Betty Williams told an audience of about a thousand people: "Right now, I could kill George Bush. No—I don't mean that. How could you nonviolently kill somebody? I would love to be able to do that." She got a standing ovation. Fewer than a dozen newspapers, mostly in Texas, mentioned her wildly applauded statement that she'd like to kill President Bush.[43]

The night George Bush gave his keynote address at the 2000 Republican National Convention, Craig Kilborn on CBS's *The Late Late Show with Craig Kilborn* ran a photo of Bush speaking over the caption, "SNIPERS WANTED."[44]

Though completely ignored by the media, during Bush's time in office, his effigy was hung, decapitated and burned at large public gatherings. T-shirts, bumper stickers and posters demanding his assassination were plentiful at anti-Bush rallies, including "Kill Bush" bags, buttons and stamps, as well as heartwarming pictures of Bush with a gun to his head. Hundreds of photos of these macabre protests were put on the Internet by citizen journalists, at sites such as Zombietime.com.[45]

When Alameda, California, resident and obsessive Bush e-mailer Michael McDonald put a life-size cardboard cutout of George Bush—with a knife in his head—on his front lawn, the local newspaper wrote a fawning editorial on this "patriotic artist." The newspaper said he just wanted people to see his work and to "engage them in thinking."[46]

If an effigy of the blessed Obama were ever hung, stabbed or decapitated at a Tea Party or other conservative event, it would receive more explosive coverage than a Romney fund-raiser in the Hamptons.[47]

The left's fantasy of an attempt on Obama's life was more than the usual liberal preening about how they were blacks' special protectors against racist America. Even liberals couldn't have believed Obama was at any greater risk of assassination than President Bush—probably a lot less, in fact.

It was to insulate a left-wing president from criticism.

Why keep burbling about racists in America and forcing people to admit there are still racists? Of course there are racists in America. What isn't there in America? It's a big country. There are also foot fetishists, trans fat–phobics and people who think a tree is more valuable than a human being.

Martin Luther King Jr. was assassinated by a racist in 1968. But more recently, in 1975, an actual president of the United States, Gerald Ford, was nearly assassinated by a tree-loving lunatic, Lynette "Squeaky"

Fromme—to stop Ford from cutting down the redwoods. Weeks later, bland, inoffensive Ford was again shot at by another crazed liberal, Sara Jane Moore, because, she said, "the government had declared war on the left."

More recently still, President Ronald Reagan was shot by John Hinckley, a kook trying to impress the actress Jodie Foster.

The historical record suggests that presidents have less to fear from white supremacists than socialists,[48] communists,[49] Palestinian activists,[50] crazed environmentalists[51] and run-of-the-mill leftists[52]—who have been responsible for all presidential assassination attempts since at least 1900. Islamic terrorists surely pose a greater danger to any U.S. president than white supremacists, who loom large only in liberal imaginations.

Of course, all public figures have a heightened risk of physical attack in a nation of 300 million people, some of whom are crazy. Presidents are in the most danger of all. But there was absolutely no reason to suppose Obama was at greater risk than any other presidential candidate. Even the Ku Klux Klan—which was being closely monitored by every media outlet from the moment Obama declared his candidacy—had only called for the wearing of black armbands to protest Obama's election. To call racism the main problem in America would be like calling cholera the main health concern. The less we have of it, the more journalists claim it's a crisis.

Liberals weren't especially worked up about the risk of assassination to other prominent black political figures, such as Clarence Thomas, Condoleezza Rice, Herman Cain or Allen West. To the contrary, they seemed to rather like the idea, with crazy CODEPINK women charging Rice at a congressional hearing and mainstream liberals eagerly publicizing slanderous, racist caricatures of Thomas and Cain. In 2012, Democratic operatives began a campaign to publicize the home addresses of Republican congressmen and their families, including black House Republican, Allen West.[53]

There is no purpose to publicizing a public figure's address other than to help deranged crackpots plot a physical confrontation. But liberals only worried about racists when it came to left-wing blacks. The imaginary racists populating liberal imaginations vanished from their memories when it came to conservative blacks.

None of these threats were of the slightest interest to the media. Not liberals' publicizing Republicans' home addresses, not mock decapitations, "Kill Bush" T-shirts, effigy burnings, "Assassins Wanted" on a late-night comedy show, a decapitated Bush head on an HBO program, an award-winning movie about President Bush's assassination or liberals' constant assertions that they'd like to kill Bush.

But during the 2008 presidential campaign, there was a hair-on-fire story about an alleged heckle against Obama at a Sarah Palin rally. The *Scranton Times-Tribune* claimed that someone in the audience shouted "Kill him!" after Palin mentioned Obama's name.

ABC, MSNBC and CNN, among many others, repeated this claim from the *Scranton Times-Tribune*. It was reporter David Singleton's moment in the sun!

This was just the sort of thing the racism hunters had been expecting! A rumored shout at a Palin rally allowed them to shift their terror over Obama's safety to rage at the Republican Party for inspiring violence with their anti-Obama rhetoric. *We are running this wonderful man for president and it's really frightening to hear him criticized.*

In fact, it was so perfect, you'd think liberals had made it up. Which, it turned out, they had.

Even before the Secret Service thoroughly debunked the allegation, it was highly implausible. The non-Fox media were scouring the Earth for dirt on McCain. The *New York Times* had put four reporters on gossip about a McCain affair, and when they turned up nothing despite months of looking, the *Times* printed a front-page story on the affair anyway, quoting the speculation of anonymous staffers.[54] It seems highly unlikely that people were shouting "Kill him!" at McCain-Palin rallies and the *New York Times* decided not to mention it to spare McCain the embarrassment.

Reporter Singleton evidently didn't realize the Secret Service takes such remarks extremely seriously. This time, one of his little pop-offs in the *Scranton Times-Tribune* was going to be fact-checked with a complete Secret Service investigation.

The agents interviewed law enforcement officers, reporters and ordinary citizens who were at the event. Not one supported Singleton's story. A dozen Secret Service agents had been spread throughout the audience, but none of them had heard it, either. Nor could Singleton produce anyone else who heard it or describe the person who had supposedly yelled it. After a massive manhunt, David Singleton remained the only person who claimed to have heard "Kill him!" shouted at the Palin rally.[55] (It's really a shame that reporters can't be outfitted with some sort of recording device capable of capturing such moments.)

Consequently, the Secret Service concluded that it never happened. "We had people all over," agent Bill Slavoski said, "and we have yet to find anyone who said they heard it."[56] As Alex Koppelman wrote in the very liberal Salon.com, "the Secret Service takes this sort of thing very, very seriously. If it says it doesn't think anyone shouted 'kill him,' it's a good bet that it didn't happen."[57]

Thanks to more bogus reporting by the *Washington Post*'s Dana Milbank, the Secret Service was also required to investigate his claim that someone in the crowd at a Palin event in Clearwater, Florida, had yelled—in an amazing coincidence!—"Kill him!" at the mention of domestic terrorist Bill Ayers's name.[58] After listening to tapes, the agents determined that Milbank had heard "Tell him!" not "Kill him!"[59]

If liberals are so worried about Obama's safety, maybe they should stop wasting the Secret Service's time by forcing them to investigate imaginative press reports about nonexistent heckles at Republican rallies.

Dozens of newspapers, TV networks and magazines had breathlessly told the original story about someone yelling "Kill him!" at a Palin rally. The story was repeated hourly on MSNBC. But apart from Fox News and CNN's Lou Dobbs, very few news outlets ever corrected the false report.

It wasn't just excitable journalists who were carrying on about the "Kill him!" hoax. It was repeated by the next president of the United States, even after he knew it was false. During the third presidential debate, McCain complained that Obama supporter, no-longer-a-hero Representative John Lewis, had compared the McCain campaign to "segregation, deaths of children in church bombings, George Wallace."

Obama defended Lewis and raised the issue of the Sarah Palin rallies, "in which all the Republicans, reports indicated, were shouting—when my name came up—things like 'terrorist' and 'kill him,'" and "your running mate didn't mention, didn't stop, didn't say 'Hold on a second, that's kind of out of line.'"[60]

Newsweek's Mark Hosenball called Obama on his baldfaced lie, noting that "even before Obama cited 'reports' of the threats at the debate, the U.S. Secret Service had told media outlets, including *Newsweek,* that it was unable to corroborate accounts of the 'kill him' remarks." Hosenball also said that "according to a law-enforcement official, who asked for anonymity when discussing a political matter, the Obama campaign knew as much."[61]

Obama thus became the second U.S. president to knowingly lie about his fellow Americans by accusing them of racism during a major presidential campaign event being watched by—in Obama's case—sixty million viewers.

The Obama campaign responded to *Newsweek*'s inquiries about the candidate's lie by saying that even if the report wasn't true, "what is true is that the tone of the rhetoric at McCain–Palin campaign events has gotten out of hand."[62] It was just like what radical lawyer William Kunstler had said of the Tawana Brawley hoax: "It makes no difference whether the attack on Tawana really happened. It doesn't disguise the fact that a lot of black women are treated the way she said she was treated."[63]

The Obama campaign was a welter of race-mongering dirty tricks, from outright lies, such as the "Kill him!" fairy tale, to hothouse-flower racial sensitivities, such as the commotion over Hillary Clinton's Bobby Kennedy remark.

It never mattered if any of the Obama campaign's charges of racism were factually true. They should have been true. To cite facts in such circumstances is to impose crime lab statistical analysis on works of imagination and musical charm.

CHAPTER 15

OBAMA, RACE DEMAGOGUE

I read Obama's books to help me understand just what it is that makes black people so afraid. Their demons. The way ideas get twisted around. It helps me understand how people learn to hate.

The above paragraph is a precise paraphrase of what Obama wrote in *Dreams from My Father: A Story of Race and Inheritance,* explaining why he read Joseph Conrad's 1902 classic, *Heart of Darkness,* with "white people" switched out for "black people."[1]

Obama's childhood consisted of a *Beverly Hills, 90210* existence at the prestigious Punahou School in Honolulu (2006 winner of "greenest" school in America!). And yet he still managed to develop a racial hair trigger. Reading about Obama's race fixation in the middle of suburban banality is akin to reading Hitler's obsessive musing on his Germanic identity.

Obama's autobiographies—there's more than one!—are bristling with anger at various imputed racist incidents. As biographer David Maraniss says, Obama sees the world through a "racial lens," presenting "himself as blacker and more disaffected than he was."[2] He's spent his life hungry for reasons to be angry.

Obama tells a story about taking two white friends from the high school basketball team to a "black party." He says they "made some small talk, took a couple of the girls out on the dance floor," but Obama found it disturbing that "they kept smiling a lot." (Probably like Rachel Maddow around a black guest.)

Then, in an incident reminiscent of the darkest days of the Jim Crow South . . . they asked to leave after spending only about an hour at the party! If having your friends want to leave a party before you do is racist, I'm practically Emmett Till.

In the car on the way home, Obama says one of his friends empathized with him, saying: "You know, man, that really taught me something. I mean, I can see how it must be tough for you and Ray sometimes, at school parties . . . being the only black guys and all." And thus Obama felt the cruel lash of racism! He actually writes that his response to his friend's perfectly amiable remark was: "A part of me wanted to punch him right there."[3]

Listen, I don't want anybody telling Obama about Bill Clinton's "I feel your pain" line.

Wanting to punch his white friend was the introductory anecdote to a full-page psychotic rant about living by "the white man's rules." (One rule he missed was: "Never punch out your white friend after dragging him to a crappy party.") Obama's gaseous disquisition on the "white man's rules" leads to this charming crescendo: "Should you refuse this defeat and lash out at your captors, they would have a name for that, too, a name that could cage you just as good. Paranoid. Militant. Violent. Nigger."[4]

For those of you in the "When will Obama play the 'N-word' card?" pool, the winner is anyone who chose page 85 of Obama's first book. Congratulations! As is usually the case, no one involved had used the N-word except the victim-wannabe Obama.

Another illustration of the racial "hang-ups" of white people, according to Obama, was a tourist to Hawaii who, upon seeing Obama swimming as a little boy remarks, "swimming must come naturally to these Hawaiians."[5] It was essentially a verbal lynching. But it was not racism when his Kenyan father praised little Obama for doing well at school, saying, "It's in the blood, I think."[6]

Luckily, Obama married into a family that was also on red alert for incidents of racism to pass down as part of the family lore. Here's the one that was worthy of inclusion in Obama's book *Dreams from My Father*: His wife's six-year-old cousin was told by some nasty little white boys that they wouldn't play with him because he was black—as opposed to the four billion other reasons kids say they won't play with other kids.[7]

The story swept like wildfire through the entire Obama extended family. They'd been waiting twenty years to feel the rush of racial victimhood and finally a six-year-old cousin-in-law of Obama's gave them their racial validation!

At Princeton, Obama's future wife, Michelle Robinson, wrote her thesis on—guess what? "How I Feel About Being a Black Person," which was fast becoming obligatory for every black college student. She wrote to four hundred black Princeton alumni, but only ninety considered the topic of "Being Black at Princeton" worthy of a reply. Robinson expressed disappointment that the ones who did reply didn't have more racial resentment, but had simply gone out and become successful. Being at Princeton was so alienating that Robinson sought to replicate the experience by going to Harvard Law School.[8]

Of course she's angry at her country. She's angry because she knows America, black and white, is snickering at her behind her back. Here she had the opportunity to get a first-class education at one of the world's most prestigious institutions, and all she could think to write about was being black.

In *Dreams from My Father,* Obama explains that the reason black people keep to themselves is that it's "easier than spending all your time mad or trying to guess whatever it was that white folks were thinking about you."[9] Here's a little inside scoop about white people: We're not thinking about you. Especially WASPs. We think everybody is inferior, and we are perfectly charming about it.

He shared with his readers a life lesson on how to handle white people: "It was usually an effective tactic, another one of those tricks I had learned: People were satisfied so long as you were courteous and smiled and made no sudden moves. They were more than satisfied, they were relieved—such a pleasant surprise to find a well-mannered young black man who didn't seem angry all the time."[10]

This forms the entire basis of Obama's political career more than a quarter of a century later.

Note that he was talking about his own mother in that passage. In his much-heralded "race" speech during the 2008 campaign, Obama disparaged the white grandmother who raised him, describing her as mired in racial stereotypes. But as Obama says: "Any distinction between good and bad whites held negligible meaning."[11] Say, do you think a white person who said that about black people could become president? White Americans voting for this guy was like a chapter out of *Men Who Hate Women and the Women Who Love Them*.

The postracial president, who was supposed to allow the country to move past race, mau-maued white America from day one of his campaign.

Indeed, the only firm evidence that there are any actual racists left in America is the fact that so many white people voted for Obama. They must have felt guilty about something. Not harboring any racist impulses, I was free to vote Republican.

Obama's 2008 campaign Web site appealed to every group in America. But not white men. There was a section for Latinos; women; First Americans; environmentalists; lesbian, gay, bisexual and transgendered people; Americans with disabilities; Asian Americans and Pacific Islanders and on and on and on. But there were no sections for either white people or male people.[12] His sole appeal to white men was to offer not to call them racists if they voted for him.

Obama's pandering calculation went like this:

- Women would get abortion and welfare;

- Latinos would get amnesty and welfare;

- Blacks would get a black president and welfare;

- Environmentalists would get no drilling, no Keystone Pipeline, no industrial advancement, and welfare;

- LGBT Americans would get gay marriage and tax breaks; and

- Asian Americans and Pacific Islanders would get affirmative action and welfare.

White men got the possibility of not being called racists.

The status of white men didn't improve after Obama became president. In a 2010 midterm election video sent to thirteen million supporters, Obama said: "It will be up to each of you to make sure that the young people, African Americans, Latinos and women who powered our victory in 2008, stand together once again."[13]

In Obama's 2008 swipe at people in small towns who "cling to their guns and religion" he also called them racist xenophobes. Although generally unnoticed because of the show-stopping "guns and religion" part, Obama said these "bitter" small town people harbor "antipathy to people who aren't like them."[14] Only liberals could attack people who are different from them by saying they dislike people who are different from them.

A few months later, Obama began warning in his stump speech that Republicans were going to attack him for being black. "They're going to try to make you afraid of me. He's young and inexperienced and he's got a funny name. And did I mention he's black?"[15] No Republican had said anyone should be "afraid" of Obama because he was black—the idea is absurd. Race mongering is the Democrats' thing. Obama was so desperate to be attacked for his race that he was launching racist attacks on himself and blaming Republicans.

Amazingly, Obama proclaimed: "We know the strategy because they've already shown their cards"—cards that were apparently so free of racism that he had to race-bait himself. "Ultimately I think the American people recognize that old stuff hasn't moved us forward. That old stuff just divides us." He was both a victim of racist attacks—delivered by himself—and a uniter against those who would make racist attacks!

Over the next month, Obama expanded on his self-race-baiting. Warming to the theme that Republicans were going to attack him because he was black, Obama said, "John McCain and the Republicans, they don't have any new ideas. The only strategy they've got in this election is to try to scare you about me. He's got a funny name. And he doesn't look like all the presidents on the dollar bills and the five-dollar bills." The press took little notice of Obama's claim that Republicans would attack him for being black until July 31, 2008, when McCain campaign manager Rick Davis called Obama on using the race card and "play[ing] it from the bottom of the deck."[16]

For the next twenty-four hours, the Obama campaign pleaded innocence, stoutly denying that Obama's dollar-bill remark had anything to do with race.[17] Maybe he'd be the first Hawaiian on a dollar bill. Apparently, there were limits to the press's credulity and eventually, the Obama campaign admitted that, yes, the dollar bill line was about race.[18]

Liberals went gaga over Obama because he was a very left-wing candidate, whose blackness could insulate him from criticism. The media would simply brand any opposition "racist." It used to be left-wing women who couldn't be attacked. But then Hillary got dumped for the left's trophy wife, Obama. *We're growing apart, Hillary. Obama makes me feel alive and opens a whole new world for me. Can't you be happy for me?* From that moment on, charges of sexism would take a backseat to charges of racism.

During the Democratic primaries, Hillary Clinton was assigned the role of Bull Connor, instead of some hapless Republican.

In March, Geraldine Ferraro, Hillary's finance chair and Walter Mondale's history-making female running mate, gave an interview in which she said: "A woman becoming president takes a very secondary place to Obama's campaign—a kind of campaign that it would be hard for anyone to run against." She said the media had gotten caught up in the idea of the first black president, adding, "if Obama was a white man, he would not be in this position . . . He happens to be very lucky to be who he is. And the country is caught up in the concept."[19]

Obama immediately pounced on Ferraro's comments. He had spent his entire life learning how to assert a black identity for purposes of advancement, and then blew up when Ferraro had the effrontery to mention it. On the NBC *Today Show,* Obama accused Ferraro of engaging in "slice-and-dice politics that's about race and about gender" and "that's what Americans are tired of because they recognize that when we divide ourselves in that way, we can't solve problems." Refusing to give up the mantle of victimhood, Obama suggested, preposterously, that it actually hurt him to be black.

In an interview with the *Morning Call* of Allentown, Pennsylvania, Obama said: "I don't think Geraldine Ferraro's comments have any place in our politics or in the Democratic Party. They are divisive. I think anybody who understands the history of this country knows they are patently absurd. And I would expect that the same way those comments don't have a place in my campaign, they shouldn't have a place in Senator Clinton's either."[20]

Obama campaign advisor David Axelrod called Ferraro's comments "offensive"[21] and demanded that she "be denounced and censured by the campaign."[22] Obama senior advisor Susan Rice called the remarks "outrageous and offensive."[23]

Even Jesse Jackson hadn't played the race card when Ferraro said the exact same thing about him during his 1988 run for president. Jackson simply said, "Millions of Americans have a point of view different from Ferraro's."[24] When you have a faster racial hair-trigger than Jesse Jackson, you might not be the man who is going to move this country past race.

Within days of the Obama campaign's attack, Ferraro was off the Clinton campaign.

A few months earlier, in December 2007, Obama-supporter Andrew Sullivan had written a much-acclaimed article in the *Atlantic,* arguing that the "logic" of Obama's candidacy was not about his policy proposals, political skills, ideology or speaking skills. Rather, it was his ability to be a "transformational" candidate—because he was black.

> What does he offer? First and foremost: his face. Think of it as the most effective potential rebranding of the United States since Reagan. . . . There is simply no other candidate with the potential of Obama to do this. Which is where his face comes in.
>
> Consider this hypothetical. It's November 2008. A young Pakistani Muslim is watching television and sees that this man—Barack Hussein Obama—is the new face of America. In one

simple image, America's soft power has been ratcheted up not a notch, but a logarithm. A brown-skinned man whose father was an African, who grew up in Indonesia and Hawaii, who attended a majority-Muslim school as a boy, is now the alleged enemy.[25]

The young Pakistani Muslim would suddenly realize that we're soft and loveable! Some Americans might have preferred that the Pakistani Muslim turn on his TV and see that America is strong and resolute, but the point was, Sullivan had cited Obama's "brown-skin" as a major selling point. We'd finally prove to the world that we weren't racists!

Isn't that what Ferraro was saying?

Why was the Obama campaign offended by Ferraro's comment that it helped him to be black when all his supporters were saying the same thing?

Not a week after the shock and awe campaign against Ferraro, another Obama supporter was droning on and on to the *New Bedford Standard-Times* about how great it was that Obama was black. The Democrats' 2004 presidential candidate John Kerry said: "It would be such an affirmation of who we say we are as a people if we can elect an African American president."

Kerry also said that Obama could have a moderating influence on the Islamic world "because he's a black man, who has come from a place of oppression and repression through the years in our own country." (Obama was born in Hawaii in 1961.) Still Kerry continued: "We only broke the back of civil rights, Jim Crow, in the 1960s here. Everybody in the world knows this is a recent journey for America too. And everybody still knows that issues of skin and discrimination still exist."[26]

So liberals considered it an advantage that Obama was black. But if anyone *else* said it was an advantage that Obama was black, it was "absurd," "offensive" and "divisive."

The day that Ferraro resigned from the Clinton campaign, also happened to be the day ABC News began revealing sermons of Obama's pastor, the Reverend Jeremiah Wright, who seemed to hate America almost as much as Michelle Obama did.

As Wright's zesty comments about America and white people became known, Obama had to engage in some quick damage control by giving a speech on race.[27]

He began his speech by talking about slavery: "And yet words on a parchment would not be enough to deliver slaves from bondage, or provide men and women of every color and creed their full rights and obligations as citizens of the United States."

All of blue-collar America said, "I wasn't there, I didn't hear any of it."

Reverend Wright and Obama are slavery nostalgics. They have no experience of slavery, lynchings, Jim Crow—anything other than abject white patronization. And yet the further slavery recedes into history, the fresher a memory it becomes!

(Indeed, as the son of a Kenyan Muslim, Obama is more likely descended from slave traders than the average American: For much of its history, the slave trade in Africa was controlled by Arab Muslims[28] and a key slave trade port, Mbasa, is located in Kenya.[29] On the eve of the Civil War in 1860, only 8 percent of Americans owned slaves.[30])

Why was Obama talking about slavery? As liberal blogger Mickey Kaus said: "We know about slavery. We want to know why Obama picked his paranoid pastor!"

In another light touch from his tedious, guilt-inducing speech, Obama compared his raving racist loon of a minister howling *"God damn America!"* to . . . poor Geraldine Ferraro. Just as some saw Wright as "a crank or a demagogue," he said, others saw Ferraro as harboring "some deep-seated racial bias." This was an outrageous smear, tempered only by its silliness. It was bad enough to score a campaign point by falsely accusing Ferraro of racism. To multiply that by claiming her obviously true remark proceeded from the same rancid racism as Reverend Wright's tirades was laughable.

Obama also compared Wright's anger to white people concerned about crime and to his grandmother who "once confessed her fear of black men who passed by her on the street."[31]

Once again, we turn to Jesse Jackson as the voice of reason on race. In a famous 1993 speech to Operation PUSH, Jackson said: "There is nothing more painful to me at this stage in my life than to walk down the street and hear footsteps and start thinking about robbery, then look around and see somebody white and feel relieved. . . . After all we have been through, just to think we can't walk down our own streets, how humiliating."[32]

According to Obama, Jackson is a racist.

It was as if the entire 1980s and the OJ verdict had never happened. Liberal racism detectors were turned on high and we were back to Jimmy the Greek–style instant-career executions for dumb remarks.

Liberal racism hunters hit a gold mine with Don Imus, who is a Mount Vesuvius of dumb remarks. In April 2007, he slimed the Rutgers women's basketball team as "nappy headed hos." (A year earlier, Imus had made an inane, grandstanding, "Stupid White Men" remark to try to get in with the brothers, telling basketball star Charles Barkley—a black man who grew up in Alabama in the 1960s: "In my view, just as a white man, it doesn't seem to me that a lot has changed since those marches in Selma."[33] I think Barkley knows the difference.)

Obama not only called for Imus's firing, but he compared Imus's stupid, comment to the mass shooting at Virginia Tech by a psychopathic student. In a speech about violence the day after the massacre, Obama said there was "another kind of violence"— the "verbal violence" of Don Imus.[34]

Al Sharpton has too much dignity to say something like that.

The OJ verdict had ripped the scales from people's eyes—but Obama put them right back. Indeed, a few years into the Obama administration, Al Sharpton, author of the Tawana Brawley hoax, was given his own show on MSNBC.

After even our racial watchdogs in the media had stopped leaping on every arrest of a black person as prima facie evidence of racism, Obama tried to turn a disorderly conduct charge against a Harvard professor into an incident of racial profiling.

The reader will recall Harvard professor Henry Louis Gates's aggressive reaction to police who responded to a neighbor's call reporting two men jimmying Gates's front door in July 2009. Gates didn't have his house keys, so he and his driver had broken in.

Sergeant James Crowley, a white police officer, showed up—along with a black and Hispanic officer—and asked Gates for identification. Anyone would have been annoyed, but Gates seems to have overreacted a tad, going on a tirade against the officer, accusing him of racial bias and saying the officer didn't know who he was messing with. He followed the officer outside to continue haranguing him, drawing a small crowd. So Crowley arrested the professor for disorderly conduct.

Gates claimed he had been harassed by racist cops, apparently unaware that there are huge areas of the country where people don't think it's heroic to bully cops after you break into your own house, for example, 99 percent of the country outside of Cambridge, Massachusetts.

A few weeks later, as the professor was vacationing in Martha's Vineyard, the black president of the United States accused Crowley of acting "stupidly" for arresting a black Harvard professor, and then going into a long soliloquy about racial profiling. (Also, for the journalists indignant over any passing reference to assassination in connection with Obama, he made a joke about his getting shot by the Secret Service if he tried to break into the White House.)

> Now, I don't know, not having been there and not seeing all the facts, what role race played in that. But I think it's fair to say, number one, any of us would be pretty angry; number two, that the Cambridge police acted stupidly in arresting somebody when there was already proof that they were in their own home; and, number three, what I think we know separate and apart from this incident is that there's a long history in this country of African Americans and Latinos being stopped by law enforcement disproportionately. That's just a fact.
>
> As you know, when I was in the state legislature in Illinois, we worked on a racial profiling bill because there was indisputable evidence that blacks and Hispanics were being stopped disproportionately. . . .

And so on.

Obama kept saying that he didn't know the facts, but he still somehow knew that the incident was an example of racism.

The country exploded in rage at this playing of the race card by the most powerful person in the universe in order to denounce a defenseless white cop, on behalf of a gilded Harvard professor, no less. We finally had a real-life version of the white power structure with all its cruel humiliations—except the power structure was black.

Instead of agreeing with Obama that Crowley had acted "stupidly," everyone wondered what might have happened to the cop if he hadn't been a model policeman, who taught diversity classes and once famously gave mouth-to-mouth resuscitation to a black athlete. They wondered what would have happened if the 911 caller *had* identified the suspected burglars as black—which it turns out she did not. What if Crowley hadn't been fully supported by other cops at the scene, including two minority officers? What if, at some point in his life, Crowley had been accused—falsely or not—of racism? His life would have been ruined.

Gates was tired, he was sick, he was cranky. And he was standing in his own house. Him, we understand. What was enraging was seeing the most powerful man in the universe stepping into the middle of an ordinary dust-up to accuse a white person of racism. That ought to be a serious charge in America.

Another state criminal matter Obama injected himself into was the 2012 claimed self-defense shooting of Trayvon Martin by a mixed-race Hispanic, George Zimmerman. During a White House news conference, the president said, "My main message is to the parents of Trayvon Martin: If I had a son, he'd look like Trayvon."

Obama looks remarkably like Michael LaSane, the kid who killed a white school teacher because he wanted her car, but there's no point in mentioning it.

It was just the encouragement the media needed. Like Captain Ahab searching for the great white whale, journalists are constantly on the hunt for proof that America was a white-supremacist wonderland.

The Hispanic instantly became white. Zimmerman was the villain, so he couldn't be "Hispanic," mixed-race or "Lah-TEE-noh." (We don't call French people *les Français* or Germans *Deutsche*—why are we suddenly speaking Spanish to identify Hispanics?) Liberals seem to imagine black victims heaving a sigh of relief when they're shot by other black people: *Thank heaven I was shot by a black so at least I wasn't a victim of racism!*

Martin's family behaved with the utmost dignity, despite it being their son who had died. Meanwhile, the media charged off, manufacturing evidence and doctoring tapes to whip up a phony race crime. Reminiscent of the KTLA Rodney King edit, NBC edited Zimmerman's 911 call about a suspicious character in his neighborhood to make Zimmerman sound like a race-obsessed bigot.

This is the actual exchange Zimmerman had with a police dispatcher during his 911 call:

> ZIMMERMAN: This guy looks like he's up to no good. Or he's on drugs or something. It's raining and he's just walking around, looking about.
>
> DISPATCHER: OK, and this guy—is he black, white or Hispanic?
>
> ZIMMERMAN: He looks black.

This is the version played on NBC:

> ZIMMERMAN: This guy looks like he's up to no good. He looks black.

The edited version, with Zimmerman reporting nothing more suspicious than a black person in his neighborhood, aired twice on the *Today*

Show, on NBC's Miami affiliate and on its Web page. The truth about NBC's deceptive editing came out only when Brent Bozell exposed it on his *Newsbusters* Web site and Fox News's *Hannity.*[35]

MSNBC gave the story nonstop coverage for two months, but as soon as the murder case against Zimmerman began to collapse, the network buried it at the bottom of the sea, never again discussing the matter in its prime-time programming.[36]

After Obama's false charges of racism against Ferraro, McCain, Palin, and various police forces around the country; Bill Clinton's false accusations of racism against the people of Arkansas and Special Forces; Bob Shrum's sleazy ad in the Maryland gubernatorial race falsely accusing a Republican of racism; Gore's loony claims of racism against Bush and the founding fathers, we didn't need a road map to notice that liberals cry "racism" for political advantage.

But we got one anyway, when, in the summer of 2010, the private chats on JournoList, were leaked, exposing the fourth estate plotting to protect Obama and smear conservatives.

The *Daily Caller* began publishing the once-secret online chats of this members-only e-mail list of liberal journalists, bloggers, activists and professors, that included *Time* magazine's Joe Klein, the *New Yorker's* Jeffrey Toobin and *New York Times* columnist Paul Krugman, as well as staffers from *Newsweek, Politico, Huffington Post,* the *New Republic,* the *Nation,* and many others.

As soon as the Reverend Wright scandal broke, there was a flurry of commentary on how to protect Obama. Chris Hayes of the *Nation* urged members working in the "mainstream media" to ignore the story, complaining that "hand wringing about just how awful and odious Rev. Wright's remarks are just keeps the hustle going."

But the poison-tipped arrow in the journalists' quiver was to randomly call Republicans "racists." Thus, Spencer Ackerman of the *Washington Independent* suggested to his fellow journalists (as if Paul Krugman needed to be reminded) that they should make false racism charges:

> What is necessary is to raise the cost on the right of going after the left. In other words, find a rightwinger's [sic] and smash it through a plate-glass window. Take a snapshot of the bleeding mess and send it out in a Christmas card to let the right know that it needs to live in a state of constant fear. Obviously I mean this rhetorically.

[T]ake one of them—Fred Barnes, Karl Rove, who cares—and call them racists. Ask: why do they have such a deep-seated problem with a black politician who unites the country? What lurks behind those problems? This makes *them* sputter with rage, which in turn leads to overreaction and self-destruction.

When some members objected that it would tarnish the Obama campaign to make accusations of racism, Ackerman clarified: "I'm not saying OBAMA should do this. I'm saying WE should do this."[37]

And that's exactly what happened.

CHAPTER 16

THE MEDIA CRY "RACIST" IN A CROWDED THEATER

As Obama played peek-a-boo with accusations of racism, the media searched for the evidence. Unable to find anything, they flung accusations anyway. Suddenly everything was racist. The word "the" was racist.

A partial list of the many, many words or actions proving a racist heart in the era of Obama are:

- stating the obvious fact that Obama was helped by his race;

- running a campaign commercial against Obama;

- mentioning that Obama's friend is Bill Ayers, a domestic terrorist;

- not electing Obama president;

- Scott Brown's pickup truck;

- opposing Obamacare;

- opposing Obama's stimulus bill;

- opposing Obama's jobs bill;

- joining the Tea Party;

- using Obama's middle name;

- demanding to see Obama's birth certificate;

- arresting a black Harvard professor;

- being a Republican;

- supporting gun rights;

- requesting documents from Attorney General Eric Holder in the administration's Mexican gun-dumping scandal;

- voter identification laws;

- references to Obama playing basketball;

- using the phrase "kitchen cabinet" in relation to a black person.

- the word "the."

The word "the" made the racist hit parade when Donald Trump said he had a "great relationship with *the* blacks." Ditto with basketball references—also from Trump, after he advised Obama to get off the basketball court and deal with high oil prices. (Obama does play basketball a lot. Trump wasn't inventing that.)

But the main proof of racism was any criticism of Obama. The media's racism divining rod brought back all the worst elements of society that flourished before the OJ verdict.

THE McCAIN PALIN CAMPAIGN

The Associated Press reported that Sarah Palin's description of Obama "palling around with terrorists carried a racially tinged subtext that John McCain himself may come to regret."[1] If AP read the news, it would know that Palin was referring to Bill Ayers, the white, privileged, upper middle class member of the Weather Underground who bombed the Pentagon and the Capitol.

When the McCain campaign ran a surprisingly effective commercial in 2008, that was called racist, too. The ad, titled "Celeb," began with clips of crowds ecstatically cheering Obama, followed by photos of Britney Spears and Paris Hilton, as the narrator called Obama "the biggest celebrity in the world." Then, the music turned ominous, and the narrator listed Obama's high-tax policies and opposition to offshore drilling, before saying that this was "the real Obama."

It must have taken hours to come up with something racist about that ad, but Jonathan Alter and Keith Olbermann set their minds to it and finally found it:

ALTER, *NEWSWEEK* COLUMNIST AT THE TIME: "The larger issue, I think, is clear—which is they're trying to portray him as being uppity. Now, is that racist? I'm not sure."

OLBERMANN: "Well if we're playing Password, if you say 'uppity,' the word that comes into my mind, that's racist, yes."[2]

Wait—who said "uppity," again? Did any Republican call Obama uppity? No. Did the ad call Obama uppity? No. ALTER SAID "UPPITY." *It's about Obama's uppitiness. That much we know. Is that racist? That's for the public to decide. I remain neutral.*

The ad had nothing to do with Obama being uppity. It was nearly the opposite, comparing him to lightweight celebrities.

CBS News's Katie Couric referred to the "Celeb" ad as "infamous," and reporter Dean Reynolds said McCain's new tone in the ad "appears to conflict with some of his more high-minded talk of the need for civility on the stump."[3]

NOT VOTING FOR OBAMA

Throughout the 2008 campaign, liberals sagely informed us that America would never make a black man president. In a cast of thousands, *Slate* magazine's Jacob Weisberg said that only if Obama won the election would children in America be able to "grow up thinking of prejudice as a nonfactor in their lives." But if he lost, Weisberg continued, "our children will grow up thinking of equal opportunity as a myth. His defeat would say that when handed a perfect opportunity to put the worst part of our history behind us, we chose not to."

Why weren't liberals worried about what children would think if Clarence Thomas's Supreme Court nomination had been defeated? No, no—only electing the most liberal person ever to seek the presidency on a major party ticket would prove that the country could "put its own self-interest ahead of its crazy irrationality over race."[4]

And guess what? Weisberg was right! Obama won and we haven't heard another peep about racism.

Not only did Obama win, he got 43 percent of the white vote—the highest of any Democrat running for president in a two-man race since 1976. Still, liberals detected racism. Immediately after whites had been mau-maued into electing the most left-wing president in U.S. history to prove they weren't racists, *Slate*'s Tim Noah was consternated that white people hadn't given a *majority* of their votes to the black candidate. The fact that McCain received 53 percent of the white vote, Noah said, was "a hidden-in-plain-sight phenomenon that warrants greater attention."[5]

The white vote for McCain, Noah said, proved that whites couldn't forgive Democrats for abolishing Jim Crow. Which the Democrats didn't abolish. Which Democrats created and preserved. And which Republicans abolished over the ferocious objections of a bunch of Democrats.

Meanwhile 96 percent of blacks voted for Obama after careful attention to the issues without any notice of race.[6] But Noah didn't think that black people's one-party vote was "a hidden-in-plain-sight phenomenon that warrants greater attention."

Then, in 2012—which happened to be a presidential election year—the *New York Times* was again promoting the theory that a vote against Obama was prima facie proof of racism.

The *Times* published the results of a "racism" study by Seth Stephens-Davidowitz that first looked for the areas of the country with the most searches for racist words and jokes on Google, and then—after excluding searches originating from Jonathan Alter and Keith Olbermann's apartments—compared the vote for Kerry and Obama in Wheeling, West Virginia (the seventh most "racist" city), to the vote in Denver, Colorado (the fourth most enlightened city).[7]

John Kerry won about 50 percent of the vote in both cities in 2004, but, four years later, while Denver voted for Obama by 57 percent, Wheeling gave Obama only 48 percent of its votes.

First of all, why are we not supposed to conclude that 7 percent of white people in Denver harbor such racist prejudices that they believed the only way to cleanse themselves was to vote for the first black president? Why else vote for Obama when you didn't vote for Kerry? Was Kerry too arrogant for them?

Second, it is simply assumed, at places like the *Times*, that only one dimension was at play in the 2008 election: Obama's race. Isn't this the sort of simplistic thinking normally associated with red-state voters?

The Stephens-Davidowitz study failed to consider, for example, the fact that Obama was the most fabulous, celebrity-backed candidate for president in recent memory. That sort of thing probably matters more to people in Denver than in West Virginia.

Not only that, but on November 2, 2008, two days before the election, Obama vowed to bankrupt the coal industry. He had actually dropped that bombshell in an interview with the *San Francisco Chronicle* much earlier in the year, but the tape was only revealed to the public days before the election.

Obama had told the Chronicle that under his "aggressive" cap and trade plan "if somebody wants to build a coal-powered plant, they can. It's just that it will bankrupt them, because they're going to be charged a huge sum for all that greenhouse gas that's being emitted."

Although the *New York Times* neglected to mention Obama's plan to bankrupt the coal industry, the tape was played many times on Fox News,[8] it was all over the Internet[9] and covered heavily in West Virginia newspapers.[10]

Mr. Stephens-Davidowitz probably wouldn't know this, but West Virginia's economy is extremely dependent on coal, providing 99 percent of the energy and 60 percent of all business taxes in the state. The average West Virginian is as well informed about the coal industry as the typical *New York Times* reporter is with the president's position on gay marriage.

The real way to test Mr. Stephens-Davidowitz's theory about West Virginians would be to run a nonflashy black candidate who had not pledged to destroy the coal industry and then compare votes.

Be that as it may, wishing to replicate Mr. Stephens-Davidowitz's experiment and bolster his results, I have compared different states' participation in the military, an institution with a high degree of racial mixing, to determine the most racist states. The surest evidence of a person's level of racial tolerance isn't a joke search, but his willingness to live in close quarters with people of other races. Residing cheek-by-jowl with black people in military barracks would be hell for racists!

Here are the study's results: The least racist states were Montana, Texas, Wyoming, Alabama, Alaska and Idaho, and the most racist were Massachusetts, New York, Connecticut, and Vermont.[11] The most racist areas of the country are Marin County, closely followed by New York City and Malibu. Of course, we can't tell the race of those joining the military from these areas (Marin County: 0.0 percent black), but nor can we tell the race of those searching for racist jokes in Mr. Stephens-Davidowitz's study.

The *New York Times* had told me the opposite was true—that West Virginians were so racist they would happily vote for a white person who promised to destroy the coal industry, but not a black one!

SUPPORTING THE TEA PARTY

The Tea Party, being composed of millions of Americans strongly opposed to Obama's policies, came in for some of the most fervid accusations of racism.

According to a batch of polls taken about the Tea Party movement in 2010, about a quarter of all Americans called themselves Tea Party supporters. (*USA Today* poll: 28 percent; *New York Times*/CBS poll: 18 percent.)[12] They were wealthier and better educated, but not much whiter than the nation as a whole.[13] (According to Gallup, Tea Party supporters were 79 percent white in a country that is 75 percent white. Less than half—49 percent—were Republicans.[14]) They were united only in believing the government was too big and Obama was taking it in a socialist direction.

Rasmussen polls showed that a majority of voters held a favorable opinion of the Tea Party movement, up to 58 percent by April 2010. By contrast, 98 percent of the political class had an unfavorable view of the Tea Partiers.[15]

It was time to panic. The media had to act fast to make the Tea Party movement toxic. So they called it racist. You might get off with a warning once, but if the media caught you agreeing with the Tea Party again, then you'd be a racist, too.

To be sure, there were a lot of white people at the Tea Parties. At no point did it flicker across liberal brains that protests against the first black president probably wouldn't draw a lot of black people, even apart from the fact that most blacks are Democrats. How many white evangelicals do Democrats have at their rallies? Complaints about Tea Partiers being white was reminiscent of the headline from the satirical magazine the *Onion,* September 20, 1990: "Iowa Family Blasted for Lack of Diversity: Exclusionary, All-White Petersons 'Deeply Offensive,' Say Activists."

This is the kind of thinking we get from people churned out by our educational system. Anything that is not "diverse" must be bad. *If Israel is such a great place, where are the Nazis?*

Unfortunately for the media, but fortunately for the country, no one was ever able to produce evidence of the much-ballyhooed Tea Party racism. We keep batting averages around here.

So the media lied. As with the endless stream of racist incidents from the seventies and eighties, all the examples of Tea Party racism triumphantly produced by the media turned out to be phony.

There were three basic categories of false "racism" charges:

1. Things that never happened;

2. Liberal infiltrators pretending to be racist Tea Partiers; and

3. Ludicrous claims of racism about anything liberals didn't like.

IT DIDN'T HAPPEN

Because many journalists are zealots, they never hesitated to believe every vile calumny about the Tea Party.

Hoping to provoke an ugly confrontation with the Tea Partiers, whom everyone kept calling racist, on the day of the Obamacare vote, Speaker of the House Nancy Pelosi marched members of the very liberal black caucus right through the middle of protesters on Capitol Hill. But the protesters didn't oblige the speaker by acting racist, so the media just lied and claimed they did.

A hue and cry went up about Representative Emmanuel Cleaver allegedly being spat on, but when video evidence proved that false, Cleaver walked back his claim.

Most outrageously, the non-Fox media said Representative John Lewis had been called the N-word fifteen times. Fifteen. I guess if you're going to invent an N-word story, you may as well go for the gold.

The protesters vehemently disputed that anyone had called Lewis the N-word, and commentator Andrew Breitbart promptly put up a $100,000 reward for anyone who could produce a video of it. Despite the media's desperate quest for anti-Obamacare racism and hundreds of cameras at the protest, no one has ever been able to produce a video of the N-word being used. To this day, the reward remains uncollected. (If only journalists had cell phone cameras!)

No matter: Hundreds of news stories on TV, in newspapers and on the Web have repeated this lie, despite the absence of evidence that it happened. On MSNBC's *The Ed Show,* Salon.com's Joan Walsh was indignant that anyone would question "whether John Lewis heard the N-word."[16] Except Lewis didn't claim he heard it. Others claimed it on his behalf.

The media kept playing bait-and-switch with the racism charges.

We have definite proof they're racist! The protesters spat on one black congressman!

Show us.

All we brought was the Stalin sign.

Where's the racist stuff?

I must have left it in the car. I'll try to remember to bring it tomorrow.

They are making the case—where's the evidence? There's nothing.

It's great that the media don't need proof. Journalists hold themselves to a Tawana Brawley truth standard. Using that criterion, why is no one talking about Chris Matthews's gay porn collection?

According to Nexis, the lie about Lewis being called the N-word has been repeated dozens of times, even long after Breitbart conclusively demonstrated it didn't happen. How many times is Chris Matthews—whose gay porn collection is way out of control—going to get away with this? How about Ed Schultz, who dates underage girls? Or Rachel Maddow, who has a major heroin problem?

These claims are based on the precise quantum of evidence that they have for the claim that anyone at the anti-ObamaCare rally called Rep. Lewis the N-word—actually less, since my slurs haven't been thoroughly investigated and disproved.

Liberals smeared vast swaths of the country for failure to go along with the whole Obama agenda. In response to slanderous attacks on the Tea Party activists as racists, a number of conservative television pundits thought it was a great retort to say: "There is the fringe on both sides."

Gee, thanks. Of course, since no one in the media was suggesting that liberals are racists, these idiots had just admitted that some conservatives were racists. Liberals have never been able to produce a single example of this alleged conservative racism, but the best our spokesmen can come up with when defamed as racists is: "Man is imperfect." Perhaps later in the taxi home, they think to themselves, "You know what I should have said? It might have been better to say 'That's a complete lie.'"

Republicans have to be trained that when they are falsely accused of racism, the proper response is: *You are a liar. That never happened.*

How about trying that?

LIBERAL INFILTRATORS

The liberal infiltrators at conservative events were always like guys who do bad gay impressions—a little too flamboyant to be believable.

Tyler Collins, liberal infiltrator at a Rand Paul event in August 2010, claimed to be a supporter of the Republican candidate chirping, "the Rand Paul campaign is a little bit racist" and calling Dora the Explorer an illegal immigrant who was "corrupting our children." He certainly enjoyed being interviewed! Collins was caught later that day, walking with supporters of Paul's opponent.[17] Then it turned out he had also written an incoherent column in a local newspaper two months earlier attacking the Tea Party.[18]

In July 2010, the George Soros–backed Center for American Progress produced a video purporting to show racism at Tea Parties. Most of the forty-three-second video showed innocuous signs, such as one saying, GOD BLESS GLENN BECK; or old clips before there was a Tea Party, such as a random man calling illegal aliens "wetbacks" in 2006; or loopy, but non-racist, signs and statements. There was only one racist clip in the entire 43-second video, so it was showed twice. It was a well-known liberal infiltrator bellowing "I'm a proud racist!"

The full video of this wacko had been posted by the Tea Partiers themselves to identify the man as a liberal plant. In the original video, the Tea Partiers surround the infiltrator, jeer at him, tell him he isn't one of them and to please go home. In a spectacularly evil fraud, Soros's people used the video, but edited all that out.[19]

Only one TV program presented the full video: Fox News's Glenn Beck show.[20] (That's probably why the Tea Partiers wanted God to bless him.)

On the very day Beck had shown the video of Tea Partiers ejecting the liberal acting like a racist—we'll generously assume he was acting—Chris Matthews announced on his show that he would believe the Tea Partiers weren't racist as soon as "just one of those Tea Party people pull down one of those racist signs at the next Tea Party rally. I'm going to just wait. Reach over, grab the sign and tear it out of the guy's hands. Then I will believe you."[21] Forget the sign, how about throwing the racist liberal out? That's what actually happened, so the media didn't report it.

IT WASN'T RACIST

Then there were the examples of putative right-wing racism that had absolutely nothing to do with race.

In August 2009, the media hysterically warned that people were bringing rifles to protests against the *first black president*. As MSNBC's Contessa Brewer put it: "Here you have a man of color in the presidency and white people showing up with guns." She continued ever more frantically, "there are questions about whether this has racial overtones . . . white people showing up with guns."

The network's culture commentator, Touré, said there was a lot of "anger about a black person being president," adding, "I'm not going to be surprised if we see somebody get a chance and take a chance and really try to hurt him." MSNBC's Dylan Ratigan concurred: "Angry at government and racism, you put those two together . . ."[22]

And sure enough, all over TV and the Web, there was a photo of a man carrying a rifle! But it was edited strangely, zooming in on the rifle, but cropping out the person holding it. When the photo was expanded on various media-watch Web sites, the armed man turned out to be . . . an African American Second Amendment supporter.

In response to Second Amendment rallies on April 19, 2010—which no one at MSNBC knows is the anniversary of the battles of Lexington and Concord—Ed Schultz claimed that the participants were rallying "on the fifteenth anniversary of the Oklahoma City bombing." He said they "are embarrassing Caucasians in this country. I'm upset that we just can't come to grips that we have a black president." Demonstrating liberals' famed racial tolerance, Schultz sneered: "They're the base. They're old. They're angry. They're white. They're scared. They're misinformed. They watch Fox."[23]

Unless the Second Amendment defenders told Ed, "Oh yes, absolutely our rally was to honor the Oklahoma City bombing—we had no idea it was the anniversary of Lexington and Concord," I'm fairly certain April 19 was chosen because it was the day the American rebels defended their armaments from British confiscation in the battles of Lexington and Concord.

What on earth does supporting gun rights have to do with not being able to "come to grips that we have a black president"?

VOTER ID LAWS

In 2011, the *New York Times* claimed in an editorial that laws requiring people to show photo identification before voting was "a modern whiff of Jim Crow."[24]

Congresswoman Debbie Wasserman Schultz, chairperson of the Democratic National Committee, said on TV that voter ID laws were proof that Republicans "want to literally drag us all the way back to Jim Crow laws and literally—and very transparently—block access to the polls to voters who are more likely to vote for Democratic candidates than Republican candidates. And it's nothing short of that blatant."[25]

From the end of the Civil War until the passage of the voting rights act in 1965, Republicans were the ones registering blacks to vote, while Democrats were blocking their vote. That's why the first black members of Congress from the South were all Republicans. The only people Republicans have tried to prevent from voting are those ineligible to vote. Now that blacks are voting for the Democrats, there's no one to stop them from voting.

The claim that modern voter ID laws were a racist Republican plot was complicated by the fact that, in 2011, such a law was enacted by Rhode Island's 85 percent Democratic legislature. The law drew its strongest support from black and Latino legislators, who cited specific examples of voter fraud.[26]

The Senate's only black member, Democrat Harold Metts, pushed the voter ID bill, saying he'd heard complaints about election fraud for years. One poll worker told him about a voter who hadn't been able to spell his own last name. In the House, the bill was supported by a black Democrat, Anastasia Williams, who had shown up to vote in 2006 and was told that she had already voted.[27] A few years later, she said she watched as a Hispanic man voted, went to the parking lot to change his clothes, and then voted again. (She said she noticed him because he was "a hottie.")[28]

As the Democratic Rhode Island legislature deliberated its voter ID bill, national Democrats begged them not to pass the bill. Wasserman Schultz called state legislators directly, asking them to kill the bill.[29]

Harold Metts and Anastasia Williams were unmoved by the national Democrats' hysteria. The bill passed, prompting liberal periodicals such as the *New Republic* to suggest that the state's African American Democrats were anti-Hispanic. Liberals are incapable of formulating an argument without accusing someone of racism. *We don't like this, so who's the racist?*

Even with Rhode Island Democrats citing specific instances of voter fraud, the *New Republic* stated, "voter impersonation has never been proven."[30] What does that mean? Do they need a signed confession?

If eyewitness accounts of voter fraud given by black Democrats isn't enough, how about a 98.2 percent voter registration in St. Louis, Missouri? Does that sound believable? How about twenty-nine voting districts in Missouri having more registered voters than voting-age people—including one county where 151 percent of the voting-age population was registered to vote in 2004?[31]

OBAMA'S MIDDLE NAME AND BIRTH CERTIFICATE

The strangest "racism" allegation concerned the use of Obama's middle name and demands to see his birth certificate.

It wasn't that "Hussein" was a black middle name: It was that it was the same name as the dictator we had just deposed in a war. It would be as if Thomas Dewey, running against FDR in 1944 and Harry Truman in 1948, had been named "Thomas Hitler Dewey." That doesn't have anything to do with race.

The birth certificate brouhaha was started by Hillary Clinton during the Democratic primaries and was quickly shot down by every respectable conservative opinion journal, including *Human Events,* the *American Spectator, National Review* and the Sweetness & Light blog.

But it was crazy to suggest that the birth certificate issue was "just another form of racism"[32] (Ed Schultz) or "borderline-racist garbage" (Rachel Maddow's blog)[33] among many other liberals claiming the birth certificate issue was racist.

Do liberals think African Americans are foreigners? Illegal immigrants perhaps?

Black people have been in the United States as long as the earliest white settlers—before the *Mayflower* arrived, with the first Africans in Virginia appearing in 1619.[34] The descendants of slavery have an American pedigree that is centuries older than the average American today.

But liberals take the position that if a conservative said it, it must be racist and reason back from there. It got to the point where some Tea Partiers began carrying signs that said, "No matter what I put on this sign, you're going to say it's racist."

JIMMY CARTER SAYS SO

In September 2009, Keith Olbermann opened his show with a breaking news bulletin: Jimmy Carter—"the 39th president of the United States"— had said: "I think an overwhelming portion of the intensely demonstrated animosity toward President Barack Obama is based on the fact that he is a black man, that he's African-American."[35]

Ah ha! What do you have to say now, racist deniers?

Who cares what Jimmy Carter says? It was as if Keith were producing a scientific study. At MSNBC, they simply can't grasp the difference between opinion and evidence. The Jimmy Carter quote amounted to Keith's saying, "Someone I think is really cool agrees with me, therefore, you have to acknowledge you're wrong." I think the more common line of reasoning would be: If, at any point Jimmy Carter agrees with me, I must be wrong.

SCOTT BROWN'S PICKUP TRUCK AND THE "KITCHEN CABINET"

In 2010, Scott Brown's pickup truck came in for a charge of racism. Olbermann said that what Scott Brown voters truly opposed was having "an African American president." When this insane point was met with gentle resistance from Howard Fineman, Keith produced the smoking gun: "What were the Scott Brown ads, though? Every one of the Scott Brown ads had him in a pickup truck."[36]

Unheralded civil rights hero Olbermann also detected "racist messages" coming from Rush Limbaugh, which he claimed had led many people to react "with just shock that anybody would say that in public."

Limbaugh had called Obama . . . a "Halfrican-American."

You could get that past the NAACP. Unable to explain what exactly was "racist" about anything Rush had said, Olbermann called it "sleek racism." Glenn Beck's statement that Obama appeared "colorless" to him, Olbermann called "an even slicker racism."[37]

Should there be civil rights statues to Keith? Because I've never heard a black person mention him.

In 2012, Mark Thompson, a guest on MSNBC's *Last Word with Lawrence O'Donnell* said that Mitt Romney's description of a black advisor as being in his "kitchen cabinet" was racist. "To talk about being in the kitchen" he said, "is really not a good metaphor to use with African-Americans." The phrase "kitchen cabinet" to mean informal advisors was coined in the early 1800s in reference to President Andrew Jackson, who was incidentally, a racist Democrat.[38]

Liberals' racism meter in the Obama era was even more delicately tuned than the racist "microaggressions" in the *American Psychologist*, ridiculed by Manhattan Institute scholar John McWhorter. As he summarized the designated "microaggressions":

> Say to someone, "When I look at you, I don't see color" and you "deny their ethnic experiences." You do the same by saying, "As a woman, I know what you go through as a racial minority," as well as with hate speech, such as "America is a melting pot." Other "microaggressions" include college buildings being all named after straight, white rich men (I'm not kidding about the straight part).

This is what "racism" had come to. As McWhorter said, "It'd be interesting to open up a discussion with a Darfurian about "microaggressions."[39]

CODE WORDS

When Republicans say something a team of scientists could study without finding racism, liberals say the Republicans are using code words.

Not only photos of Paris Hilton and Scott Brown's pickup truck, but standard Republican positions on small government, low taxes and tough-on-crime policies are supposed to be proof of racism. That's convenient. Since there is nothing objectively racist about these policy stances, liberals explain that they are "dog whistles" "slick racism," "subtle racism" or "code words" that secretly convey: "I hate black people."

This is as opposed to liberals who actually make racist statements all the time—but they have good hearts, so it doesn't count.

We had Biden calling Obama "the first mainstream African American who is articulate and bright and clean." Senator Harry Reid praised Obama for not having a "negro dialect, unless he wanted to have one," while Bill Clinton said a few years ago, Obama "would have been getting us coffee."[40] Former CBS newsman Dan Rather said the argument against

Obama would be that "he's very articulate . . . but he couldn't sell water-melons if you gave him the state troopers to flag down the traffic."[41]

But because they are liberals, their use of actually racist phrases be-comes code for "I love black people!"

As French philosopher Jean-François Revel said of the left, while most regimes are judged on their records, only communism is judged only by its promises. Similarly, modern liberals are judged on their motives; conser-vatives are judged on what liberals claim we really meant.

The Tea Party was held responsible for every single person who showed up at their rallies, including random nuts or liberal infiltrators as if it proved something about the whole movement. Meanwhile, the explosion of sexual assaults, drug overdoses and property damage at Occupy Wall Street events were never thought to impugn the admirable motives of that group. (The first month of Occupy Wall Street protests included more than a dozen sexual assaults; at least half a dozen deaths by overdose, suicide or murder; and millions of dollars in property damage.[42])

Hordes of young liberal nitwits sport T-shirts featuring Che Guevara, a vile racist who described blacks as "indolent," spending their "meager wage on frivolity or drink" who lack an "affinity with washing." This isn't a big secret: He wrote it in his book *The Motorcycle Diaries*. No one calls the liberal nitwits racist.

When it comes to black conservatives, liberals drop the subtlety and tell us that blacks are stupid, unqualified and oversexed. It's as if all the fake fawning over black nonentities creates a burning desire in liberals to call some black person an idiot—and all that rage gets dumped on black con-servatives.

Democratic Senator Harry Reid called Clarence Thomas "an embar-rassment to the Supreme Court," adding, "I think that his opinions are poorly written." Name one, Harry.

White liberal *Washington Post* reporter Mary McGrory dismissed Thomas as "Scalia's puppet." The *New York Times*'s Bill Keller called Justice Thomas an affirmative action appointment.

Bill Clinton slyly demeaned Colin Powell by citing him as a product of "affirmative action," slipping it in during a televised town hall meeting in his 1997 "national conversation" on race. "Do you favor the United States Army abolishing the affirmative action program that produced Colin Powell?" he asked. "Yes or no?"[43]

When Bush made Condoleezza Rice the first black female secretary of state, there was an explosion of racist cartoons portraying Rice as Aunt

Jemima, Butterfly McQueen from *Gone with the Wind*, a fat-lipped Bush parrot and other racist clichés. Joseph Cirincione, with the Carnegie Endowment for International Peace, said Rice "doesn't bring much experience or knowledge of the world to this position." (Unlike Hillary Clinton, whose experience for the job consisted of being married to an impeached, disbarred former president.) Democratic consultant Bob Beckel—who ran Walter Mondale's campaign so competently that Mondale lost forty-nine states—said of Rice, "I don't think she's up to the job."

When Michael Steele ran for governor in Maryland, the Democratic Senatorial Campaign Committee dug up a copy of his credit report—something done to no other Republican candidate. He was depicted in blackface and with huge red lips by liberal blogger Steve Gilliard. Oreo cookies were rolled down the aisle at Steele during a gubernatorial debate.

And of course, both Clarence Thomas and presidential candidate Herman Cain were slandered with racist stereotypes out of a George Wallace campaign flier.

But a Republican drives a red pickup truck and that's "racist."

Liberals step on black conservatives early and often because they can't have black children thinking, "Hmmm, the Republicans have some good ideas, maybe I'm a Republican."

The basic set-up is:

Step 1: Spend thirty years telling blacks that Republicans are racist and viciously attacking all black Republicans.

Step 2: Laugh maliciously at Republicans for not having more blacks in their party.

Republican positions are not code words for racism. Rather, liberals use "racism" as a code word for Republican positions. The basic difference between the parties is that Republicans support small government, low taxes, and tough-on-crime policies, while Democrats prefer behemoth national government with endless Washington bureaucracies bossing us around, taxes through the roof and releasing criminals.

Republicans also oppose abortion and gay marriage, but those are touchy issues for Democrats since black people don't like them either. So those aren't "code words."

In lieu of arguing with Republicans, Democrats simply brand all words describing their positions as a secret racist code, visible only to liberals. (To be fair, they should know.)

Bill Moyers distributed tapes of Martin Luther King's adulterous affairs to the press. But this sensitive soul claims Republicans hated LBJ's Great

Society program because they hated black people. Yes—Republicans were only pretending to care about bankrupting the country. That was a pretext, but deep down they didn't care one way or another about a gargantuan, useless government spending program, requiring heavily staffed Washington bureaucracies. What reason, other than racism, could Republicans have for objecting to that?

How has the War on Poverty improved black people's lives again? Try comparing how black people were doing before and after the Great Society before answering that.

Democrats claim "states' rights" is racist code, but they are the only ones who ever used the phrase as a front for racism. Democrats love enormous, metastasizing national government for everything under the sun[44]—but, strangely, they wanted "states' rights" for their Jim Crow policies. Republicans want a tiny federal government with the states running everything else. The only times in the last century that Republicans have supported a broad federal remedy was when the Democrats were denying black people their civil rights in the South.

As has been overwhelmingly demonstrated over the past few decades, when Republicans talked about things like "states' rights," "law and order" and "welfare reform," what they meant was: states' rights, law and order and welfare reform. And as soon as their policies were implemented— most aggressively during the post–OJ verdict paradise—blacks suddenly had better lives and started being murdered a lot less. There are your Republican racists.

CHAPTER 17

WHITE GUILT KILLS

White people using elections to prove that they like black people has never turned out well. It does not move us beyond race. What moves the country beyond race is to move beyond race. But, to make up for what a small band of racist Democrats did, we keep being asked to wreck the country.

Consider a few examples.

Liberal New York Mayor John Lindsay (in office January 1, 1966—December 31, 1973) "made every issue a matter of race," the Manhattan Institute's Fred Siegel says, and "treated New York's outer-borough Catholics as right-wing racists."[1] Even vandalism had to be celebrated as a tribute to cultural diversity, with Lindsay's parks commissioner nonjudgmentally explaining, "Some people like to sit on the benches; others like to tear them up."[2]

Lindsay was one of the principal authors of the Kerner report on the black riots of 1967. When the Irish staged bloody, racist draft riots during the Civil War, President Abraham Lincoln sent federal troops to New York to smash the riots. When Newark and Detroit were nearly burned to the ground by black rioters in 1967, we got a report explaining the rioters' grievances and calling for new government spending programs.

Under Lindsay, the official NYPD approach to dealing with race riots was to refuse to call them "riots." To preserve his presidential aspirations, the mayor simply defined them out of existence, then turned around and boasted that New York was a sea of ethnicities living in peace and harmony. The only downside was that cop killers walked free and the crime rate skyrocketed.

On Lindsay's watch, the head of the Black Liberation Army, Twyman Meyers, murdered four New York City policemen and sprayed another police car with machine gun fire in front of witnesses. When Meyers's license plate number was released to the press, the cop-killer—Meyers, not

Lindsay—responded by mailing the plate to the *New York Times* with a note vowing to "mete out justice in the fashion of Malcolm X" to "the fascist state pig police."[3]

The official position of the New York Police Department was to deny that there was a movement to kill cops. That was New York City policing before Giuliani.

Lindsay spurned working class whites, hard hats and the middle class, instead appealing to rich, Manhattan elites and angry blacks. His idea of solving the race problem was to put "much of the city's African-American community on to the dole"—as Siegel and E. J. McMahon put it in the *Public Interest*.[4] The very term "limousine liberal" was coined to describe Lindsay.

Under Lindsay, New York got its first income tax, the murder rate exceeded one thousand for the first time in history and he bequeathed a bankrupt city to his successors. The symbol of New York during the Lindsay administration should have been piles of garbage and a dead cop.

But like Obama, Lindsay was elegant, telegenic and looked good in a suit. All the people who went totally nuts over Lindsay are the same ones going nuts over Obama today. At the end of his two terms, the next man to be elected mayor, Abe Beame, ran on the slogan, "Had Enough Charisma?" The *New York Times* wrapped its editorial arm around Lindsay, brooking no criticism for its matinee idol.

Lindsay did incalculable damage not only to New York, but to the entire nation, which foolishly followed the recommendations of the Kerner report. That was when the country decided that instead of punishing black rioters, we would hear them out and lavish black neighborhoods with those oh-so-helpful government programs.

Another beneficiary of liberal race mongering was David Dinkins, who ran for mayor of New York about fifteen years after Lindsay left the city in tatters, so he could finish the job.

On August 23, 1989, in the middle of the Democratic primary pitting Dinkins against incumbent Ed Koch, a black sixteen-year-old named Yusef Hawkins was fatally shot by a group of white thugs in Bensonhurst, Brooklyn. This set off massive protests led by Al Sharpton, who was looking for a new gig a year after his work on the Tawana Brawley hoax had concluded so triumphantly.

The white gang had been lying in wait to attack a romantic rival—a black or Hispanic youth allegedly dating a neighborhood girl. It was Yusef's bad luck that he happened to be walking past the girl's house that

night, on his way with three black friends to see a used car. Yusef was sin-
gled out by the white toughs as the putative boyfriend, with one of the
whites asking, "Is this the one?"

No one—not the responding police officers, the witnesses, the black
commissioner of police Benjamin Ward (of the Farrakhan mosque incident), not the girl who had inspired the attack—believed there was a racial
element to the shooting.[5] As Shelby Steele described the case in a PBS
Frontline documentary, there was nothing racial about the murder—until
Al Sharpton made it so.

When the people of Bensonhurst failed to act sufficiently racist in front
of TV cameras as hundreds of blacks marched through their town, Sharpton appeared to taunt the onlookers.[6] Bensonhurst residents so detested
Sharpton that they forgot the press was there and began shouting epithets
and waving fists and watermelons at him—just the sort of footage TV networks eat up with a spoon. The mostly Italian American crowds didn't
mind black people. They didn't mind blacks marching in their town. It was
Sharpton they loathed.

Yusef's funeral became a political extravaganza with a dozen politicians in attendance, Sharpton acting as concierge and Farrakahn's Fruit of
Islam doing security. Sharpton the Peacemaker eulogized Hawkins by saying, "I don't know who shot Yusef, but the system loaded the gun." He said:
"I want you to know, Yusef, we're not going to let you down. They're going
to pay this time."[7]

In a strange moment during an event that was full of them, one black
preacher demanded "freedom" not just in Bensonhurst, but "in Wappingers Falls"—the site of the Tawana Brawley hoax, long since disproved.

All the white politicians were booed by the crowd at the funeral service.
Only Dinkins got a big cheer. Mayor Ed Koch was booed; mayoral candidate
Rudy Giuliani was booed; Governor Mario Cuomo was booed. Pursuant to
the blacks-can-never-do-anything-wrong policies in force at the time,
Cuomo later praised the blacks who had booed him, commending them for
their restraint and saying, "they treated me better than I expected."[8]

The parents and brothers of the boy who was lying in the coffin didn't
speak at the funeral—this was a political rally. Yusef's father, Moses Stewart, had warned Dinkins, "You do not take my son's death as a political
thing to take potshots at other politicians."[9] Stewart was gracious to Mayor
Koch, offering to walk out of the church with him[10] and later told the *New
York Times* that if he were going to endorse anyone, it would have been
Koch. Dinkins, he said, "came to me to campaign."[11]

Despite Stewart's desires, his son's death was a huge political spectacle
—and it worked.

While Sharpton was out causing a ruckus, Dinkins could utter sweet
nothings and be hailed as a racial healer. In a world of Sharptons, Masons
and Maddoxes, Dinkins came across as the kinder, gentler black man. Just
like Obama.

Suddenly, newspapers were full of references to "the historic nature" of
Dinkins's candidacy and bubbling with enthusiasm at the prospect of Dinkins becoming "New York City's first black mayor."

Is this sounding familiar?

Even as Dinkins refused to disassociate himself from Jesse Jackson and
Al Sharpton, both of whom had made remarks causing consternation in
Jewish communities, he was publicly endorsed by Gilbert Klaperman, former president of the New York Board of Rabbis. Klaperman held a press
conference to announce that he had "committed a major sin," by looking at
the color of Dinkins's skin.[12]

It should have been a premonition of things to come that the general
election pitting Dinkins against Giuliani turned into an ethnic slugfest,
but, alas, was not. Voters were desperate to believe that having a black
mayor would calm racial tensions. As Ken Auletta wrote in the New York
Daily News at the time, even if Giuliani would make a better mayor, you
had to vote for Dinkins or blacks would say it was racist[13]—just what Jacob
Weisberg said about Obama twenty years later.

Dinkins won the election and, in no time managed to turn a city that
was already dysfunctional into Dante's inner circle of hell.

The hope that his election would bring an end to raging racial wars
turned out to be unfounded. Dinkins's reign was marked by constant racial tumult—marches, riots, protests and a string of alleged racist incidents, with the mayor invariably taking the side of criminals against the
police. No accusation of racism was too implausible to prevent a Dinkins
press conference denouncing racism.

Although he is usually remembered for his weak indecisiveness, it
should also be recalled that Dinkins was a whirlwind of activity whenever
there were fake victims of racism to be comforted.

Dinkins not only fueled racial strife by pandering to race agitators, but
he raised the ugly specter of racism on his own behalf over petty political
disputes. (Again: Sound familiar?) In 1993, Dinkins responded to Senator
Daniel Patrick Moynihan's speech on social disorder by implying that the
speech was racist.

Moynihan had compared the murder, welfare and illegitimacy rates in the city in 1943 to 1993, asking: "What in the last fifty years in New York City is now better than it was?"

Dinkins responded by saying that in Moynihan's "good old days, I wore the uniform of a U.S. Marine and I had to sit in the back of the bus."[14]

So there you have it. Blacks were discriminated against once, so don't worry about skyrocketing murder, welfare and illegitimacy rates.

When another Democrat, Governor Mario Cuomo, threatened to have the Financial Control Board take over New York City's budget if Dinkins couldn't win any concessions from government unions, Dinkins threatened race riots, saying he would "bring in Jesse Jackson and make this a real black-white thing."[15]

Yet and still, Dinkins almost won reelection on white guilt. As Michael Tomasky wrote in *New York* magazine, "Bad as the previous four years were—about 1,700 private-sector jobs lost every week on average, homicides surpassing 2,000 per year, more than 1 million residents on welfare—just about half the city was reluctant to give up on its first black mayor."[16]

In case there wasn't enough racial intimidation in the Dinkins campaign, President Bill Clinton came to town to accuse New Yorkers of racism if they didn't reelect Dinkins. Beginning with a phony disclaimer—"this is not as simple as overt racism"—Clinton then accused New Yorkers of supporting Giuliani just because he was white. In the standard liberal use of the word "we" to mean "you," he said: "It's this deep-seated reluctance we have, against all our better judgment, to reach out across these lines."[17]

This was the *re*-election campaign for the city's first black mayor. New Yorkers had already voted for him once. Had they not realized Dinkins was black in 1989? But unless voters stuck with a disastrous black mayor, they were racists.

If Dinkins had not been defeated by Giuliani in 1993, the same liberal policies of the previous thirty years would have continued unabated and about 28,000 more people would have been murdered between then and now, most of them black.

Noticeably, successful black public servants are never helped by white guilt. The clearest cases are black Republicans. No white guilt aided their rise.

And yet look at what that has produced! To name a few, there's Representative Allen West, Representative Tim Scott, Lieutenant Governor and Republican National Committee chair Michael Steele, Secretary of State Condoleezza Rice, presidential candidate Herman Cain, Judge Janice Rogers Brown, and, saving the best for last, Supreme Court Justice Clarence Thomas—whom Shelby Steele calls "the freest black man in America."[18]

With neither blacks nor self-righteous liberals to vote for her, Mia Love became the first black mayor of Saratoga Springs, Utah, in 2009. In the middle of a national economic meltdown, she cut the city's deficit from $3.5 million to $779,000 and won the highest possible bond rating for her city.

If your tastes run toward Democrats, there is Cory Booker, mayor of Newark and the most impressive elected Democrat in the nation. It wasn't white guilt that got Booker his job: In his first two mayoral runs, Booker ran against black Democrats and was attacked for not being black enough.[19] The second time, in 2006, Booker won, becoming the nation's only postracial Democrat.

Since being elected mayor, Booker has produced an almost Giuliani-like transformation of one of the most crime-ridden cities in the nation. Within two years, Booker had reduced murders in Newark by 36 percent, shootings by 41 percent, rapes by 30 percent, and auto thefts by 26 percent.[20] By 2009, Newark was back to 1959 murder rates.

On his way to a Fourth of July barbecue one year, Booker spotted a woman buying drugs on the street in front of children. He had his security detail pull over, so he could arrest her.[21]

And that's to say nothing of Booker's advocacy of charter schools and his help getting downtown Newark its first grocery store in more than twenty years—a crucial quality of life matter in the inner city.[22]

It's not just in the political world that white guilt kills. The minority doctor who took Allan Bakke's place at medical school was so incompetent that his medical license was eventually revoked for "gross negligence, incompetence and repeated negligent acts."

Patrick Chavis had been touted by Senator Teddy Kennedy, the *New York Times* and the *Nation* as the doctor admitted in Bakke's place. As Kennedy put it, he was the "perfect example" of affirmative action because he was "serving a disadvantaged community and making a difference in the lives of scores of poor families."

Dr. Chavis made a difference to the community by sending half a dozen of his patients, bleeding and vomiting, to the emergency room and killing one of them.[23] There's your affirmative action success story.

White guilt has never produced anything but catastrophe.

White guilt fueled the liberal crime policies that resulted in tens of thousands, maybe hundreds of thousands of murders, to say nothing of maimings, burnings and rapes. White guilt got us huge tower blocks of public housing that are fortresses of social pathology. It produced the entire entitlement-dominated politics we have now.

It's led the nation to turn a blind eye to the ticking time bomb of exploding illegitimacy rates.

It got us the *George Lopez Show* and we don't even owe the Hispanics anything.

It got an acquittal for OJ as a result of the trial being moved to a venue that would produce more black jurors than the courthouse in the jurisdiction where the crime occurred.

It produced a destructive welfare state that was untouchable for decades. It got us anxiety, anger, fear and a major political party incapable of making an argument more sophisticated than: "You racist!"

And it got us the most left-wing president America has ever seen.

When there were so few cases of white-on-black hate crimes that liberals had to start making them up, wasn't that a clue that the Klan wasn't preventing black progress anymore? If white people could be shorn of all racism overnight, it's not clear how that would improve the black condition.

On the other hand, if all black people woke up tomorrow morning with the cultural predilections of Korean Americans, all sociological disparities—income, crime rates, out of wedlock births—would vanish within ten years. Both thought experiments are unfair, but one at least has a practical resonance to it.

As Shelby Steele has said: "Whites don't think they have the moral authority to ask anything of black people, certainly not to judge them. But there's something wrong with people who have a 70-percent illegitimacy rate. This is a group of people who are lost. But we are surrounded by whites who refuse to tell us that."

The national obsession with racism is a self-inflicted punishment that has resulted in disaster, for everyone, but most of all for black people. The initial lie from which all other lies flow is the idea that black people's condition in America depends on white people's beneficence. It's Bull Connor's last revenge.[24]

ACKNOWLEDGMENTS

Thanks go, first of all, to my publisher, Adrian Zackheim, for taking on a lightning-speed publishing schedule after the idea for this book struck me like a thunderbolt in April. He and his editorial assistant, Eric Meyers, have done an amazing job, along with a team of long-suffering copy editors and production staff, whose names I don't even know yet. Whatever errors remain—it would have been a lot worse without them. (We plan to correct any additional mistakes after Media Matters does its painstaking fact-checking the day the book is released.)

A number of my friends have read or commented on sections of the book—often in first-draft form, and my first drafts are abominable. They became less so, thanks to: Trish Baker, Jim Hughes, Jeremy Rabkin, Jim Moody, Marshall Sella, Younis Zubchevich, David Friedman, Allan Ryskind, Hans Bader and Ned Rice.

Other friends have helped in a thousand small ways with this book, other books, my columns, my life—with title ideas, helpful insults, enthusiasm and, most important, interest. Jon Tukel told me he started reading one chapter in the middle of the workday and couldn't stop. When you're not sure if you've become Jack Nicholson in *The Shining*, a comment like that is important. These friends include: Steve Gilbert; James Higgins; James Mann; Miguel Estrada; Robert Caplain; Jonathan Tukel; Jon Caldara; Gene Meyer; Bill Armistead; Melanie Graham; Barry Puckett; David Limbaugh; my current agent, Mel Berger; my agent for life, Joni Evans; Beda Koorey; Mallory and Thomas Danaher; Lee and Allie Hanley and my brothers, John and Jim.

1948 ELECTION

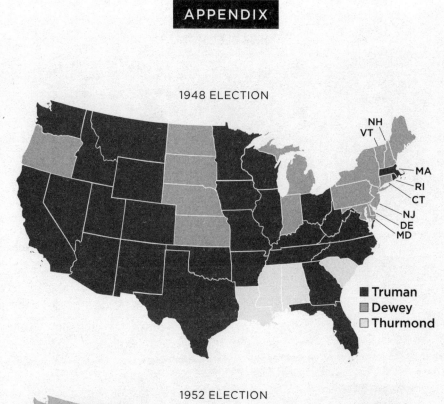

NH
VT
MA
RI
CT
NJ
DE
MD

- Truman
- Dewey
- Thurmond

1952 ELECTION

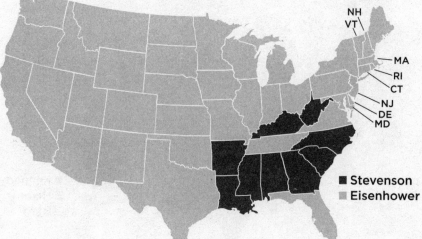

NH
VT
MA
RI
CT
NJ
DE
MD

- Stevenson
- Eisenhower

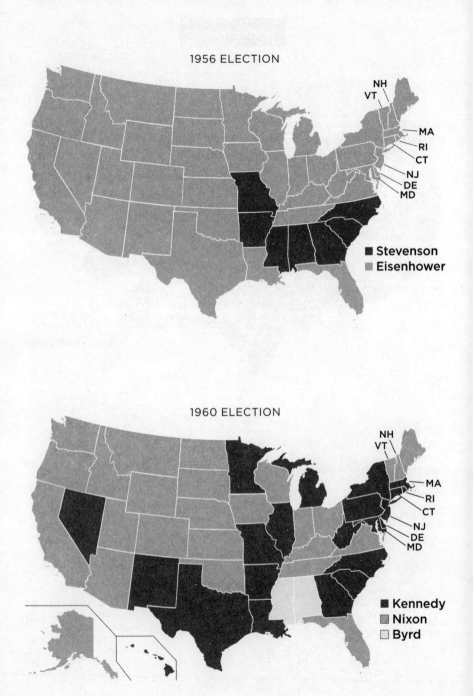

1956 ELECTION

NH
VT
MA
RI
CT
NJ
DE
MD

■ Stevenson
■ Eisenhower

1960 ELECTION

NH
VT
MA
RI
CT
NJ
DE
MD

■ Kennedy
■ Nixon
□ Byrd

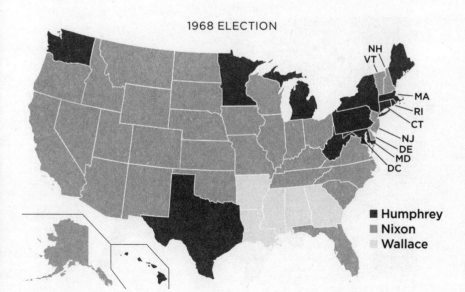

1964 ELECTION

NH
VT
MA
RI
CT
NJ
DE
MD
DC

■ Johnson
■ Goldwater

1968 ELECTION

NH
VT
MA
RI
CT
NJ
DE
MD
DC

■ Humphrey
■ Nixon
■ Wallace

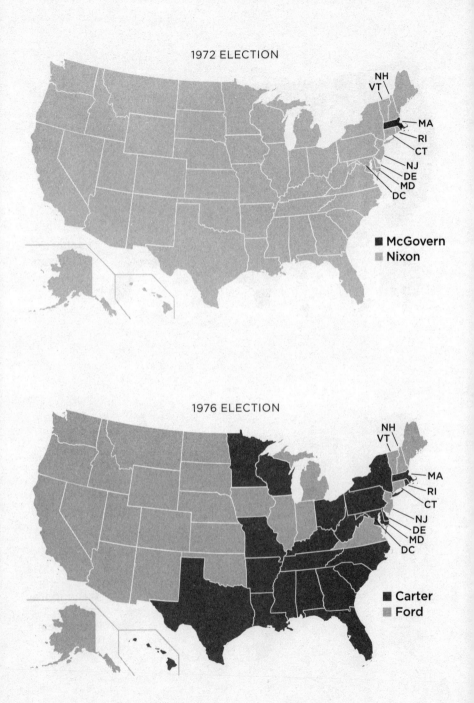

1972 ELECTION

NH
VT
MA
RI
CT
NJ
DE
MD
DC

■ McGovern
■ Nixon

1976 ELECTION

NH
VT
MA
RI
CT
NJ
DE
MD
DC

■ Carter
■ Ford

1980 ELECTION

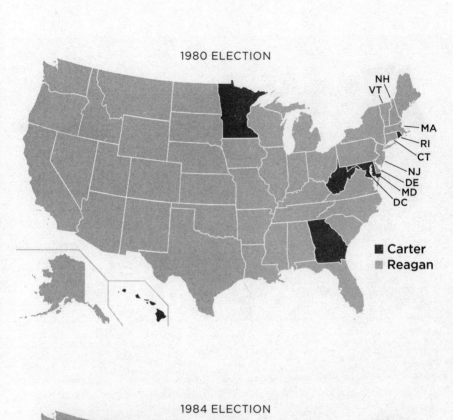

NH
VT
MA
RI
CT
NJ
DE
MD
DC

■ Carter
■ Reagan

1984 ELECTION

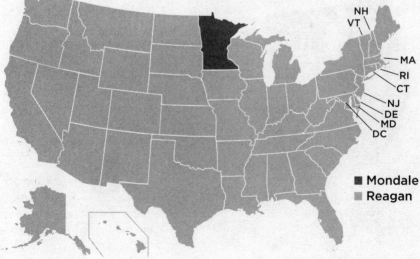

NH
VT
MA
RI
CT
NJ
DE
MD
DC

■ Mondale
■ Reagan

1988 ELECTION

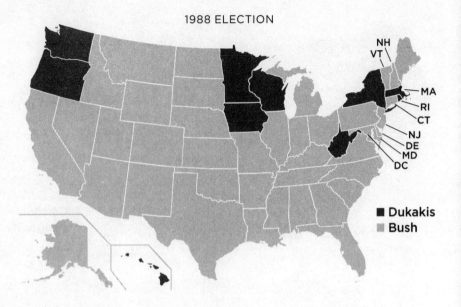

NH
VT
MA
RI
CT
NJ
DE
MD
DC

■ Dukakis
■ Bush

1992 ELECTION

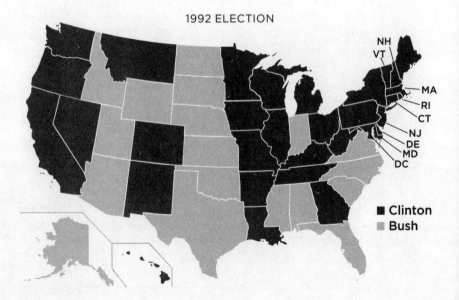

NH
VT
MA
RI
CT
NJ
DE
MD
DC

■ Clinton
■ Bush

1996 ELECTION

NOTES

CHAPTER 1: RACE WARS OF CONVENIENCE, NOT NECESSITY

1. In Eisenhower's first election, Republicans also picked up six House seats in Virginia, ten in North Carolina, one in Florida and five in Texas. (Michael Barone, *Our Country* at 711, f1.) It was then that Republicans began to think that "if they were no longer quite so strong in some of their old citadels in the North like Pennsylvania, they were now capable of wining elections in modern-thinking towns in the South like Roanoke and Charlotte, St. Petersburg and Dallas." (Michael Barone, *Our Country* at 262.)
2. Henry A. Rhodes, "An Analysis of the Civil Rights Act of 1964: A Legislated Response to Racial Discrimination in the U. S." (Yale–New Haven Teachers Institute, 1982, available at http://www.yale.edu/ynhti/curriculum/units/1982/3/82. 03.04. x.html).
3. Robert A. Caro, *The Years of Lyndon Johnson, Vol. 3: Master Of The Senate* (Paperback).
4. Ibid., at xv.
5. Reagan's magnificent 1981 tax cuts passed with a vote of 323–107 in the majority Democratic House, and 89–11 in the Senate, where Republicans held a bare majority of fifty-two seats. Edward Cowan, "Reagan's 3-Year, 25% Cut in Tax Rate Voted by Wide Margins in the House and Senate," *New York Times*, July 30, 1981.
6. During the campaign, Nixon had been polling at 42 percent, Humphrey at 29 percent and Wallace at 22 percent. On election day, Nixon's percentage held steady at 43.4 percent. Wallace's had dropped to 13.5 percent, while Humphrey's jumped to 42.7 percent. Patrick J. Buchanan, "The Neocons and Nixon's Southern Strategy," *The American Conservative*, December 30, 2002. See also Michael Barone, *Our Country*, at 449 (Nixon's "status as a longtime supporter of civil rights, in the Eisenhower administration and at the 1960 national convention, made it difficult for him to steal away Wallace's votes").
7. Conrad Black, *The Invincible Quest: The Life of Richard Milhous Nixon* (McClelland & Stewart, 2007) at 647.
8. *Hannity & Colmes*, FOX News, November 17, 2004.
9. Walter V. Robinson, "Professor's Past in Doubt: Discrepancies Surface in Claim of Vietnam Duty," *Boston Globe*, June 18, 2001.
10. Adrian Havill, *Deep Truth: The Lives of Bob Woodward and Carl Bernstein* (Birch Lane Press, 1993) at 19–20 and 221–23.

11. Thomas Sowell, *Black Rednecks and White Liberals* (Encounter Books, 2005), Chapter 1, passim. See also David Hackett Fischer, *Albion's Seed* (Oxford University Press, 1989) and James Webb, *Born Fighting: How the Scots-Irish Shaped America* (Broadway Books, 2004).
12. Sowell, *Black Rednecks*
13. Ibid. at 22.
14. Ibid. at 23.
15. Fischer, *Albion's Seed* at 737.
16. *Albion's Seed* at 770.
17. Webb, *Born Fighting* at 168.
18. Sowell, *Black Rednecks* at 25 (internal quotations omitted).
19. The verdict from the jury of eleven blacks and one white was "not guilty by reason of insanity." 83 percent of Americans disagreed with the verdict, according to an ABC poll the day after the verdict. Doug Linder, "The Trial of John W. Hinckley, Jr.," UMKC Faculty Projects (2008), available at http://law2.umkc.edu/faculty/projects/ftrials/hinckley/hinckleyaccount.html.
20. Kerwin Swint, *Mudslingers: The Twenty-Five Dirtiest Political Campaigns of All Time* (Union Square Press, 2008) at 228.
21. See, e.g., Rick Bragg, "Quietly, Alabama Troopers Escort Wallace for Last Time," *New York Times*, September 17, 1998; "George C. Wallace" (1963–67, 1971–79, 1983–87), Encyclopedia of Alabama, available at http://www.encyclopediaofalabama.org/face/Article.jsp?id=h-1676.
22. *Black Rednecks* at 1.
23. Fred Siegel, *The Future Once Happened Here* (Encounter Books, 1997) at 38.
24. Only between 1960 and 1966, more then 600,000 blacks migrated out of the South to the North and West. Report of the National Advisory Commission on Civil Disorders, Summary of Report, Chapter 6.
25. "The Negro Crime Rate: A Failure in Integration," *Time,* April 21, 1958, 16–20. Quoted in Michael W. Flamm, "'Law and order' at Large: The New York Civilian Review Board Referendum of 1966 and the Crisis of Liberalism," *The Historian*, March 22, 2002.
26. Sowell, *Black Rednecks* at 121–22.
27. Erol Ricketts, "The Origin of Black Female-Headed Families," *Focus*, Spring/Summer 1989, 32–37, available at http://www.irp.wisc.edu/publications/focus/pdfs/foc121e.pdf.
28. Siegel, *The Future Once Happened Here.*
29. Mickey Kaus, *The End of Equality* (Basic Books, 1995) at 111.
30. Kaus, *The End of Equality* at 110–12.
31. Ricketts, "The Origin of Black Female-Headed Families" at 32–37.
32. Thomas Sowell, *The Vision of the Anointed: Self-Congratulation as a Basis for Social Policy* (Basic Books, 1995) at 61.
33. Ricketts, "The Origin of Black Female-Headed Families" at 32–37.
34. About 6 percent of both blacks and whites were widowed; 15 percent of blacks were divorced or separated, compared to 11.9 percent of whites. America's Families and Living Arrangements: 2010, U.S. Census, 2010, Table A1, available at http://www.census.gov/population/www/socdemo/hh-fam/cps2010.html.
35. Josh Getlin, Joyce: "Celebrity of Homeless Dispute in N.Y.," *Los Angeles Times*, December 20, 1987.

36. Siegel, *The Future Once Happened Here* at 205.

37. *The Future Once Happened Here* at 206.

38. William J. Stuntz, "The Pathological Politics of Criminal Law," *Michigan Law Review*, December 1, 2001 (citing U.S. Dep't Of Justice, Crime In The United States 1972: Uniform Crime Reports, 1973, at 61 table 1).

39. Brent Staples, "When Only Monsters Are Real," *New York Times*, November 21, 1993.

40. Pew Social Trends, "Optimism about Black Progress Declines," November 13, 2007, available at http://pewsocialtrends.org/files/2010/10/Race-2007.pdf; See also Juan Williams, "One Race Divisible," *Washington Post*, November 14, 2007; Gary Kamiya, "Is Race Dying?" Salon.com, November 26, 2007.

CHAPTER 2: INNOCENT UNTIL PROVEN WHITE

1. Robert F. Williams, *Negroes with Guns* (Marzani & Munsell, 1962).

2. Eric Pace, "Jimmy (the Greek) Snyder, 76, Is Dead: A Sports Oddsmaker," *New York Times*, April 22, 1996.

3. Vera Haller, "Judge to Decide Case Against Policeman Who Shot Woman During Eviction," Associated Press, January 12, 1987.

4. Selwyn Raab, "State Judge Dismisses Indictment of Officer in the Bumpurs Killing," *New York Times*, April 13, 1985.

5. Selwyn Raab, "Angry Outburst by Spectators Disrupts Start of Bumpurs Trial," *New York Times*, January 13, 1987.

6. Frank J. Prial, "Amid Protest, Bumpurs Case Nears Its End," *New York Times*, February 18, 1987; Raab, "Angry Outburst by Spectators Disrupts Start of Bumpurs Trial."

7. "Testimony Barred in Graffiti Arrest," *New York Times*, November 2, 1983.

8. "Account Is Read of Officer's Bid to Curb Stewart," *New York Times*, August 20, 1985.

9. Isabel Wilkerson, "Gross Testifies on Alcohol's Role in Stewart Death," *New York Times*, October 17, 1985.

10. Editorial: "Transit Police on Trial," *New York Times*, June 9, 1984.

11. Sam Roberts, "Death Stirs Police Burtality Charges," *New York Times*, September 29, 1983.

12. Philip Shenon, "Juror Says Prosecutors Fought Murder Counts," *New York Times*, August 25, 1984.

13. "12 Cases: Synopses of the Issues and the Panel's Conclusions," *New York Times*, April 24, 1985; Richard Levine, "Charge Against Officer in Stewart Case Is Dropped," *New York Times*, October 28, 1987; Kevin Sack, "New York Regents Drop Charges Against Former Medical Examiner" *New York Times*, July 28, 1990.

14. "12 Cases: Synopses of the Issues and the Panel's Conclusions," *New York Times*, April 24, 1985

15. The accusations against Dr. Gross led to state and city investigations into the examiner's conduct. He responded with defamation suits against the *New York Times* and various pathologists, and in the end he was mostly cleared, accused of mismanagement by the state health board and fired by Mayor Ed Koch. Dr.

Gross's libel suit was dismissed because of the impossible standard for such claims by public figures.

16. Editorial: "Transit Police on Trial."

17. Editorial: "How to Remember Michael Stewart," *New York Times*, November 26, 1985.

18. "Voices from the Jury Box," *New York Times*, January 15, 1986.

19. Isabel Wilkerson, "Stewart Decision In, the Trial Goes on Trial," *New York Times*, December 1, 1985.

20. Samuel G. Freedman, "To Some, Davis Is 'Hero' Amid Attacks on Blacks," *New York Times*, January 2, 1987.

21. Editorial: "The Message of the Davis Case," *New York Times*, November 25, 1988.

22. Editorial: "How to Remember Michael Stewart."

23. Editorial: "The Crown Heights Acquittal," *New York Times*, October 31, 1992.

24. Donatella Lorch, "2d Officer Recounts Details of Arrest in Crown Heights," *New York Times*, October 1, 1992.

25. See, e.g., Charles J. Hynes, district attorney, Kings County, "Letter to the Editor: Crown Heights Trial Had Vigorous Prosecution." *New York Times*, April 7, 1998.

26. Robert D. McFadden, "Teen-Ager Acquitted in Slaying during '91 Crown Heights Melee," *New York Times*, October 30, 1992.

27. Donatella Lorch, "Inquiries Set in '91 Slaying in Crown Hts.," *New York Times*, October 31, 1992.

28. Andy Newman, "In Twist, Defendant Admits to Stabbing in Crown Hts. in '91," *New York Times*, April 29, 2003.

29. Editorial: "The Crown Heights Acquittal," *New York Times*, October 31, 1992.

30. "Is This Justice?" (New York) *Newsday*, October 31, 1992.

31. McFadden, "Teen-Ager Acquitted in Slaying."

32. See, e.g., Bob Liff, "PBA Head: Dinkins Poured Gas on Riot," *Newsday* (New York), July 14, 1992; Samuel Maull, "DA: Washington Heights Cop Cleared Because Witnesses Unreliable," Associated Press September 10, 1992.

33. James Dao, "Tension in Washington Heights," *New York Times*, July 8, 1992.

34. Peter Hellman, "The Cop and the Riot," *New York* magazine, November 2, 1992.

35. See, e.g., "District Attorney's Findings Regarding the Police Killing of Jose Garcia," *New York Times*, September 11, 1992; M. P. McQueen, "Calm on Clear Day," *Newsday* (New York), September 11, 1992.

36. Hellman, "The Cop and the Riot."

37. Connie Chung and Giselle Fernandez, "Violence Breaks Out in New York in a Case of Police Brutality," CBS Evening News, July 7, 1992.

38. Dennis Hevesi, "Upper Manhattan Block Erupts after a Man Is Killed in Struggle with a Policeman," *New York Times*, July 5, 1992.

39. James Dao, "Angered by Police Killing, a Neighborhood Erupts," *New York Times*, July 7, 1992.

40. Alfred Lubrano, "He Didn't Want to Die in New York," (New York) *Newsday*, July 6, 1992.

41. Jim Dwyer, "Lies, Whispers in Garcia Case," (New York) *Newsday*, July 6, 1992.

42. See, e.g., "District Attorney's Findings Regarding the Police Killing of Jose Garcia" and "Calm on Clear Day."

43. Hellman, "The Cop and the Riot."

44. See, e.g., "District Attorney's Findings Regarding the Police Killing of Jose Garcia."
45. Maull, "DA: Washington Heights Cop Cleared Because Witnesses Unreliable."
46. McQueen, "Calm on Clear Day."
47. "No Inquiry in Heights Case," *New York Times*, September 18, 1992; Rose Marie Arce, "Garcia Kin Want Probe," (New York) *Newsday*, September 18, 1992.

CHAPTER 3: GUILTY UNTIL PROVEN BLACK

1. Jill Nelson, "Up Against the System," *Washington Post*, May 10, 1987. (Full quote: Maddox is "making all of us confront the barriers of our own racism and this is particularly difficult for progressive whites, because we're so self-serving about our racism.")
2. Column reprinted in Nelson George, *Buppies, B-boys, Baps, and Bohos: Notes on Post-Soul Black Culture* (Da Capo Press, 2001) at 223–40.
3. George at 239.
4. Gary Langer, "Tale of Two Worlds, and One Tragedy," Associated Press, June 23, 1985.
5. George at 238.
6. Jane Rosen, "Shooting Deepens Race Fears: Killing Black Youth by White Policeman in New York Sparks Race Violence Fears," (London) *Guardian*, June 17, 1985.
7. Editorial: "The Death of Edmund Perry," *New York Times*, June 23, 1985.
8. Tom Morganthau, "Two with Too Much to Lose," *Newsweek*, July 15, 1985.
9. See, e.g., Crystal Nix, "Inner City, Elite Campus: How 2 Worlds Jar," *New York Times*, January 4, 1986.

   "The tensions of living in two worlds became part of the story of 17-year-old Edmund Perry, an honors graduate at Phillips Exeter Academy who was shot to death by a plainclothes police officer near Morningside Park last summer in what the police described as an attempted robbery."
10. "Using the Stage to Voice Feelings about Racism," *New York Times*, April 30, 1989.
11. Dorothy J. Gaiter, "To Be Black and Male Is Dangerous in U.S.," *Miami Herald*, July 11, 1985.
12. See, e.g., Michael Coakley, "Violence Ends a Black Success Story," *Chicago Tribune*, August 15, 1985.
13. Tom Morganthau, "Goetz: Victim or Villain?" *Newsweek*, April 1, 1985.
14. See, e.g., Robert D. McFadden, "Justice Drops All Major Charges Against Goetz in Shooting on IRT," *New York Times*, January 17, 1986; Samuel Maull, "Defense Lawyer Argues That Charges Against Goetz Be Dropped," The Associated Press, November 26, 1985 (citing Darrell Cabey's interview with the *Daily News*'s Jimmy Breslin that "his three friends intended to rob Goetz because 'he looked like easy bait. . . . He looked like he had money.'").
15. In addition, a secretary who had been sitting on a nearby park bench testified that just before the shooting, two black men passed her and she heard someone say, "Give me what you have." M. A. Farber, "Testimony Ends in Assault Trial of Jonah Perry," *New York Times*, January 17, 1986.
16. M. A. Farber, "Officer Tells of Shooting Honors Student to Death," *New York*

Times, January 14, 1986; M. A. Farber, "Last Arguments Offered in Trial of Jonah Perry," *New York Times*, January 22, 1986.

17. M. A. Farber, "Jonah Perry Acquitted of Mugging Officer Who Fatally Shot Brother," *New York Times*, January 23, 1986.

18. George at 232.

19. According to Department of Justice statistics, for example, in 1985—the year Perry was shot—black males committed nearly as many murders (6,043) as white males (6,943), although blacks are only 12 percent of the population. C. Puzzanchera and W. Kang (2011). "Easy Access to the FBI's Supplementary Homicide Reports: 1980–2009." Available at http://www.ojjdp.gov/ojstatbb/ezashr/.

20. Jill Nelson, "Up Against the System," *Washington Post*, May 10, 1987.

21. See, e.g., "Police Reportedly Left Barry Investigation on Their Own," United Press International, January 11, 1989; Robert Pear, "2d Investigation Touches Capital Mayor," *New York Times*, January 1, 1989.

22. Vincent McCraw, "Rally Gives Barry Hero's Welcome, *Washington Times*, July 3, 1990.

23. See, e.g., McCraw, "Rally Gives Barry Hero's Welcome"; Karl Vick, "Barry Fights to Regain Respect Despite Trial, (Florida) *St. Petersburg Times*, July 6, 1990.

24. Vick, "Barry Fights to Regain Respect."

25. Ibid.

26. Stephanie Saul, "Barry Trial Accents Race Issue," (New York) *Newsday*, July 19, 1990.

27. Gregory Freeman, "Marion Barry's Battle for Public Opinion Engrosses Many Blacks," (Missouri) *St. Louis Post-Dispatch*, July 6, 1990.

28. Vick, "Barry Fights to Regain Respect."

29. Ibid.

30. Freeman, "Marion Barry's Battle for Public Opinion."

31. Vick, "Barry Fights to Regain Respect."

32. Elsa Walsh and Barton Gellman, "Chasm Divided Jurors in Barry Drug Trial," *Washington Post*, August 23, 1990.

33. Ibid.

34. Michael Abramowitz and Rene Sanchez, "Barry Basks in Glow of 'Donahue,'" *Washington Post*, November 1, 1990.

35. Howard S. Gantman, "NAACP Director Decries 'Harassment' of Black Officials," United Press International, July 8, 1990.

36. Abramowitz and Sanchez, "Barry Basks in Glow of 'Donahue.'"

37. Lynn Sherr, "Who Is Ed Summers? Carjack Killer or Framed Innocent?" *20/20*, ABC News, June 3, 1994.

38. Barbara Campbell, "In Cold Blood?" *New York* magazine, March 7, 1994. Available at http://books.google.com/books?id=XOMCAAAAMBAJ&pg=PA32&source=gbs_toc_r&cad=2#v=onepage&q&f=false.

39. Joseph Berger, "Man Guilty on All Counts in Carjacking," *New York Times*, December 16, 1994.

40. John Sullivan, "Abduction Suspect Wanted a Car, But Would He Kill for It?" *New York Times*, March 21, 1996.

41. Chambers's famed "Fifth Avenue townhouse," for example, was one apartment in a townhouse on 90th St. acquired through the miracle of another rent-controlled apartment going co-op. Before Giuliani, 90th St. was getting pretty close to Har-

lem. At the time of Chambers's arrest, his mother was many months behind in rent. Nonetheless, Chambers was consistently described as living in a "Fifth Avenue townhouse." See, generally, Linda Wolfe, *Wasted: The Preppie Murder* (iUniverse, 2000).

42. See, e.g., Samuel G. Freedman, "Darkness Beneath the Glitter: Life of Suspect in Park Slaying," *New York Times*, August 28, 1986; Esther Pessin, "Accused Central Park Killer Charged With Burglaries," United Press International, December 16, 1986; Margot Hornblower, "A Murder among Manhattan's Elite," *Washington Post*, August 30, 1986.

43. Editorial: "The Dirty Little Secret," *New York Times*, December 23, 1986.

44. Gary Langer, "Civic Leaders Call for Calm in Face of Racial Attacks," Associated Press, December 24, 1986.

45. Gary Langer, "Racial Attack Victim Grimes Is Arrested on Assault Charge," Associated Press, December 27, 1986.

46. Jack Beatty, "Howard Beach Portents," *New York Times*, January 7, 1987.

47. Dan Collins, "A Bitter Bite of the Big Apple," *U.S. News & World Report*, January 12, 1987.

48. Sydney P. Freedberg, "Marchers Denounce Racism: Queens Protesters Met by Hostility," *Miami Herald*, December 28, 1986.

49. "Homicide Trends in the U.S., Trends by Race," Bureau of Justice Statistics. Available at http://bjs.ojp.usdoj.gov/content/homicide/tables/ovracetab.cfm.

50. "Week in Review: Not So Simple as a Lynching," *New York Times*, December 28, 1986.

51. See, e.g., Todd S. Purdum, "Man Held in Design Student's Murder," *New York Times*, May 3, 1986; *People v. Anthony Neal Jenkins*, Sup. Ct. NY, APP DIV, 2d Dept, September 30, 1991. Available at http://ny.findacase.com/research/wfrm-DocViewer.aspx/xq/fac.19910930_0050508.NY.htm/qx.

52. Samuel G. Freedman, "New York Race Tension Is Rising Despite Gains," *New York Times*, March 29, 1987.

53. Jimmy Breslin, "Ugliness of Birmingham Returns—in New York," *Toronto Star*, January 4, 1987.

54. See, e.g., Josh Getlin, "Rage and Outrage: Jimmy Breslin's Racist, Newsroom Pique Provokes a Nationwide Furor," *Los Angeles Times*, May 15, 1990.

55. Jack Beatty, "Howard Beach Portents."

56. Robert D. McFadden, "The Howard Beach Inquiry: Many Key Questions Persist," *New York Times*, December 28, 1986.

57. Virginia Byrne, "Police Sent to Howard Beach as Murder Charges Dropped," Associated Press, December 30, 1986.

58. See, e.g., Editorial: "Victory for Reason on Howard Beach," *New York Times*, August 5, 1989; "Convictions, Sentences Upheld for Howard Beach Defendants," Associated Press, July 31, 1989.

59. Charles J. Hynes, *Incident at Howard Beach* (iUniverse, 2011) at 47.

60. Mark Mooney, "Howard Beach Case Ringleader Deported," *Daily News*, August 16, 2001.

61. See, e.g., "No Remorse, No Sense of Guilt," (New York), *Newsday* January 23, 1988.

62. "In 2 Other Assault Cases, No Resolution Yet," *New York Times*, October 26, 1987.

63. "Mayor Gets Angry Reaction at Howard Beach Church," Associated Press, December 29, 1986, Monday, PM cycle.

64. "Police Report Racial Attack in Brooklyn," Associated Press, December 29, 1986, Monday, AM cycle.

65. "Racial Incidents on Rise," *Washington Post*, January 7, 1987.

66. "8 Blacks Attack White Cabbie in N.Y. Race Retaliation," *Chicago Tribune*, December 25, 1987.

67. "New York: 2 Black Men Assault White Wife of Officer," *Miami Herald*, January 4, 1988; "Police Say Robbery Was Racially Motivated," *New York Times*, January 3, 1988.

68. Dirk Johnson, "Slain Woman Found in Pool of Connecticut Home," *New York Times*, December 12, 1986, (511 words); Howard W. French, "2 Held in Connection with Death of Woman at New Canaan Home," *New York Times*, December 15, 1986 (363 words); "2d Murder Charge Filed in Drowning," *New York Times*, January 1, 1987 (113 words).

69. On July 23, 2007, ex-cons Joshua Komisarjevsky, 26, and Steven J. Hayes, 44, assaulted and bound Dr. William A. Petit Jr., 50, in his Cheshire, Connecticut home and proceeded to sexually assault his wife, Jennifer Hawke-Petit, 48, and one of their daughters before murdering Mrs. Hawke-Petit and both daughters Hayley, 17, and Michaela, 11. The men set the house on fire and were caught fleeing the premises. Both were given the death penalty. In response to the heinous crime, idiot Democrats repealed the death penalty in Connecticut: Peter Applebome, "Death Penalty Repeal Goes to Connecticut Governor," April 11, 2012.

70. See, e.g., "Woman Meets Flaming Death at Hands of Tormentors," Associated Press, October 4, 1973. Available at http://news.google.com/newspapers?nid=1665&dat=19731004&id=0T5PAAAAIBAJ&sjid=WyQEAAAAIBAJ&pg=7073,3010511).

71. Kathryn Shattuck, "What's On Today," *New York Times*, February 17, 2011.

72. Associated Press, "Tennessee: Killer Sentenced to Death," *New York Times*, October 31, 2009.

73. Column reprinted in Nelson George, *Buppies, B-boys, Baps, And Bohos: Notes on Post-Soul Black Culture* at 223–40.

CHAPTER 4: HEY, WHATEVER HAPPENED TO THAT STORY . . .

1. Dan Jacobson, United Press International, March 23, 1987.

2. Thomas Morgan, "50 Arrested in Anti-Racism Protest at Columbia," *New York Times*, April 22, 1987.

3. "23 Seized in Protest on Columbia Clash," *New York Times*, April 8, 1987.

4. "Racial Bias Protest at Columbia," *New York Times*, April 5, 1987.

5. Barbara Kantrowitz with Bill Turque, "Blacks Protest Campus Racism," *Newsweek*, April 6, 1987.

6. Robert Marquand, "School Colors: Uneasy Gray Between Black and White," *Christian Science Monitor*, June 14, 1988.

7. "Emory Students Hold Rally for Hospitalized Student," United Press International, April 13, 1990.

8. "Police Say Racist Threats Were Faked," *Chicago Tribune*, June 3, 1990; "Misspelling Is Cited in Threat." *New York Times*, June 2, 1990.
9. "Racial Attacks Leave Freshman in Severe Shock," *New York Times*, April 22, 1990.
10. Editorial: "Discipline in Black and White," *Boston Herald*, February 23, 1993; "A Test of Racism Produces an Uproar," *New York Times*, February 17, 1993.
11. Jodi Wilgoren, "Christian College Secludes Students after Hate Letters," *New York Times*, April 23, 2005.
12. See, e.g., "Black Student Sends Threats, Police Say," (Ohio) *Akron Beacon Journal*, April 27, 2005.
13. Sydney H. Schanberg, "Scoop-Hungry Press Fans the Flames of Hate," *Newsday* (New York), March 15, 1988.
14. Holly Planells, United Press International, February 27, 1988.
15. "'We, the Grand Jury:' Text of Its Conclusions in the Tawana Brawley Case," *New York Times*, October 7, 1988.
16. Les Payne, "Tawana Made It Up," (New York) *Newsday*, April 27, 1989.
17. Michael Winerip, "Hidden Victim in Brawley Case Is Civil Rights," *New York Times*, October 11, 1988.
18. "Al Sharpton Defends Himself Against Cocaine Deal Charges," CNN *Crossfire*, July 23, 2002.
19. See, e.g., Dave Goldiner, Sharpton on Drug Sting Tape, *Daily News*, July 23 2002.
20. Reverend Al Sharpton discusses various political issues, NBC's *Meet the Press*, August 25, 2002.
21. Michael Winerip, "Our Towns: As a Mob Howls, One in Yonkers Pleads for Sanity," *New York Times*, February 2, 1988.
22. James Feron, "Yonkers Housing Advocate Held in Fake Death Threats," *New York Times*, December 1, 1988; "Yonkers 'Lone Voice' Admits Fake Threats," *New York Times*, April 27, 1989.
23. Maria Newman, "Officials Pledge Drive to Counter Bias Attack," *New York Times*, January 8, 1992.
24. See, e.g., White Teens Paint Black Children White," United Press International, January 6, 1992.
25. Peter Moses, "2 Sides Clash over Bias Puzzle," *New York Post*, February 7, 1992.
26. Joseph A. Gambardello, "White Trio Beats Latino Boy," (New York) *Newsday*, January 14, 1992.
27. Maria Newman, "Police Puzzled by Lack of Leads in Bias Attacks on Black Youths," *New York Times*, February 6, 1992.
28. Ibid.
29. Peter Moses, "2 Sides Clash over Bias Puzzle"; "The Bronx Bias Investigation," *New York Post*, February 7, 1992. Moses also says there was a porno theater across the street from the location of the attack and the security cameras on the outside of the building indicated that no such crime had occurred. (Phone call with Peter Moses, July 28, 2010.)
30. Maria Newman, "Police Puzzled by Lack of Leads In Bias Attacks."
31. "Leads Have Run Out in Youth Bias Attacks," *New York Times*, May 10, 1992.
32. Maria Newman, "Victim of Bias Attack, 14, Wrestles with His Anger," *New York Times*, January 9, 1992.

33. Jim Dwyer, "Race Victim's Mom: I Wanted a Better Life for My Kids," (New York) *Newsday*, January 8, 1992.

34. Anna Quindlen, *Thinking Out Loud: On the Personal, the Political, the Public and the Private* (Ballantine Books, 1994) at 12–13.

35. Frank Wolfe, "Others Don't Recall What Clinton Does," (Little Rock) *Arkansas Democrat-Gazette*, June 9, 1996.

36. Michael Fumento, "The Great Black Church-Burning Hoax, 1998." Available at http://fumento.com/racism/column8.html.

37. "Clinton's Speech Accepting the Democratic Nomination for President," *New York Times*, August 30, 1996.

38. "Remarks by President Bill Clinton at Boys and Girls Nation Ceremony, the East Room, the White House," Federal News Service, July 18, 1996.

39. "Transcript of Remarks by President Clinton to Northern California DNC Gala, July 23," U.S. Newswire, July 24, 1996.

40. "Transcript of Remarks by President Clinton to Little Rock, Ark." U.S. Newswire, September 3, 1996.

41. "Army OKs Discharge of Soldier Accused of Painting Swastikas," (Quincy, Massachusetts) *Patriot Ledger*, December 18, 1996.

42. Sonya Ross, "Jackson Says He Is Ready to Return to Civil Rights Stage," Associated Press, January 21, 2001.

43. Bill Press, Tucker Carlson, *The Spin Room*, CNN, January 18, 2001.

44. *Hannity & Colmes*, "Did Jesse Jackson Misuse Rainbow/PUSH Funds?" FOX News Network, January 24, 2001.

45. Mary A. Mitchell, "Jackson Should Slow His Speedy Recovery," *Chicago Sun-Times*, January 23, 2001.

46. Marc Santora, "Columbia Professor in Noose Case Is Fired on Plagiarism Charges," *New York Times*, June 24, 2008; Murray Weiss, "Noose 'Ties' Eyed," *New York Post*, March 31, 2008.

47. Wayne King, "FILM:Fact vs. Fiction in Mississippi," *New York Times*, December 4, 1988.

48. Joan Biskupic, "Hate Crime Laws Face Free-Speech Challenge," *Washington Post*, December 13, 1992.

49. Lynda Richardson, "61 Acts of Bias: One Fuse Lights Many Different Explosions," *New York Times*, January 28, 1992.

50. See, e.g., Dennis Hevesi, "Girl Is Raped in Bias Case, Police Report," *New York Times*, January 15, 1992; Richardson, "61 Acts of Bias."

51. Tom Collins, "Cops Find Car in Bias Rape," (New York) *Newsday*, January 17, 1992.

52. David Kocieniewski, "Cops Call Bias Attack Report a Lie," (New York) *Newsday*, January 18, 1992.

53. Mary B. W. Tabor, "Police Say Brooklyn Man Faked Bias-Attack Story for Attention," *New York Times*, January 18, 1992.

54. Alison Mitchell, "Police Find Bias Crimes Are Often Wrapped in Ambiguity," *New York Times*, January 27, 1992.

55. Anemona Hartocollis, "'It Could Happen to Me,'" *Newsday* (New York), January 19, 1992.

56. Sheryl McCarthy, "Hey Guv: Only the Players Are Different in This Game of Hate," (New York) *Newsday*, January 20, 1992.

57. Glenn Smith, "'He's Getting Off Free in a Way,' Father Says," (Charleston, SC) *Post and Courier*, December 2, 2008.
58. Jim Finkelstein, "Police Arrest Final Suspect in 1992 Race-Based Slaying," *Detroit Free Press*, October 20, 1994.
59. "N.Y. Defendant Keeps His Own Counsel," *Washington Post*, January 27, 1995.

CHAPTER 5: THAT OLD BLACK MAGIC

1. Dudley Clendinen, "The Electoral Evangelism of Pat Robertson," *New York Times*, September 21, 1986.
2. Chris Hedges, "Feeling the Hate with the National Religious Broadcasters," *Harpers*, May 30, 2005.
3. James Kirchick, "Where's the Outrage? Blacks Lifted Calif.'s Anti-Gay Rights Measure," *USA Today*, November 12, 2008.
4. Jake Tapper, "The Skeletons and Suits in Sharpton's Closet," Salon.com, June 21, 2003.
5. "US Legislators Set to Vote on Same-Sex Marriage Bill," Agence France Presse, July 12, 1996. Clinton himself had given an interview to the gay magazine the *Advocate* in which he blamed Republicans for the "divisive" law, but was able to avoid charges of simultaneous flip-flopping by virtue of the press not reporting that. His full interview is available only at the Web site of the Queer Resources Directory. "A Letter from President Clinton" dated August 15, 1996, available at http://www.qrd.org/qrd/usa/federal/doma/1996/clinton.letter-08.07.96.
6. Randy Jurgensen and Robert Cea, *Circle of Six* (Disinformation Co., 2007) at 51.
7. Jurgensen at 45–46.
8. See generally Jurgensen and Cea, *Circle of Six*; Sam Roberts, "The Mosque, the Mayor and Great Moments on the Playing Field," *New York Times*, October 29, 2006.
9. Jurgensen at 233.
10. Marshall Kilduff and Phil Tracy, "Inside Peoples Temple," *New West*, August 1, 1977, available at http://jonestown.sdsu.edu/JonestownPDF/newWestart.pdf.
11. Rebecca Moore, "The Demographics of Jonestown," in "Alternative Considerations of Jonestown and Peoples Temple," Department of Religious Studies at San Diego State University. (Adapted from "Demographics and the Black Religious Culture of Peoples Temple," in *Peoples Temple and Black Religion in America* (Bloomington: Indiana Press University, 2005), 57–80, eds., Rebecca Moore, Anthony Pinn and Mary Sawyer, available at http://jonestown.sdsu.edu/AboutJonestown/JTResearch/demographics.htm.
12. See, e.g., Sid Moody and Victoria Graham, Associated Press, November 26, 1978.
13. Ibid.
14. Stephen Frazier, "The Onliest One Alive," CNN, August 10, 1997.
15. Stephen Schwartz, "Deaths in Waco Recall Jonestown Nightmare," *San Francisco Chronicle*, April 20, 1993.
16. Robert Lindsey, "Jim Jones: From Poverty to Power of Life and Death," *New York Times*, November 26, 1978.
17. Marshall Kilduff and Phil Tracy, "Inside Peoples Temple."
18. Robert Lindsey, "Jim Jones."

19. "Inside Peoples Temple."
20. Lindsey, "Jim Jones."
21. Wallace Turner, "Little Attention Paid to Warnings by Sect's Leader," *New York Times*, November 21, 1978.
22. Lindsey, "Jim Jones."
23. Genoa Barrow, "A Survivor's Story," *Sacramento Observer*, March 18, 2010.
24. Sid Moody and Victoria Graham, Associated Press, November 26, 1978.
25. Kenneth L. Woodward, "Temple Trouble." *Newsweek*, August 15, 1977.
26. "U.S. Congressman, Four Others Killed in Guyana Ambush," Facts on File World News Digest, November 24, 1978.
27. Charles A. Krause, "Bodies in Guyana Cause Confusion."
28. Peter Arnett, Associated Press, November 27, 1978.
29. See e.g., Michael Taylor, "20 Years Later, Jonestown Survivor Confronts Horrors," *San Francisco Chronicle*, November 2, 1998.
30. Lindsey, "Jim Jones."
31. Fielding M. McGehee, comp. The Death Tape, Jonestown Audiotape Primary Project: Transcripts, available at http://jonestown.sdsu.edu/AboutJonestown/Tapes/Tapes/DeathTape/Q042.html.
32. See, e.g., Sid Moody and Victoria Graham, Associated Press, November 26, 1978.
33. "Garry Visits Jonestown: I Have Been to Paradise," *The Sun Reporter*, November 10, 1977, available at http://jonestown.sdsu.edu/AboutJonestown/JonestownReport/Volume9/efreinBefore/images/efreinBefore3-4A.pdf.
34. Associated Press, "Chas. Garry, Attorney for the Black Panthers," *Los Angeles Times*, August 17, 1991.
35. Gerald Nicosia, *Home to War* (Crown Publishers, 2001) at 221; Richard Stacewicz, *Winter Soldiers: An Oral History of the Vietnam Veterans Against the War* (Twayne Publishers, 1997) at 294–95.
36. "Nation: Messiah from the Midwest," *Time*, December 4, 1978.
37. The Rachel Maddow Show, MSNBC, November 14, 2008.
38. Lester Holt, "Thirty-Year Anniversary of Jonestown Massacre," NBC Nightly News, November 9, 2008.
39. "Jury Acquits 2 Members Of Philadelphia Cult," *New York Times*, July 23, 1981.
40. Lee Linder, "MOVE Defendant Accuses Court of Racial Prejudice," Associated Press, January 2, 1980.
41. See, e.g., Selwyn Raab, "Philadelphia Officials Vary In Explaining Siege Tactics," *New York Times*, May 19, 1985; Bill Peterson, "Huge Fire Destroys House of Philadelphia Radicals: Police Helicopter Drops Explosive Device," *Washington Post*, May 14, 1985.
42. Dan Blake, "Sharpton, Others Call for Indictments in 1985 MOVE Bombing," Associated Press, November 5, 1988.
43. Jamal E. Watson, "Louima, Others Decry Police Brutality," *Boston Globe*, December 10, 2000.
44. Michelle Cliff, "Street Justice," *Village Voice*, September 15, 1998.
45. "Supporting the MOVE Prisoners," Earth First!, June 30, 2002.
46. See Andrew Sullivan: "The Daily Dish: Wright in Context," the *Atlantic*, March 21, 2008, "The Daily Dish: The Polling on Wright," March 21 2008, "The Daily Dish: Two Wright Decisions," March 14, 2008, "The Daily Dish: Theology, Poli-

tics, Wright and Obama," March 16, 2008, "The Daily Dish: The Evidence on Wright," March 16, 2008 and passim.

47. Editorial: "Mr. Obama's Profile in Courage," *New York Times,* March 19, 2008.
48. Maureen Dowd, "Black, White and Gray," *New York Times,* March 19, 2008.
49. Janny Scott, "A Candidate Chooses Reconciliation Over Rancor," *New York Times,* March 19, 2008.

CHAPTER 6: PEOPLE IN DOORMAN BUILDINGS SHOULDN'T THROW STONES

1. John H. McWhorter, "Why Blacks Don't Need Leaders," *City Journal,* Summer, 2002.
2. Thomas Sowell, *The Vision of the Anointed: Self-Congratulation as a Basis for Social Policy* (Basic Books, 1996) at 158.
3. Ramsey Clark, *Crime in America: Observations on its Nature, Causes, Prevention and Control* (Simon & Schuster, 1970) at 220; (cited in Thomas Sowell, *The Vision of the Anointed: Self-Congratulation as a Basis for Social Policy* (Basic Books, 1996) at 23.
4. Sowell, *The Vision of the Anointed* at 27.
5. Sowell, *The Vision of the Anointed* at 26.
6. Editorial: "A Man Who Can Be Mayor," *New York Times,* May 13, 1965.
7. Vincent Cannato, *The Ungovernable City,* (Basic Books, 2002) at 64.
8. Robert D. McFadden, "John V. Lindsay, Mayor and Maverick, Dies at 79," *New York Times,* December 21, 2000.
9. Fred Siegel, *The Future Once Happened Here* (Encounter Books, 1997) at 4.
10. Jan M. Chaikan and Marcia R. Chaikan, "Varieties of Criminal Behavior," RAND Corporation, August 1982, at 215 (cited in Attorney General William Barr, "Remarks to the Young Republican National Federation," J. W. Marriott, Federal News Service, March 20, 1992).
11. Bureau of Alcohol, Tobacco and Firearms, "Protecting America: The Effectiveness of the Federal Armed Career Criminal Statute," 1992.
12. Bob Sipchen, "Putting a Price on Violence," *Los Angeles Times,* June 5, 1994.
13. John J. DiIulio, "Activist Judges Earn Dunce Caps for Their Prison Caps," Philly. com, October 31, 1994. Available at http://articles.philly.com/1994-10-31/news/25870404_1_prison-cap-prison-violence-crime-bill.
14. "Truth in Sentencing in State Prisons," U.S. Department Of Justice, January 10, 1999.
15. John J. DiIulio, "Activist Judges Earn Dunce Caps For Their Prison Caps."
16. "The Left Starts to Rethink Reagan," Daily Beast, May 3, 2008. Available at http://www.thedailybeast.com/newsweek/2008/05/03/the-left-starts-to-rethink-reagan.html.
17. Quoted in Michael W. Flamm, "'Law and Order' at Large: The New York Civilian Review Board Referendum of 1966 and the Crisis of Liberalism," *The Historian,* March 22, 2002.
18. Joseph P. Viteritti, "Police, Politics, and Pluralism in New York City: A Comparative Case Study" (Beverly Hills, 1973), at 12. (Cited in Michael W. Flamm, "'Law and Order' at Large.")

19. Confidential survey for Roy Wilkins by John F. Kraft Inc., August 1966, "Harlem, 1966–67," Box 32A, Group IV, NAACP Papers, LOC. (Cited in Michael W. Flamm, "'Law and Order' at Large."

20. Spiro T. Agnew, Statement at Conference with Civil Rights and Community Leaders, reprinted in *ChickenBones: A Journal*, available at http://www.nathaniel-turner.com/agnewspeakstoblackbaltimoreleaders1968.htm.

21. Ibid.

22. Quoted in "'68: The Fire Last Time," Part 4 (narrated by Sunni Khalid). See, Baltimore '68: Riots & Rebirth, available at http://archives.ubalt.edu/bsr/archival-resources/documents/wypr-part-4.pdf.

23. Marvin Olasky, "History Turned Right Side Up, *World* magazine, February 13, 2010. Available at http://www.worldmag.com/articles/16346.

24. C. Clark Kissinger, *Discover the Networks: A Guide to the Political Left*, available at http://www.discoverthenetworks.org/individualProfile.asp?indid=1386.

25. "Victim Claims No Robbery Plans: Mother Says No Hard Feeling," Associated Press, January 11, 1985.

26. United Press International, "Goetz 'Looked Like Easy Bait,'" *Chicago Tribune*, November 27, 1985.

27. Esther Pessin, "Goetz Says His Alleged Victim Was 'Stupid to Commit Crime," United Press International, October 31, 1985.

28. See, e.g., Selwyn Raab, "4 Youths Shot by Goetz Faced Criminal Counts," *New York Times*, January 10, 1985; George P. Fletcher, *A Crime of Self-Defense: Bernhard Goetz and the Law on Trial* (University of Chicago Press, 1990) at 107.

29. Todd S. Purdum, "2 of Those Shot by Goetz Face New Jail Terms," *New York Times*, April 9, 1986.

30. William Johnson, "Subway Vigilante Struck a Nerve," (Canada) *Globe and Mail*, January 18, 1985 (citing *Daily News* poll). According to a *New York Newsday* poll, both groups favored Goetz, but whites were more favorable, supporting Goetz 56 percent to 26 percent, compared to 45 percent to 33 percent, among blacks. Robert D. McFadden, "Poll Indicates Half of New Yorkers See Crime as City's Chief Problem," *New York Times,* January 14, 1985 (citing *Newsday* poll).

31. Phil McCombs, "The Vigilante Mystique: Exploring an American Phenomenon, from Gunslingers to Goetz," *Washington Post*, January 17, 1985.

32. Paul Galloway, "Bearing Arms: The Rewards, the Risks," *Chicago Tribune*, February 24, 1985.

33. John Leo and Jack E. White, "Behavior: Low Profile for a Legend Bernard Goetz," *Time*, January 21, 1985.

34. Carol Vecchione, untitled article, United Press International, February 23, 1985.

35. Galloway, "Bearing Arms."

36. David E. Sanger, "The Little-Known World of the Vigilante," *New York Times*, December 30, 1984.

37. Tom Morganthau with Lynda Wright, "A Goetz Backlash," *Newsweek*, March 11, 1985.

38. Richard Cohen, "What Was Goetz Thinking?" *Washington Post*, March 2, 1985.

39. Untitled article, *Chicago Tribune*, Associated Press, January 2, 1985.

40. Margot Hornblower, "Wounded Youth Denies Intent to Rob New York City 'Subway Vigilante,'" *Washington Post,* January 11, 1985.

41. Esther B. Fein, "For Goetz Victim's Mother, Worry and Self-Doubt," *New York Times* January 12, 1985.

42. Ibid.

43. George P. Fletcher, *A Crime of Self-Defense: Bernhard Goetz and the Law* at 182–83.

44. Kirk Johnson, "Youth Shot in Subway Says He Didn't Approach Goetz," *New York Times*, May 20, 1987.

45. Fletcher, *A Crime of Self-Defense* at 182–83.

46. Joseph R. Tybor, "Message of Fear: Goetz's Acquittal Reflects American Beliefs," *Chicago Tribune*, June 21, 1987.

47. Ibid.

48. David E. Pitt, "Blacks See Goetz Verdict as Blow to Race Relations," *New York Times*, June 18, 1987.

49. Ibid.

50. McWhorter, "Why Blacks Don't Need Leaders."

51. *Grutter v. Bollinger* 539 U.S. 306 (2003), et al. (Thomas J., concurring and dissenting;) (quoting "What the Black Man Wants: An Address Delivered in Boston, Massachusetts, on 26 January 1865," reprinted in 4 The Frederick Douglass Papers 59, 68, (J. Blassingame and& J. McKivigan, eds., 1991).

52. Bill Keller, "Mr. Diversity," *New York Times*, June 28, 2003.

CHAPTER 7: LIBERAL-BLACK RELATIONS: THEIR LANDLORD *AND* THEIR FRIEND

1. See, e.g., Michael Barone, "The New Continental Divides," *U.S. News & World Report*, November 6, 1994 (noting that the Irish have done well in hierarchies, but "haven't fared as well in free-market commerce").

2. Jonathan Eig, *Opening Day: The Story of Jackie Robinson's First Season* (Simon & Schuster, 2008) at 7.

3. Marvin Olasky, "History Turned Right Side Up, *World* magazine, February 13, 2010. Available at http://www.worldmag.com/articles/16346.

4. Michael Moore, *Stupid White Men: And Other Sorry Excuses for the State of the Nation!* (Regan Books, 2004) at 79.

5. Chris Dixon, "Vows: Sarah Staveley-O'Carroll and Michael Matthews," *New York Times*, April 1, 2010.

6. Mary Vespa, "Tom Wicker & Pam Hill: A Mixed-Media Marriage Changes Their Luck," *People* magazine, April 28, 1975.

7. Patricia McCormack, "Kids Lean to Reagan, Anderson, Informal Polls Show," United Press International, November 1, 1980. Reagan also won nationally in high schools and junior high school polls. Meanwhile, the *Washington Post* called the elderly "a bedrock of Carter's southern base." See Edward Walsh, "Carter Says Reagan Can't Be Trusted With Presidency," *Washington Post*, October 11, 1980.

CHAPTER 8: RODNEY KING—THE MOST DESTRUCTIVE EDIT IN HISTORY

1. KTLA-TV, Los Angeles, "Rodney King: Videotaped Beating." Peabody Awards, Winners, 1990s. Available at http://www.peabody.uga.edu/winners/winners_1990s.php.
2. Lou Cannon, *Official Negligence: How Rodney King and the Riots Changed Los Angeles and the LAPD* (Basic Books, 1999) at 39.
3. Cannon, *Official Negligence* at 25.
4. Trial Testimony of Rodney King, available at Los Angeles Police Officers' (Rodney King Beating) Trials, University of Missouri School of Law. Available at http://law2.umkc.edu/faculty/projects/ftrials/lapd/kingownwords.html.
5. Cannon at 43.
6. Unable to use intermediate force, female law enforcement officers are much more likely to shoot civilians than their male counterparts. John R. Lott Jr., "Does a Helping Hand Put Others at Risk? Affirmative Action, Police Departments and Crime," *Economic Inquiry*, April 1, 2000.
7. Cannon at 38.
8. Karl Vick, "Another Acquittal Would Be No Surprise," (Florida) *St. Petersburg Times*, August 6, 1992.
9. Sergeant Stacey Koon, *Presumed Guilty: The Tragedy of the Rodney King Affair* (Regnery Publishing, 1992), quoted in Los Angeles police officers' (Rodney King beating) trials, University of Missouri School of Law, available at http://law2.umkc.edu/faculty/projects/ftrials/lapd/kingownwords.html.)
10. "Nightline: In the Mind of the Jury," ABC News, March 8, 1993.
11. Roger Parloff, "Maybe the Jury Was Right," *American Lawyer*, June 1992.
12. Cannon at xix–xx.
13. Walter Williams, "TV Deception in Rodney King Case," *Dallas Morning News*, January 2, 1993.
14. *Official Negligence* at 21 and 23.
15. Address to the Nation on the Civil Disturbances in Los Angeles, California, Public Papers of the President, May 1, 1992.
16. "Two Juries, Two Verdicts," ABC News, April 27, 1993.
17. John Hurst and Leslie Berger, "Four Officers—Their Paths to Trial," *Los Angeles Times*, February 3, 1992.
18. "Nightline: In the Mind of the Jury," ABC News, March 8, 1993.
19. News Conference with the Joint Center For Political and Economic Studies and Home Box Office re: Comprehensive Assessment of Views of African American Electorate in the 1992 Presidential Year, Federal News Service, July 8, 1992.
20. "The Times Poll; 'Moral Leadership' Needed in Inner Cities, Voters Say," *Los Angeles Times*, May 23, 1992.
21. Three officers were acquitted, and the jury failed to reach a verdict on the fourth officer.
22. David Whitman, "The Untold Story of the LA Riot," *U.S. News & World Report*, May 31, 1993.
23. Ibid.
24. Edward J. Boyer, "In Bradley's Wake, a Heated Rivalry Boils," *Los Angeles Times*, July 18, 1993.

25. Eugene Yi, "LA Riots, in Our Own Words," KoreAm April 29, 2012. Available at http://iamkoream.com/april-issue-la-riots-in-our-own-words/.
26. Douglas P. Shuit, "Waters Focuses Her Rage at System," *Los Angeles Times,* May 10, 1992.
27. See, e.g., Robert Rector, "The Size and Scope Of Means-Tested Welfare Spending," The Heritage Foundation, August 1, 2001. Available at http://www.heritage.org/Research/Testimony/The-Size-and-Scope-Of-Means-Tested-Welfare-Spending; Chris Edwards, "Food Subsidies, Cato Institute: Downsizing the Federal Government," July 2009. Available at http://www.downsizinggovernment.org/agriculture/food-subsidies.
28. David Whitman, "The Untold Story of the LA Riot," *U.S. News & World Report,* May 31, 1993.
29. Brandi Hitt, "From the KTLA Vaults: The Rodney King Beating, 20 Years Later," March 3, 2011. Available at http://www.ktla.com/news/landing/ktla-rodney-king-20-years,0,6945898.story.
30. Brandi Hitt, "From the KTLA Vaults: The Rodney King Beating, 20 Years Later."
31. Cannon at 22.
32. Richard Horgan, "Idiot Box: Lingerie Models Warm Up KTLA Morning Forecast," February 14, 2012. Available at http://www.mediabistro.com/fishbowlla/ktla-morning-news-mark-kriski-henry-dicarlo-fredericks-hollywood-valentines-day_b53211.
33. POW Pledge from ABC, May 1993, http://www.aim.org/publications/aim_report/1993/05b.html.
34. Jim Newton and John L. Mitchell, "Symbolism Alters Image of Suspects in Denny Beating, *Los Angeles Times,* December 27, 1992.
35. John McWhorter, *Losing the Race: Self-Sabotage in Black America* (Free Press, 2000) at 69.
36. William Hamilton, "King, Denny Cases: To Many, a Contrast in Black and White," *The Washington Post,* February 25, 1993.
37. Cannon at 609.
38. Jay Nordlinger, "Shrill Waters; Move Aside, James Carville: Big Bad Max Is the Loudest, Toughest, Meanest Clinton-Defender of Them All," *National Review,* January 25, 1999.
39. Editorial: "The Crown Heights Acquittal," *The New York Times,* October 31, 1992.
40. See, e.g., John R. Lott Jr., "Analysis: Reckless Mortgages Brought Financial Market to Its Knees," September 18, 2008, available at http://www.foxnews.com/story/0,2933,424945,00.html#ixzz1ulnTqidV.

CHAPTER 9: THE TRIAL OF THE CENTURY: MARK FUHRMAN'S FELONY CONVICTION

1. PBS *Frontline*: "The O.J. Verdict." Available at http://www.pbs.org/wgbh/pages/frontline/oj/view/.
2. BBC, "On This Day, 1995: O. J. Simpson verdict 'Not guilty.'" Available at http://news.bbc.co.uk/onthisday/hi/dates/stories/october/3/newsid_2486000/2486673.stm.
3. See, e.g., Michael Sneed, *Chicago Sun-Times,* September 27, 1995; Timothy Ap-

pleby, "Mistrust of Police Simpson's Big Hope," (Canada) *Globe and Mail*, September 25, 1995.

4. See, e.g., Will Bunch, "The Great Divide," *Philadelphia Daily News*, October 4, 1995.

5. Bill Smith, "Moment in Time: Verdict Broadcast Grips St. Louis," (Missouri) *St. Louis Post-Dispatch*, October 4, 1995.

6. "Students Charged in Attack after O.J. Verdict Read," (Missouri) *St. Louis Post-Dispatch*, October 6, 1995.

7. "Racial Division Appears Deep at O.J. Verdict," (Tennessee) *Chattanooga Free Press*, October 4, 1995.

8. "O.J. Verdict Sparks Beating in Colo.," United Press International, October 6, 1995.

9. Mark Fuhrman, *Murder in Brentwood* (Regnery Publishing, 1997) at 122–23.

10. Fuhrman, *Murder in Brentwood* at 268–71.

11. "Sex in Sacramento," *Newsweek*, April 3, 1995.

12. Cochran compared Fuhrman to Adolf Hitler, saying:

> "There was another man, not too long ago in the world, who had those same views, who wanted to burn people, who had racist views and ultimately had power over people in his country. People didn't care. People said, 'He's just crazy, he's just a half-baked painter.' And they didn't do anything about it. This man, this scourge, became one of the worst people in the history of this world, Adolf Hitler, because people didn't care or didn't try to stop him. He had the power over his racism." *Nightline*, ABC News, September 28, 1995.

13. Fox Butterfield, "A Portrait of the Detective in the 'O. J. Whirlpool,'" *New York Times*, March 2, 1996.

14. Butterfield, "A Portrait of the Detective in the 'O. J. Whirlpool.'"

15. Ibid.

16. "Panel Discussion on the Perjury Trial of Former Los Angeles Detective Mark Fuhrman," *Rivera Live*, CNBC, October 2, 1996.

17. "Simpson Jurors Speak Out on How They Reached a Verdict," ABC News, October 4, 1995.

18. "Fuhrman Plea-Bargain an Outrage That Taints Criminal Justice System," (Fort Lauderdale, Florida) *Sun-Sentinel*, October 4, 1996.

19. Editorial: "Fuhrman's Tap on Wrist," *Seattle Post-Intelligencer*, October 4, 1996.

20. "Fuhrman Plea Is a Travesty," *Florida Times-Union* (Jacksonville), October 4, 1996.

21. "Disgraced Cop in Simpson Case Deserved Jail," *Buffalo News* (New York), October 4, 1996.

22. "Editorial: Mark Fuhrman, His Own Tangled Web," (Durham, NC) *Herald-Sun*, October 4, 1996.

23. "Another Injustice from O.J. Simpson's Murder Trial," (Idaho) *Lewiston Morning Tribune*, October 5, 1996.

24. William Raspberry, "Justice Deferred and Denied," *Washington Post*, October 07, 1996.

25. Carl T. Rowan, "A Slap on the Wrist," *Chicago Sun-Times*, October 6, 1996.

26. "Ex-Juror Predicts Simpson Deadlock; Court Investigates Allegations That Panel Improperly Discussed Case," Washington Post, April 7, 1995.

27. "Excerpts of Testimony Given by Dismissed Juror to Judge Ito," Associated Press, April 13, 1995.

28. Bob Pool and Amy Pyle, "Case Was Weak, Race Not Factor, Two Jurors Say," *Los Angeles Times*, October 5, 1995.

29. "Will the Real Mark Fuhrman Stand Up?" *The Geraldo Rivera Show*, April 23, 1997.

30. "Fred, Patti and Kim Goldman Discuss the Simpson Trials and Their New Book," *Rivera Live*, February 17, 1997.

31. Editorial: "Fuhrman's Perjury Revisited," *San Francisco Chronicle*, October 4, 1996.

32. "Fuhrman Plea-Bargain an Outrage."

33. Editorial: "Fuhrman's Tap on Wrist."

34. Editorial: "Fuhrman's Price for Perjury Doesn't Cover the Harm Done," (Indiana) *South Bend Tribune*, October 13, 1996.

35. Editorial: "Mark Fuhrman, His Own Tangled Web."

36. See, e.g., Rowan, "A Slap on the Wrist" ("The judge in the civil trial now will probably find it impossible to deny Simpson's lawyers the right to tell the jury about Fuhrman's role in citing alleged evidence of Simpson's guilt.")

37. Stuart Taylor Jr., "Prosecute Him for Perjury?" *Legal Times*, February 10, 1997.

38. "The Tale of the Tape: O.J. Speaks, Panelists Discuss Simpson's Just-Released Videotape Proclaiming His Innocence," *The Geraldo Rivera Show*, February 22, 1996.

39. "Panel Discussion on the O.J. Simpson Criminal Trial," *Rivera Live*, CNBC, May 28, 1996.

CHAPTER 10: POST-OJ VERDICT: PARADISE

1. See, e.g., Jeff Jacoby, "Bradley's Homage to a Race-Baiter," *Boston Globe*, December 6, 1999.

2. See, e.g., Jay Nordlinger, Power Dem; The strange rise of a hatemonger, National Review, March 20, 2000.

3. Michael Slackman and Marjorie Connelly, "Sharpton Claims Success But Reassesses," *New York Times*, March 3, 2004.

4. See, e.g., "Dean Bears Brunt of Opponents' Vitriol in Debate Aimed at Minority Voters," The Bulletin's Frontrunner, January 12, 2004.

5. Gayle White, "Yale Roommate Vouches for Dean on Race," *Atlanta Journal-Constitution*, January 15, 2004.

6. Dudley Clendinen, "U.S. a Cathedral for Jackson Speech," *New York Times*, July 19, 1984.

7. "Decision 2000: Democratic National Convention," MSNBC, August 15, 2000.

8. See, e.g., Larry McShane, "After a Decade, the Tawana Brawley Case Goes to Court," Associated Press, November 9, 1997.

9. Ronald Sullivan, "Defendant Told of Jogger Rape, Detective Says," *New York Times*, November 28, 1990.

10. Cathy Connors, "Tawana's Team Sued for 30 Mil," *New York Amsterdam News*, March 2, 1996.

11. Alan Feuer, "Adviser in Tawana Brawley Case Pays Off Defamation Award," *New York Times*, November 7, 2001. ("Mr. Sharpton paid off the judgment against him

in June with the help of a group of supporters that included Percy E. Sutton, the former Manhattan borough president, the lawyer Johnnie L. Cochran Jr. and Earl Graves Jr., the president of Black Enterprise magazine. [T]he check that satisfied Mr. Maddox's debt was signed by John Beatty, the owner of the Cotton Club, a nightclub in Harlem. . . .")

12. Fred Siegel, *The Prince of the City: Giuliani, New York, and the Genius of American Life* (Encounter Books, 2006) at 104.

13. Ibid.

14. *Turnaround : How America's Top Cop Reversed the Crime Epidemic* (Random House, 1998), chapter one at http://www.nytimes.com/books/first/b/bratton-turnaround.html.

15. Siegel, *The Prince of the City* at 104.

16. Alison Mitchell, "With Defense of Police at Mosque, Giuliani Moves to Isolate 2 Critics," *New York Times*, January 15, 1994.

17. James C. McKinley Jr., "Praise of Innis Wins Rebuke for Giuliani," *New York Times*, January 22, 1994.

18. Editorial: "Tests for Mr. Giuliani, *New York Times*, January 18, 1994.

19. Clifford Krauss, "New York City Crime Falls But Just Why Is a Mystery," *New York Times*, January 1, 1995.

20. "Editorial: Re-Elect Mayor Giuliani," *New York Times*, October 26, 1997.

21. Chris Matthews, "Cheap, Plentiful Gas and an SUV in Every Garage: Do Americans Want It All for Nothing?" MSNBC: *Hardball*, May 18, 2001.

22. James Traub, "Giuliani Internalized," *New York Times*, February 11, 2001.

CHAPTER 11: LIBERALS ARE THE NEW BLACKS

1. Neil J. Young, "Equal Rights, Gay Rights and the Mormon Church," *New York Times*, June 13, 2012.

2. Judge H. Lee Sarokin, a Democratic-appointed federal judge, ruled that discrimination against smelly, frightening homeless people violated the equal protection clause because it had a "disparate impact" on people who refuse to bathe compared to those who bathe regularly. *Kreimer v. Bureau of Police for the Town of Morristown*, 765 F. SUPP. 181 (D.N.J. 1991), REV'D, 958 F.2D 1242 (3RD CIR. 1992).

3. Peter Singer, *Unsanctifying Human Life: Essays on Ethics* (Wiley-Blackwell, 2002) at 80.

4. U.S. Equal Employment Opportunity Commission, Charge Statistics FY 1997 Through FY 2011, available at http://www.eeoc.gov/eeoc/statistics/enforcement/charges.cfm.

5. Jonathan Rauch, "Offices and Gentlemen," *New Republic*, June 23, 1997, citing Walter K. Olson, *The Excuse Factory* (Free Press, 1997).

6. *Brown Transport Corp. v. Commonwealth*, 578 A.2d 555, 562 (Pa. Commw. Ct. 1990).

7. Kentucky Commission on Human Rights, Human Rights Report, Spring 1994, at 2.

8. See, e.g., Supreme Court nomination of Samuel Alito. "After His Toughest Week, Bush Comes Out Fighting," Economist.Com, November 2, 2005.

"The left will portray [Alito] as out of the mainstream, in favour of weakening the ability of women and minorities to seek protection in America's civil-rights laws and, of course, chipping away at a woman's right to an abortion. The case that will receive the most scrutiny is *Planned Parenthood v. Casey*, in which Mr. Alito voted to uphold a requirement that would have forced women to notify their husbands (in most cases) before getting an abortion"; "Alito Pick Stirs Passions," *Contra Costa Times* (California), November 1, 2005. "'Alito's confirmation could shift the court in a direction that threatens to eviscerate the core protections for women's freedom guaranteed by *Roe v. Wade*, or overturn the landmark decision altogether,' NARAL President Nancy Keenan said."; Jonathan Riskind and Jack Torry, "Fight Brewing over Nominee," *Columbus Dispatch* (Ohio), November 1, 2005 "Senate Democrats and civil-rights and abortion-rights organizations denounced the Alito nomination, pointing out that he has a reputation for having one of the most conservative legal minds on the federal bench. He voted in 1991 to uphold most of a restrictive Pennsylvania abortion law, including a requirement that a woman needed to inform her husband before having an abortion."

9. David M. Halbfinger, "Kerry Is Grilled on Gay Marriage and Attacks Bush on Sept. 11 Commission," *New York Times*, March 8, 2004.
10. Peter Brimelow, *Alien Nation: Common Sense About America's Immigration Disaster* (Harper Perennial, 1996).
11. See George J. Borjas, "Immigrants In, Wages Down—How to Do the Figuring," *National Review,* May 8, 2006.
12. National Center for Education Statistics, "Fast Facts: Dropout Rates," citing U.S. Department of Education, National Center for Education Statistics, 2011, *The Condition of Education 2011* (NCES 2011-033), Indicator 20, available at http://nces.ed.gov/fastfacts/display.asp?id=16.
13. Cord Jefferson, "How Illegal Immigration Hurts Black America," February 10, 2010.
14. *Anderson Cooper: 360*, CNN, April 11, 2006.
15. Richard Perez-Pena, "70 Abortion Law: New York Said Yes, Stunning the Nation," *New York Times*, April 9, 2000.
16. *Bray v. Alexandria Women's Health Clinic*, 506 U.S. 263 (1993).
17. Jennifer A. Dlouhy, "House Member's Father Faces Stiff Judicial Confirmation Test," *Congressional Quarterly Daily Monitor*, October 29, 2001.
18. Ana Radelat, "Opposition Grows to Bush Judicial Nominee," Gannett News Service, October 24, 2001.
19. Danny Hakim, "Spitzer Pushing Bill to Shore Up Abortion Rights," *New York Times*, April 26, 2007.
20. See *United States v. Morrison*, 529 U.S. 598 (2000).
21. H. R. Conf. Rep. No. 103-711, at 385.
22. Jan Vertefeuille, "Testing the Legal Limits," *Roanoke Times* (Virginia), March 24, 1996.
23. Jeremy Rabkin, "Christy on the Brink," *American Spectator,* January 1997.
24. Linda Greenhouse, "Battle on Federalism," *New York Times*, May 17, 2000.
25. Department of Justice, Criminal Victimization in the United States, 1997 Statistical Tables, Table 42, available at http://bjs.ojp.usdoj.gov/content/pub/pdf/cvus97.

pdf; Department of Justice, Criminal Victimization in the United States, 1999 Statistical Tables, Table 42, available at http://bjs.ojp.usdoj.gov/content/pub/pdf/ cvus98.pdf; Department of Justice, Criminal Victimization in the United States, 2003 Statistical Tables, Table 42, available at http://bjs.ojp.usdoj.gov/content/pub/ pdf/cvus0302.pdf; Department of Justice, Criminal Victimization in the United States, 2004 Statistical Tables, Table 42, available at http://bjs.ojp.usdoj.gov/ content/pub/pdf/cvus0402.pdf; Department of Justice, Criminal Victimization in the United States, 2005 Statistical Tables, Table 42, available at http://bjs.ojp. usdoj.gov/content/pub/pdf/cvus0502.pdf; Department of Justice, Criminal Victimization in the United States, 2006 Statistical Tables, Table 42, available at http://bjs.ojp.usdoj.gov/content/pub/pdf/cvus0602.pdf; Department of Justice, Criminal Victimization in the United States, 2007 Statistical Tables, Table 42, available at http://bjs.ojp.usdoj.gov/content/pub/pdf/cvus0702.pdf; Department of Justice, Criminal Victimization in the United States, 2008 Statistical Tables, Table 42, available at http://bjs.ojp.usdoj.gov/content/pub/pdf/cvus0802.pdf.

26. Tom Sorensen, "It's Time to Get to Truth of Duke Scandal," *Charlotte Observer* (North Carolina), March 31, 2006.

27. Richard Brookhiser, "A Supreme Court without a WASP," *New York Post,* May 17, 2010, available at http://www.nypost.com/p/news/opinion/opedcolumnists/supreme_court_without_wasp_vW4PHHXIky4pUolRNgGRnI.

28. KC Johnson, "Group Profile: The Cultural Anthropologists, Durham-In-Wonderland," August 20, 2007, available at http://durhamwonderland.blogspot.com/2007/08/group-profile-cultural-anthropologists.html.

29. See generally, KC Johnson, "Group Profile: William Chafe, Durham-In-Wonderland," August 27, 2007, available at http://durhamwonderland.blogspot.com/2007/08/group-profile-william-chafe.html.

30. Stuart Taylor and KC Johnson, *Until Proven Innocent: Political Correctness and the Shameful Injustices of the Duke Lacrosse Rape Case* (Thomas Dunne Books, 2007) at 341.

31. http://www.amazon.com/Empire-Michael-Hardt/dp/0674006712/ref=sr_1_1?s=books&ie=UTF8&qid=1337975972&sr=1-1.

32. Charlotte Allen, "Duke's Tenured Vigilantes," *Weekly Standard*, January 29, 2007.

33. Cathy N. Davidson, "In the Aftermath of a Social Disaster," *News & Observer* (Raleigh, North Carolina), January 5, 2007.

34. *Nancy Grace Show,* CNN, April 18, 2006.

35. *Scarborough Country,* MSNBC, April 5, 2006.

36. *The Situation with Tucker Carlson,* MSNBC, June 5, 2006.

37. Ibid., May 24, 2006.

38. Susan Brownmiller, *Against Our Will: Men, Women, and Rape* (Ballantine Books, 1993; first published in 1975) at 366. "False Allegations of Sexual Assault," Brent E. Turvey and Michael McGrath in *Rape Investigation Handbook,* 2nd ed., John O. Savino and Brent E. Turvey, eds (Academic Press, 2011) at 275. (All claims of a 2 percent rate of false rape allegations can be traced back to Brownmiller's book.)

39. Crime Index Offenses Reported, Section II, Department of Justice Uniform Crime Reporting, 1996 at 22. Data on "unfounded" rape complaints after 1996 does not seem to be available.

40. Eugene J. Kanin, "False Rape Allegations," *Archives of Sexual Behavior,* February

1994. Available at http://falserapearchives.blogspot.com/2009/06/archives-of-sexual-behavior-feb-1994.html.

41. Charles P. McDowell, "False Allegations," *Forensic Science Digest* 11, no. 4, December, 1985 (a publication of the U.S. Air Force Office of Special Investigation); Bruce Gross, "False Rape Allegations: An Assault on Justice," *Annals of the American Psychotherapy Association*, December 22, 2008.

42. *The Situation with Tucker Carlson*, December 22, 2006.

43. Howard Kurtz, "The Press Turning Up Its Nose at Lame Duck," *Washington Post*, February 5, 2007.

44. See, e.g., "I Guess It's a Jungle in Here Too, Huh?" Feministe Blog, 2008, available at http://www.feministe.us/blog/archives/008/04/25/i-guess-its-a-jungle-in-here-too-huh/

CHAPTER 12: CIVIL RIGHTS CHICKEN HAWKS

1. Andrew Ferguson, *Fools' Names, Fools' Faces* (Atlantic Monthly Press, 1996).

2. Ronald Kessler, *Inside the White House: The Hidden Lives of the Modern Presidents and the Secrets of the World's Most Powerful Institution* (Simon & Schuster, 1995) at 33.

3. E. W. Kenworthy, "Civil Rights Bill Passed, 73–27: Johnson Urges All to Comply; Dirksen Berates Goldwater," *New York Times*, June 19, 1964.

4. Ibid.

5. At the beginning of the campaign, polls had shown Nixon at 42 percent, Humphrey at 29 percent, and Wallace at 22 percent. On election day, Nixon's percentage remained virtually unchanged at 43.4 percent. Wallace lost nearly half his support and ended up with 13.5 percent of the vote. Humphrey picked up 12 percentage points—just a little bit less than Wallace lost—giving him 42.7 percent of the votes cast. Just four years after Goldwater's run, the segregationist vote went right back to the Democrats. Patrick J. Buchanan, "The Neocons and Nixon's Southern Strategy," *The American Conservative*, December 30, 2002.

6. In 1964, Goldwater won Georgia, South Carolina, Mississippi, Alabama and Louisiana. In 1980, Reagan lost Georgia and barely beat Carter in Mississippi, 49.4 to 48.1 percent; Alabama, 48.8 to 47.4 percent; and South Carolina, 49.4 to 48.1 percent. See, e.g., "The Election of 1980," American Presidency Project, University of California, Santa Barbara. Available at http://www.presidency.ucsb.edu/show-election.php?year=1980.

7. "Reagan Bush Youth Chairman Is LSU's Homecoming Queen: Says Youth Will Vote Republican in Nov.," *The Morning Advocate*, Folder, Louisiana Box 387, Research Unit, PP-RRL, Simi Valley, Ca.

8. Arthur Schlesinger Jr., "How McGovern Will Win," *New York Times*, February 11, 1968.

9. George McGovern, Address Accepting the Presidential Nomination at the Democratic National Convention in Miami Beach, Florida, July 14, 1972. Available at http://www.presidency.ucsb.edu/ws/index.php?pid=25967#axzz1zoNNrGgk.

10. Michael Barone, "GOP Poised to Reap Redistricting Rewards," *Creators Syndicate*, November 7, 2010.

11. *Booknotes with Brian Lamb*, Paul Greenberg, *No Surprises: Two Decades Of Clinton Watching*, July 7, 1996.
12. Bart Barnes, "Barry Goldwater, GOP Hero, Dies," *Washington Post*, May 30, 1998.
13. See, e.g., Robert A. Caro, *The Years of Lyndon Johnson, vol. 3: Master of the Senate* (Vintage, 2003).
14. These Democrats all voted against allowing a vote on Eisenhower's 1957 civil rights bill. Caro at 905.
15. Earl Black and Merle Black, *The Rise of Southern Republicans* (Belknap Press/Harvard University Press, 2002) at 93; see also James Lee Annis, *Howard Baker: Conciliator in an Age of Crisis* (Madison Books, 1994) at 46.
16. To Recommit H.R. 6400, The 1965 Voting Rights Act, Prohibiting the Denial to Any Person of the Right to Register or to Vote Because of His Failure to Pay a Poll Tax or Any Other Such Tax, 89th Congress July 9, 1965, roll call vote available at http://www.govtrack.us/congress/votes/89-1965/h86.
17. Eric Foner, *Reconstruction: America's Unfinished Revolution, 1863–1877* (Harper Perennial Modern Classics, 2002) at 425.
18. See, e.g., Jeffrey Leonard, "Earlier Agnew Took Moderate Stances," *Harvard Crimson*, October 10, 1973; Associated Press, "George Mahoney, 87, Maryland Candidate," *New York Times*, March 21, 1989.
19. Spiro Agnew, "The American Presidents." Available at http://www.theamericanpresidents.net/agnew.html.
20. Hackett Fischer, *Albion's Seed*, Kindle edition at 14311.
21. President Jimmy Carter, Address at Commencement Exercises at the University of Notre Dame, May 22, 1977, available at www.presidency.ucsb.edu http://www.presidency.ucsb.edu/ws/index.php?pid=7552#ixzz1zQzVHUF7.
22. Robert Caro, *The Years of Lyndon Johnson* at xv.
23. John Nichols, "Robert Byrd's American Journey," the *Nation*, June 28, 2010. Available at http://www.thenation.com/blog/36753/robert-byrds-american-journey#.
24. Donald Baer and Steven V. Roberts, "The Making of Bill Clinton," *U.S. News & World Report*, March 22, 1992.
25. Adam Nossiter, "For South, a Waning Hold on National Politics," *New York Times*, November 11, 2008.
26. Eugene Robinson, "Will Racism Keep Obama from Being President?," *Fort Wayne Journal Gazette*, December 17, 2007.
27. Joe Klein, "Powell's Race Problem," *Newsweek*, June 24, 1996.
28. Naftali Bendavid and Stephen Miller, "Remembrances: A Strong Voice for the Senate, His State," *Wall Street Journal*, June 29, 2010.
29. See, e.g., Kyle Longley, *Senator Albert Gore, Sr.: Tennessee Maverick* (Louisiana State University Press, 2004) at 90–93 and 102.
30. The White House, Office of the Press Secretary, Text of President's Remarks in Tribute to Sen. Fulbright, U.S. Newswire, May 7, 1993.
31. Caro, *Master of the Senate* at 548.
32. Attacks on McCarthy weren't run-of-the-mill Democratic blarney: Robert Kennedy worked for McCarthy and Senator John F. Kennedy refused to censure McCarthy.
33. Meacham, "A Man Out of Time."
34. "The First President to Entertain a Negro, Booker T. Washington Dined," *Washington Bee*, October 19, 1901. Available at http://www.whitehousehistory.org/

decaturhouse african-american-tour/content/The-First-President-to-Entertain-a-
Negro-Booker-T-Washington-Dined.

35. For party platforms, see John Woolley and Gerhard Peters, the American Presidency Project, University of California, Santa Barbara. Available at http://www
.presidency.ucsb.edu/platforms.php.

36. Non-southern Democrats voting against Eisenhower's 1957 Civil Rights Act: Senators Wayne Morse of Oregon, Warren Magnuson of Washington, James Murray of Montana, Mike Mansfield of Montana and Joseph O'Mahoney of Wyoming. Caro at 905.

37. Baer and Roberts, "The Making of Bill Clinton."

38. The White House, Office of the Press Secretary, Text of President's Remarks in Tribute to Sen. Fulbright, U.S. Newswire, May 7, 1993.

39. Ibid.

40. Joshua R. Preston, "Hoodwinked: Race and Robert Byrd Ku Klux Klan Inspired a Life in Politics," *Human Events*, December 12, 2005.

41. Eric Zimmermann, "Clinton says Byrd joined KKK to Help Him Get Elected," *The Hill*, July 2, 2010.

42. Editorial, *Hartford Courant*, April 16, 2004.

43. See, e.g., Lynette Holloway, "Why Is the Black Abortion Rate So High?" *The Root*, December 20, 2010, available at http://www.theroot.com/views/why-black-abortion-rate-so-high.

CHAPTER 13: YOU RACIST!

1. Jon Meacham, "A Man Out of Time: Trent Lott and the GOP Grew Up Together in the South." *Newsweek*, December 23, 2002.

2. Bob Herbert, "Racism and the G.O.P.," *The New York Times*, December 12, 2002.

3. Keith Olbermann and Chris Matthews, "Decision '08" Interview with Former President Jimmy Carter," MSNBC, August 27, 2008.

4. Irv Randolph, "McCain Interjects Race into Campaign," *Philadelphia Tribune*, August 8, 2008.

5. Roger Simon, "A Measure of Racism: 15 Percent?" Politico.com, April 21, 2008.

6. *The Ed Show*, MSNBC, March 23, 2010.

7. "Candidates' Labor Day Speeches Mark Start of Presidential Race," *Washington Post*, September 1, 1980.

8. Steven Komarow, "Bush Hits Dukakis as Weak on Defense, Dukakis Campaigns in South," Associated Press, August 5, 1988.

9. Ibid.

10. G. G. LaBelle, The Associated Press, September 1, 1980. (The media quickly corrected Reagan's joke, noting that the Klan did not *originate* in Tuscumbia, though that was the current location of the Klan's national headquarters.)

11. "Grand Klan Wizard Says Reagan Appealing to Black Vote," The Associated Press, September 3, 1980.

12. See Roger Simon, "How A Murderer and Rapist Became the Bush Campaign's Most Valuable Player," *Baltimore Sun*, November 11, 1990. (Excerpt from Roger Simon, *Road Show* (Farrar, Straus & Giroux, 1990). Available at http://articles.bal-

timoresun.com/1990-11-11/features/1990315149_1_willie-horton-fournier-mi-chael-dukakis.

13. Ibid.
14. See Roger Simon, "How A Murderer and Rapist Became the Bush Campaign's Most Valuable Player."
15. Dorothy Gilliam, "Bush's Restrictive Covenant," *Washington Post*, November 3, 1988.
16. "Bob Jones University Drops Interracial Dating Ban," *Christianity Today*, March 1, 2000.
17. The Carter administration had ordered the IRS to withdraw BJU's tax-exempt status over the ban—an exemption granted to more than a million organizations, including those that advocate for abortion, environmental mandates, an end to logging, more foreign aid spending, and national health care. But one little Christian school prohibiting interracial dating because an Asian family complained was a bridge too far. President Reagan restored the tax exemption on the grounds that nothing in the law prohibited it, the case went to the Supreme Court and a divided court found that the dating ban prohibited the school from receiving a tax exemption by reading into the statute a requirement that organizations seeking tax-exempt status "demonstrably serve and be in harmony with the public interest." Abortion is in harmony with the public interest, but a ban on interracial dating is not.
18. "Full Text of Republican Debate," *New York Times*, January 8, 2000.
19. Ann Gerhart, "Rebel Y'all," *Washington Post*, February 2, 2004.
20. Shelby Foote, "The Art of Fiction," *Paris Review*, Summer 1999. Interview by Carter Coleman, Donald Faulkner, William Kennedy.
21. Fischer, *Albion's Seed*. (Kindle edition, 14005–14009.)
22. Terri D. Reeves, "Memory of Ex-Slave, Confederate Soldier Is Revived," *St. Petersburg Times* (Florida), February 25, 2003; Adam J. Carozza, "Remembrance and Honor: An Interview with Mary Wilder Crockett," *Southern Scribe*, 2003. Available at http://www.southernscribe.com/zine/culture/remembrance_honor.htm.
23. James Webb, *Fields of Fire* (Bantam, 2001) at 34.
24. Byron York, "The Democratic Myth Machine," *National Review*, April 19, 2004.
25. Steven Thomma and Ron Hutcheson, "Right-to-Life, Gun-Advocacy Groups Also Running Anti-McCain Campaigns," Knight Ridder, February 16, 2000; "Gore 2000 Criticizes Tenor of Bush Campaign," U.S. Newswire, April 26, 2000.
26. "Interview with Paul Krugman," *The Charlie Rose Show*, December 26, 2007.
27. Deroy Murdock, "Reagan, No Racist," *National Review*, November 20, 2007.
28. Jon Meacham, "A Man Out of Time: Trent Lott and the GOP Grew Up Together in the South." *Newsweek*, December 23, 2002.
29. Jonathan Alter, "Forum: Was It Ever Going To Be Easy?" *Newsweek*, May 5, 2008.
30. Todd S. Purdum, "Striking Strengths, Glaring Failures," *New York Times*, December 24, 2000.
31. Joe Klein, "Putting Clinton's Legacy to a Vote," *New York Times*, March 17, 2002.
32. Clifford Krauss, "New York City's Gift to Clinton: A Lower National Crime Rate," *New York Times*, September 1996.
33. Michael Cooper, "DNA Evidence Links Rape Suspect to 17 Attacks in Region, Authorities Say," *New York Times*, April 9, 1999.
34. Cragg Hines, "Clinton Details Effort to Halt Police Racism: Plan Follows Inci-

dents of Excessive Force," *Houston Chronicle*, March 14, 1999, Sunday four-star edition.

35. Federal News Service, March 25, 1999, Thursday. Weekly Media Availability with Attorney General Janet Reno, Department of Justice, Washington, DC.

36. Weiser, Benjamin, "Final Frisking Policy of the Police Faces Scrutiny," *New York Times*, March 19, 1999.

37. Heather MacDonald, "America's Best Urban Police Force," *City Journal*, Summer 2000.

38. "Puerto Rican Demonstrators Demand Pardon for Jailed Terrorists," *The Bulletin's Frontrunner*, August 30, 1999. "Tapes Indicate Prisoners Will Return to Violence." *Newsweek* (9/6) reported, "The most damning evidence against the nationalists, *Newsweek* has learned, is still-secret audio tapes made by the Bureau of Prisons." The tapes "record at least some of the prisoners saying that 'as soon as they get out of there, they are going to return to violence,' one law enforcement official said."

39. Anderson Cooper, "State of Texas to Retain Polygamist Children: Clinton to Obama: 'Toughen Up,'" CNN, April 18, 2008.

40. *Anderson Cooper, 360*, CNN, May 2, 2008.

41. Christopher Andersen, *American Evita: Hillary Clinton's Path to Power* (Wm. Morrow, 2004) at 16–17.

CHAPTER 14: DREAMS OF MY ASSASSINATION

1. Steve Kroft, Interview with Barack and Michelle Obama, CBS, *60 Minutes*, February 11, 2007.

2. This was a theory pushed by Representative Maxine Waters. See Craig Delaval, "Cocaine, Conspiracy Theories & the C.I.A. in Central America," PBS *Frontline*, available at http://www.pbs.org/wgbh/pages/frontline/shows/drugs/special/cia.html.

3. Peter Knight, *Conspiracy Theories in American History: An Encyclopedia*, vol. 1 (ABC-CLIO, 2003) at 38. "It was suggested that [Church's Fried Chicken] (whose franchises were located primarily in urban areas and had a sizable black customer base) was owned by racist whites who added an ingredient to the chicken that would cause black men to become sterile. A parallel theory held that the makers of Tropical Fantasy, a low-cost soft drink marketed principally in largely black urban areas, was owned by the KKK and added an ingredient to its product that would sterilize or cause impotence in black men."

4. John King, "Racism: Personal Safety Factors in Obama's Deliberations," CNN.com, January 19, 2007.

5. Frank Rich, "The Terrorist Barack Hussein Obama," *New York Times*, October 12, 2008.

6. Bob Herbert, "Roads, High and Low," *New York Times*, May 27, 2008.

7. "Obama Will Be Assassinated if He Wins: Nobel Winner Lessing," Agence France-Presse February 9, 2008.

8. Allison Samuels, "Daring to Touch the Third Rail," *Newsweek*, January 28, 2008.

9. Jeff Zeleny, "In Memories of a Painful Past, Hushed Worry about Obama," *New York Times*, February 25, 2008.

10. Eileen Sullivan, "Obama Has More Threats than Other Presidents-Elect," The Associated Press, November 15, 2008.

11. Steve Gilbert, "AP: Obama Gets Most Death Threats Ever," Sweetness & Light, November 15, 2008.

12. Rachel Weiner, "Obama's Secret Service Agent Most Influential Man in the World," the Huffington Post, December 26, 2008. Available at http://www.huffingtonpost.com/2008/11/25/idetailsi-obamas-secret-s_n_146325.html.

13. Frank Rich, "The Terrorist Barack Hussein Obama."

14. Leonard Pitts, "Racism Lurks in the Shadows for Obama," *Orlando Sentinel* (Florida), May 8, 2007.

15. ABC News Now, *Perspectives*, "Speak Freely," May 11, 2007.

16. Jeff Zeleny, "In Memories of a Painful Past, Hushed Worry About Obama."

17. Matthew Jaffe, "Obama Security Challenge as Popularity Grows," ABC News, February 28, 2008, http://abcnews.go.com/Politics/Vote2008/ story?id=4350538&page=1#.T_ufu45Sbao.

18. Scout Tufankjian, "Guarding Obama," Slate.com, January 2009. Available at http://www.slate.com/articles/arts/gallery/2009/01/guarding_obama.html.

19. Robert Lindsey, *New York Times*, November 14, 1979; the Associated Press, November 13, 1979.

20. Katharine Q. Seelye, "Kennedy Comment Sends Clinton into Damage Control," *New York Times*, May 26, 2008.

21. Kenneth J. Moynihan, "Was Outrage over RFK Remark Launched by Obama Campaign?" *Telegram & Gazette* (Massachusetts), May 29, 2008.

22. Kenneth R. Bazinet, "Firestorm? Blame It on Bam," *Daily News* (New York), May 26, 2008.

23. Bob Herbert, "Roads, High and Low," *New York Times*, May 27, 2008.

24. Roger Cohen, "The Obama Connection," *New York Times*, May 26, 2008.

25. Eugene Robinson, "Clinton's Grim Scenario," *Washington Post*, May 27, 2008.

26. Keith Olbermann, *Countdown with Keith Olbermann*, MSNBC, May 23, 2008.

27. The United States Secret Service and Presidential Protection: An Examination of a System Failure. Hearings Before the Committee on Homeland Security, 111th Cong. (December 3, 2009) (testimony of Mark J. Sullivan, director, United States Secret Service).

28. *Newsweek*'s Mark Hosenball traced the rumor of increased threats against Obama to author Ronald Kessler, who had claimed in a 2009 book that threats against the president rose by 400 percent after Obama took office, but the Obama-threat hysteria long preceded Kessler's book. Mark Hosenball, "Threats Against Obama Drop to Normal Levels," *Newsweek*, November 9, 2009. Available at http://www.thedailybeast.com/newsweek/blogs/declassified/2009/11/09/threats-against-obama-drop-to-normal-levels.html.

29. "WP Makes Up Hate Site 'Explosion' Story," Sweetness & Light, June 22, 2008, citing Eli Saslow, "Hate Groups' Newest Target," *Washington Post*, June 22, 2008.

30. Ibid.

31. Marisol Bello, "White Supremacists Target Middle America," *USA Today*, October 20, 2008.

32. Mark Preston, "White Supremacists Watched in Lead Up to Obama Administration," CNN, January 16, 2009.

33. Ed Schultz, MSNBC, *The Ed Show*, June 11, 2009.

34. Kathy Shaidle, "Holocaust Museum Shooter von Brunn a 9/11 'Truther' Who Hated 'Neo-Cons,' Bush, McCain," *The Examiner*, June 10th, 2009. Available at http://www.examiner.com/conservative-politics-in-national/holocaust-museum-shooter-von-brunn-a-9-11-truther-who-hated-neo-cons-bush-mccain.

35. "When Right-Wing Extremism Moves Mainstream," National Public Radio (NPR), March 25, 2010.

36. Kirk Johnson and Eric Lichtblau, "Officials See No 'Credible Threat' to Obama in Racist Rants," *New York Times*, August 27, 2008.

37. See, e.g., Woody Baird and Andrew DeMillo, "Authorities Say Skinhead Plot Wasn't Fully Formed," *Abilene Reporter-News* (Texas), October 29, 2008; Richard A. Serrano," "Pair Accused of Plotting to Kill Obama, 102 Blacks," *Los Angeles Times,* October 28, 2008.

38. Stephanie Schendel, "Election, Economy Spark Explosive Growth of Militias," MSNBC.com, March 7, 2012. Available at http://usnews.msnbc.msn.com/_news/2012/03/07/10602763-election-economy-spark-explosive-growth-of-militias.

39. "Potok Claims 'Explosive Growth' of Militias," Sweetness & Light, March 8, 2012. Available at http://sweetness-light.com/archive/potok-claims-explosive-growth-of-militias.

40. Leon Wieseltier, "The Extremities of Nicholson Baker," *New York Times*, August 8, 2004; Linton Weeks, "A Novel's Plot Against the President," *Washington Post*, June 29, 2004.

41. MacKenzie Weinger, "Bush Decapitated in 'Game of Thrones,'" Politico.com, June 13, 2012.

42. TV Sound Bite, The Hotline, October 9, 2006.

43. James Hohmann, "Nobel Laureate Calls for Removal of Bush: Irish Peace Activist's Speech at Dallas Event Gets Standing Ovation," *Dallas Morning News*, July 12, 2007.

44. Lynn Elber, CBS: "Violent Anti-Bush Graphic Was 'Regrettable,'" Associated Press, August 9, 2000.

45. "Death Threats Against Bush at Protests Ignored for Years," ZombieTime.com. Available at http://www.zombietime.com/zomblog/?p=621.

46. Jonathan B. Opet, [untitled], *Alameda Sun*, March 2, 2007. Available at http://alamedasun.com/local-and-hometown/1139-patriotic-artist-gets-read-the-patriot-act.

47. There appears to have been two lone kooks who hung Obama effigies. One was the crazy pastor in Florida who created an international incident by burning a Koran in 2012, and the other was an anti-government nut who hung a slew of politicians (mostly local) in effigy in his yard in North Carolina and on a flatbed truck to protest, as he claims, a government cover-up of several of his family members being murdered by law enforcement officers. He added Obama to his gallery of hanging effigies sometime in 2012. Mike Opelka, "Why Is a Hangin' Truck Driving Around NYC with President Obama on a Noose?" *The Blaze*, May 4, 2012.

48. Leon Czolgosz, who killed President William McKinley in 1901, was a socialist; Giuseppe Zangara attempted to assassinate president-elect Franklin Roosevelt because he was a "capitalist."

49. Lee Harvey Oswald, who shot President John F. Kennedy, was a communist.

50. Senator Robert Kennedy was killed on June 5, 1968, by Sirhan Sirhan, a Palestinian extremist angry with Kennedy for his support of Israel.

51. Charles Manson follower Lynette "Squeaky" Fromme, shot at President Gerald Ford in 1975 because she was incensed about the plight of the California redwood.

52. Sara Jane Moore tried to kill President Ford because "the government had declared war on the left."

53. Alex Isenstadt, "GOP Unnerved by Democrats' Candid Camera Techniques," Politico.com, July 9, 2012; "Liberal Media Posts Allen West's Home Address," *Fox News Nation*, June 25, 2012, available at http://nation.foxnews.com/allen-west/2012/06/25/liberal-media-posts-allen-west-s-home-address#ixzz21ChIewuW.

54. Jim Rutenberg, Marilyn W. Thompson, David D. Kirkpatrick and Stephen Labaton, "For McCain, Self-Confidence on Ethics Poses Its Own Risk," *New York Times*, February 21, 2008. "Correction: . . . *The article did not state, and the Times did not intend to conclude, that Ms. Iseman had engaged in a romantic affair with Senator McCain or an unethical relationship on behalf of her clients in breach of the public trust.*"; see also Clark Hoyt, "What That McCain Article Didn't Say," *New York Times*, February 24, 2008.

55. See also "In It for the Long Haul," The Hotline, October 16, 2008; "The Journal Editoral Report," Fox News Network, October 18, 2008; Jack Kelly, "The Media Misrepresent McCain and Palin Rallies," *The Blade* (Toledo,Ohio), October 18, 2008; *Lou Dobbs Tonight*, CNN, October 16, 2008.

56. "Secret Service Says 'Kill Him' Allegation Unfounded," *Times Leader*, October 15, 2008. Available at: http://www.timesleader.com/news/breakingnews/Secret_Service_says_Kill_him_allegation_unfounded_.html.

57. Alex Koppelman, "Did Anyone Really Yell 'Kill Him'"? Salon.com, October 16, 2008.

58. Dana Milbank, "Unleashed, Palin Makes a Pit Bull Look Tame," *Washington Post*, October 7, 2008.

59. "Hammering Home Their Percentage Point," The Hotline, October 16, 2008 ("Secret Service spokesperson Eric Zahren said 10/15 that listening to tapes of the Florida rally, the Secret Service heard "tell him" or "tell them," but never heard "kill him.")

60. "Transcript: The Third Presidential Debate," *New York Times*, October 15, 2008.

61. Mark Hosenball, "The Death-Threat Debate," *Newsweek*, October 27, 2008. Available at http://www.thedailybeast.com/newsweek/2008/10/18/the-death-threat-debate.html.

62. Ibid.

63. James B. Jacobs and Kimberly Potter, *In Hate Crimes: Criminal Law & Identiy Politics* (Oxford University Press, 2000) at 143.

CHAPTER 15: OBAMA, RACE DEMAGOGUE

1. Barack Obama, *Dreams From My Father: A Story of Race and Inheritance* (Crown, 2007) at 103. "I read the book to help me understand just what it is that makes white people so afraid. Their demons. The way ideas get twisted around. It helps me understand how people learn to hate."

2. Quoted in Michiko Kakutani, "The Young Dreamer, with Eyes Wide Open," *New York Times*, June 4, 2012 (reviewing David Maraniss, *Barack Obama: The Story* (Simon & Schuster, 2012).

3. *Dreams* at 83–85.

4. Ibid.

5. *Dreams* at 25.

6. *Dreams* at 65.

7. *Dreams* at xix.

8. See, e.g., Evan Thomas, "Alienated in the U.S.A.," *Newsweek*, March 12, 2008.

9. *Dreams* at 98.

10. *Dreams* at 94.

11. *Dreams* at 85.

12. "White Men Can Vote," the *Economist*, July 3, 2008. Available at http://www.economist.com/node/11670719.

13. Julie Mason, "Obama's Election Year Pitch Leaves Out White Males," *Washington Examiner*, April 27, 2010. Available at http://washingtonexaminer.com/article/14619.

14. Mayhill Fowler, "Obama: No Surprise That Hard Pressed Pennsylvanians Turn Bitter," the Huffington Post, April 11, 2008. Available at http://www.huffingtonpost.com/mayhill-fowler/obama-no-surprise-that-ha_b_96188.html.

15. Caren Bohan, "Obama Says Republicans Will Use Race to Stoke Fear," Reuters, June 20, 2008.

16. See, e.g., *World News With Charles Gibson*, ABC News, July 31, 2008.

17. See, e.g., "Barack Obama Campaign Conference Call: The Launching of a New Website and Discussing How the McCain Campaign Is Taking the Low Road." (Participants: David Plouffe, Obama for America campaign manager; Susan Eisenhower), Federal News Service, July 31, 2008.

18. Mark Mooney, "Obama Aide Concedes 'Dollar Bill' Remark Referred to His Race," ABC News, August 1, 2008. Available at http://abcnews.go.com/GMA/Politics/story?id=5495348&page=1#.T_bYV45Sbao

19. Jim Farber, "Geraldine Ferraro Lets Her Emotions Do the Talking," *Torrance Daily Breeze*, March 7, 2008.

20. Josh Drobnyk and John L. Micek, "Skin Color Is Not a Campaign Issue, Obama Warns," *The Morning Call*, March 12, 2008.

21. Jayson K. Jones and Ana C. Rosado, "Obama Campaign Criticizes Ferraro Comments," *New York Times*, March 11, 2008.

22. Robin Abcarian, "Ferraro Quits Clinton Campaign After Obama Remarks," *Los Angeles Times*, March 13, 2008.

23. Jayson K. Jones and Ana C. Rosado, "Obama Campaign Criticizes Ferraro Comments," *New York Times*, March 11, 2008.

24. Ben Smith, "A Ferraro Flashback," Politico, March 11, 2008.

25. Andrew Sullivan, "Goodbye to All That: Why Obama Matters," *Atlantic*, December 2007.

26. Obama: How much damage was done, MSNBC's First Read, March 20, 2008, available at http://firstread.msnbc.msn.com/_news/2008/03/20/4437326-obama-how-much-damage-was-done .

27. "Transcript: Barack Obama's Speech on Race," *New York Times*, March 18, 2008.

Available at http://www.nytimes.com/2008/03/18/us/politics/18text-obama. html?_ r =1&pagewanted=print.

28. See, e.g., Neely Tucker, "Descendants Hold to Ex-Slaves' Dream," *Detroit Free Press*, November 5, 1997 "The Rev. David Mwambila, a Kenyan living on the Indian Ocean coast . . . In 1874, Matthew Wellington, his great-grandfather . . . had been captured by Arab slave traders. . . ."; Erica Poff, Country Profile: The Republic of Kenya, Ohio University, Center for International Studies, September 18, 2007 at 4, available at http://www.internationalstudies.ohio.edu/activities-outreach/files/Kenya.pdf. "Arabs had been trading African slaves for over 1000 years, taking them to the Arabian Peninsula, Persian Gulf, and other regions of Asia. European slave traders came later in the 17th century, taking African slaves to various islands in the Indian Ocean and the Americas."; Cynthia McKinney, Expectations for U.N. Conference Against Racism, CNN International, September 1, 2001; "WALTER MBOTELA, DESCENDANT OF FREED SLAVE:' . . . [I]t was a terrible thing what the Arabs did to Africans.'"

29. See, e.g., Erica Poff, Country Profile: The Republic of Kenya, Ohio University, Center for International Studies, September 18, 2007 at 4, available at http://www.internationalstudies.ohio.edu/activities-outreach/files/Kenya.pdf. "One of the most important aspects of early trade and cultural interaction in Kenya was the evolution of the slave trade in East Africa"; Cynthia McKinney, Expectations for U.N. Conference Against Racism, CNN International, September 1, 2001. "To an area when control of what is now Kenya came first under Arab rule, then Portuguese, before Arabs regained the upper hand in the late 17th century. Through it all, Mbasa served as a key port in Africa's slave trade."; Kevin Mwachiro, Remembering East African slave raids, BBC, March 30, 2007, available at http://news.bbc.co.uk/2/hi/africa/6510675.stm. "There was not much slave-raiding along the Kenyan coast but it was a vital transit point for slaves who were captured further inland, due to its proximity to the main market in Zanzibar".

30. Results from the 1860 Census, The Civil War Home Page, available at http://www.civil-war.net/pages/1860_census.html; See also Jenny B. Wahl, Slavery in the United States, Economic History Association, February 1, 2010, available at http://eh.net/encyclopedia/article/wahl.slavery.us.

31. Ibid.

32. Mary A. Johnson, "Crime: New Frontier; Jesse Jackson Calls It Top Civil-Rights Issue," *Chicago Sun-Times*, November 29, 1993.

33. Bernard Goldberg, *Crazies to the Left of Me, Wimps to the Right: How One Side Lost Its Mind and the Other Lost Its Nerve* (Broadside Books, 2008). at 30–31.

34. Ben Smith, "Obama on Virginia Tech, and 'Violence,'" Politico, April 17, 2007.

35. NBC Staff, "Bozell on Hannity 'Media Mash': NBC Deliberately Skewed Travyvon Martin Story with Selective Editing," March 30, 2012; available at http://newsbusters.org/blogs/nb-staff/2012/03/29/bozell-irresponsible-media-skewing#ixzz20TrewbRw.

36. Noah Rothman, "MSNBC *Primetime* Makes Zero Mentions of Trayvon Martin Case After Pro-Zimmerman Evidence Surfaces," Mediaite.com, May 23, 2012.

37. Jonathan Strong, "Documents Show Media Plotting to Kill Stories about Rev. Jeremiah Wright," The Daily Caller, July 20, 2010, available at http://dailycaller.com/2010/07/20/documents-show-media-plotting-to-kill-stories-about-rev-jeremiah-wright/print/#ixzz0uI7TXbTr.

CHAPTER 16: THE MEDIA CRY "RACIST" IN A CROWDED THEATER

1. Douglass K. Daniel, "Analysis: Palin's Words Carry Racial Tinge," Associated Press, October 5, 2008.
2. *Countdown* with Keith Olbermann, MSNBC, August 4, 2008.
3. Katie Couric, *CBS Evening News,* July 31, 2008.
4. Jacob Weisberg, "If Obama Loses, Racism Is the Only Reason McCain Might Beat Him," Slate, August 23, 2008, available at http://slate.com/id/2198397.
5. Timothy Noah, "What We Didn't Overcome," Slate, November 10, 2008.
6. See David Paul Kuhn, "Exit polls: How Obama Won," November 5, 2008.
7. Seth Stephens-Davidowitz, "How Racist Are We? Ask Google," *New York Times,* June 9, 2012.
8. See, e.g., *Hannity & Colmes,* Fox News Network, November 3, 2008.
9. The coal interview story was broken by Brent Bozell's *Newsbusters*; P. J. Gladnick, "Audio: Obama Tells *SF Chronicle* He Will Bankrupt Coal Industry," *Newsbusters,* November 2, 2008, available at http://newsbusters.org/blogs/p-j-gladnick/2008/11/02/hidden-audio-obama-tells-sf-chronicle-he-will-bankrupt-coal-industry#ixzz20YouLcsF.
10. Chris Dickerson, "Coal Official Calls Obama Comments 'Unbelievable'," *West Virginia Record,* November 2, 2008.
11. Tim Kane, "Who Are the Recruits? The Demographic Characteristics of U.S. Military Enlistment, 2003-2005," The Heritage Foundation, October 27, 2006, available at http://www.heritage.org/research/reports/2006/10/who-are-the-recruits-the-demographic-characteristics-of-us-military-enlistment-2003-2005.
12. See, e.g., "Talk of the Nation: The Tea Party, a Modern Movement," National Public Radio (NPR), April 29, 2010.
13. Kate Zernike, "Doing Fine, But Angry Nonetheless," *New York Times,* April 18, 2010.
14. Jonathan Gurwitz, "A Tea Party Movement That's Strong, More Focused—and Much Different from Its Caricature," *St. Paul Pioneer Press* (Minnesota), April 17, 2010.
15. Joe Schoffstall, "Poll Shows Support for Tea Party Movement Continues to Grow," cnsnews.com, April 22, 2010.
16. *The Ed Show,* MSNBC April 13, 2010.
17. David Weigel, "Tea Party Infiltration Done Wrong," Slate.com, August 9, 2010. Available at http://www.slate.com/content/slate/blogs/weigel/2010/08/09/tea_party_infiltration_done_wrong.html.
18. Alex Pappas, "Infiltrator Trying to Pass as Rand Paul Fan Wrote Column Bashing Tea Party," the Daily Caller, August 11, 2010. Available at http://dailycaller.com/2010/08/11/infiltrator-trying-to-pass-as-rand-paul-fan-wrote-column-bashing-tea-party/#ixzz20OTrMFgt.
19. Lachlan Markay, "Far-left Think Progress Fabricates Examples of Tea Party Racism for Bogus Video," *Newsbusters,* July 16, 2010, available at http://newsbusters.org/blogs/lachlan-markay/2010/07/16/far-left-think-progress-fabricates-examples-tea-party-racism-bogus-v.
20. Glenn Beck, Fox News Network, July 19, 2010.
21. *Hardball* with Chris Matthews, MSNBC, July 18, 2010.
22. Kyle Drennen, "MSNBC: ObamaCare Protesters 'Racist,' Including Black Gun-

Owner," *Newsbusters,* August 18, 2009, available at http://newsbusters.org/blogs/
kyle-drennen/2009/08/18/msnbc-no-mention-black-gun-owner-among-racist-
protesters#ixzz21KhK8M00.

23. *The Ed Show,* MSNBC, April 19, 2010. Available at http://www.msnbc.msn.com/
id/36663015/ns/msnbc_tv-the_ed_show/t/ed-show/#.T_6BQo5Sbao.

24. "Editorial: They Want to Make Voting Harder?" *New York Times,* June 5, 2011.

25. *Washington Watch with Roland Martin,* TV One, June 5, 2011.

26. Simon van Zuylen-Wood , "Why Did Liberal African-Americans in Rhode Island
Help Pass a Voter ID Law?" *New Republic,* February 7, 2012.

27. David Scharfenberg, "Who Passed Voter ID?" *Providence Phoenix,* May 16, 2012.

28. Simon van Zuylen-Wood, February 7, 2012.

29. David Scharfenberg, May 16, 2012.

30. Simon van Zuylen-Wood, "Why Did Liberal African-Americans in Rhode Island
Help Pass a Voter ID Law?" *New Republic,* February 7, 2012.

31. Complaint in *U.S. v. Missouri,* U.S.D.C. (Western Dist of Mo Central Div) available at http://www.justice.gov/crt/about/vot/nvra/mo_nvra_comp.php; *U.S. v.
Missouri,* U.S.D.C. (CD MO) (2007) (case dismissed for naming wrong parties—
state instead of counties—under National Voter Registration Act of 1993). Available at http://www.sos.mo.gov/elections/laughrey_ruling.pdf.

32. *The Ed Show,* MSNBC, May 22, 2012.

33. Steve Benen, "What's the Matter with Arizona?" *The Maddow Blog,* May 18, 2012.

34. See, e.g., David Hackett Fischer, *Albion's Seed: Four British Folkways in America*
(Oxford University Press, 1991) at 6372–6375, e-book edition. ("The first Africans
appeared in the colony [of Virginia] as early as 1619; a census of 1625 enumerated
23 blacks. There were fewer Africans in the Chesapeake than in New England or
New Netherlands. Their legal status remained very unclear.")

35. *Countdown with Keith Olbermann,* September 15, 2009.

36. Mark Finkelstein, "Massachusetts: Olbermann Cries Racism," NewsBusters.org,
January 19, 2010, available at http://newsbusters.org/blogs/mark-finkelstein
/2010/01/19/massachusetts-olbermann-cries-racism#ixzz20Mqfv855.

37. *Countdown with Keith Olbermann,* MSNBC, February 15, 2007.

38. Jeff Poor, "MSNBC Guest Suggests Romney's Use of the Term 'Kitchen Cabinet' Is
Racist," the *Daily Caller,* July 12, 2012, available at http://dailycaller.com/
2012/07/12/msnbc-guest-suggests-romneys-use-of-the-term-kitchen-cabinet-is-
racist/#ixzz20X52N2PB.

39. John McWhorter, "Racism in Retreat," *New York Sun,* June 5, 2008.

40. John Heilemann and Mark Halperin, *Game Change: Obama and the Clintons,
McCain and Palin, and the Race of a Lifetime* (Harper, 2010) at 36.

41. *"The Chris Matthews Show,"* (syndicated) March 7, 2010.

42. See OccupyWallStreet.org ("Occupy Wall Street is a people-powered movement
that began on September 17, 2011, in Liberty Square in Manhattan's Financial
District"); Jillian Dunham, #OccupyWallSt Roundup, Day 59, November 14, 2011;
Just Like the Tea Party: A List of Occupy Mayhem Sorted by Type, November 16,
2011, Verum Serum, available at http://www.verumserum.com/?p=33490.

43. James Bennet, "Clinton, at Meeting on Race, Struggles to Sharpen Debate," *New
York Times,* December 4, 1997.

44. Eric Foner, *The Story of American Freedom* (W.W. Norton and Company, 1999) at
193 ("Under Roosevelt's guidance [in 1932], the Democratic Party was trans-

formed from a bastion of localism and states' rights into a broad coalition of farmers, industrial workers, the reform-minded urban middle class, liberal intellectuals, *and, somewhat incongruously, the white-supremacist South, all committed to federal intervention . . .*) (emphasis added)

CHAPTER 17: WHITE GUILT KILLS

1. Fred Siegel, "Ground Zero for Big Government," *The American Enterprise*, June 1, 2002.
2. As usual, it was white liberals who drove a truck through this hole. A Lindsay aide hired "Yippie" leader Abbie Hoffman as a "community liaison" and Hoffman responded "by writing giant 'F—k You's' on the walls of Grand Central Station." Fred Siegel, "Ground Zero for Big Government," *The American Enterprise*, June 1, 2002.
3. Jurgensen at xviii.
4. E. J. McMahon and Fred Siegel, "Gotham's Fiscal Crisis: Lessons Unlearned," *Public Interest,* January 1, 2005.
5. See, e.g., Ralph Blumenthal, Black Youth Is Killed by Whites; Brooklyn Attack Is Called Racial, the *New York Times*, August 25, 1989.
6. Don Kowet, A close-up of race issue as media spectacle, the *Washington Times*, May 15, 1990 (reviewing "Seven Days in Bensonhurst," PBS's *Frontline).*
7. Elizabeth Kolbert, "Youth's Funeral Focuses on Racial Divisions," the *New York Times*, August 31, 1989.
8. Ibid.
9. Walter Goodman, "Review/Television: Examining the Bensonhurst Killing," the *New York Times*, May 15, 1990.
10. Elizabeth Kolbert, Youth's Funeral Focuses on Racial Divisions, August 31, 1989.
11. M. A. Farber, "In Son's Slaying, a Father Finds His Mission," the *New York Times*, September 28, 1989.
12. Celestine Bohlen, "Dinkins Stresses His Appeal for Harmony," the *New York Times*, September 7, 1989.
13. Ken Auletta, "Mayoral Flight's Ready for Takeoff and I'm Getting on with Dinkins," the *New York Daily News*, October 29, 1989 (quoted in Jared Taylor, *Paved With Good Intentions: The Failure of Race Relations in Contemporary America* (Carroll & Graf Publishers 1992) at 265.
14. Fred Siegel, *The Prince of the City: Giuliani, New York and the Genius of American Life* (Encounter Books 2006) at 74.
15. Ibid.
16. Michael Tomasky, "The Day Everything Changed," *New York Magazine*, October 6, 2008.
17. "Clinton Hits a Nerve on Race," the *New York Times*, September 30, 1993.
18. Margaret Wente, Interview: Shelby Steele, Harvard Academic And Black Conservative, *Globe and Mail* (Canada), October 20, 2007. ("Q: 'Is there any prominent black figure who doesn't wear the mask?' . . . Steele: 'Clarence Thomas. He wears no mask at all. He's not a bargainer or a challenger. He's his own man. He has deep and profound convictions. You can take them or leave them, but he is unwavering. He is a rather heroic figure—the freest black man in America.'")

19. "The Crisis of Black Political Succession," *Washington Informer,* May 8, 2002.
20. Sean Gregory, Why Cory Booker Likes Being Mayor of Newark, July 27, 2009, available at http://www.time.com/time/magazine/article/0,9171,1910983,00.html #ixzz20RI8sz6K.
21. Ibid.
22. Glenn Townes, "Booker to deliver State of the City address," *New York Amsterdam News,* March 1, 2012.
23. See, e.g., Douglas Martin, "Patrick Chavis, 50, Affirmative Action Figure," the *New York Times,* August 15, 2002; Abraham H. Miller, "Clinton's Silenced Dialogue on Race," *World and I,* June 1, 1998.
24. This is a paraphrase of Peter Brimelow's remark on the first page of his book *Alien Nation:* "There is a sense in which current immigration policy is Adolf Hitler's posthumous revenge on America." Peter Brimelow, *Alien Nation: Common Sense About America's Immigration Disaster* (Harper Perennial 1996) at xvii, available at http://www23.us.archive.org/stream/Alien_Nation/alien-nation-peter-brimelow _djvu.txt.

Index